THE FILMS OF JOHN HUGHES

A history of independent screen production in Australia

JOHN CUMMING

ATOM Moving Image Series

Publishing

The Moving Image | Number 12, 2014

ISBN 978 1 876467 23 4

THE MOVING IMAGE is published by the Australian Teachers of Media in association with its various publishing partners which includes RMIT's School of Media and Communication, the Australian Film Television and Radio School (AFTRS), Deakin University's School of Communication and Creative Arts, the Australian Centre for the Moving Image (ACMI) and the Australian Teachers of Media (ATOM).

Our aim is to promote knowledge, appreciation and enjoyment of screen culture and media, with particular emphasis on Australian film.

Address all correspondence to: The Editor, THE MOVING IMAGE, ATOM, PO Box 2040, St Kilda West Post Office, St Kilda Vic 3182, Australia.

Statements of fact and opinion appearing in THE MOVING IMAGE are made on the responsibility of the contributors alone, and do not imply the endorsement of the editorial board or the publisher.

Copyright © 2014 Australian Teachers of Media (ATOM)

Managing Editor: Peter Tapp <editor@atom.org.au>

Editors: Julie Stafford and Will Allen

Commissioning Editorial Board:
Lisa French (Chair), Deputy Dean, (Media), School of Media & Communication, RMIT
Felicity Collins, Reader/Associate Professor, Creative Arts and English, School of Humanities and Social Sciences, La Trobe University
Ben Goldsmith, Senior Research Fellow in the ARC Centre of Excellence for Creative Industries and Innovation, QUT
Jane Landman, Senior Lecturer, School of Communication and the Arts, Victoria University
Belinda Smaill, Senior Lecturer in Film and Screen Studies in the School of Media, Film and Journalism, Monash University.

Layout, Design and Cover: Pascale van Breugel

Printing: Everbest Printing China

Trade Enquiries: ATOM – Tel (03) 9525 5302 / Fax (03) 9537 2325

*Dedicated to
Rosemary and Stuart Cumming*

Editorial

The Moving Image is Australia's premier series of monographs on film, television and multimedia, covering current practice, history, theory, analysis and criticism.

Australian film/television/multimedia is the principal, but not exclusive, focus of **The Moving Image** series, which is a key site for the publishing of academic research, particularly on Australian cinema. The choice of topics is informed by international developments in the areas of theory, criticism, history and practice of film/video/multimedia as well as issues of Australian national/cultural identity.

Each monograph is refereed and consists of about 30,000 to 50,000 words and deals with a specific topic. Most issues are single-authored, although joint or edited collections will be considered. The writing is scholarly while also being accessible to an interested general readership.

The monographs have readers and subscribers from all over the globe, and ATOM is particularly keen that a number of individual issues would have relevance to tertiary or secondary education.

The Moving Image is published annually by ATOM in association with its publishing partners. ATOM is a not-for-profit organisation, but **The Moving Image** is part of the publications arm operating as a commercial publisher. Profits, when they occur, do, however, go towards commissioning new books in the series.

We would welcome contributions and proposals for monographs, which will enable us to continue this project.

The Editorial Board

CONTENTS

IX	**Acknowledgements**
1	**Introduction**
19	**Chapter 1:** Cybernetic Synergies
41	**Chapter 2:** *Menace*
57	**Chapter 3:** *November Eleven*
79	**Chapter 4:** *Film-Work*
101	**Chapter 5:** *Traps*
121	**Chapter 6:** *All That is Solid*
143	**Chapter 7:** *One Way Street*
155	**Chapter 8:** *What I Have Written*
167	**Chapter 9:** *Some Aspects of Australian Racism*
187	**Chapter 10:** *The Archive Project*
205	**Chapter 11:** *Indonesia Calling* and *Love & Fury*
235	**Appendix I:** Acronyms and Abbreviations
238	**Appendix II:** Filmography and Media Works – John Hughes
242	**Appendix III:** Bibliography – John Hughes
244	**Appendix IV:** References
269	**Appendix V:** Index

Acknowledgements

John Hughes has been enormously patient as I have wrestled with the tale of his many films. Much of the informational value of this book is due to his generosity. Lisa French has provided immeasurable support and patience in seeing this work to completion. For guidance and insight, thanks also go to Lisa, to Rick Thompson, Felicity Collins, Belinda Smaill, and Jane Landman. Gillian Leahy, Adrian Danks, Deane Williams, Adrian Martin, Anny Mokotow, Andrew Preston, Keith Beattie, Sian Prior and Peter Tammer also provided invaluable responses along the way. Graeme Cutts' approach to thinking about films and history has been in my mind throughout this project.

Thanks to my other colleagues and friends for their support and encouragement, especially Matthew Allen, Estelle Barrett, David Ritchie, Jennifer Radbourne, Francis Treacey, Louise Johnson, Michael Meehan, Angela O'Brien, Denise Varney, Michael Victory, Simon McLean, Chris Knowles, Dirk De Bruyn, Stephen Goddard, Gen Bailey, Saidin Salkic and Simon Wilmot.

The staff and invaluable resources of AFI Research, the ACMI Collection and Deakin University, La Trobe University, University of Melbourne and Australia Council libraries were second in importance only to Hughes' personal archives. Technical assistance was readily and generously provided by Marina Minns, Kris Paterson, Jane Garner, Eileen Wall, Liz Tucker, Dennis Claringbold, Rachel West, Josipa Crnic, Bob Tyler, Colin Savage, Robert Pitman, Gary Murin and, at ATOM, Will Allen and Zak Hamer. Thanks also to Samantha Lang, Sandra Levy and Katrina Sedgwick for supporting this project.

Peter Tapp and the ATOM staff kindly shared their office with me for the indexing and last stages of production. Julie Stafford thoroughly proofread the final iterations of the manuscript and patiently corresponded on numerous questions and changes. Nicole Snelleksz artfully remastered and enhanced a mountain of image files. Thanks to Deb Verhoeven and Deakin University for making that work possible and to Pascale van Breugel for bringing text and image together so elegantly. Professor Mary Luckhurst kindly provided insights on the art of indexing – using words.

I am indebted to Peter Hughes (no relation) for providing the first substantial essay on John Hughes' oeuvre. He is one of a number of writers, editors and publishers who have consciously and consistently paid attention to otherwise unheralded Australian independent films. Likewise, Bill Mousoulis and John Flaus are to be thanked for the inspiration they give all who make or write about films in Melbourne.

My deepest appreciation goes to Yoni Prior, whose wisdom has been called upon regularly, and our son Reuben for having graciously shared his childhood with this work.

INTRODUCTION

NEWSREEL IMAGES FILMED BY JOHN HUGHES IN 1970.

Around noon on the 15 October 1970, John Hughes, a 21-year-old news cameraperson, was hurriedly dispatched to the site of the worst accident in Australia's industrial history. Hughes found himself filming the immediate aftermath of the collapse of Melbourne's Westgate Bridge. Two thousand tons of concrete and steel and fifty men had plunged into the Yarra River. Thirty-five construction workers and engineers were dead.[1] Their colleagues, passersby and emergency workers were hauling bodies and survivors from thick black mud. Hughes looked on through the 16 mm cine camera viewfinder as a witness repeatedly told journalist Martyn Goddard how he was unable to reach workmates who were screaming for help from within a crumpled burning shed. Hughes doesn't have a great deal to say about this event. The account here comes largely from the original nine-minute news story that can now be found on YouTube.[2]

While Hughes experienced the Westgate assignment as a nightmare, he recalls a superior in the Cine-camera Department congratulating him on the footage and exclaiming with enormous pride, 'That was broadcast in Russia!' The guilelessness of this response confirmed doubts Hughes was already having about the prospect of a career in the mainstream media. Within a few months, on another assignment with Goddard, an astute social worker convinced them that, however diligent they were in recording a background story on drug abuse, it would be distorted, sensationalised and do more harm than good.

Back in the camera car, Hughes and Goddard decided to make their own film on the subject. John's life as an independent filmmaker had begun.

John Hughes is now one of Australia's most eminent filmmakers. Spanning four decades, his filmography (see Appendix II) includes the unique and critically acclaimed dramatic feature *What I Have Written* (1995),

JOHN HUGHES AND ERIKA
ADDIS FILMING *TRAPS*.

THE ELECTION TALLY ROOM IN *TRAPS* (1985).

together with nearly 30 non-fiction films that have seen him honoured with the most prestigious documentary awards in Australia – a country with a strong tradition of documentary production. Hughes has also been recognised by the academic community with honorary positions at two leading universities. The subjects of these films include international figures such as philosopher Walter Benjamin – *One Way Street* (1992) – and filmmaker Joris Ivens – *Indonesia Calling: Joris Ivens in Australia* (2009). Among other themes, *Menace* (1976) and *Traps* (1985) investigate the impact of secret service activities on the function of democratic institutions at either end of the Cold War period. One group of films explores the history and institutional practice of racism in Australia. This includes *After Mabo* (1997), which chronicles a chapter in the national struggle over Indigenous land rights. A triptych of works deals with the history and culture of independent filmmaking itself by tracing a number of filmmakers' organisations across the post-war decades.

Universal themes, such as the legacy of colonialism and the representational practices and political function of the media, underlie the specific local situations that these films examine. Beyond the stories they tell, the entire body of work serves as an ongoing investigation of filmmaking: as a process, as a social and industrial practice and as an art form. Each film is an exploration of what it is possible for the filmmaker to do within the conceptual, technical, institutional, financial and commercial conditions of the particular historical moment in which it is made. The stories in this book should therefore be relevant both to emerging filmmakers who are determined to experiment and challenge preconceptions and also to wider communities as they grapple with the challenge of cultural sustainability in the contemporary world.

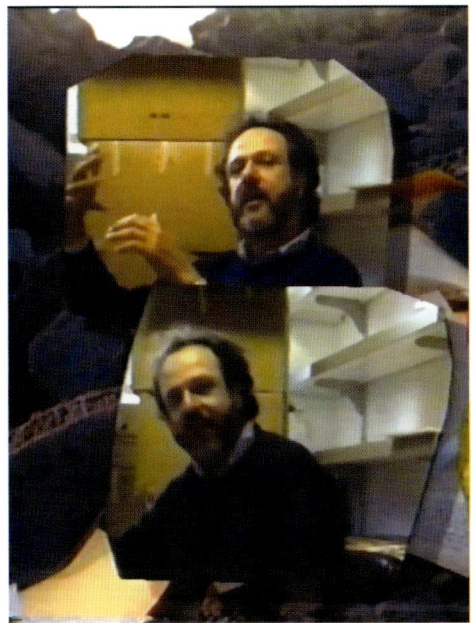

ANSON RABINBACH IN *ONE WAY STREET* (1992).

THE SHOOTING SCRIPT FOR *WHAT I HAVE WRITTEN* (1995).

The pioneering documentary filmmaker Alberto Cavalcanti said in 1955, 'Without experimentation, the documentary ceases to exist.'[3] Experimentation is evident in every aspect of John Hughes' films and this is why I think they deserve close attention. The ride is not always smooth or safe but it is much more interesting than following the routines of tried and proven formula. Hughes pays careful attention to history and ideas. His films employ a range of approaches to dramatisation, a multifaceted approach in visual design, and detailed work upon the space of the picture frame itself. These factors tell their own story about the mediation of ideas and the creative exploitation of new technologies across half a century. Since the 1960s there has been a great deal of interest in hybrid forms, such as the essay film, the formally innovative independent documentary and the experimental feature. Hughes offers an entire oeuvre to this enterprise.[4] Rather than being classified solely as a maker of 'art films', however, Hughes has been careful to locate most of his practice within the established documentary industry and tradition. In this context he has been able to produce a substantial body of work that honours Cavalcanti's understanding of the flexibility and vitality of documentary form and process.

One of the lessons Hughes took from his early experiences in television news media is that the most valuable thing the independent filmmaker can offer an audience is the integrity of their own editorial autonomy. As the producer of the films he directs, Hughes has maintained an unusually high level of creative independence. His films are grounded in traditions of politically engaged independent filmmaking and grassroots collective cultural activism. A substantial part

ABOVE: CAROLYN HOWARD WITH A STEENBECK 16 MM FILM EDITING MACHINE IN *TRAPS* (1985).

RIGHT: MARGOT NASH AND KEITH GOW IN *FILM-WORK* (1981).

of his filmmaking has been dedicated to chronicling the history of those traditions in Australia. *Indonesia Calling: Joris Ivens in Australia* (2009), *The Archive Project* (2006) and *Film-Work* (1981) form a triptych of films about socially progressive filmmaking of the 1940s and 1950s. At the time of writing, Hughes – in the fifth decade of this particular undertaking – is working on a film about the filmmakers' co-operative movement of the 1960s and 1970s. This will turn the collection into a quartet. Whatever forms creatively and socially engaged screen production take in future, these films provide vital historical background. The stories they tell do not appear in the dominant narrative of Australia's feature film industry.

The traditions of documentary, experimental and short filmmaking in Australia are at least as strong as those of the theatrical feature film. In fact, since World War II, the documentary has had greater historical continuity here than the feature. Hughes' films also show that non-feature filmmaking traditions underpin much of Australia's contemporary screen culture. The independent film culture that Hughes' films trace shares its origins with Australia's first international film festival and a practice of writing about cinema that long preceded academic involvement and that thrives beyond the bounds of mainstream publication. Since the 1900s such film cultures have been based on international social, artistic and intellectual networks, and on a mixture of voluntary, collective and artisanal practices with largely spasmodic support from government and non-government institutions, trade unions or private patrons. The small-scale practices and world-wide networks of such independent practice have more relevance to many of today's young innovators than do the institutions, economics and power structures that continue to drive most of the world's mainstream film and electronic media industries today.

The work of an independent filmmaker has always included a great deal more than directing films. Working in an artisanal mode, he or she often performs, or has a hand in, every aspect of craft at the same time as engaging in discussion and organisation around the

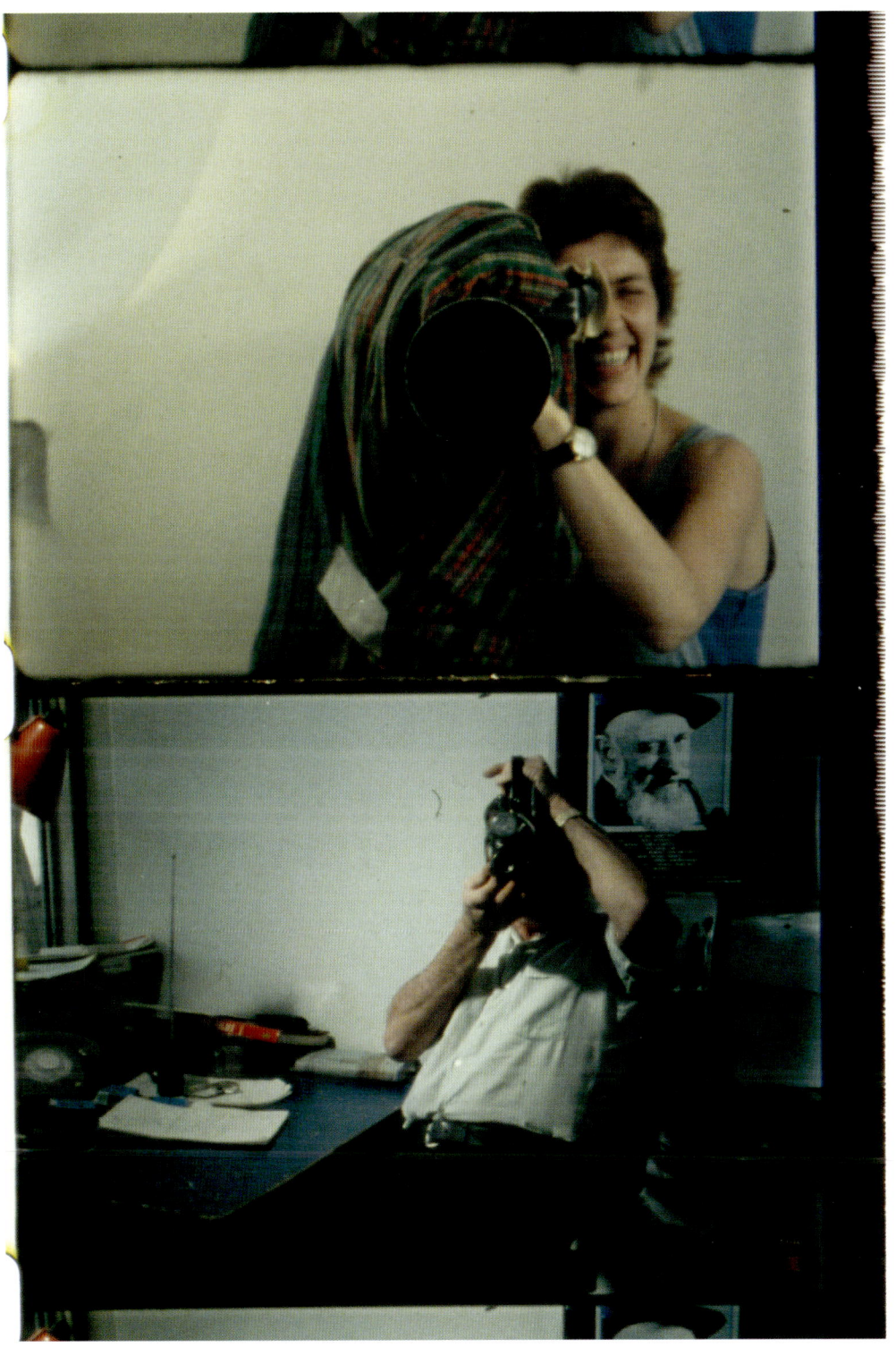

NOVEMBER 11 (1979).

JOURNALIST PHILLIP ADAMS, PIONEER PRODUCER OF THE 1970S FEATURE FILM REVIVAL, DISCUSSES THE DEMISE OF THE NATIONALIST AGENDA FOR AUSTRALIAN CINEMA IN *THE ARCHIVE PROJECT* (2006) DVD EXTRAS.

wider sphere of screen culture and industry. In addition to having proficiency as a producer, photographer, sound recordist, editor, distributor and exhibitor of films, there is research, organisation, lobbying, entrepreneurship and mentoring to be done. As an independent producer-director, Hughes has engaged in all of these activities – often simultaneously. He is also a scholar, writer, organiser, activist and teacher. As a television bureaucrat he was both eminent and innovative, and through his filmmaking he has become a leading historian of Australian documentary cinema. The ongoing story of Hughes' work illustrates the delicate balance of individual, collective and corporate agendas that many contemporary artists need to negotiate.

To better understand this kind of independent filmmaking and the context of the films discussed in this book, it may be helpful to briefly consider the wider history of filmmaking in Australia. In the silent era, Australia had one of the world's most successful entrepreneurial motion picture industries.[5] Scholars even speculated that the first-ever feature film might have been made in Australia.[6] British and American film corporations (or combines), however, had effectively strangled the Australian feature film industry early last century through their vertical integration of production, distribution and exhibition.[7]

After World War II, a dynamic film societies' movement, together with new waves of immigration from continental Europe, put a dent in the Anglo-American hegemony of Australian screen culture. A taste for global cinema was nurtured among the generation of enthusiasts who drove the burgeoning local television and advertising industries. From the late 1950s these enterprises attracted new infrastructure and personnel to screen production, whilst a small and scattered community of independent filmmakers continued to make documentaries, some shorts and the occasional feature. The early 1960s saw an injection of momentum and creative talent from a younger generation of artists and cinephiles with many different kinds of cinema in mind. Their grassroots activity found a focus in the filmmakers' co-operative movement, as the following chapter shows.

NOVEMBER 11: ON SACRED LAND (1983).

Together with the access video movement, the co-ops pointed to a possible cultural future of decentralised, community-based, globally networked production and reception of moving-image work in a myriad of forms. In the early 1970s, after decades of reviews and inaction, and just as the countercultural co-op movement began to gain traction, Australian governments invested in a revival of local feature film production. This revival was based on a nationalistic agenda aimed at the establishment of a commercial feature film industry. Over time, this small local industry was expected to find a niche in a largely unregulated global market dominated by multinational media corporations with massive influence and spending power. The whole range of other filmmaking practices that flourished around the self-sufficient film societies and filmmakers' co-ops in the 1960s were also boosted momentarily by the first injection of public funds in the 1970s. Initial finance for the newly emergent Australian film industry came, with few strings attached, through the aptly named Experimental Film and Television Fund (EFTF). A number of internationally acclaimed feature film directors subsequently emerged from the milieu of EFTF funding and co-op filmmaking.[8] Their work, however, represents only one of many trajectories that filmmakers of that generation took. Hughes' filmmaking represents one other.

Throughout the 1970s and 1980s most professional small-scale Australian film productions (shorts, documentaries and low-budget features) were subsidised but broadly independent.

Individual producers, often working on original ideas as, or with, writer-directors, formed small production companies and worked with relatively low budgets. Those who developed creative ideas maintained a high degree of autonomy and creative control. Over time, budgets increased and the number of production subsidies, especially for short, experimental, documentary and low-budget feature films dwindled. Subsidy for documentary production became almost exclusively linked to 'commercial' investment – mainly from public broadcasters. Throughout this period and into the twenty-first century, the lion's share of public film funding – and an enormous amount of volunteer labour – has been channelled into the Australian commercial feature film enterprise. In a process that can take decades, and much unpaid effort, a small portion of the feature film projects that are developed secure finance and go into production. Less than ten per cent of Australian writers, producers and directors have made more than three feature films. Most have seen only one of their feature film projects go into production.[9]

In 2006 a government review foreshadowed a restructuring of federal funding support that attenuated the trajectory described above. The objective was to transform Australian filmmaking 'from a cottage industry to one that is based on successful business enterprise'.[10] Hughes describes this as driven by neoliberal ideology in which 'audiences are seen as consumers, rather than, say, citizens'.[11] Taxpayer subsidies are now channelled towards supporting larger, more profit-oriented companies and productions. This strategy seems to ignore the fact that local production is and always has been totally dwarfed by the American industry it is supposed to ape – an industry that largely controls and determines what is on our screens. Younger producers and directors who work in this context do so, increasingly, as employees or contractors, with limited creative control or experience of leadership. Those who are creatively entrepreneurial are left to make their own way, without subsidy, and in a situation of independence that profoundly favours social and economic privilege. The range of 'voices' that appears on Australian screens today is accordingly limited. For most promising filmmakers, 'credit card' production or budget-less filmmaking based on donations and favours is either not an option or is difficult to sustain beyond one or two projects.

The production and exchange of digital films using low cost, high-definition equipment and online services demonstrate that tools for production and distribution on an artisanal or 'cottage industry' basis are more accessible than ever before. The preparation costs for cinema or broadcast release of such work, however, still run into tens or hundreds of thousands of dollars. Without an effective system of public funding to leverage the potential of this contemporary practice, then, most independent filmmakers remain largely without access to mainstream markets. They are free, however, to make films in any way and in any form they choose and to explore alternative approaches to financing, distribution and exhibition. In both regards, John Hughes' work is instructive: he has navigated the ever-changing waters of independent filmmaking for decades and has used every project to explore new methods and new approaches. Hughes' first film was self-funded, but it is unlikely that we would have his subsequent films if it were not for some form of government subsidy. Most significantly, we have these films because of Hughes' capacity to push at the boundaries of funding policy and to negotiate with financial controllers and cultural gatekeepers.

A range of factors has defined the conditions of production for independent filmmakers over the past half-century. In the history told here, certain cultural opportunities have been discovered, developed and defended. Others have been traded or lost amidst a complex of shared and competing interests and perceptions. It is hardly possible to speak of success and failure in this field. Rather, there are hierarchies of marginalisation, differentials of opportunity and influence, and irregular opportunities for assistance in making do. The broad trajectory of the first thirty years of Hughes' working life – from oppositional filmmaker and media activist in the early 1970s, to television executive in the late 1990s – is typical of many among his generation who have established successful careers in the Australian film and television industry. A parallel trajectory that sees Hughes working as an academic in the late 1970s and again in the 1990s is characteristic of others from his generation of independent filmmakers. However, the combination of both these paths, together with a creative output of over twenty independent films is far from typical, while his voluntary return from salaried employment to the vagaries of freelance independent production in middle age is most unusual. Hughes' films bear the traces of all these trajectories and his filmmaking is better described as a vocation than a career.

My own introduction to screen culture began in the late 1970s, just after the legendary (and somewhat mythologised) Melbourne Filmmakers Co-operative (MFC) was shut down. As a student I was introduced to the idea of independent filmmaking by Peter Tammer and Nigel Buesst at Swinburne Film and Television School and later by the young virtuoso documentary filmmaker Brian McKenzie at Rusden State College (now Deakin University). In the 1980s, influenced particularly by Tammer's approach to film form, I made short experimental films that mixed actuality and dramatisation. There were also collective projects including a dissident essay film about the re-enactment of the arrival of the first fleet of convicts in Australia.[12] So this study is written from, and is limited by, the perspective of one of the generation of independent filmmakers and screen-culture

JOHN HUGHES IN *FILM-WORK* (1981).

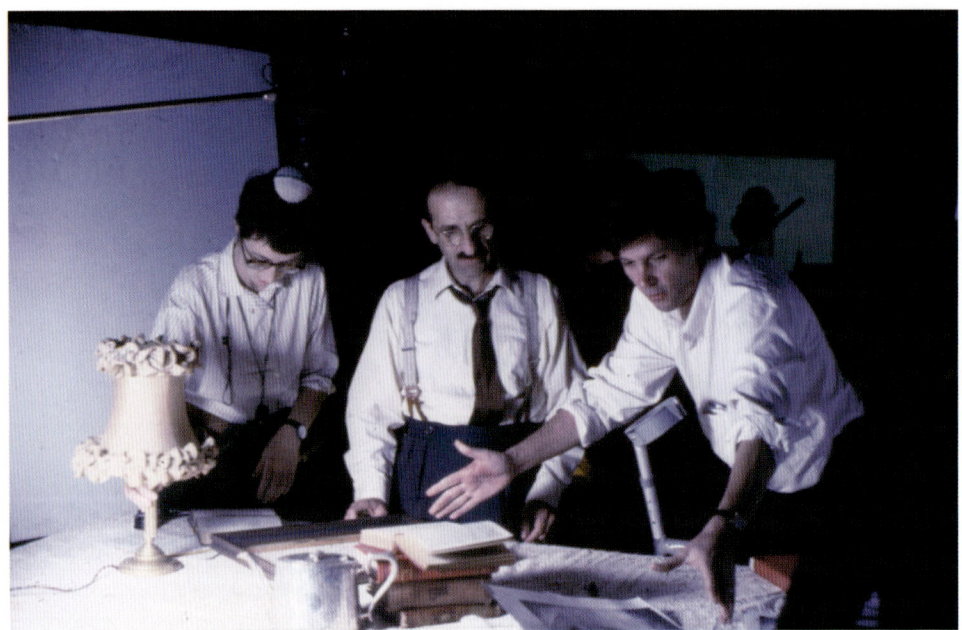

NICOLETTE FREEMAN, NICO LATHOURIS AND JOHN HUGHES PREPARING A SCENE FOR *ONE WAY STREET* (1992).

activists who immediately followed the Co-op generations to which Peter and John belong. At Rusden, Hughes presented *Film-Work* (1980) on the invitation of another significant mentor, film lecturer and historian, Graeme Cutts. Sitting in on Graeme's classes I was also introduced to the work of two filmmakers from earlier generations who play an important role in the story of Hughes' work: Giorgio Mangiamele (whom Cutts was instrumental in seeing properly recognised within Giorgio's lifetime) and Joris Ivens, whose *Indonesia Calling* Graeme was researching as much as possible whilst its key protagonists were still alive. From 1982 to 1985 Hughes and I volunteered together on the Independent Film Action Committee (IFAC). The filmmakers that IFAC represented were concerned with film as an art form and also as a vehicle for local, marginal, oppositional and personal voices, often through the production of short films and documentaries. Sustained at that time by a trickle of government funding, independent filmmaking was a largely unpaid, but nonetheless professional enterprise. Subsidy for the Australian film industry was increasingly being directed to feature film production, according to business models that reflected a global industry dominated by multinational corporations. In the spirit of acting locally and thinking globally, IFAC, in league with similar organisations in other states and other countries, campaigned for the recognition of diverse, modest-scale, regional production sectors. We did this through screenings, workshops and seminars and by critiquing and contributing to the cultural and industrial policies of state and federal governments and institutions.

The perspective of this book is also conditioned by a much younger generation of independent filmmakers with whom both Hughes and I have had the opportunity to work. They explore

FILMMAKER MARGOT NASH WORKING ON *MENACE* (1976).

the potential of the digital realm and some show an unprecedented capacity to engage with international markets. Yet, as producers in their own right, these young filmmakers are alienated from the major avenues of public and commercial support for Australian film production. When they do attempt to engage with the film-financing establishment, their experience is often one of being patronised, thwarted or exploited. So questions about independence are as relevant today as they ever were. Government-funding bodies have all but abandoned support for short and very low-budget filmmaking, even as a 'training ground'. The emergence of inexpensive digital video cameras, desktop editing and online distribution is seen as serving this function. In 2002 Clare Stewart described the position of emerging filmmakers in the era of 'new digital freedom' as passive supplicants before the talent scouts of a global entertainment industry that they subsidise.[13] These self-funded filmmakers have no formal links to industry and must cover the cost of development and production, which usually means working with unpaid crew. Stewart argued that the numerous competitive events, such as the Tropfest film festival, that constitute the cultural community to which today's emerging filmmakers still supposedly belong, are part of a network that primarily plays to corporate interests. The competitively conformist and markedly masculine culture of Tropfest is not representative.[14] Among the 'emerging' generation of independent filmmakers there is a will to create coherent practitioner communities and a hunger for dialogue around the form, function, ethics and politics of filmmaking.[15] The channels of support and nourishment for these impulses are limited and the impulses themselves are constantly at risk of being subsumed by commercial discourses. These discourses insistently construct independent filmmaking as a market niche or as the bottom rung on a career ladder

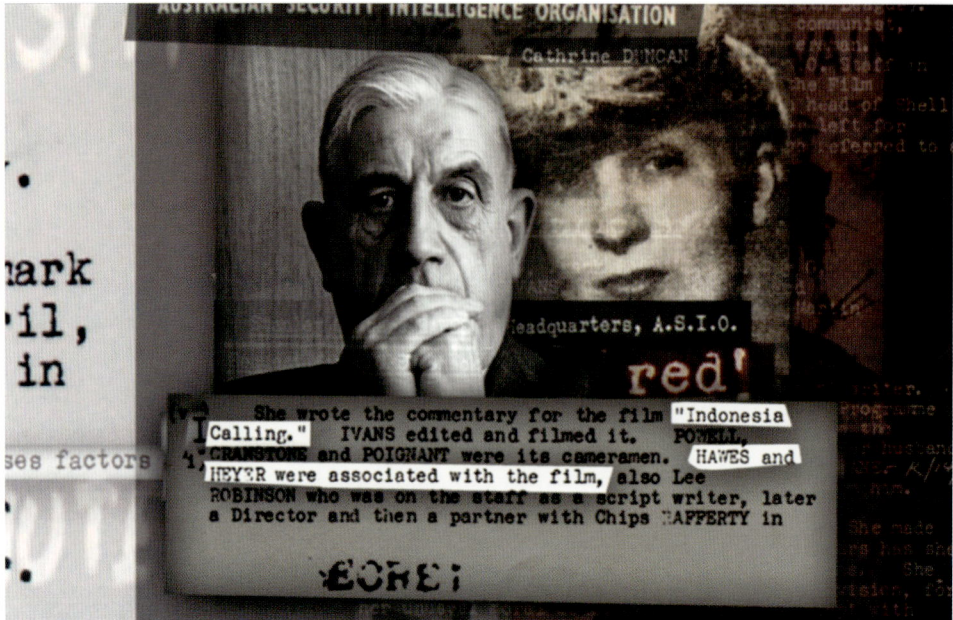

INDONESIA CALLING: JORIS IVENS IN AUSTRALIA (2009).

rather than as a space within which alternative and oppositional practices can be explored, developed and sustained.

Hughes' case is instructive in the contemporary context because, when the economic base for independent documentary production in Australia shifted from grant-based funding to investment by public television broadcasters, he was able to maintain an unusually high level of creative autonomy, producing films outside the constraints that accompany most commissions for television. He also adapted to roles on both sides of the negotiating table, taking up an executive position commissioning documentaries for SBSi (Special Broadcasting Service Independent) from 1999 to 2001. The new generation of documentary filmmakers he worked with at SBSi faced the highly competitive environment described above, without the identifiable community of peers and mentors that Hughes had found in the days of filmmakers' co-operatives (see Chapter 9).[16]

As both Ross Gibson and Peter Hughes have noted, John Hughes' films stem from *a desire to engage with the world*.[17] Hughes' films form a compendium of social, political, philosophical and artistic concerns. In content, they reveal aspects of history, culture and social practice otherwise largely ignored, repressed or forgotten. In form, they reflect a century of innovative art-making. They extend into twenty-first century television production the constructivist project of interdisciplinary art forms that foreground and explore the politics of representational processes. There is a complex interplay in these films between a wide range of cultural codes and modes of creative expression. The exploration of film form this body of work traces extends over decades

FOOTAGE FROM THE REALIST FILM UNIT OF THE 1950s IN *THE ARCHIVE PROJECT* (2006).

and continues to reflect the inclusive and pluralistic nature of the artist co-operative culture from which Hughes emerged as a filmmaker and as an activist for access video in the early 1970s.

Throughout the 1970s and 1980s feminist filmmakers also built on the traditions of political art, theatre and cinema to reveal histories and ideas that have been excluded from or marginalised within mainstream cultural discourse.[18] Hughes saw his work as following a parallel path. He sought the collaboration of innovators in community theatre to make *November Eleven: an Australian History* (1981), *Traps* and *All That is Solid*. These films combined documentary and dramatic elements in a drive to achieve what media historian Peter Hughes identified as an 'apposite, rigorous, conjunction of form and content'.[19] This is a defining characteristic of John Hughes' films that continues to be shared by much of the work in alternative theatre today.

In my view, Hughes' most innovative contribution to film craft, at an international level, lies in his work with screen design. From the never released *Some Aspects of Australian Racism* (1973, see Chapter 9) to *Love & Fury* (2013, see Chapter 11), Hughes has experimented with simultaneously arranging and layering multiple images and text within the space of a single frame. In this collage work, he strives to resolve an aesthetic tension between didactic or expository style and a more poetic dimension in documentary cinema. Within this aesthetic, subtle but profound innovations have emerged in the very process of the production of meaning within televisual form, especially since *One Way Street* (1992) and *After Mabo* (1997). In a rare instance for an Australian feature film, a stylised approach to screen design is also carried into *What I Have Written* (1995).

PAUL ENGLISH AND HELEN MORSE IN *LOVE & FURY* (2013).

Also significant – particularly in the Australian context – is Hughes' persistent experimentation with dramatisation and performance. During the 1980s this exploration was one of creative risk-taking that took his work well beyond the conventional demarcations of documentary and fictional form. That experience is distilled, in Hughes' later work with performers, in both the dramatic fiction *What I Have Written* and the apparently straightforward but subtle and highly sophisticated documentary *Love & Fury*. A particular interest of my study are questions that this aspect of Hughes' work provokes about the dialectical potential of relationships between the elements of dramatisation, performance and actuality within film form.

Hughes' unique approach to collage within the frame has a similar dialectical capacity. Its genesis might lie in 'strange displays' that John remembers his father, Stan, creating in the window of the family's cake shop on Saturday afternoons during the 1950s. He says there would be a topical dimension to these found object installations such as the Melbourne Olympic Games of 1956. John's recollection suggests that there was something dialectical about Stan's compositions because he says they usually included 'a small questioning gesture' – skepticism about the world and the things commonly presented.[20] Stan Hughes was a window-dresser and graphic artist before the war. Should we then imagine the shop window displays that John remembers as amateur or professional works? If they were personal reflections without commercial function, as his son suggests, were they art? Even if we had access to these displays today it is likely that there would be no clear answer to these questions: questions that might equally be applied to the works of many independent filmmakers and other artists whose means and modes of production and exhibition are often comparable. Stan Hughes had found a form of creative play through which his relationship to the world could be negotiated, in a space that was at once private and open to public view – rather like television. Meanwhile, Australians had their first opportunity to view the world from the privacy of their homes, with the introduction of television timed to coincide with the Melbourne Olympic Games.

Hughes describes his family as having little sense of inheritance or history. His forbears, who included Welsh railway workers, a Liverpool mariner and domestic workers, were (like a swathe of their class and generation) 'particularly damaged' by both the First World War and the Depression of the 1930s.[21] During World War II both his parents did factory work in protected industries but maintained an interest in creative pursuits. Hughes remembers that during the 1950s, after long days of toil in the cake shop, they spent nights working at the kitchen table on concepts, words and music for musical theatre shows. Around the time of the shop window displays that John Hughes recalls, the Tivoli Theatre in Melbourne presented *Olympic Follies* (1956), a mainstream theatre production based on an idea by John's mother, May Hughes.[22] So both his parents were engaged in weaving creative compositions – in text, design, drama and music – around this topical international event that had its origins in the ancient world and was the focal point for the introduction of television to Australian culture.

Stan and May Hughes also encouraged the creative life of their two children. Stan helped his sons build a photographic enlarger using cake tins. While he encouraged John's interest in drawing, boys at Brighton Technical School threw punches and abuse at John and a classmate as they attended art classes at the adjacent girls' school. Hughes recalls being very disturbed by such experiences at school. However, encouraged by English literature teachers who offered alternative ways to view the world, he wrote poetry attacking the brutal, hierarchical and authoritarian culture of the schoolyard.

Hughes says his parents were skeptical about organised religion but encouraged his involvement in a local church community through a basketball team and Sunday school. He remembers conversation about how different meanings might be found in Bible stories. In the mid-1960s, at fourteen years of age, he read Bertrand Russell's *Why I Am Not a Christian*.[23] Having decided not to be confirmed, he was surprised to have his views treated with respect by the church minister. At around this time he began to frequent the Committee for International Co-operation and Disarmament (CICD) and other haunts of Melbourne's nascent counterculture – the peace, beat, folk and blues movements. So, coming from a broadly liberal-humanist background, Hughes encountered politics at an early age. Since adolescence, he has been attuned to the zeitgeist of international left-wing thought. Through film and video, he has joined efforts to democratise media and to locate and help build access to mass audiences. While these were quests within contemporary culture, they also led to a study of early twentieth-century socialist culture.

Despite such internationalism, Australian independent work remains unrecognised in historical surveys of international independent documentary and avant-garde film and video. In English language publications concerned with these practices, the Anglo-American bias is arguably even more entrenched than it is in international scholarship of mainstream cinema. Significant documentary, short and experimental works from countries like Australia, are rarely if ever acknowledged in global surveys of these genres, and only occasionally receive attention in surveys of national cinema. It is as if global cultural memory is impermeable to its smaller constituents, no matter how profoundly they are engaged with global trends and with each other. Contributing to this situation is the fact that Australian independent films, together with those of many other smaller screen cultures, have been largely absent from multinational as well as local distribution channels. These films have tended to be available to audiences, critics and scholars largely through one-off festival screenings and occasional exposure on broadcast television within a year or so of completion. For many years all but Hughes' most recent films, like most Australian independent works, were largely out of circulation. In February 2011, however, all of Hughes' previously released works were made available by Kriszta Doczy who, with encouragement from veteran independent filmmaker Peter Tammer, has begun to address this market gap through her educational distribution company Artfilms. Since then, video copies of early films by Tammer and many of the other filmmakers referred to in this book have become available on DVD and more recently via internet streaming.[24] The not-for-profit Australian Teachers of Media (ATOM) also now hosts online streaming by filmmakers and organisations.

In the early 2000s, I conducted a series of interviews with John Hughes as part of a research project that traced both his filmmaking and his involvement in the polemics, culture and organisation of independent film in Australia during the previous thirty years.[25] These and subsequent discussions are the source of many of Hughes' statements in this book.

Contemporary low-budget digital filmmaking, like independent work of decades past, often involves or draws upon documentary practice. It calls for experimentation and engages with questions and interests that go beyond the concerns of established commercial production.

Hughes' filmmaking provides a model of perseverance but also of a preparedness to take creative risks alongside a critical approach to practice that is always open to new possibilities and to renewal based upon ongoing research across a range of fields, including the history of film itself. For these reasons, this book is written as much for contemporary practitioners and cinema enthusiasts as it is for scholars and students of film history.

Endnotes

[1] West Gate Bridge Committee, The West Gate Bridge Memorial, Melbourne, 2013, <http://www.westgatebridge.org>, accessed 10 January 2013.
[2] Martyn Goddard, 'Westgate Bridge collapse', *ABC News*, Camera John Hughes, 15 October 1970, Melbourne, <http://www.youtube.com/watch?v=UR8eYevYcg8 >, accessed 10 January 2013. Hughes' account is from Ken Linnett, 'Taming of the Left in Australia', film review, *The Melbourne Times*, 5 March 1986, p. 10.
[3] Alberto Cavalcanti, 'Alberto Cavalcanti: His Advice to Young Producers of Documentary', *Film Quarterly*, no. 9, 1955, pp. 354–355, cited by Pat Laughren 'Debating Australian Documentary Production Policy: Some Practitioner Perspectives', *Media International Australia*, no. 129, 2008, pp. 116–128.
[4] In discussing this genre, Australian film scholars most often cite Helen Grace's *Serious Undertakings* (1982), Ross Gibson's *Camera Natura* (1985), Sarah Gibson and Susan

Lambert's *Landslides* (1986) and the films of John Hughes. See, for example, Peter Hughes 'The Documentary Project and Postmodernity', thesis (PhD), School of Arts and Media, La Trobe University, Bundoora, 1997 and Tony Barta 'Making it Strange: *Camera Natura, One Way Street* and *The Refracting Glasses* as Realism, Surrealism and the Poetics of History in Film', in John Benson, Ken Berryman & Wayne Levy (eds), *Screening the Past: The Sixth Australian History and Film Conference Papers*, Melbourne, La Trobe University, 1993, pp. 205–210.

5. Jeannette Delamoir, 'The Explosive Life of an Exploiteer: Franklyn Barrett Tours North Queensland with 'The Ten Commandments', *Australia's Living Archive*, 2011, National Film and Sound Archive, Canberra, <http://www.nfsa.gov.au/research/papers/>.

6. See 'The First Long Picture in the World' in Ina Bertrand & William D Routt. *The Story of the Kelly Gang*, The Moving Image, ATOM, St Kilda, 2007.

7. Mike Walsh, 'The Motion Picture Distributors Association of Australia and the conversion of Sir Victor Wilson', first release, selected papers from the Film and History Conference, Adelaide, November 2002. *Screening the Past*, no. 16, 2004, La Trobe University, 7 May, <http://tlweb.latrobe.edu.au/humanities/screeningthepast/firstrelease/fr_16/mwfr16.html>, accessed 19 December 2013. See also Delamoir, op. cit.

8. Feature film directors whose early experimental or short films were supported by the EFTF include Bruce Beresford, Tim Burstall, Jan Chapman, Richard Franklin, Scott Hicks, Richard Lowenstein, Chris Noonan, Phillip Noyce, Peter Wier and – at 16 years of age – Alex Proyas. See Alex Gerbaz, 'The Legacy of the Experimental Film and Television Fund, 1970–78', National Archives of Australia, Canberra, 2009.

9. Screen Australia Research, activity of producers, directors and writers of Australian feature films, 1970–2011, <http://www.screenaustralia.gov.au/research/statistics/oefilmmakersffactivity.aspx>, accessed 31 January 2013.

10. Department of Communications, Information Technology and the Arts, 'Review of Australian Government Film Funding Support, issues paper', 2006, p. 9, <http://arts.gov.au/sites/default/files/pdfs/australian–film–review.pdf>, accessed 22 February 2013.

11. John Hughes, 'After *Indonesia Calling*', PhD exegesis, School of Media and Communication, College of Design and Social Context, RMIT University, Melbourne, November 2012.

12. John Cumming, Jane Madsen & James Swinson, *First Time Tragedy, Second Time Farce*, 1989, 16 mm, colour, 75 minutes, Counter Productions (Australia) & Zero One (UK), Executive Producer Russell Porter, Camera John Cumming, John Gulliver, Vicki Hastrich & James Swinson, Sound John Cruthers, Piers Douglas, Andrew Howie, Jane Madsen, Mark Nash & James Swinson, Music Steve Skaith, Editor Jane Madsen. Featuring Bart Willoughby, Robyn Archer. Produced with assistance from Film Victoria.

13. Stewart, Clare, 'SPAA Fringe: independence contested', *Real Time/On Screen*, no. 47, March 2002, p. 17. In 2002 Stewart became the first head of film programs at the Australian Centre for the Moving Image (ACMI). She went on to become director of the Sydney Film Festival, head of exhibition at the British Film Institute (BFI) and was appointed director of the London Film Festival in 2012.

14. Tropfest is promoted as 'Australia's most prestigious short film festival' and an 'iconic cultural event'. Of the 141 finalist films in Tropfest from 2005 to 2013, only 22 were directed by women. This is 2% below the representation of women as professional feature film directors

in the period 2007–2011. See Tropfest Australia. The world's largest short film festival, Sydney, 2013, <http://tropfest.com>, accessed 13 February 2013.

15 See, for example, Genevieve Bailey & Benj Binks, Doco3000, Melbourne, 2013, <https://http://www.facebook.com/Doco3000>, accessed 14 February 2013.

16 Hughes was involved in the development of a large number of innovative projects during his time with SBSi. A review of that legacy would require a volume on its own.

17 Peter Hughes, 'A way of being engaged with the world: the films of John Hughes', *Metro*, no. 93, Autumn 1993, pp. 46–55. Ross Gibson, 'Life as a Project of Montage', *Filmnews*, November 1992, pp. 17, 18.

18 See the collection of writings on women's independent filmmaking in Australia, edited by Annette Blonski, Barbara Creed and Freda Freiberg, *Don't Shoot Darling! Women's Independent Filmmaking in Australia*, Greenhouse, Melbourne, 1987. Despite its exclusive focus on work by women, this is the most comprehensive monograph and reference work on Australian independent filmmaking of this period.

19 To date, Peter Hughes' 1993 nine-page article for *Metro* magazine (op. cit.) is the only sustained overview of Hughes' oeuvre.

20 Interview with John Hughes, conducted by John Cumming, Melbourne, 1 August 2000.

21 ibid.

22 Hughes, May, Ralton R James & David N Martin, 'Olympic Follies', Tivoli Theatre, Melbourne, 1956. Cinema and Theatre Historical Society, <http://www.caths.org.au/archives/archives.htm>, accessed 11 June 2013.

23 Bertrand Russell, 'Why I Am Not a Christian', in Paul Edwards (ed.), *Why I Am Not a Christian: and other essays on religion and related subjects,* Allen & Unwin, London, 1957.

24 Such releases need to continue in order to redress an imbalance in institutional and private collections that have come to be dominated by a welcome but overwhelming flood of retrospective releases from Europe and North America.

25 John Cumming, 'A long road to the small screen: John Hughes and the independent film and video movement in Australia', thesis (MA), Cinema Studies, La Trobe University, Melbourne, 2004.

CHAPTER 1:
Cybernetic Synergies

While working in television, John Hughes became involved with independent cinema through the artists and filmmakers co-operative movement of the 1960s. His first 16 mm short film *Nowhere Game* (1972) was a self-funded documentary that won a national award and screened in a commercial cinema. As the camera operator on an experimental feature film *Dalmas* (Deling, 1973), Hughes saw how the form and process of conventional filmmaking could be radically challenged. This chapter traces these early adventures in filmmaking and also explores the local film culture of Melbourne, including the work of the Melbourne University Film Society (MUFS, now Melbourne Cinémathèque), the Carlton filmmakers and the Melbourne Filmmakers Co-operative (MFC). This brief introduction to aspects of post-war film culture and production in Melbourne from the 1950s to the 1970s will also provide a context for discussions of wartime and post-war independent filmmaking that occur in subsequent chapters.

After leaving school at fifteen years of age, Hughes recalls that he worked on the railways, but kept up with his artwork, exhibiting and selling paintings at the Emerald Hill Gallery in South Melbourne. Around 1967 he started work as a trainee at the Australian Broadcasting Commission (ABC), which had its television studios near his family's home in Elsternwick. He recalls that his first position in this very thorough apprenticeship was with the dispatch department. Here, by repeatedly navigating the corridors of the television station to make deliveries, Hughes learnt the structure of the organisation. In his next position, with television staging, he met artists and artisans from all the creative departments.

Finally, in the cine camera department, Hughes was introduced to the latest technology of 1960s filmmaking. By the mid-1960s the ABC was beginning to adopt crystal-sync technology. This enabled sound synchronisation between autonomous 16 mm film cameras and ¼-inch sound tape recorders – without the use of cables. Throughout the post-war period the range and availability of 16 mm equipment, supplies and processing had expanded enormously. Extensive military use of this economical lightweight medium during World War II transformed what was formerly a home-movie gauge into an industrial one ideally suited to production for television. This also made the tools of professional production much more affordable and manageable for independent filmmakers, photographers and other visual artists. No longer the preserve of avant-garde artists with wealthy benefactors, personal artisanal filmmaking began to flourish as a popular form. Hughes soon developed an interest in such independent filmmaking and sometime before 1970 he persuaded the ABC administration to allow him to organise a guest presentation to ABC trainees. The guest was Giorgio Mangiamele, a pioneer of independent production in Australia whose work Hughes thinks he may have read about in a newspaper.

Mangiamele was an Italian immigrant who, during the 1950s and 1960s, produced a number of poetic films that explored migrant experience in Australia.[26] He was arguably the most accomplished independent maker of narrative film in Melbourne at the time, having made three feature length and six short dramatic films between 1953 and 1970. In the early 1960s Mangiamele worked as cinematographer for his English-born contemporary and friend Tim Burstall, on the children's television series *Sebastian the Fox* and on two of the many short films on modern Australian art that Burstall also made for television throughout the decade.[27] I will begin to set the scene into which Hughes was about to enter with a brief consideration of these pioneering independents. They both produced and directed their films – as Hughes would do – and were key figures of Australian filmmaking at the end of the 1960s.

Mangiamele was one of the first Australian directors to have a feature film accepted into competition at the prestigious Cannes Film Festival.[28] He also won some AFI Awards but otherwise attracted limited recognition within the Australian film industry. The importance of Mangiamele's work – both as filmmaking and as cultural intervention – is now widely acknowledged and a number of his films have been restored and released on DVD.[29] Leaving aside the institutionalised racism of post-war Australia and the almost complete neglect of local independent filmmakers by television broadcasters at the time, the commercial potential of his films was constrained by a singular, personal, artistic vision steeped in the ideology and aesthetic of Italian neorealism. Mangiamele was resolutely a maker of art cinema.

Burstall graduated from The University of Melbourne a year or so before 1948 when the film society MUFS was established. By that time, Burstall and his wife Betty were part of the community that developed around the famous artists' colony of Montsalvat in the semi-rural area of Eltham, where they built their own home from mud bricks and scrap.[30] He also wanted to make artistic films but came to independent filmmaking later than Mangiamele with an award-winning, forty-five minute independent drama *The Prize* (1959). Whilst very much the 'Eltham' filmmaker, Burstall played an important part in the Carlton scene when he began to direct plays at La Mama theatre, which his wife Betty established in the late 1960s as 'a place where new ideas, new ways of expression can be tried out; a place where you can hear what people are thinking and feeling'.[31] After the punishing box-office failure of his first feature film *2000 Weeks* (1969), Burstall took a resolutely populist direction and is widely regarded as having been instrumental in re-establishing commercial feature filmmaking in Australia.[32] Accounts that claim this was the first feature made by Australians 'since Charles Chauvel's *Jedda* in 1955', however, ignore films including his friend Mangiamele's *Clay* (1965).[33] Burstall's third feature *Alvin Purple* (1973), which Mangiamele thought 'appalling' and a 'sell out', remains one of the highest grossing Australian films.[34] Mangiamele, on the other hand, was unable to secure finance for any feature projects after *Beyond Reason* (1970).

From 1952 Gil Brealey and Ian Jones built a small 16 mm MUFS production facility, made a number of short films and helped fund and produce the first film that Barry Humphries appeared in.[35] At least until the late 1960s, MUFS was the primary enclave for the theoretical and critical consideration of cinema in Melbourne. In that decade it had between 1200 and 1500 members, including the central group of 'Carlton' filmmakers. Two MUFS cinephiles that turned to filmmaking in the early 1960s were Sasha Trikojus and Bert Deling. They embodied the idea of a critically informed practice. Barrett Hodsdon writes that with the support of 'MUFS veterans' Brian Davies and Bob Garlick, their critical writing in MUFS journal *Annotations* was 'almost ahead of the international currency of the [French] New Wave'.[36] *Annotations*, unlike its Sydney University Film Group's *Bulletins*, included interviews with local independent filmmakers and reviews of their work.[37] Trikojus, Deling and Garlick also revitalised the MUFS' production subcommittee and set up the Unifed (a film society trust created with Melbourne Film Festival income), providing small grants for several 'Carlton films' throughout the 1960s.[38] Student organisations at other universities and the State Film Centre of Victoria also provided a modest degree of institutional support for local independent films.[39] Bruce Hodsdon has dubbed the 'Carlton filmmakers', many of whom were also connected in some way to La Mama theatre, as the 'Carlton ripple' because they did not constitute a wave or movement – more an 'energy centre'.[40] An account by Nigel Buesst, a key Carlton independent filmmaker, suggests that while this ripple was composed of a divergent set of individuals, they took their lead from the 'French new wave' rather than from the traditional neorealist filmmaking of Mangiamele or the more commercial direction that Tim Burstall took.[41]

The continuity Victorian filmmakers enjoyed, between the personnel and activities of film organisations as far back as the 1940s, did not exist to the same extent in NSW. In 1965 the Ubu group emerged from the inner-urban artists community of the Yellow House in Sydney. Ubu championed contemporary 'underground' and 'experimental' filmmaking and conducted lightshows and film screenings. The Ubu artists were particularly entrepreneurial. Their events often attracted attention from the censors and, in turn, from the mainstream media and they regularly drew audiences of over one thousand people. They relied on their wits, a counterculture market, and a beneficent commercial film laboratory. Members of Ubu started the Sydney Filmmakers Co-operative (SFC), informally, in 1966.[42] The London Filmmaker's Co-op was officially registered that year.[43] Both followed the model of the New York Film-maker's Coop (NYFC, registered in 1962) where the emphasis was on a non-narrative, formalist, poetic and personal/diarist 'experimental' filmmaking.[44] In recent years, Corinne Cantrill has confirmed the American influence upon local enthusiasts of experimental film during the 1960s, saying that 'the real dynamic' was in America.[45] But the idea of a film co-operative was not new in Australia. Research discussed in Chapter 4 shows that moves were made to establish a filmmaking co-op with a documentary bent, through the trade union movement, as early as 1957.[46]

The film co-op movement was made popular globally by packages of 16 mm films from the New American Cinema. Hughes later learned that these were sponsored by the Ford Foundation, distributed through diplomatic channels and quite possibly sanctioned by the CIA (see Chapter 3).[47] Australian films also started to travel – often in filmmakers' suitcases and without any official infrastructure or funding. In 1967 Ubu conducted a 'Sydney Underground Movies' screening in Melbourne's Dendy Cinema. Carlton filmmaker Peter Tammer responded with a screening of Melbourne films, *A Breath of Fresh Air*, also at the Dendy.[48] Tammer, also a freelance editor who had worked with Burstall at Eltham films, soon took a job at the Commonwealth Film Unit (CFU) in Sydney, where he got some help from local film people, including Kit Guyatt and Sandra Levy, to screen the program in Sydney's Union Theatre, a venue Ubu also used.[49] Tammer was

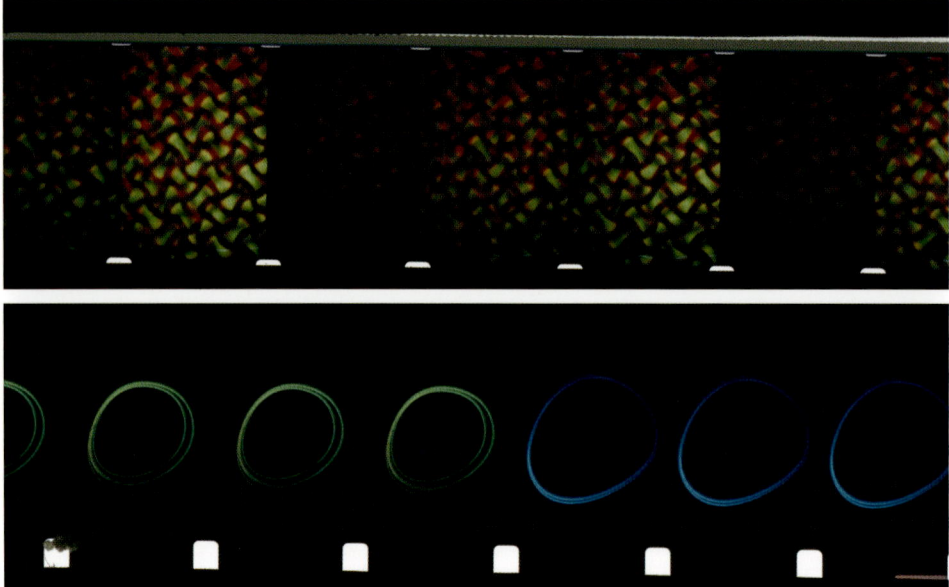

CYBERNETIC SYNERGY (1976).

stimulated by some of the Ubu work and keen to show that there was independent filmmaking in Melbourne too, and that it was different. Whilst sometimes taken in earnest, this kind of rivalry may have been one stimulus for the formation of the MFC a few years later.[50] Leading Ubu filmmaker Albie Thoms characterised the Melbourne filmmakers as being 'more concerned with social conscience than personal expression [or technical] or aesthetic experiment'.[51] Tammer doesn't accept this caricature of the filmmakers in either city nor of rivalry between them at the time, citing Sydney filmmakers like Kit Guyatt as both socially committed and supportive.[52] Tammer had been making independent short films since 1964, and like many of the other Carlton filmmakers, crossed freely between narrative, documentary and experimental forms.[53]

1970 was a watershed year for independent film in Melbourne, as it was for John Hughes, with the beginnings of the Melbourne Filmmakers Co-operative (MFC) in screenings conducted by visual artists, filmmakers and cinephiles at the Pinacotheca art gallery in Richmond.[54] These gatherings synthesised the post-war film society movement, which MUFS epitomised, with the artists' co-op movement that had also gained momentum in Australia during the 1960s. The screenings featured a wide range of local and international independent films and some of the first independent video recordings made in Australia. While Hughes worked in television, he was also among those who came to the Pinacotheca screenings with a background in the visual arts. At just 20 years of age, the aspiring filmmaker and television cameraperson had his formative cinema experiences at the MFC and saw some 'extremely strange films' that revealed 'a whole other world'.[55]

MFC founders included the gallery's owner Bruce Pollard and filmmakers Jim Wilson, Tammer, Trikojus and Deling, together with Fred Harden – a recent graduate from the RMIT photography school who was interested in filmmaking and was (or would soon be) working for an advertising agency.[56] Tammer insists that visual artists were central to the film activity at Pinacotheca and to the early life of the Co-op.[57] James (Jim) Clayden was beginning a diverse life of professional creative activity in painting, sculpture, performance art, theatre and filmmaking and was soon working on a multi-screen projection piece.[58] Born in Germany, Jonas Balsaitis attended Preston Institute of Technology, Prahran College of Technology, completed his studies at the National Gallery School in 1969, and had his first exhibition of paintings at Pinecotheca in 1970. Like Michael Lee, he had begun experiments with film animation.[59] Lee, who had come to Melbourne in 1968 to study film at Swinburne Technical College, 'was never concerned with characterisation or narrative but with the communication of emotions and moods'.[60] Like Hughes, these artists were in their early twenties. They used Super-8 film, an amateur gauge format that was much cheaper and easier to use than 16 mm, and unlike portable video technology at that time, afforded impressive full-colour projection.[61] Alongside these artists' films, MFC hosted screenings of more conventional narrative and documentary work.

A week before the Westgate Bridge collapse, Hughes attended a projection that Bert Deling had arranged at the Co-op on 'double head' – with the sound and picture on separate reels. The film was *Beginnings* (1970) – the now legendary documentary of student protest against the American War in South East Asia made by Rod Bishop, Gordon Glenn, Scott Murray and Andrew Pecze at La Trobe University.[62] The film was followed by 'video interviews', 'a dialogue on Politics & the Image Industry' and Deling collected donations at the door for a print of the film to be made.[63] Here was an independent filmmaking community at work. Through it, Hughes was meeting a wide range of dedicated enthusiasts and innovators. The film editor of *Beginnings*, nineteen-year-old Scott Murray, was also writing for *Cinema Papers*, a La Trobe student tabloid that, with Murray as its editor, became the major Australian film magazine for three decades.[64]

Early in 1971 a permanent base was established for the MFC at 161 Spring Street. Co-op organiser and internationally recognised painter Don Laycock rented this large space in Melbourne's theatre district. He called it Babylon. The volunteer organisers built a cinema with a bio box, together with a more informal screening space. Tammer recalls that old seating was brought in from the Balwyn Cinema and a large artists' stretcher with a canvas was professionally made as a screen.[65] One of the Co-op directors, Ian McRae, gave it the name Mind's Eye Cinema, and the Melbourne Filmmakers Co-operative was officially incorporated on the 5 July 1971.[66] Its terms of trade were modelled on those of the Sydney Filmmakers Co-operative (SFC), which was registered in March 1970. The filmmakers' co-ops were non-profit, collectively owned organisations and filmmakers were to receive 75% of any returns. In both cases, registration came about partly in response to the lure of federal funding which would relieve the considerable workload on the handful of volunteers driving each organisation.[67]
The MFC's aims were to exhibit, distribute and 'ultimately assist in the production of members films'.[68] Harden, the first chair of the MFC, recalls full-house attendances of up to 150 to events at Spring Street.[69]

ABOVE AND TOP RIGHT: *NOWHERE GAME* (1971); **BELOW RIGHT:** RAYNOR ELLINGHAUS IN *NOWHERE GAME*.

In Melbourne, the co-operative movement gave continuity to some of the activities that had been taking place through the film societies in previous decades, but it also brought a cultural shift, broadening the cinematic palette to include experimental work and experiments with film by visual artists.[70] In doing so, the co-op movement marked out as 'independent' a broad field of activity that embraced a wide range of aesthetics, ideologies and ambitions and did so through organisations that were created by and for a broad range of filmmakers. According to the historical records and accounts, however, the MFC was an organisation almost completely dominated by men in its early days. Women were around, however, and beginning to organise the next big cultural shift.

Hughes recalls making a number of short Super-8 films from around 1969.[71] In 1971 the first government film grants were provided. In that year Hughes made his first 16 mm film *Nowhere Game*. But he did so without a grant. While he was among the younger generation of co-op filmmakers who would become conversant with government funding regimes, Hughes made his first professional film in the wholly independent mode of the founding co-op filmmakers. That year, in his role as an ABC cameraperson, Hughes accompanied journalist Martyn Goddard, who had been given a brief to develop a news magazine story on illicit drug use in Melbourne. At the Buoyancy Foundation they met Rod Patterson and Robin Laurie who ran the crisis drop-in centre there.

From this meeting, Patterson became something of a mentor for Hughes. Laurie, an actor and filmmaker, had been president of the otherwise rather masculinist MUFS in the mid-1960s. She was already – or soon became – a friend of Hughes.[72] Hughes and Goddard were persuaded that a news story, according to the ABC brief, was unlikely to be helpful. The sensational depictions of drug use in the media at the time, said Patterson and Laurie, were 'part of the problem.'[73] After the meeting they decided that they could collaborate with Buoyancy in making a documentary independently that might advocate an alternate viewpoint. In their spare time, and with their own funds (about A$2000 for film and laboratory costs), they borrowed equipment and recruited an ABC assistant editor to cut the film.

In the opening scene of *Nowhere Game* Buoyancy Foundation director Father Jim Armstrong explains that young people turn to drugs because 'there's nothing else to do and nowhere

IMAGES FROM *NOWHERE GAME* (1971). NOTE THE TRACES OF LOW-BUDGET PRODUCTION IN THE FINAL FILM PRINT HERE: ORIGINAL CAMERA FILM, SPLICED WITH ADHESIVE TAPE.

else to go – it's a great big nowhere game.'[74] Later in the film a discussion is staged in a park between Armstrong and three heroin addicts. Armstrong tends to play devil's advocate in his inquiries about addiction. Meanwhile, Rod Patterson exemplifies the spirit of partisan work of advocacy that drives the film. Patterson and Buoyancy solicitor Raynor Ellinghaus make extended statements about the complexities of teenage drug abuse and their frustration at the stereotyping, ignorance and intolerance towards the problem in the wider community and media.

In 1976 Hughes described *Nowhere Game* as a short documentary intended to 'de-mystify some of the attitudes that had grown up as a result of press campaigns about drug addicts'.[75] In the film, Patterson leads a discussion on the floor of a tiny apartment with two young women who have just taken heroin – Mary Anne lies unconscious on a mattress for much of the time while Patterson, cigarette in hand, probes the other woman's reason for spending most of her time in the room. She describes her sense of the 'pointlessness' of living. Much of this discussion plays out in a continuous four-minute shot. The 16 mm cine camera has a distinct presence in the film as a benign and confiding eye. This effect is arguably enhanced by the technical limitation of the borrowed device's noisy mechanism as it rattles away underneath the conversations. Hughes' camerawork is otherwise passive and observational, but his subjects seem to be consciously engaging with the camera without self-consciously playing to it. The filmmaker/cinematographer

NOWHERE GAME (1971).

is behind the camera, evoking an effect that Peter Watkins pioneered, also with 16 mm news cameras, on *Culloden* (1964) and *The War Game* (1965).

Colin Bennett, *The Age* newspaper film critic and an Australian Film Institute (AFI) board member, had seen *Nowhere Game* – possibly at a Filmmakers Co-op screening. Bennett contacted Hughes, told him about the AFI and suggested he enter the film in their AFI Awards. Hughes later learned that he and Goddard had been acknowledged with an AFI Award. Subsequently, Hughes actively marketed *Nowhere Game* in a way that was and remains typical of the makers of self-funded films. As is so often the case, however, cost recoupment was minimal. ABC Television rejected the film but the Victorian Department of Health bought six prints for training and educational purposes. Perhaps in fear of the film's contentiousness, it decided that only health professionals should view these. *Nowhere Game* had a non-theatrical life through MFC screenings and distribution by the MFC. In 1974 it was exhibited theatrically at the Athenaeum, an independent commercial cinema in the city centre, where it supported Roman Polanski's *The Fearless Vampire Killers* (1974).[76]

In 1967 when he announced the establishment of the Australia Council for the Arts (ACA), the Liberal prime minister Harold Holt described its role as to 'increase, at a national level,

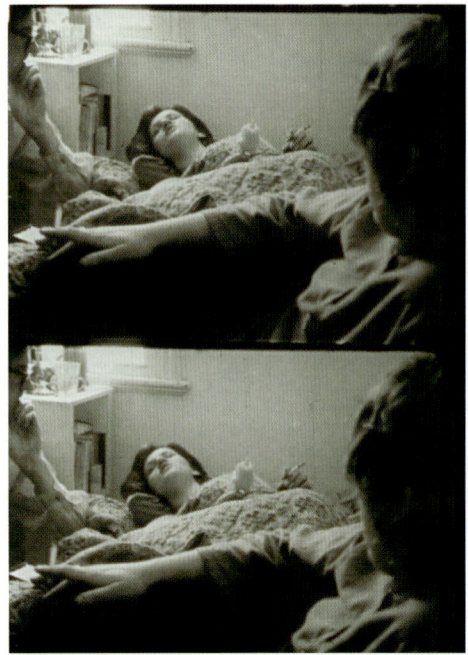 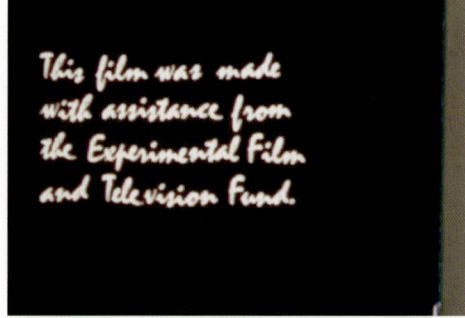 

CLOCKWISE FROM TOP LEFT: *NOWHERE GAME* (1971); *CYBERNETIC SYNERGY* (1976); JOHN HANSEN, 'WHAT SOCIETY USES AN ENGINEER FOR TOTALLY STIFLES CREATIVITY.' *CYBERNETIC SYNERGY*.

Commonwealth patronage of the Arts without creating a monolithic structure'.[77] The ACA's remit followed recommendations from the 1963 'Vincent Report' and included support of 'filmmaking for television with an educational and cultural emphasis'.[78] The Council's founding chairman, Dr HC 'Nugget' Coombs, was a socially progressive advocate of a lively, diverse, democratic, national culture.[79] Long before Gough Whitlam, Coombs lent authority to these popular aspirations with clarity and a scope of vision that, perhaps ironically, included an apparent skepticism towards institutions. Coombs and other powerbrokers were focused on the long-term establishment of a conventional commercial cinema. They saw the vibrant Australian experimental cinema of the day as a means to this end.[80] This aspiration is explicit in the Australia Council's 1969 Interim Report, the foundation document of federal film funding in Australia, and underlies the historical trajectory of independent production and the checkered fortune of Australia's subsidised commercial film industry over subsequent decades.[81] The re-establishment of a commercial feature film industry was not universally supported. At the time, a range of people saw this model as neither sustainable nor desirable. The celebrated Hollywood biographer Charles Higham was, at that time, a leading Sydney film critic. He put the case for the establishment of Australian cinema along avant-garde rather than Hollywood lines.[82] Referring to the Sydney Co-op, filmmaker and academic Gillian Leahy has outlined the crossroads that Australian film culture came to in the late 1960s as one:

[…] *between the Hollywood model for Australian film and the low-rent model espoused by those that formed the Co-op; the division between those interested in filmmaking and distribution funded and run by experts and entrepreneurs, versus filmmaking and distribution run on democratic lines by filmmakers and film workers.*[83]

In his early history of the Sydney Filmmakers Co-op, Albie Thoms describes a consultative meeting about Arts Council support for film in which he found 'that opinions had already been largely formulated'.[84] In 1969 Holt's successor, John Gorton, adopted the Australia Council's recommended three-pronged approach to support for the Australian film and television industries: a National Film and Television School, an Australian Film and Television Development Corporation (later AFC, now Screen Australia) and an Experimental Film and Television Fund (EFTF). The Interim Council for a Film and Television School (ICFTS) and later the Film, Radio and Television Board (FRTB) of the Australia Council oversaw these developments.

This schema of state institutions was to shape Australian film culture into the twenty-first century just as the community-based exhibition activities of the film society movement had shaped its development in the post-war years (see Chapter 4). Independent film and access video were initially sponsored through the relatively liberal regimes of the EFTF. Colin Bennett wrote the guidelines for the fund.[85] However, as Helen Grace explained in the early 1980s, such diversity was subordinate to an 'imaginary unity, the industry' of commercial feature film production that would become 'dominant over other possible film practices'.[86] Over time, the activities of the EFTF and other programs with a cultural rather than a commercial or training focus would be phased out. The early 1970s, then, was a unique time of state support for a wide range of practices and initiatives.

Extraordinarily, as Thoms points out, however, the Film and Television Board of ACA sought to secure the distribution rights to films it sponsored through the EFTF. Lisa French and Mark Poole point out that the intent was to bolster the AFI's Vincent Library function as a national distributor.[87] However, the reason that organised filmmakers including Thoms protested so vigorously was not so much to protect their individual rights, but to maintain control of the distribution that underpinned (in the case of Sydney) or could underpin (in the case of Melbourne and other states) their co-operative organisations. The concept of the EFTF came from a British model of the time but the fund itself, administered initially by the AFI, had an Australian precursor in Unifed Productions. Unifed was a special assistance scheme established in the early 1960s by filmmakers themselves through MUFS. It channelled Melbourne Film Festival revenue into productions via small grants administered by the AFI.[88] Ultimately, such grassroots initiatives – and much of the social basis of the burgeoning independent film culture from which they emerged – would be subsumed by the structures of government 'support'.

A diverse cohort of people provided the momentum behind the video access movement. Technically minded artists, who had created psychedelic lightshows that were so popular in the late 1960s and early 1970s, joined social activists and pioneers of electronic music who had begun explorations in electronic visual synthesis. One such artist, John Hansen, began explorations into what would become known as video art.

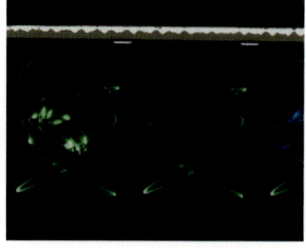

ELECTRONIC EQUIPMENT BUILT BY HANSEN. *CYBERNETIC SYNERGY* (1976).

AN ELECTRONIC IMAGE CREATED BY JOHN HANSEN IN *CYBERNETIC SYNERGY* (1976).

Cybernetic Synergy: The Kinetic Art of John Hansen

In 1972 Hughes received the first of two Experimental Film and Television Fund (EFTF) grants, totalling A$1432, for the production of a film about the kinetic video and electronic sculpture work of John Hansen.[8] Hansen, an engineer turned artist, had built a visual synthesiser by modifying sound devices and domestic television sets. In 1974 Hansen, also with a small grant from ACA, created a colour video synthesiser.[90]

The imagery in one scene oscillates between realism and surrealism as hotel patrons are interviewed amid one of Hansen's psychedelic light displays.

The long closing scene of the film is an abstract sequence of Hansen's kinetic synthesised video imagery that could stand alone as a seminal work of electronic art. The sequence sits quite oddly at the end of this short documentary film. This is the closest Hughes has come to abstract filmmaking in his own work. Hughes now sees this film as an example of the kind of work from the Co-op period that confounds conventional distinctions between an abstract, materialist cinema and one 'engaged with advocacy' at a social-political level.[91]

In the Co-op years, radical directions were being explored in film structure, the filmmaking process and the constituents of a screen culture. Explorations by the Marxist cultural avant-garde of Russia and Germany in the early twentieth century, particularly the work of Bertolt Brecht, had been revisited in post-war European political cinema, especially after 1968.[92] For many Melbourne filmmakers of the early 1970s, these ideas first became prominent through screenings at the MFC. Hughes recalls publications by the British Film Institute (BFI) and the journal *Jump Cut* as being important at the time. He says, 'One of our favourite films at the time was *British Sounds*.'[93] Later-period Godard films like *British Sounds* had a status among Co-op members similar to what the early French new wave cinema had for MUFS. That film had a direct influence on Hughes' *Some Aspects of Australian Racism* (see Chapter 9). The stylistic influence of Godard and Gorin's Dziga Vertov Group is explicit in the work of a number of MFC films at the time, including Bert Deling's legendary first feature film.

ABOVE LEFT AND CENTRE: HANSEN INSTALLATIONS AMID FUTURISTIC HOTEL DECOR IN *CYBERNETIC SYNERGY* (1976); **RIGHT:** THE FILM'S TITLE PLACED WITHIN THE OPENING FRAME OF *CYBERNETIC SYNERGY*.

Dalmas (Bert Deling, 1973)

In 1972 Bert Deling received a grant from the EFTF for his first feature film *Dalmas* (1973). Sasha Trikojus, the director of photography, was looking for a 16 mm camera operator. Hughes recalls arriving at Deling's flamboyantly countercultural household for a rather unconventional job interview. He was invited to work on the project and had to do some strenuous negotiation to take leave from the ABC.

The opening scene in *Dalmas* features a single take, static shot of a long monologue by Baba Ram Das, an American guru and former colleague of Timothy Leary.[94] This scene is a full-screen re-filming from recordings of filmmakers and counterculture figures that Trikojus and Deling began making in 1971 with an early videotape recorder (VTR) purchased with some of the first EFTF funds. Hughes' recollection is that he saw some of these tapes at the Melbourne Co-op. The *Dalmas* shoot provided Hughes with an experience he describes as 'extraordinary'.[95] The film begins as a detective story: an ex-cop descends into a psychedelic, counterculture underworld where a collective of young actors called Tribe functions like a Greek chorus.[96] Gradually, Detective Dalmas becomes one of the tribe as the film slides into an exposition of its own process of production. Deling's first feature adheres to Annette Blonski's claim that a defining characteristic of independent filmmaking in all genres at the time was a self-consciousness about how films are made.[97]

Bruce Hodsdon recently wrote of *Dalmas* and Dave Jones' *Yackety Yack* (1974): 'These two films remain to my knowledge the only fully reflexive features in Australian cinema'.[98] In 2000 Hughes told me:

I mean the thing is so self-reflexive that there was a series of script workshops that would go on the night before the next day's shoot, which would be coming out of what was actually taking place on the set. There's a scene in Dalmas on the beach which is an apt parody of a John Hughes character … in which the documentary cameraman refuses to shoot a certain scene – insisting on saving the life of a drowning man rather than filming it – and declaring the director a fascist.[99]

This scene echoes some of Hughes' professional experience at the time and, in particular, his former colleague's excitement about the international success of the footage from the Westgate Bridge disaster.

A major energising factor behind the counterculture activity of the late 1960s and early 1970s was the escalation of the American war in Vietnam. Australia was a key US ally in that conflict in Vietnam and Australian youth were conscripted to fight. At the time, dissenters understood, correctly, that the scale of US aerial bombing campaigns in South East Asia was unprecedented.[100] The responses to this mechanised atrocity among artists and activists of the counterculture was akin, in some respects, to that of the Dada movement in the era of World War I and sometimes referred to or borrowed from Dada directly. Even the use of hallucinogenic drugs could be seen as an act of defiance against the 'rational' thinking of a highly organised civilisation that poured resources into industrial-scale destruction of civilian life. While there is no explicit anti-war message in *Dalmas*, the form, content and production process of the film reflect a rejection of the conventions, authoritarianism and conservative values associated with the social establishment – and conventional filmmaking – at the time.

Robin Laurie worked on *Dalmas* as an actor and as assistant director, and had helped Deling with the script.[101] She recalls 'we all went down to Lake Tyers, took LSD and left the camera on the table so that anybody could film anything'.[102] For the last part of its 103 minutes, *Dalmas* becomes a collection of personal diary films by the members of Tribe and the crew. In an old guesthouse at Lake Tyers, Deling explains, 'What's been suggested, as a result of the trip yesterday, is that we've been really trying to structure things even more than we thought.' He hands the remaining film stock over to the cast and crew, suggesting that when half of it is used they 'drop another trip or whatever the equivalent is' and use the remaining film in one day. What follows is a string of scenes, discussions, tableaux, skits and sketches in which the only continuity is the gaze of the camera.

From 1972 until early 1974, MFC activities were centred on its Spring Street base. The small core of active members was becoming worn out. There were successful events and screenings without an audience. A screening at the University of Melbourne Union theatre had to be cancelled because it was Co-op policy not to register films for censorship. Many Australian films were being hacked to pieces because of puritanical censorship regimes against which there had been a long-running national campaign. In July 1972 officers of the vice squad attended a screening of Sydney filmmaker Kit Guyatt's *Phallic Forest* (1970).[103] A year later, John Mathews, the Co-op manager who seems to have often worked for a merely token wage, was charged to appear in court as an unregistered exhibitor and for showing an unregistered film. Activities appear to have continued, however, with an A$500 grant from the EFTF to cover advertising and promotion. By this time, both the Health Department and the Fire Brigade had made adverse assessments of Babylon as a cinema venue.[104] There was a regular turnover of personnel on the management committee. Frustration about lack of support from the general membership made fortnightly open meetings untenable and led to the committee to start to act unilaterally.

At a general meeting in April 1973, Deling was elected chair and John Hughes was elected to the MFC committee of management. Ann Wookey, the only woman on the new committee, was elected treasurer.[105] By the end of the year Pat Longmore responded to a Co-op notice that read as a 'cry for help'.[106] She had done a course in 16 mm filmmaking and had recently attended a women's liberation meeting from which the Melbourne Women's Film Group was formed with the intent of making a film about abortion. Longmore took a leading role at the Co-op organisationally and put enormous energy into dragging it from what one MFC newsletter described as 'doldrums'.[107] Eventually an old funeral parlour at 380–382 Lygon Street Carlton was secured. Some people would now refer to the MFC as the 'Carlton Film Co-op', reinforcing the identity of the Carlton filmmakers. Reopening in June of 1974 with weekly screenings and monthly general meetings, the MFC also hosted a national conference of film co-ops with representatives from every capital city in Australia.

Meanwhile a similar rejuvenation was taking place in the Sydney Co-op with a number of energetic feminist filmmakers steering it from its masculinist avant-garde roots. By the mid-1970s, Hughes' generation had brought a more overt political agenda to the filmmakers' co-ops, developing them as institutions for social change and as a base for political documentary production. At the same time, Hughes and his peers were cultivating a more symbiotic – and arguably fatal – relationship between the co-ops and funding bodies.

On a panel together with Longmore in 1982, Fred Harden, the first chair of the MFC, gave an account that was partly based on false recollections.[108] He pointed, however, to a tension that some others associated with the MFC, including Hughes, probably felt. Harden described a 'big push' to turn the Co-op into a more professional cinema operation, while 'idealists' like himself retreated to one end of the space with their Super-8 equipment.[109] A July 1972 MFC Newsletter reports 'with a move to a more commercial emphasis in the large theatre', Jim Clayden, Peter Tammer, Fred Harden and others created 'Patmos', a separate theatre that would be equipped with a new dual gauge 8 mm projector purchased with money from Unifed.[110] In 1972 Harden and Corinne Cantrill published an article decrying the 'expansionist mentality' at the MFC as anathematic to the spirit of the co-ops.[111] Harden also suggested that this expansionism came from industry professionals; however, Tammer says 'there was no sense of division in my mind between experimenters and professionals' and points out that Harden himself worked in the advertising industry.[112] As Hughes has noted, conventional fictional narratives tended not to be identified with the Co-op movement at a time when convention in Australian film culture was largely set by a conservative television industry. In this context, Co-op filmmaking was undertaken in a personal rather than industrial mode and could be radical in form and content.

Like many of the filmmakers discussed here, Tammer is interested and conversant in all forms of filmmaking. Arthur and Corinne Cantrill have a more specialised interest. By the early 1970s they had established an international reputation – with their unparalleled output of nearly fifty meticulous experimental films and multi-screen exhibitions, performances and workshops – long before and quite independently of the Co-op. Corinne's *In This Life's Body* (1984) remains the exemplary autobiographical essay documentary. Their long-running journal *Cantrills Filmnotes* provided an invaluable platform for writing by and about the work of independent filmmakers 'with emphasis on experimental film, video art, digital media, and associated work in performance and installation art'.[113] For decades they were the pre-eminent exponents of experimental film in Australia. This focus is critical to the success of the efforts they have made. The Cantrills supported a very wide range of filmmaking practices and practitioners, but the Melbourne Filmmakers Co-op was a collective attempt to create an even broader church and a survey of the remaining screening programs would suggest that it was never exclusivist. Unlike Tammer, however, Hughes did perceive the split that Harden and Cantrill characterised in their writings of 1972. In 2001 he described it along the lines of a conventional dichotomy between high art and political art.

There were two camps in the co-ops; a visual art oriented one, initially inspired by European art cinema but increasingly leaning towards New York avant-gardism, and a social change orientated group.[114]

Such a dichotomy had been identified in independent filmmaking circles around the world, most famously in the contentious 1975 essay of English theorist and filmmaker Peter Wollen 'The Two Avant-Gardes'.[115] Overall, the milieu of eclectic independent filmmakers of the 1960s and 1970s – in Melbourne at least – resists such caricature. Filmmakers like Deling, Tammer, Buesst and (in Sydney) Guyatt and Ubu filmmaker David Perry were interested, each in their own way, with both art and social critique, but they did not make purely abstract or didactically political films. The MFC screened feature films by new wave European directors alongside local and international experimental films and documentaries.

As Annette Blonski wrote in 1987:

It would be false to assume that there was fundamental division or struggle between the experimentalists and the political filmmakers [of the early 1970s]. It was not nearly so simple: important alliances were forged, cross fertilisation was inevitable, and provided one of the most interesting aspects of this period. Debates about representation, realism and narrative were common amongst most filmmakers of this period […]. [116]

The MFC retained a diverse membership in a milieu that encouraged an exploration of film form and a sense of artistry, even amongst the most polemically inclined filmmakers. In this context, independent filmmaking represented an underground activity and had little to do with profession or career. The co-ops were, at least in theory, open to anyone who wanted to get involved. It was in this open co-op milieu that Hughes began his vocation as a filmmaker.

The stories of the filmmakers' co-ops, *Nowhere Game* and *Dalmas*, reflect the enthusiasm of a generation of intelligent, socially engaged young people to challenge established power structures, conventions and stereotypes in art, politics and the media. In each case, experiments were being made with grassroots democracy, with new social formations and new ways of seeing and communicating. Hughes' main focus was on the political use of film. He was skeptical about experimental cinema associated with the American avant-garde to the extent that the US corporate, security and diplomatic establishment had endorsed abstraction in art. As the following chapters will show, however, the formative influence of the whole diversity of the Carlton arts scene, counterculture and international film co-op milieu is evident throughout his work.

Endnotes

26. Gaetano Rando & Gino Moliterno, *Celluloid Immigrant: Italian Australian Filmmaker Giorgio Mangiamele*, The Moving Image, ATOM, St Kilda, 2011. Raffaele Lampugnani, Giorgio Mangiamele: Cinematographer of the Italian Migrant Experience, Connor Court Publishing, Ballan, Victoria, 2012.
27. ibid., Rando & Moliterno, p. 26.
28. ibid.
29. Giorgio Mangiamele, *The Giorgio Mangiamele Collection: Five Provocative Works by an Italian Filmmaker in Post-War Australia*, 2011, DVD, Australia. Distributed by NFSA and Ronin Films.
30. Montsalvat, Home page, Eltham, 2010, <http://www.montsalvat.com.au>, accessed 7 January 2013.
31. Liz Jones, Betty Burstall & Helen Garner, History, La Mama, 1988, <http://lamama.com.au/about/history/>, accessed 7 January 2013.
32. Jake Wilson, 'Carlton + Godard = Cinema: An Interview with Nigel Buesst', *Senses of Cinema*, no. 27, 2003, Senses of Cinema Inc., <http://sensesofcinema.com/2003/27/carlton_plus_godard/>, accessed 4 January 2013.
33. Richard Brennan, 'Tim Burstall', Screen Australia, 2004, Australian Film Commission (AFC) archive, <http://afcarchive.screenaustralia.gov.au/newsandevents/afcnews/feature/tim_burstall/newspage_113.aspx>, accessed 8 January 2013. Author not attributed, 'Tim Burstall: Film writer, producer, director', Obituaries, 2004, Milesago: Australasian Music & Popular Culture 1964–1975, <http://www.milesago.com/Obits/frames7.htm>, accessed 7 January 2013.
34. Rando, op. cit., p. 28, Film Victoria, 'Australian Films at the Australian Box Office', 8 June 2011.
35. Adrian Danks, 'Arrested Developments or from The Heroes are Tired to The Tomb of Ligeia: Some Notes on the Place of the Melbourne University Film Society in 1960s Film Culture', in Seamus O'Hanlon (ed.), *Go: Melbourne in the Sixties*, Circa, Beaconsfield, 2012, pp. 101–114. Gil Brealey went on to work in television and play a central role in the Australian feature film revival as founding director of the South Australian Film Corporation. Gil Brealey, 'SAFC 40th Anniversary Speech', Australian International Documentary Conference (AIDC), 27 February 2012, Adelaide Studios, <http://www.safilm.com.au/library/Gil Brealey Speech 40th Anniversary AIDC Opening Night_0.pdf>, accessed 24 February 2013.
36. Barrett Hodsdon, *Straight Roads and Crossed Lines: The Quest for Film Culture in Australia from the 1960s?* Bernt Porridge Group, Shelton Park, 2001, p. 66. Robert Garlick later worked on Mangiamele's last feature *Clay* (1970). Rando, op. cit., p. 93.
37. ibid., p. 73.
38. ibid., p. 78.
39. Graham Shirley & Brian Adams, *Australian Cinema: The First Eighty Years*, 2nd edn, Angus & Robertson, Sydney, 1989, p. 225.
40. Bruce Hodsdon, 'The Carlton Ripple and the Australian Film Revival', *Screening the Past*, 23 November, 26 April 2009, La Trobe University, Melbourne, <http://www.latrobe.edu.au/screeningthepast/23/carlton-australian-revival.html>, accessed 24 February 2013.

41. Wilson, op. cit.
42. Peter Mudie, *Ubu films: Sydney underground movies 1965–1970*, UNSW Press, Sydney, 1997, p. 14.
43. Stephen Dwoskin, 'Film-Related Organizations: Filmmakers Co-op', *Filmwaves*, no. 3, 3 February 1998.
44. Jonas Mekas, Filmmaker's Cooperative: a brief history, The New American Cinema Group, The Film-makers' Coop, 2000 <http://film-makerscoop.com/about/history>, accessed 6 February 2014.
45. Donna McLachlan & David Bates, 'Interview with Arthur and Corinne Cantrill', *Verbatim*, 11 May, 5 pm, 2002, ABC Radio National, Australia.
46. Lisa Milner, *Fighting films: a history of the Waterside Workers' Federation Film Unit*, Pluto Press, North Melbourne, Vic., 2003.
47. John Hughes, 'Albie's blind eye to the why', *Nation Review*, 3–9 November 1978, p. 22 Eva Cockroft, 'Abstract Expression, Weapon of the Cold War', *Artforum*, June 1974, pp. 39–41.
48. Mudie, op. cit., p. 80. Shirley & Adams, op. cit., pp. 223–4.
49. Peter Tammer, Notes on the Melbourne Filmmakers Co-op, email to John Cumming, Kyneton, 20 November 2011.
50. Albie Thoms, 'Ten Years of the Sydney Film-maker's Co-op', in Albie Thoms (ed.), *Polemics for a New Cinema*, 1978, p. 353.
51. Shirley & Adams, op. cit., p. 223.
52. Tammer, op. cit.
53. MIF, Peter Tammer, Melbourne Independent Filmmakers, Bill Mousoulis (ed.), Innersense, Melbourne, May 2008, <http://www.innersense.com.au/mif/tammer.html>, accessed 9 January 2013.
54. Fred Harden recollected early events 'at an Arts Co-op in Carlton, in an old church hall on the corner of Nicholson and Victoria Streets'. Barbara Hall, Fred Harden & Pat Longmore, 'An oral history of the Melbourne Filmmakers Co-operative', in Barbara Creed, John Davies, Freda Freiberg, David Hanan & Kim Montgomery (eds), *Papers and Forums on Independent Film and Asian Cinema*, La Trobe University, Melbourne, ASSA, AFTRS, 1982, pp. 141–155. These are likely to have been in 1969. Tammer has no recollection of these and may not have been involved at that time. Tammer, op. cit.
55. John Hughes, *Nowhere Game*, interview conducted by John Cumming, Melbourne, 1 August 2000.
56. Harden's account has him 'fresh out of R.M.I.T. photography school' at the earlier Carlton events. Tammer recalls Harden as 'working for an Ad agency' by 1972. Harden in Hall et al., op. cit., Tammer, op. cit.
57. Tammer, ibid.
58. MIF, James Clayden Biography, Melbourne Independent Filmmakers, Bill Mousoulis (ed.) Innersense, Melbourne, 2005, <http://www.innersense.com.au/mif/tammer.html>, accessed 9 January 2013.
59. Jonas Balsaitas, 'Biography', Charles Nodrum Gallery, 2012, Melbourne, <http://www.charlesnodrumgallery.com.au/artist–biography.asp?idArtistInfo=383&idArtist=1088>, accessed 9 January 2013.

60 Michael Lee, Critical Overview, Melbourne Independent Filmmakers, Bill Mousoulis (ed.) Innersense, Melbourne, 2003, <http://www.innersense.com.au/mif/lee.html>, accessed 9 January 2013.

61 Uses for Super-8 film were also found in the mainstream production industry. For example, Mike and Mal Leyland produced the outback adventure television series *Ask The Leyland Brothers* from 1976 to 1984 in this 8 mm format. Author not attributed, 'Mike Leyland dies, aged 68', *Perth Now*, 14 September 2009, News Limited, <http://www.perthnow.com.au/news/mike-leyland-dies-aged-68/story-e6frg12c-1225772917208>, accessed 14 February 2013.

62 Bruce Hodsdon, op. cit.

63 ibid., MFC, *Beginnings* screening flyer, Pinacotheca, Richmond, Melbourne Filmmakers Co-op, c. 1970. This roughly pasted flyer for an event on Thursday 8 October at 8 pm has images of abstract pictures on the gallery walls that look like Balsaitis' *Image of a Point Seen Through* (1970). Like all the other MFC documents I've located from the early 1970s, it is headed 'Melbourne Film-Makers' Co-Op' showing use of the name before the Co-op's incorporation at Spring Street in 1971. A handwritten note says '– believe this is 1970 OR 1971'. It is most likely to have been in 1970, the year *Beginnings* was completed. Pollard purchased 10 Waltham Place, Richmond in January 1970. See Trevor Fuller, 'Bruce Pollard and Pinacotheca: psychological content', *Artlink*, vol. 26, no. 4, 2006.

64 Scott Murray, 'Interview', Peter Malone's website, 6 November 1998, 30 May 2012, <http://www.signis.net/malone/tiki-index.php?page=Scott+Murray&bl>, accessed 6 January 2013.

65 Tammer, op. cit.

66 MFC, Formation of a filmmakers co-op., notice, Melbourne Filmmakers Co-op, Babylon, Melbourne, 3 June 1971.

67 Mudie, op. cit., p. 14. Harden in Hall et al., op. cit., p. 141.

68 MFC, Notice of General Meeting, Melbourne Filmmakers Co-op, Babylon, Melbourne, 5 July 1971.

69 Harden recalls paying Chris Löfvén A$180 from door takings for a screening of his work. Harden, op. cit. Löfvén, who started making 16 mm films as a sixteen-year-old in 1964, photographed some of the Carlton films and started a long career making music clips. Chris Löfvén, Filmography, Melbourne Independent Filmmakers, Bill Mousoulis (ed.) Innersense, Melbourne, 2012, <http://www.innersense.com.au/mif/lofven.html>, accessed 10 January 2013. In 1970 Löfvén made a 70-minute experimental feature *Part One – 806*.

70 According to Adrian Danks, MUFS had paid little attention to avant-garde or oppositional cinema. See Danks, op. cit.

71 Hughes remembers getting a favourable response from Fred Schepisi to one of these films 'a kind of music clip to Dylan's "Visions of Johanna".' Schepisi was an EFTF selector in the early 1970s, but Hughes does not recall applying for a grant in the 1971 round. He may have shown this film to support a later application. John Hughes, The early 1970s, email to John Cumming, Melbourne, 30 May 2002. Bob Dylan, 'Visions of Johanna', *Blonde on Blonde*, Columbia Records, USA, 1966.

72 Laurie co-wrote and worked on the short documentary *Monash 66* in 1966. Hughes may have already met Laurie at the MFC or at La Mama, where she performed in a number of plays from 1969 and throughout the 1970s. See Bruce Hodsdon, 2009, op. cit.; Robin

Laurie, 'Some recollections of Life in the APG', *The Pram Factory: Australian Theatre History. The Australian Performing Group at the Pram Factory*, 2005, Suzanne Ingleton, <http://www.pramfactory.com/memoirsfolder/Laurie–Robin.html>, accessed 6 February 2013; Tim Robertson. *The Pram Factory*, Melbourne UP, Melbourne, 2001.

[73] John Hughes, *Nowhere Game*, interview conducted by John Cumming, Melbourne, 1 August 2000.

[74] John Hughes & Martyn Goddard, *Nowhere Game*, 1972, 16 mm, b&w, 23 minutes, Magic Dragon Productions, Melbourne, Scriptwriters John Hughes & Martyn Goddard, Camera John Hughes.

[75] Quoted in Chris Warner, Cynthia Connop & Ginny Brook, 'Filmmaking in Australia', *Farrago*, Friday 9 July 1976, p. 12.

[76] Athenaeum, advertisement, *The Sun*, Saturday 20 July 1974, p. 19.

[77] Rt Hon. Harold Holt, Cultural Activities, The House of Representatives, Australia, press release, Canberra, 1967.

[78] Victor Vincent, Hartley Cant, Samuel Cohen, Thomas Drake-Brockman, George Hannan, Douglas McClelland & Reginald Wright, Report from the Select Committee on the Encouragement of Australian Productions for Television, Canberra, 1963, p. 1.

[79] See, for example, Dr HC Coombs, The Australia Council for the Arts – Progress and Plans, UNESCO, Australia Council, pamphlet file, Canberra, 1969. See also John Hughes' film *Love & Fury: Judith Wright & 'Nugget' Coombs* (2013).

[80] See also Herbert C Coombs, *Trial Balance*, Macmillan, South Melbourne, 1981.

[81] ACA, Interim Report: Film Committee, Australia Council for the Arts, Sydney, 1969.

[82] Albie Thoms, 'Ten Years of the Sydney Film-maker's Co-op', in Albie Thoms (ed.), *Polemics for a New Cinema*, 1978, p. 361.

[83] Gillian Leahy, 'Collective amnesia: A brief, sporadic history of the first twenty-five years of independent filmmaking in Australia', in Jefferey Cook (ed.), *Community and Independent Television*, Metro Television Ltd, Sydney, 1993, p. 54.

[84] Thoms, op. cit., p. 361.

[85] Lisa French & Mark Poole. *Shining a Light: 50 years of the Australian Film Institute*, The Moving Image, Australian Teachers of Media (ATOM), St Kilda West, 2009, p. 42.

[86] Helen Grace & James Kesteven, 'The Public Wants Features!': Creative Underdevelopment of Australian Independent Film Since the 1960s, in Barbara Creed, John Davies, Freda Freiberg, David Hanan & Kim Montgomery (eds), *Papers and Forums on Independent Film and Asian Cinema*, Australian Screen Studies Association (Victoria), Australian Film and Television School, La Trobe University, Melbourne, 1982, pp. 16–36.

[87] French, op. cit., p. 45.

[88] Bruce Hodsdon, 2009, op. cit. Through MUFS, Trikojus, Garlick and Deling negotiated with the Victorian Federation of Film Societies and the AFI for some of the surplus revenue from the Melbourne Film Festival to be channelled into filmmaking through the Unifed. Barrett Hodsdon, op. cit., p. 78. Buesst has referred to this as the UniFed Film Foundation. See Jake Wilson, 'Carlton + Godard = Cinema: An Interview with Nigel Buesst', Senses of Cinema, no. 27, 2003, Senses of Cinema Inc., <http://sensesofcinema.com/2003/27/carlton_plus_godard/>, accessed 4 January 2013.

[89] ACA, Annual Report (calendar year), Australia Council for the Arts, Sydney, 1974. Hansen

had received a Special Project grant of A$5000, also from the Film, Radio and Television Board (FRTB) of the Australia Council to develop his synthesiser. This report incorrectly describes this film as 35 mm and black and white. See also Ken Berryman, 'Allowing young filmmakers to spread their wings: The Educational Role of the Experimental Film and Television Fund', thesis (MEd), Centre for the Study of Education Communication and Media, La Trobe University, Melbourne, 1985.

[90] Stephen Jones, John Hansen, D*Hub, Powerhouse Museum, Sydney, 2006, <http://www.dhub.org/articles/150>, accessed 19 June 2013.

[91] John Hughes, SBSi and after, interview conducted by John Cumming, Melbourne, 9 February 2004.

[92] Brecht developed an approach to acting and collective theatre-making that sought to establish a dialectical relationship between the audience, the process of theatre-making, contemporary politics and history. See the discussion of Epic Theatre in Chapter 5.

[93] John Hughes, *Film-Work,* interview conducted by John Cumming, Melbourne, 12 September 2000.

[94] John Hughes, MFC, Access Video and EMA, interview conducted by John Cumming, Melbourne, 16 January 2002.

[95] John Hughes, *Film-Work*, interview conducted by John Cumming, Melbourne, 12 September 2000.

[96] Tribe sometimes performed at La Mama theatre. See Robin Laurie, op. cit. Also, see Leslie Rees, *A History of Australian Drama:* Australian Drama in the 1970s, vol. 2, Angus & Robertson, Melbourne, 1978.

[97] Annette Blonski, 'At the Government's Pleasure: Independent Cinema', in Blonski, Creed & Freiberg, op. cit., p. 59.

[98] Bruce Hodsdon, op. cit.

[99] John Hughes, op. cit.

[100] This was officially confirmed in 2000 when the US Clinton administration revealed that the bombardment of Cambodia alone amounted to over 2.7 million tons. This is more than the two million tons of munitions (conventional and nuclear) dropped by the Allies during all of World War II. Taylor Owen & Ben Kiernan, 'Bombs Over Cambodia', The Walrus, The Walrus Foundation, Canada, 2006, p. 67, <http://www.walrusmagazine.com/articles/2006.10 history–bombing–cambodia/>, accessed 24 February 2013.

[101] Robin Laurie, op. cit.

[102] ibid.

[103] *The Phallic Forest* toured as a double bill with Phil Noyce's twin-screen documentary *Good Afternoon*. See Artfilms, Kit Guyatt Films: *President Johnson's Visit* (1967), *Balmain* (1969) and *The Phallic Forest*, Kit Guyatt Films, Kriszta Doczy (ed.) Contemporary Arts Media, 2012, <http://www.artfilms.com.au/Detail.aspx?ItemID=4927>, accessed 10 January 2013.

[104] MFC, Minutes of General Meeting, Melbourne Filmmakers Co-op, Babylon, 161 Spring Street, Melbourne, 1973.

[105] The minutes state that Margaret Thompson 'stood down in favour of Ann Wooley' and a number of men declined nomination. Of the 27 people recorded as present, ten were women. MFC, Minutes of General Meeting 11 April, Melbourne Filmmakers Coop, Babylon, 161 Spring Street, Melbourne, 1973.

[106] Hall et al., op. cit., pp. 141–155.
[107] MFC, Newsletter, Melbourne Filmmakers Co-op, 1973.
[108] Harden claimed that Deling, Tammer and Longmore instigated this 'push'. However, Longmore and Tammer both independently expressed surprise at this account, saying that Longmore became involved after Tammer and Deling had largely withdrawn from the Co-op. See Hall et al., op. cit., and Peter Tammer, notes on the Melbourne Filmmakers Co-op, op. cit.
[109] Barbara Hall, Fred Harden & Pat Longmore, 'An oral history of the Melbourne Filmmakers Co-operative', in Barbara Creed, John Davies, Freda Freiberg, David Hanan & Kim Montgomery (eds), *Papers and Forums on Independent Film and Asian Cinema*, La Trobe University, Melbourne, ASSA, AFTRS, 1982, pp. 141–155.
[110] MFC, op. cit.
[111] Fred Harden and Corinne Cantrill, 'The Alternative Cinema and the Film Co-ops … Are the two compatible?' *Cantrills Filmnotes*, no. 12, December 1972, pp. 18–21. Arthur and Corinne Cantrill, who had been experimenting with film since the late 1950s, joined the MFC after a creative fellowship with the Australian National University in Canberra (during 1969 and 1970) and earlier experience at the Drury Lane Arts Laboratory in London. Shirley & Adams, op. cit., p. 258.
[112] Tammer, op. cit.
[113] Arthur Cantrill & Corinne Cantrill, Cantrills Filmnotes, Melbourne, 2011, <http://www.arthurandcorinnecantrill.com/filmnotes.html>, accessed 10 January 2013.
[114] John Hughes, The Melbourne Filmmakers Co-op, interview conducted by John Cumming, Melbourne, 20 September 2001.
[115] Peter Wollen, 'The Two Avant-Gardes', *Readings & Writings: Semiotic Counter-Strategies*, Verso, London, 1982. Originally published Studio International, December 1975. American independent filmmaker Jon Jost also characterises such a schism in his account of the Chicago-based Newsreel collective of the late 1960s in Ian Christie, *Jon Jost: a voice from the margins*, 1983, Eleventh Hour television program, Visions, Large Door, Channel 4 TV, London.
[116] Annette Blonski, 'At the Government's Pleasure: Independent Cinema', in Blonski et al., op. cit., p. 51.

CHAPTER 2:

Menace

The early- to mid-1970s was a time in which, as young adults, John Hughes and his peers were beginning to explore and assert themselves politically through community-based organisations such as the filmmakers' co-ops and the access video movement. The end of twenty-three years of conservative government boosted the confidence of those engaged in a range of campaigns for social change. During this time Hughes also secured finance to cover the production costs of three short documentaries, including *Cybernetic Synergy* (1974), a portrait film of one of Australia's pioneering video artists (see Chapter 1). At this time video technology became available and Hughes was active in the movement to democratise the production of moving image media. He made a video recording about an international judicial inquiry into American war crimes in Vietnam. Hughes' concern for the fate of Australia's first progressive post-war government (Whitlam's Labor government) saw him immersed in historical research that underpinned his first feature length documentary film *Menace* (1976), a film about Australia's own era of McCarthyism. The counterculture generation to which he belonged had been largely disillusioned with conventional politics, but Hughes took an interest in understanding why the traditional left in Australia had apparently failed.[117] With *Menace* and then *Film-Work* (1981) he sought to provide a historical context for contemporary activism and was largely concerned with the history of progressive social movements in the immediate post-World War II period.

While the gradual withdrawal of Australian troops from Vietnam was already underway, Australian involvement in the war, military conscription and moral support for the ongoing American bombing were brought to an immediate end with the election of the Labor government of Gough Whitlam in 1972. From 1972 to 1975 progressive social policy in Australia flourished and then floundered. During this time Hughes had firsthand experience of the limits of government involvement with citizen-controlled initiatives and with the socially innovative use of new media. As a volunteer organiser, trainer and advocate, Hughes chronicled the experience of the access video movement in Melbourne in a number of submissions and published accounts. This work was grounded in his reading of contemporary debates in media, cultural and social theory.

As a news camera operator, Hughes had discovered that radio and television broadcasts did not provide a reliable way of learning about what was happening in the world. He felt like 'a cog in the wheel that makes news' and from this developed a contempt for the pretence of objectivity and balance that exists in mainstream media.[118] As he explained to Peter Hughes in 1993:

[…] *what doesn't appear on the TV screen is the fact that the premier is drunk, is the fact that the journalist and the premier, before they begin, agree not to discuss certain matters, is the fact that they share a bonhomie of conceit in relation to the exclusivity that they share.*[119]

He said his superiors were astonished by the young camera assistant's inquiries about editorial interference by politicians, while the journalists appeared to be complacently amused. On the other hand, Hughes also learnt of serious investigative work that some journalists were doing outside the confines of mainstream media. As he reflected in 1976, he was able to synthesise a 'particular perspective' on film and television from his early experiences as a trainee in ABC Television and from his involvement with the Melbourne Filmmakers Co-op (MFC) in the late 1960s.[120] Subsequent to the main shoot of *Dalmas*, Hughes borrowed Trikojus' cumbersome video machine and recorded the tape *Ted Laurie on American War Crimes in Vietnam* (1972).[121] Robin Laurie's father – a barrister known as Red Ted – had returned from the 4th hearing of the International Inquiry into US War Crimes in Indo-China held in Copenhagen in October 1972.[122] Hughes' tape was recorded at a press conference where, as far as he recalls, there were no other cameras present. Hughes claims that there was 'no way' Laurie's account would have been aired on broadcast television at the time.[123] He describes this alternative newsreel recording as 'early community video'.[124] The idea for *Menace* may have germinated at this time as the film is concerned with a historic court case that Ted Laurie had fought twenty years earlier.

In the early 1970s Hughes and others saw creative and aesthetic possibilities in the new technology of video and a potential means to establish a democratic screen culture. As Sydney-based documentary filmmaker Tom Zubrycki explains, video was seen as a means of 'enabling social change'.[125] Videotape recording equipment, while primitive, soon became relatively cheap and simple to use. Many small organisations could raise funds for such equipment. By 1970 publications had begun to emerge from North America about experiments in communal use of the new technology, and the federal funding bodies were taking an interest. Such reports inspired Hughes to begin working on a speculative enterprise in cultural politics. This became known as the community access video movement, one of the foundations of the community television sector.[126]

All over the industrialised Western world in the 1970s, concepts of access video evolved through engagement, by community activists and filmmakers, with the ideas of influential forward thinkers in fields other than art and cinema. Hughes happened upon Paulo Freire's book *Pedagogy of the Oppressed*, an important new text for educators and social reformers that led him to think about 'media literacy' and 'the possibility of a democratic practice in media'.[127] The language Hughes used to write about access video in the mid-1970s was markedly Freirean. For him, Freire's ideas about education were 'completely in opposition' to what mainstream television did.[128]

In 1974 Hughes wrote of 'a continuing discussion group oriented towards ways and means of humanising one area of the communications media'.[129] The Video Exchange had its gestation in the Learning Exchange, a progressive community-based organisation that supported the access video movement with experience from the Media Access Centre of the Portola Institute in California and Downtown Community Television in Toronto.[130] Since 1971 Hughes and Robin Laurie had been working with community organisations committed to community development and social justice, such as the Fitzroy Free Legal Service. In 1972 they were among those who helped Deling and Trikojus prepare an application to the Interim Council for a Film and Television

School (ICFTS) 'for financial support for a national video network based on open access'.[131] In 1973 Hughes wrote articles about access video in the Learning Exchange's widely distributed, community-based newspaper and submitted an application to the Community Arts committee of the Australia Council for the Arts (ACA) seeking finance for three projects in inner city areas.[132] Volunteers pursued a raft of projects with support and equipment loans from La Trobe University Media Centre and Melbourne College of Education (MCE, later Melbourne State College) where Laurie started working. Hughes ran workshops at the five-day Action for World Development Exhibition and with the Fitzroy Residents' Association and the Housing Commission Tenants Union.

The Video Exchange was formed amidst this activity and culminated in a detailed submission to the Film, Radio and Television Board (FRTB) of the Australia Council for funding to establish a video access centre in Melbourne. The group soon became mired by the machinations of bureaucracy. It seemed that sponsorship by the state of this idealistic and inclusive initiative might be achievable, but the incompatible imperatives of larger institutions eventually held sway. Despite the Whitlam government's ostensible support for community-based initiatives, community control was not seriously entertained. The imperatives of commerce and the politics of administration within the institutions of government made state sponsorship of video access centres and the filmmakers' co-ops a poisoned chalice. As early as 1974, Hughes made the following observation about this phenomenon:

The problems we experienced are common to people working toward citizens' control of social environments. It is very easy for an organisation to internalise the presumptions of our highly institutionalised society. In his book The Abstract Society*, Anton C. Zijderveld speaks of Bureaucracy taking over the role of religion " … as the general coercive force in pluralistic society that keeps this society together as a functionally integrated whole." It also creates, he goes on to say, "systems of domination and subordination throughout all of society".*[133]

As we shall see, this account could describe the fate that was to come to a number of citizens' initiatives in Australian screen culture throughout the last half of the twentieth century. Hughes later wrote: 'The funding bodies' role was one of containing, constraining and domesticating the potential of the movement at its origin'.[134] The federal government effectively took control of the emerging community video sector by establishing, controlling and managing video access centres of its own. The facility that emerged from the groundwork laid by the Video Exchange was called the Carlton Access Video and Resource Centre (CAVRC).[135] In 1976, after a lengthy struggle, community groups began to regain control of these centres that were the focal point for a wide range of activity that utilised Portapak video equipment.

Despite the government's inability to embrace citizen control, notions of access and equity in its public services underpinned many of the Labor government's reforms. Hughes says that it was under their Early Leavers scheme that he was accepted as a mature age student at La Trobe University, even though his secondary school education was incomplete. He also got a job at the Melbourne College of Education (MCE) on in-house productions and community projects that dovetailed with his Video Exchange activity. In July 1974 a columnist for Melbourne

RALPH GIBSON AND JOHN HUGHES IN *MENACE* (1976).

daily newspaper, *The Sun*, reported on the use of new video technology at MCE. Caroline Ross writes of watching Hughes edit 'a fortnight's taping by video on Dr Bertram Wainer and the abortion issue'.[136] Hughes describes this project as *Abortion a Woman's Decision* (1972), 'an informational film for use within Bert Wainer's fertility clinic'.[137] He employed a hybrid of film and video technologies for this project. In the early 1970s, video provided a low-cost means of recording, while 16 mm film provided a reliable format for editing and projection.

In the mid-1970s Rod Patterson referred Hughes to the writings of Walter Benjamin and Hans Magnus Enzensberger. Enzensberger's 'Constituents of a Theory of the Media' (first published in 1970) heralds the zeitgeist to which Hughes was attuned. It pays tribute to Benjamin and Bertolt Brecht for their seminal work on 'the consciousness industry' and embraces El Lissitzky's vision for automated new media and anticipates the technological convergence that has become the internet.[138] Enzensberger calls for a new decentralised socialist vision, including collective use of the media, in which the specialist becomes redundant and transmission gives way to interaction. He decries the 'cultural archaism' of the New Left with its exclusive adherence to a 'manipulation thesis' of the media and its inherent fear of the masses.[139] For Enzensberger, Marshall McLuhan's phrase 'the medium is the message', is an 'ideologically sterile' expression from a bourgeois culture that 'wants the media *as such* and *to no purpose*'.[140] Like Hughes, he saw much of the American artistic avant-garde as giving symbolic expression to this wish. Enzensberger influenced and provided some of the intellectual underpinning for the community media movement in the 1970s and for digital activism today.

In *British Sounds* (1969) Godard and Gorin created a juxtaposition that echoed the events in Paris during May 1968. They placed the ideas of trade unionist factory workers next to those of New Left university students. Godard, the haute-bourgeoisie intellectual, had acknowledged and recorded a glimpse of the intellectual and political life of working-class people. In the early 1970s, Hughes made films largely informed by his contact with artists and intellectuals, but he was keen to learn more about the working-class movement in Australia. The countercultural milieu of Melbourne's film society, film co-op and alternative theatre scene with its centre in the inner suburb of Carlton, evolved initially from the campus culture of the University of Melbourne. While largely, but by then not exclusively middle class, this culture had its roots in the city's own haute-bourgeoisie. Around 1970 there came from the suburbs a vigorous Maoist push upon this scene. According to Brian Adams and Graham Shirley, this push was launched not by factory workers but by students from the outer suburban Monash University.[141] Among these student protesters there were young theatre workers who saw themselves as engaged in an anti-imperialist, anti-authoritarian and anti-hierarchical class struggle.[142] This culture provided the milieu through which Hughes, who had left school at 15 years of age, encountered other young artists and intellectuals. Despite their left-wing attitudes, however, many of these people had little familiarity with the history, traditions, activities and consciousness of the working-class movement. By the mid-1970s it was the initiative of this movement that came to interest Hughes the most and caused him to embark, with *Menace*, on a lifelong project of research.

TED LAURIE, *MENACE*

Menace (1976)

Hughes began the investigations that led to *Menace* late in 1974. At this time, he says, the fate of the Whitlam Labor government was becoming clear and a number of researchers, including Hughes, were looking closely at the events of 1949 that led to the downfall of the Labor government of Ben Chifley.[143] Hughes found the events surrounding the Victorian government's Royal Commission into Communism in 1949 to be particularly revealing about 'how we got to the state of mind that had maintained a Liberal-Country Party government for 23 years'.[144]

Robin Laurie's father, Ted Laurie, was the Queen's Counsel who represented the Victorian Branch of the Communist Party at the Commission. A communist himself, Laurie (like many people who became involved

A CONTEMPORARY CARTOON CELEBRATING THE 1951 DECISION OF THE AUSTRALIAN HIGH COURT TO OUTLAW MENZIES' COMMUNIST PARTY DISSOLUTION BILL IN *MENACE* (1976).

'THE "RESPECTABLE" VIEW WAS REALLY A PRO-HITLER ONE IN THE THIRTIES. THIS IS WHAT PEOPLE DON'T UNDERSTAND.' PAT COUNIHAN IN *MENACE*.

in this political, legal and constitutional struggle) argued that civil liberty and fundamental democratic rights were at stake.

At this time, Australians were largely unaware of the totalitarian reality of the Soviet Union under Stalin. Soviet forces had paid the heaviest price in the fight against Nazi Germany. In Australia, communists where pitching thier ideals against the harsh realities and inequities of life for working-class people (see Chapter 10). Likewise, opposition to communism was ideological – based on the threat that communism posed towards the established order of economic and religious power.

The origins of communism in Australia were largely independent of the Soviet Union. They lay in the labour and peace movements and in campaigns against the compulsory military conscription of boys as young as twelve years of age, prior to and during World War I. Communists saw that the real purpose of that war, on the part of the aristocratic and capitalist classes of the European empires, was to halt the spread of revolution and avoid the fate of the Tsarist regime in Russia. Patriotism was largely a fabrication whereas the allegiances of class were evident in the lived experience of material and social relations. From the 1920s to the 1950s numerous leading writers, artists, educators and trade unionists joined the Communist Party of Australia (CPA) and many other progressive thinkers found themselves aligned with the CPA on a range of issues. The communist movement was internationalist and therefore seen as the only credible opposition to ultranationalist fascism. Communists were active supporters of Aboriginal people in their campaign for equal rights, decades before serious attention was paid to that issue in mainstream media and politics.

The Victorian Royal Commission and the 1951 national referendum (to give the federal government the power to ban the Communist Party in Australia) were important chapters in a long history of attempts to silence political dissent in Australia. The outcomes of both were victories for democracy in general and for the labour movement in particular. John Hughes wanted to make this film

MENACE (1976).

because it told a story that, unlike many accounts of labour movement history, was one of success.

Menace was originally going to be a film about Ted Laurie and the Victorian Commission but the focus shifted to include the federal Communist Party Dissolution Bill. For Hughes, it was important to include Ted Laurie's daughter, his friend Robin Laurie, in *Menace*. In this way the film was to become 'a study of the effect of Australian McCarthyism' on his own generation.[145]

In 1977 Hughes said:

It soon became clear that, before we made the film, we had to document what actually had been done, the events of the period are so little known. […] To do that, you need a whole lot of knowledge about what happened. I think The Cold War happened in every street, in every head. I hope this film will make people talk about it. […] The thing that has been internalised can be equated with the hidden curriculum of our schools. […] it generates a 'culture of silence'.[146]

Interviews, news clippings, newsreel footage and voice-over narration are used to encapsulate much of the political detail of this intriguing period. Narration, which is used sparingly, explains

ABOVE: *MENACE* (1976). MENZIES SAW THE PEACE MOVEMENT AS A VEHICLE OF COMMUNISM DESIGNED TO 'SOFTEN UP' THE DEMOCRATIC WORLD.[147] **RIGHT:** *MENACE*.

that after the outbreak of war in Korea, prime minister Robert Menzies announced that Australia should be prepared for a third world war within three years. The narration also reveals that Menzies' interior minister, Kent Hughes, made himself well known as a fascist in the 1930s and believed that Australia must become the 49th state of America. The tenacity and thoroughness of Hughes' approach to historical detail is evident throughout *Menace*. In one scene, Ralph Gibson recounts how, in 1930 during the Depression – 'while thousands of people were literally starving, the state machinery was used quite shamelessly to help the rich through the crisis'. From off-camera, Hughes can be heard quickly providing the prompt 'the Premier's Plan' – a reference to rapid cuts to government spending, wages and pensions carried out in the 1930s. Gibson immediately takes up this prompt as evidence for his claim.

After World War II the Communist Party of Australia had a membership in the tens of thousands and communists led the trade unions that fought hardest for the forty-hour week and significant wage rises for working-class people. *Menace* argues that it was these gains, as much as ideology or a concern about Soviet aggression, that pitched the establishment – represented by big employers and Menzies' Liberal Party – into a vicious campaign against the Communist Party of Australia (CPA).

Menzies' attacks on opposition to his government went beyond the CPA. He claimed, for example, that the peace movement was orchestrated by the CPA under direction from Moscow. A number of the interviewees in *Menace* were active in the peace movement during the 1950s. Some were also leading figures in the CPA and were likely to have known exactly what the CPA's role was – yet Hughes does not put such claims to them. They are open and insightful about the broader political landscape and the impact that Menzies' push to criminalise their politics had on them personally. Their testimony reveals nothing, however, about what only they knew: the machinations of the CPA and its relationship to Stalin's USSR.

Many Australians saw friendship with communist countries as a step towards world peace. They did not accept the idea, vigorously promulgated in the West, that the Soviet Union – whose

ABOVE: JOHN HUGHES AND LLOYD EDMUNDS IN *MENACE* (1976). **OVERLEAF:** PAUL HAMPTON AND SUSY POTTER IN *THE GOLDEN HOLDEN* (PRAM FACTORY, 1975) IN *MENACE*.

population was more severely wounded by war than any other – had the will or capacity to initiate a campaign of military aggression on a global scale. American historians and writers have confirmed this intuition more recently. Gore Vidal, reflecting on both the historical record and his experience in America's political circles throughout the post-war period, concludes that the Cold War was a tool of manipulation for political and economic gain by 'the lords of the defence industry' and 'a small group at the heart of the National Security State'. They 'knew just how weak the Soviet economy was and how far behind us they were in modern weaponry' whilst popularising the opposite perception. By the 1960s President John Kennedy was refusing Soviet proposals for disarmament and actively seeking theatres of war such as Cuba and Vietnam.[148]

In Australia, the range of individuals, organisations and activities that could have been outlawed under the Communist Party Dissolution Bill 1950 was astonishing. It sought to outlaw not only the Party, but also any individuals (declared persons) or organisations associated with it or its objectives, any advocacy of associations outlawed under the Act and any public speaking or 'words represented or reproduced in any visible form' that advocates the objectives of a banned organisation.[149] It included provision to search for and confiscate any property, including books, documents or papers, belonging to the unlawful association. Declared persons would be barred from employment or contracts with the Commonwealth, its authorities in a wide range of 'vital industries' (including mining, construction, transport and power) or industrial organisations such as trade unions.[150] The legislation could have seen many unions shut down and the whole union movement crippled. A jail term of five years was to be applicable for any activities deemed by the Act to be communist in nature. The interviewees in Menace recount the very real fear of overnight house raids, the scale of which would require the establishment of concentration camps to accommodate a significant cross-section of Australian citizens.

Hughes conducted most of the interviews for Menace in people's homes. These settings, together with the use of personal photographs, evoke the social network of support around those targeted in government investigations and serve to reinforce the sense of violation brought to their lives. In the 1930s Dorothy Gibson met refugees from German fascism and came to see the communist movement as the only effective means to peace. Lloyd Edmunds joined the International Brigade to help fight fascism in Spain. They describe the Cold War struggle of Australian communists and democrats as a direct continuation of the experience of anti-fascists generally during the 1930s Depression.

Hughes wanted to address a remnant anti-communism he perceived in media culture during the 1970s. He felt that archive footage from the period could be used as 'a reminder that cinema is not innocent of ideology'.[151] His research revealed evidence of a covert dimension to the foreign control of Australian cinema that was of such great concern to advocates of a homegrown Australian film culture. The film's title derives from an anti-communist propaganda film, ostensibly produced by the Department of Interior in 1952 and (as an introductory text explains) 'edited, scripted and narrated at 20th Century Fox in Sydney.' Fox subsidiary Hoyts funded it. Hughes claims that when he attempted to gain access to the negative for Menace (1952), which, like that of most Commonwealth films was held by Film Australia, permission to use it was denied – by Eric Davis, the managing director of 20th Century Fox in Australia at the time.[152] The soundtrack to Hughes' Menace begins

CLOCKWISE FROM TOP: RALPH GIBSON WITH EDWARD AMBROSE DYSON CARTOON; GEORGE SEELAF; 1970s MELBOURNE MAY DAY MARCH, APG CONTINGENT. *MENACE*.

with a part of Fox's signature drum roll looped and repeated in such a way that it has the quality of a jackhammer. This sound is reflected at the end of the film by the jarring percussive sound of the 'break out' scene in the play *The Golden Holden*, a contemporary Pram Factory theatre production, including Robin Laurie.[153]

The shadow of Stalin and the institutional hierarchy of the Communist Party itself are an oddly unacknowledged and unexplored off-screen presence in the world of Hughes' *Menace*.[154] While the film is almost entirely concerned with events in the 1950s, the last part of the film is centred around Robin Laurie and Mick Counihan, both of whose parents are interviewed earlier in the film. Counihan describes his confrontation with his parents over their own alliance with Stalinism through the Communist Party. These complicating elements, presented by Hughes' peers, are attached at the end of the film. It's as if Hughes knows this material is important but cannot digest or manage the complexities these revelations threaten to bring to bear upon what, up until Mick Counihan's statement, has been a totally partisan film. The screen is a contestable space, and what Hughes is most compelled to achieve upon it is an idea of justice, more so than an idea of truth. Despite the potential complication of the Counihan scene, this imperative gives the film coherence and makes it a useful antidote to the persistent and dominant historical view that Hughes' *Menace* throws into question.

Thirteen people were interviewed for *Menace*, which, at 96 minutes, is Hughes' first feature length film. Most were artists and intellectuals. In search of trade unionists who were involved in the Royal Commission, Hughes was referred to George Seelaf, a leader whose perspective became an important reference point within the film. Seelaf established the Trade Union Clinic

1970s MELBOURNE MAY DAY MARCH – SOCIALISTS MARCH IN SUPPORT OF INDEPENDENCE FOR EAST TIMOR IN THE MID-1970s, *MENACE* (1976).

MELBOURNE MAY DAY MARCH, *MENACE*.

and Research Centre in Footscray that later became the Western Suburbs Community Health Centre. Rod Patterson worked there as a social planner and during the 1970s Seelaf employed Hughes at the clinic to record video of social programs. Hughes came to know Seelaf well and developed great respect for his enormous achievements in developing cultural activities for working people through the trade unions. In 1985 Seelaf became the subject of *Is It Working?* (see Chapter 4).

Menace shows how an attempt to ban an opposition political party triggered a local articulation of an international struggle for the fundamental human and democratic right to freedom of opinion, expression and association that was taking place in the immediate post-war period.[155] At the time the film was made, the access video movement sought to enable community development through a wider facilitation of these rights and the right to participate freely in the cultural life of a democratic society through contemporary media. At the same time, the Whitlam government, which generally supported these ideas, was under threat. Through *Menace*, Hughes found parallels between these two moments in Australia's social history. His reading saw him investigating debates within the left on the potential of new media, participatory democracy and citizens' control. His experience in broadcast news, the work with pioneering video artists and his involvement as an organiser and activist in the campaign for community-controlled access to video resources, imbued his work with an acute awareness of ideology and how the manipulation of knowledge and perception is disguised within the conventional patterns of social interaction, including those of mainstream media production and filmmaking. All of this research would feed into a number of future projects, including historical studies of independent filmmaking units that had their origins in the working-class movement. It also led to a series of meditations on the demise of the Whitlam Labor government, known as the *November Eleven* tapes.

Endnotes

[117] Albie Thoms said the emergence of the counterculture could be attributed to 'the failure of the traditional left to effectively challenge conservative control'. Danni Zuvela & Albie Thoms, 'The Ubu Moment: An Interview with Albie Thoms', *Senses of Cinema*, no. 27, 2003, Senses of Cinema Inc., Melbourne, <http://www.sensesofcinema.com/2003/27/albie_thoms/>, accessed 24 February 2013.

[118] Quoted in Chris Warner, Cynthia Connop & Ginny Brook, 'Filmmaking in Australia', *Farrago*, Friday 9 July 1976, p. 13.

[119] Quoted in Peter Hughes, 'A way of being engaged with the world: the films of John Hughes', *Metro*, no. 93, Autumn 1993, p. 49.

[120] Quoted in Chris Warner, op. cit.

[121] Margot Nash, Judi Stack, Rae Walker, Brian Walsh & Diana Wolthers (eds), *Melbourne Independent Videotape Catalogue*, Melbourne Access Video & Media Co-operative, Carlton, 1976, p. 15. This dates the tape 1970. According to John Hughes, October or November 1972 is the more probable date.

[122] The inquiry was established in 1970 with the intention of creating an International War Crimes Commission. See Peter S Cook, *Red Barrister: A Biography of Ted Laurie QC*, La Trobe University Press, Bundoora, 1994.

[123] John Hughes, MFC, Access Video & EMA, interview by John Cumming, Melbourne, 16 January 2002.

[124] ibid.

[125] Tom Zubricki, 'Documentary: a personal view', in Geoff Burton & Raffaele Caputo (eds), *Second Take*, Allen & Unwin, St Leonards, 1999, p. 179.

[126] Melbourne's community television station, Channel 31, began regular broadcasting, with a low-power transmitter, in 1994 and commenced digital transmission in 2010. See Melbourne Community Television Consortium, 2010, <http://www.mctcltd.org.au/aboutus.html>, accessed 19 June 2013.

[127] Paulo Freire, *Pedagogy of the Oppressed*, Penguin, London, 1972, p. 31.

[128] John Hughes, *Nowhere Game*, interview by John Cumming, Melbourne, 1 August 2000, p. 31.

[129] John Hughes, 'What to do with a Greek bearing gifts', *Learning Exchange*, December 1974, p. 4.

[130] John Hughes, 'General Background of the Formation of the Video Exchange', submission to the Film, Radio and Television Board of the Australia Council for the Arts for the establishment of a Community Video Exchange – Appendix 1, Video Exchange, Melbourne, 1973, p. 7.

[131] ibid.

[132] John Hughes, 'Community Use of Video', *Learning Exchange*, March 1973, pp. 14–15.

[133] Hughes, op. cit.

[134] John Hughes, Opening Lines: *What to do with a Greek bearing gifts*, letter to Kaye Griffin (Open Channel), personal archives of John Hughes, East Brunswick, 10 November 1993.

[135] It is likely CAVRA distributed Ted Laurie on American War Crimes in Vietnam, as the video was in the collection of the MAVMC from 1976. CAVRA evolved into the screen resource organisation for the state of Victoria, Open Channel, <http://www.openchannel.org.au>, accessed 14 February 2013.

[136] Caroline Ross, 'It's a video world', *The Sun*, 20 July 1974, p. 24.

[137] John Hughes, *Film-Work*, interview conducted by John Cumming, Melbourne, 12 September 2000.

Another film with a similar title was made at about this time: Virginia Coventry (Vic) *Abortion – a Woman's Business*, 16 mm, b&w, 15 minute social comment documentary with an A$1000 grant from the EFTF. See ACA Annual Report (calendar year), Australia Council for the Arts, Sydney, 1974.

[138] Hans Magnus Enzensberger, 'Constituents of a Theory of the Media', *Raids and Reconstructions: Essays in Politics, Crime & Culture*, Stuart Hood (trans.), Pluto Press, London, 1976, pp. 41–51. Enzensberger writes that in 1923, Lissitzky imagined the 'electro-library' or database together with 'auto-vocalising and kino-vocalising representations,' which were still only emergent in the early twenty-first century.

[139] ibid., p. 27.

[140] ibid., p. 44.

[141] Monash was an important hub for the anti-war movement and Maoism was boosted there by strong support for North Vietnam and the National Liberation Front of South Vietnam (NLF). Two of the leading Monash Maoists were Albert Langer and Michael Hyde. See Haydn Keenan, *Persons of Interest: ASIO's dirty war on dissent*, 2013, 4 episodes, Smart Street Films, Sydney, Producer Gai Steele. Featuring Roger Milliss, Michael Hyde, Gary Foley and Frank Hardy. Produced with assistance from the SBS-TV. Distributed by <http://www.smartstreetfilms.com.au>.

[142] Graham Shirley & Brian Adams, *Australian Cinema: The First Eighty Years*, 2nd edn, Angus & Robertson, Sydney, 1989. Originally published 1983, p. 223. For a discussion of the political culture of the La Mama theatre company and the Australian Performing Group (APG) at this time, see Tim Robertson. The Pram Factory, Melbourne UP, Melbourne, 2001, pp. 43–62. For a firsthand account see Robin Laurie, 'Some recollections of life in the APG', *The Pram Factory: Australian Theatre History*. The Australian Performing Group at the Pram Factory, 2005, Suzanne Ingleton, <http://www.pramfactory.com/memoirsfolder/Laurie–Robin.html>, accessed 6 February 2013.

[143] Mike Richards, 'Interview with John Hughes', ABC Radio, July 1977.

[144] ibid.

[145] Barbara Hall, 'In Every Street, In Every Head', interview with John Hughes, *Filmmaker*, 1977, p. 3.

[146] ibid.

[147] Author not attributed, 'Prime Minister Condemns Peace Convention', *The Canberra Times*, Thursday 17 September 1953, p. 1.

[148] Gore Vidal, 'At Home on the Hudson in the Cold War' in *Palimpsest, a memoir*, Penguin, Melbourne, 1996, pp. 235–238.

[149] Parliament of Australia, *Communist Party Dissolution Act 1950*, Act no. 16, section 25.

[150] ibid., sections 22 & 13.

[151] John Hughes, *Menace*, program notes, 1977.

[152] In a 1977 interview with Barbara Hall, Hughes discussed other anomalies in Australia's film archives, pointing to a 'lack of archive material generally'; the fact that 'There are no Australian owned newsreel archives'; and traces of a likely collusion between 'US multinationals and the Department of the Interior' in Cold War manipulation. Specifically, '30 newsreels' that Hughes had identified from catalogue entries as relevant were physically 'missing' from the Movietone and Cinesound collections. See Hall, op. cit.

[153] *The Golden Holden*, Writer John Romeril, Director Lindsay Smith, Music Buzz Leeson, Lighting Jon Hawkes, Kelvin Gedye. Cast: Carol Porter, Robin Laurie, Susy Potter, Paul Hampton, Roz de Winter, Neil Giles, The Theatre of Fact, Pram Factory, Front Theatre, November–December 1975.

[154] At the time Hughes was making *Menace* (1977), film scholar Graeme Cutts recorded an interview on reel-to-reel videotape that takes up this issue. Hughes found a place for Cutts' footage thirty years later in *The Archive Project* (see Chapter 10).

[155] United Nations, *The Universal Declaration of Human Rights*, Paris, 10 December 1948, <http://www.un.org/en/documents/udhr/index.shtml>, accessed 19 June 2013.

BANNERS AND VIDEO MONITOR IN THE FIRST *NOVEMBER ELEVEN* INSTALLATION.

CHAPTER 3:

November Eleven

Each of the trilogy of *November Eleven* videotapes was made as a component of gallery installation works that John Hughes created in collaboration with artist Peter Kennedy. The titles *November Eleven* (1979), *November Eleven: Work in Progress* (1981) and *November Eleven: On Sacred Land* (1983) refer to the dismissal in 1975 of the democratically elected Whitlam Labor government by the Australian Governor-General Sir John Kerr. The installations are audio-visual meditations on that event and significant in Hughes' oeuvre for a number of reasons. The projects provide a kind of laboratory in which formal devices are explored. They employ video technology and draw aesthetic inspiration from early modernist movements in theatre, film and the visual arts. They also brought Hughes into an engagement with contemporaries in progressive theatre that would extend across a number of his films. The influence of constructivist tendencies in theatre and Dadaist bricolage is clearly evident in the first of the tapes. The projects also carry a commitment – one that had crystallised during the making of *Menace* (1976, Chapter 2) – to the social values and political mythologies of the labour movement.

Whilst the first *November Eleven* video is composed entirely of 'quotations' – documentary material from a range of sources – these videos would fit more comfortably into the category of video art than that of documentary. The tapes serve to remind, or pique interest in, historical events rather than to chronicle them. Here, Hughes seems to have been less concerned with presenting evidence than with recording and keeping alive the outrage that had flared across the

GOUGH WHITLAM 1974: 'WE CANNOT DISCLOSE ANY MORE ABOUT THEIR PURPOSES, BECAUSE THEY'RE NOT OUR SECRETS.' *NOVEMBER ELEVEN*.

social fabric of a nation. Consequently, this chapter begins with an exposition of the historical record – as it was available to Hughes in 1979, and as it has been added to over time. The impact the change of government had on independent media and filmmaking will also be traced. I will then turn to some of the technological developments and artistic influences behind the *November Eleven* tapes before discussing the videos themselves.

Whitlam's Labor government eliminated military conscription and capital punishment and instituted robust systems for the provision of universal health care, legal aid and access to university education without fees. It also expanded the federal arts budget and gave the arts a central place in the national agenda. Whitlam opened the door to land rights for Aboriginal and Torres Strait Islander people saying 'their case is beyond argument' and 'all of us are diminished' while they are 'denied their rightful place in this nation'. Furthermore, Australia's longest-serving judge, and the inaugural chairman of the Australian Law Reform Commission, has described Whitlam's commitment to 'changing Australia's perception of itself as an active participant in international affairs'.[156] On being sworn in as prime minister, Whitlam said of foreign policy:

Our thinking is towards a more independent Australian stance in international affairs and towards an Australia which will be less militarily oriented and not open to suggestions of racism, an Australia which will enjoy a growing standing as a distinctive, tolerant, co-operative and well-regarded nation not only in the Asia Pacific region but in the world at large.[157]

After 23 years in opposition, Labor initiated the recognition of land rights for Indigenous Australians and ratified fifteen United Nations treaties, engaging Australia in enforceable international human rights law together with treaties on the non-proliferation of nuclear weapons and environmental conservation.

In 1974, having been defeated in a referendum to control prices and wages and in the wake of the international oil crisis of 1973, Labor presided over spiralling inflation and growing unemployment.[158] Conservative forces, aggravated by the government's reforms, blamed its spending. Whitlam's opponents also exploited the inexperience of his team by capitalising on a series of ministerial 'scandals'.

On 11 November 1975, after the opposition blocked supply in the Senate, the Australian Governor-General Sir John Kerr made the unprecedented move of sacking the prime minister. Kerr then appointed opposition leader Malcolm Fraser in a caretaker role. This is the event Hughes and others still refer to as 'the coup'. Indeed, there are parallels between the events leading to the demise, by non-democratic means, of the Whitlam Labor government in Australia and of the democratically elected Unidad Popular government of Salvador Allende in Chile. The coup in Chile on 11 September 1973 was a military one, whereas in Australia the power of the monarchy was invoked to usurp a legitimate democratic government. In both cases vested interests – both local and international – were at work behind the scenes.

In the last years of America's rampage in Indochina and after the US backing of Augusto Pinochet's murderous coup d'état in Chile – in which the Labor government discovered its own agents were complicit – there was suspicion of US Central Intelligence Agency (CIA) involvement in undermining Whitlam's Cabinet. In a 2005 paper *Beyond Conspiracy Theory: US presidential*

FROM TOP: SIR JOHN KERR, 18TH GOVERNOR-GENERAL OF THE COMMONWEALTH OF AUSTRALIA (11 JULY 1974 – 8 DECEMBER 1977); KERR REIMAGINED; WHITLAM RESPONDS TO A READING OF KERR'S ANNOUNCEMENT ON THE STEPS OF PARLIAMENT HOUSE, CANBERRA ON 11 NOVEMBER 1975, REFERRING TO MALCOLM FRASER AS 'KERR'S CUR'; PROTESTORS ARE QUICK TO DRAW PARALLELS BETWEEN THE CONSTITUTIONAL COUP IN AUSTRALIA WITH THE MILITARY COUP D'ÉTAT IN CHILE IN *NOVEMBER ELEVEN* (1979).

CLOCKWISE FROM TOP LEFT: 16 MM CELLULOID FILM COUNTDOWN LEADER REPROCESSED ELECTRONICALLY; REMEMBRANCE DAY AS MILITARISTIC CELEBRATION; F1-11 FIGHTER JETS FLY SYMBOLICALLY OVER THE AUSTRALIAN CAPITAL ON 11 NOVEMBER 1975; COUNTDOWN FRAMES PUNCTUATE THE MONTAGE, THEIR ROTATING GRAPHICS EVOKING THE SCAN OF A RADAR SCREEN IN *NOVEMBER ELEVEN* (1979).

archives on the Australian press, national security and the Whitlam government, Professor Stephen Stockwell wrote:

Those investigating the events that led to the fall of the Whitlam government in 1975 are often accused of an obsession with conspiracy, but documents from the presidential archives from the Eisenhower to Ford administrations provide evidence of the complex inter-relationship between the Australian press, security services and Whitlam's opponents. Recent archival work clearly establishes the ready complicity of the Australian press and a role for the US National Security Council in Whitlam's demise.[159]

According to Arthur Tange, Secretary of the Australian Defence Department from 1970 to 1979, Whitlam had 'a deep antipathy' to CIA involvement in destabilising left-wing governments.[160] Nor could his government trust the Australian Security Intelligence Organisation (ASIO). Attorney-General Lionel Murphy had long been critical of the ASIO Act that left the Director-General of ASIO 'in no way subject to Ministerial or Parliamentary control'.[161] In 1973, as preparations were made for a visit by the communist Yugoslav prime minister Dzemal Bijedic, Murphy was told that ASIO was continuing with policies of the former government with regard to the anti-communist activities of the Croatian Ustasha in Australia. He was led to believe that ASIO had been

SIR JOHN KERR, COMMANDER-IN-CHIEF OF THE AUSTRALIAN DEFENCE FORCE, REMEMBRANCE DAY, 1975. *NOVEMBER ELEVEN* (1979).

withholding information he had been requesting for two weeks about a terrorist threat to Bijedic.[162] As Jenny Hocking explains, Bijedic's safety was ASIO's responsibility, 'but it was ultimately Murphy's responsibility as the Minister in charge'.[163] Murphy sent Commonwealth Police to ASIO's Melbourne offices to secure safes and files.[164] The 'Murphy raid' sent shock waves through the international intelligence community.[165] America and Britain had enjoyed access to ASIO intelligence without effective ministerial oversight for decades.[166] When Whitlam sought to learn what US bases in Australia were being used for, there was further alarm. These facilities were, in President Richard Nixon's words, 'Our most direct stakes in Australia …'[167] The bases had been at the centre of US-Australian relations since the early 1960s.

Less than a month after being elected, Whitlam – who had flown bombing missions as a flight lieutenant during World War II – wrote to Nixon questioning 'most earnestly' whether the bombing that concentrated on Hanoi and Haiphong for twelve days around Christmas 1972 would lead to 'the return of the North Vietnamese to the negotiating table'.[168] US Secretary of State, Henry Kissinger, described this campaign as equivalent to 'a 4000 plane raid in World War II'.[169] Their explosive force was equivalent to that of the atomic bomb dropped on Hiroshima. US presidential archives reveal that the Nixon administration was outraged by Whitlam's suggestion that the US and Hanoi be appealed to – on equal terms – to negotiate peace in Vietnam.[170]

FROM TOP: 'THE WHITLAM GOVERNMENT IS A DERANGED, INDECENT, DISHONEST GOVERNMENT. PROMISCUOUS IN THE FULL SENSE OF THE WORD.' DOUG ANTHONY, LEADER OF THE COUNTRY PARTY (DEPUTY PRIME MINISTER 1971–1972 AND 1975–1983); 'AUSTRALIANS CAN TURN BACK, TURN THE CLOCK BACK – GO BACK TO ALL THAT OLD HOPELESSNESS, FLATNESS AND STALE FUTILITY ...' GOUGH WHITLAM (1975); FORMER LIBERAL PRIME MINISTER BILLY MCMAHON AND HIS WIFE SONIA CAMPAIGNING FOR FRASER IN 1975. *NOVEMBER ELEVEN*.

The US administration soon received deputations and correspondence from powerful Australians declaring their support for the US bombing and distancing themselves from the Labor government. Nixon's communications director reported that Sir Frank Packer, who controlled Australian Consolidated Press, had offered 'any use you may like of his magazines and network.'[171]

Within a year of the election of a Labor government, Nixon appointed Marshall Green as US Ambassador to Australia.[172] Green, a specialist in counterinsurgency, was a hardened veteran of America's Cold War campaign against communism in Asia. He was ambassador to Indonesia during the coup d'état there and provided weapons used in the mass 'eradication of communists' that continued after that event.[173] Later, in 1973, Whitlam met with Nixon (a president in the midst of being disgraced through his abuse of power in the Watergate scandal) and returned home to hose down the hostility in his own party towards the secret bases. Meanwhile, Henry Kissinger was able to report of the meeting a 'promise of "cosmetic changes" to give the impression of Australian control ...'[174]

When Labor was re-elected in the double dissolution election of 1974, left-wing Cabinet members including Jim Cairns became more prominent and Green warned Washington that there could be a move towards 'neutrality and the removal of American bases from Australian shores.'[175] Rupert Murdoch, at that time a powerful national – rather than global – media mogul had supported the election of a Labor government in 1972, but soon became disillusioned with it. Late in 1974, Kerr, while being entertained by Murdoch, is said to have provided a 'very detailed and elaborate outline' of his constitutional powers as Governor-General in the event that the opposition was able to block the budget in the Senate.[176] Hearsay? WikiLeaks, has recently revealed that on 15 November 1974 Murdoch did confidently tell the US Ambassador (in Green's words) 'Australian elections are likely to take place in about one year, sparked by refusal of appropriations in the Senate. All signs point to a Liberal-Country victory ...'[177]

WHITLAM ON US BASES, 'THEY WILL NOT BE USED TO MAKE WAR ON ANY COUNTRY ...' *NOVEMBER ELEVEN* (1979).

In September and October 1975, ASIO and Australian Secret Intelligence Service (ASIS) chiefs were sacked. On 2 November, under President Gerald Ford, the CIA chief William Colby was sacked. That day, Whitlam claimed publicly that the leader of the National Party, Doug Anthony, and Richard Stallings, the American who had founded the Pine Gap base and whom Whitlam had just learnt was a CIA agent, were closely associated.[178]

Whitlam was now coming closer to learning that US bases in Australia were not merely used to monitor missiles, spacecraft and the like. They were (and presumably still are) also used to monitor radio and telephone communications across Asia and within Australia.[179] Stockwell concludes 'Whitlam was astounded that the US had misled him and offended that he had been duped into misleading his party'.[180] The prime minister demanded the names of CIA operatives in Australia and publicly revealed that the American Joint Defence Space Research Facilities at Pine Gap and Nurrungar were used by the CIA.

Labor cabinet minister Clyde Cameron believed that American fear of a refusal by Whitlam to renew the leases for installations would have been sufficient motivation for them to make moves to destabilise the government.[181] Tange acknowledges, but plays down the status of a CIA telex

CLOCKWISE FROM TOP LEFT: WHITLAM; PRIME MINISTER WHITLAM DEMANDED THE NAMES OF CIA OPERATIVES IN AUSTRALIA AND PUBLICLY REVEALED THAT THE CIA USED THE AMERICAN JOINT DEFENCE SPACE RESEARCH FACILITIES AT PINE GAP AND NURRUNGAR; SIR JOHN AND LADY ANNE KERR, REMEMBRANCE DAY CEREMONY, 11 NOVEMBER 1975; MALCOLM FRASER. *NOVEMBER ELEVEN* (1979).

to ASIO, just two days before a federal parliamentary debate was due on the American satellite bases 'extravagantly predicting serious consequences for Australia's relations which could follow the prime minister's disclosures'.[182] That was on 10 November.

In 1976 the US Senate Church Committee reported that CIA intervention in foreign, political, press and trade union culture was routine and that between 1961 and 1975 the agency had conducted 900 'major' projects and thousands of smaller ones overseas.[183] In 1977 the US Senate Select Committee on Intelligence conducted an investigation into allegations of CIA involvement in the dismissal of the 1975 Australian government but never made public its findings.[184] Accounts by a number of ex CIA officials indicate that Nixon distrusted the Whitlam government, and covert activity against it is likely to have occurred.[185]

The election of Fraser's conservative Liberal-National Party coalition government in December 1975 had a much greater significance for the non-feature and film culture arena than had that of Whitlam's progressive team in 1972. Under Fraser, total government expenditure was not substantially reduced but funding cuts were many and visible across a wide range of social and cultural programs. In 1976 the responsibilities of the Australia Council's Film, Radio and Television Board (FRTB) were transferred to the commercially oriented Australian Film Commission (AFC),

CLOCKWISE FROM TOP LEFT: THE LAST NUMERIC FRAME OF FILM COUNTDOWN LEADER; MALCOLM FRASER, 1975; THE COUNTDOWN SEQUENCE IN *NOVEMBER 11* ENDS WITH A RED FRAME AND A REPEATING SOUND LOOP OF THE GOVERNOR-GENERAL'S OFFICIAL SECRETARY READING THE DATE. *NOVEMBER ELEVEN* (1979).

with a reduction in funds.[186] This was the beginning of a dark age for 'underground cinema' as film producer and cultural commentator Phillip Adams predicted that July.[187] For independent film and community media this change heralded the beginning of a period of increasing competition and demarcation of artistic, political and social territory. In 1978 Hughes circulated a discussion paper about the new order of federal funding for independent production under the AFC. He bemoans the loss of state commitment to the broad range of 'non-commercial film':

We can expect funding to established and establishment filmmakers to produce narrative films on the one hand and to filmmakers operating in a space called avant-garde on the other. The concept of the middle level will become increasingly under pressure from each, until finally it's crushed.[188]

Hughes distributed his discussion paper to like-minded individuals in Melbourne and Sydney, encouraging their participation as a 'client community' in the 'decision-making operations' of the AFC's Creative Development Fund (CDF). Implicit in this strategy of building an alliance between politically active and astute documentary filmmakers is a vaguely identified 'avant-garde' that Hughes saw as also having ties to reactionary establishment forces.

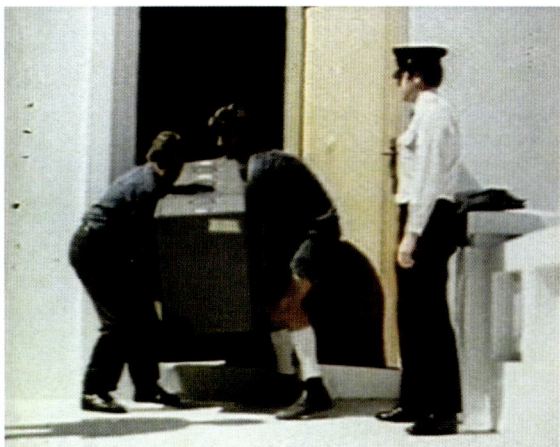

CLOCKWISE FROM LEFT: MELBOURNE FILMMAKERS' CO-OP FAÇADE, 1977; WHITLAM'S OFFICE IS CLEARED, 11 NOVEMBER 1975. *NOVEMBER ELEVEN* (1979).

The Melbourne Filmmakers Co-op (MFC), like many groups, had come to depend on federal funding to employ a small number of staff and to underwrite the cost of its exhibition and distribution activities. The AFC started a 24-year process of 'rationalisation' of distribution for independent film in Australia. That process would see the country stripped of all three of its subsidised, non-profit distributors, each of which was established by groups of enthusiasts before the advent of federal arts funding. The first phase was withdrawal of funding from filmmaker-controlled co-ops: Melbourne in 1977 and Sydney in 1985.

In mid-1977, after disputes over accountability for funds provided by it, the AFC decided not to continue the financial support that the MFC had become dependent on. Staff continued without pay after the announcement, working at the shop-front cinema in Lygon Street to present, in August 1977, a fundraising season of *Menace*. This event was used to publicise the co-op's plight and to gather signatures on a petition.[189] Visual artist Peter Kennedy made a banner that read 'Save the Film Co-op; another federal cut-back victim'.[190] This was strung across the MFC shop front. Together with photographer Barbara Hall, who was also an MFC organiser and Hughes' partner at the time, Hughes

FROM TOP: HALL & HUGHES' PHOTOMONTAGE OF THE KENNEDY BANNER ACROSS THE SYDNEY HEADQUARTERS OF THE AUSTRALIAN FILM COMMISSION; WHITLAM CAMPAIGNING FOR RE-ELECTION IN DECEMBER 1975; A NEWSREEL IMAGE OF WHITLAM AUGMENTED AND REPROCESSED IN *NOVEMBER ELEVEN* (1979)

made photomontages of this banner stretched across centres of power in the Australian film industry, including the AFC's Sydney headquarters. A series of postcards from these images was sent to influential members of the film industry over a twelve-month period. The short life of Melbourne's film co-op, however, was over.[191]

Meanwhile, Hughes was looking for alternative ways to reach audiences and was attracted to the idea of exhibiting video work in art galleries. In the *November Eleven* triptych, Hughes and Kennedy explored this opportunity. In addition to making paintings, Peter Kennedy made installation pieces. He had also produced a number of video works in collaboration with Mike Parr that were exhibited in art galleries internationally in the early 1970s. Kennedy shared Hughes' view of the 'coup' and proposed the first of an ongoing series of collaborative projects dealing with Australian history. Kennedy secured funds from the Australia Council's Visual Arts Board to assist with some of the production costs of the first of three installations the pair made together.[192] There is an aesthetic development across the trilogy, from modernist montages of contrasts and climaxes to the post-modern pastiche of blended intensities that characterise the last tape. This shift reflects one that was taking place in discourses on art in Australia in the 1980s and might also be symptomatic of the related emergence of a discrete practice of video art generated within the technical domain of analogue video mixing.

In 1979 Hughes was employed at Melbourne State College (MSC) where he worked on sponsored projects such as *Gunana*, a Super-8 documentary about an Aboriginal dance group from Mornington Island, which he directed. As with the work he did at MSC in the early 1970s, a hybrid of film and video technology was used. By this time, however, more precise editing and easy-to-use replay equipment was made possible through the introduction of cassette-based ¾-inch videotape. This U-matic format was quickly and widely adopted for non-broadcast educational use and became a viable format for distribution. Trolleys carrying playback decks and TV screens began emerging alongside the 16 mm

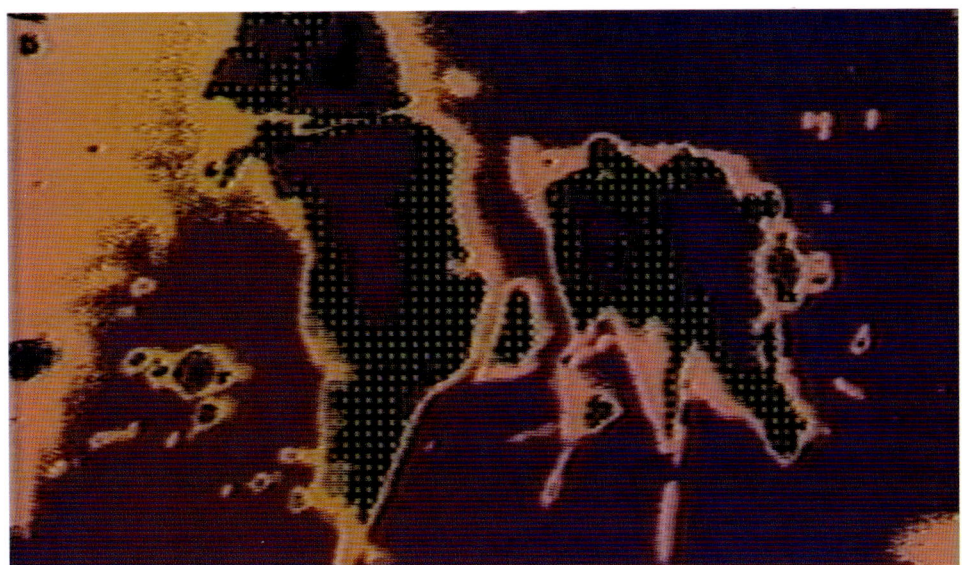

FROM TOP: VIDEO EFFECTS BROUGHT TO *NOVEMBER ELEVEN* BY RANDALL, BENDINELLI AND SCOLLO.

film projectors used in schools, colleges and universities. Whereas *Abortion: A Woman's Decision* (1974, see Chapter 2) was shot on reel-to-reel J-format video and edited and shown on 16 mm film, *Gunana* was shot on 8 mm film and edited and displayed from U-matic video cassettes. For a project shot at a location accessed by small plane, a Super-8 sound camera was practical, inexpensive, did not require mains power and rendered daylight scenes more faithfully than any affordable video format of the twentieth century.

Hughes' reading at this time included the journals *Telos*, *Screen*, *Jump Cut* and *New Left Review*.[193] In 1979 Martin Esslin, playwright, journalist and professor of drama at Stanford University, visited the college and delivered lectures on the work of cultural theoretician and playwright Bertolt Brecht.[194] Hughes traces his interest in Russian and German Constructivism of the 1920s to *The New Sobriety*, a book by another scholar of Brecht's milieu, John Willett.[195] In the 1920s, constructivist artists such as Egon Erwin Kisch and El Lissitzky were committed to a practice that engaged with the world. In reaction to the psychologism of German Expressionism, they adopted an impersonal approach to literature and art. In 1924, amid the euphoria of discovering mass media and revolutionary collectivism, El Lissitzky wrote, 'Much as I respect the individual touch [in art] it must have no personal element'.[196] The idea of reportage, championed by Erwin Kisch, was one in which the artist is 'an impersonal screen, a neutral observer'.[197] In contrast to the supposed 'objectivity' of the news journalist, the artist consciously embraces a political point of view from which to observe. This is how Hughes had already been learning to construct himself as a filmmaker.

CLOCKWISE FROM TOP LEFT: US AMBASSADOR TO AUSTRALIA ED CLARK ACCEPTING 'ONE PEPPER CORN' RENT FROM AUSTRALIAN PRIME MINISTER HAROLD HOLT AT THE OFFICIAL OPENING OF US NAVAL COMMUNICATION STATION NORTH WEST CAPE IN SEPTEMBER 1967; JOHN HALFPENNY, SECRETARY OF THE AMALGAMATED METAL WORKERS' UNION, DEMANDS THAT THE AUSTRALIAN COUNCIL OF TRADE UNIONS (ACTU) 'TAKE AUSTRALIA-WIDE INDUSTRIAL ACTION' IN RESPONSE TO KERR'S SACKING OF WHITLAM; WHITLAM'S EVENTUAL SUCCESSOR AS LEADER OF THE ALP AND THE NEXT LABOR PRIME MINISTER, ACTU PRESIDENT BOB HAWKE, WATCHES THE TALLY BOARD AS WHITLAM FALLS. 'THIS IS NOT THE TIME FOR PRECIPITATE INDUSTRIAL ACTION.'; MARGARET WHITLAM LOOKING ON IN 1974 AS GOUGH DECLARES '… THESE SECRETS WILL NOT BE REVEALED UNLESS THE AMERICANS AGREE. *NOVEMBER ELEVEN* (1979).

November Eleven

The *November Eleven* triptych brings together the work of artists in painting, film, video art and sound. Hughes describes the first *November Eleven* (1979) videotape as a Dadaist piece that uses 'the detritus of culture, the material in the air, the broadcasts' to present a 'counter text in the tradition of Joris Ivens and Heartfield'.[198] The banners that Kennedy made for the *November 11* gallery installation are echoed in the video's declamatory, sloganeering style and in its status as a document of protest. Some of the images are subjected to extreme colour distortion effects provided by video artists Robert Randall and Frank Bendinelli.[199] Another video maker, Andrew Scollo, is credited as co-director for his work on the project. The video is a montage of found television and radio material reporting on the dismissal of the Whitlam government, angry street protests and the election of the Fraser government.[200] The sound montage is a work of musique concrète created by Robert Moore together with Hughes' long-time friend John Scott. In a longer iteration, it also served as a work for radio.[201] The filmmakers' commentary on the events depicted lies in the selection and combination of images and spoken word. For Hughes, the

CLOCKWISE FROM TOP LEFT: OUTRAGED AT THE GUSTO WITH WHICH MURDOCH BACKED FRASER IN 1975, PRINT WORKERS RIP BUNDLES OF NEWSPAPERS FROM DELIVERY TRUCKS UNDER BANNERS DEMANDING THE NATIONALISATION OF MEDIA 'UNDER WORKERS' CONTROL'; POSTURE AND GESTURE ARE DISTILLED THROUGH GRAPHIC LAYERING AND ELECTRONIC PROCESSING; MALCOLM FRASER WAVING AT A CAMPAIGN RALLY IN 1975. *NOVEMBER ELEVEN* (1979).

events of 1975 are emblematic of the issue of centralised media power that concerned him as a young news camera operator and that had been a motivation for the access video movement.

The form Hughes, Scollo, Moore and Scott explored with *November Eleven* can be seen as preempting the scratch video phenomena of the early 1980s. But it can also be seen, like scratch video itself, as an extension, in an electronic form, of the collage work of experimental or 'avant-garde' filmmakers like Len Lye, Joseph Cornell, Arthur Lipsett and Bruce Conner.[203] Conner's films came to Australia in the early co-op years as part of a package of New American Cinema. His found-footage music clip for pop group *Devo* was also playing on Australian television at the time *November Eleven* was made.[204]

By the late 1970s Hughes had become suspicious of the libertarian international avant-garde, having learnt of connections between Ford Foundation sponsorship and CIA cultural policy and personnel, in which the New American Cinema package that came to Australia was implicated. In an article he wrote in 1978, Hughes cites Eva Cockcroft who had established in 1974 that in the Cold War context, international cultural exchange was symbolically loaded and subject to scrutiny. She claimed that senior personnel within the art establishment and the CIA, 'recognised that dissenting intellectuals who believe themselves to be acting freely could be useful tools in the international propaganda war'.[205] Abstraction in art was seen as apolitical and helped create an image of America as a liberal society on the international stage. It is ironic, then, that *November Eleven* was later included in an exclusive retrospective compilation of Australian avant-garde film and video art. A further irony is that by placing work that is designed to be instantly replayable (video) into the ephemeral context of art gallery exhibition, *November Eleven* has, to date, achieved a greater longevity of exposure in that context than most of Hughes' more substantial works on film.[206]

November Eleven: Work in Progress

The Dada-inspired approach to montage and found footage of the earlier *November Eleven* tape is evident throughout the second of this trilogy, *November Eleven: Work in Progress* (1981). Much of the newsreel footage of the earlier tape is included here. The video begins with one of Melbourne's massive anti-war marches of the late 1960s or early 1970s. In a scene reminiscent of marches that Hughes recalls filming as a cameraperson at the Australian Broadcasting Commission (ABC), young protesters in whiteface chant the name of the veteran Vietnamese independence leader 'Ho, Ho, Ho Chi Minh!'[207] This is possibly the street theatre group Flying Wedge that included Robin Laurie, John Duigan and some of the Maoist theatre workers from Monash University referred to in Chapter 2.[208] This is followed by an animated advertisement for the Bank of America, the graphic style of which – ironically – resembles the style of Fernand Léger's 'Charlot Cubiste' (Cubist Charlie Chaplin) sequence in the Dadaist film of 1924 *Ballet Mécanique*. A television commercial for Coca-Cola follows, featuring young female shoppers, a pop group, and a beach buggy. The Coke commercial blends the youthful energy of the protesters with the ideology of the Bank of America advertisement. The protesters become at once anti-realist actors and caricatures of public political performance. Like everything else in this tape, these images can be viewed as concrete artefacts of daily life – the tickets, spools of cotton and cigarette butts Walter Benjamin noted in still life collages of Dada art.[209]

In *The New Sobriety, 1914–33: Art and Politics in the Weimar Period*, Willett notes that multimedia elements – 'projected texts, film, the treadmill stage and other devices' – were an important part of Erwin Piscator's 'documentary drama'. The constructivist aesthetic allowed such visual devices to be wheeled or projected onto the modernist theatre's bare stage. Hughes literally places this bare stage onto the small screen in *November Eleven: Work in Progress*. Actors Carolyn Howard and Paul Davies are filmed in a blue-screen television studio with just three props (a couch, a television and a folded newspaper) to suggest a domestic setting. They debate the morality of Soviet imperialism while watching footage of the 1968 Russian invasion of Czechoslovakia. Chroma key is used to create an uneasy montage of projections within the frame by placing the television images all around the characters. For one shot, the chroma is keyed to black so that the characters and their television appear to be floating in a void. Newsreel footage is also superimposed into scenes of Howard and Davies from *Exits* (1980), a film they had made with Pat Laughren about the dismissal of the Whitlam government (see Chapter 5).

Jonathon Holmes claimed to see a shift between the first and second iterations of the Kennedy/ Hughes' *November Eleven* project, from a banner and videotape that 'partake of mythologising' to ones that are 'much more interested in demythologising'.[210] The central statement of the project, however, presents a totalising grand narrative of mythic proportion:

THE HISTORY OF STRUGGLE
OF THE AUSTRALIAN PEOPLE
INSPIRES TODAY'S STRUGGLE
FOR NATIONAL INDEPENDENCE
AND SOCIALISM.

This text from Kennedy's banner is revealed, line-by-line, throughout the duration of Hughes' videotape as a core authorial statement. A highly selective view of Australian history, the statement's fantastical nature, is reinforced in a story-time sequence in which a child's voice, backed by Carolyn Howard's, reads about the Australian labour movement from a children's book. The text describes how the oppositional forces of nineteenth-century Australian politics were absorbed through a liberal-capitalist constitution, such that 'Genuine socialist demands were placed outside what passed as political debate.' No reference is made in this video to shameful chapters of Australia's socialist history, such as the labour movement's role in establishing and maintaining the 'White Australia' policy.

It may seem an anomaly in late twentieth-century culture – years after Fluxus, Pop Art and Punk for a work of art that carries such earnest, utopian, nationalist content to draw its formal devices and spiritual heritage from the mercurial, anti-doctrinaire spirit and form of Dada. In doing so, *November Eleven: Work in Progress* harks back to a specific and short-lived historical nexus between art, utopian political organisation and the state. Willett had shown that in 1920s Germany and Eastern Europe the Dada and Constructivist art movements served the artistic arm of the Communist Party and the early Soviet state.[211] He also highlighted, however, the unsteady nature of this relationship, the internationalist quality of these movements, and their disenfranchisement under the rise of both fascism and Stalinism in the 1930s.

At the time he made *November Eleven: Work in Progress,* Hughes might have agreed with a formulation that Paulo Freire articulated several years later in *Pedagogy of Hope*:

To me ... the element of failure in the experience of 'realistic socialism', by and large, was not its socialist dream, but its authoritarian mould – which contradicted it, and of which Marx and Lenin are also guilty, and not just Stalin – just as what is positive in the capitalist experience has never been the capitalist system, but its democratic mould.[212]

The coup d'états in Chile and Australia in the early 1970s can be seen, with this formulation in mind, as instances of capitalism asserting itself in an authoritarian mould. In Australia the values of the capitalist establishment were asserted through the colonialist office of an unelected governor. In Chile, as in fascist Germany, Italy and Spain, authoritarian capitalism adopted the guise of military dictatorships. The threat that Allende – and to a lesser extent Whitlam – posed to

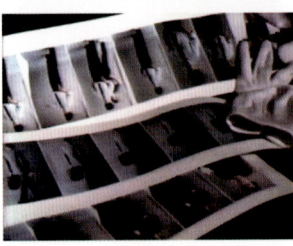

FROM TOP: IMAGES FROM *NOVEMBER ELEVEN: ON SACRED LAND* (1983).

global capitalist hegemony was that it offered a socialist experience within a democratic mould. This challenged the myth that democracy and global capitalism are somehow interdependent. It also exposed the neoliberal conceit that cloaks the imperatives of powerful commercial interests in the guise of democratic ones.

November Eleven: On Sacred Land

(1983)

Following from the theme of a Eurocentric construction of history in *November Eleven: Work in Progress*, the third Kennedy/Hughes' installation is concerned with the historical struggle of Indigenous Australians. Hughes' video borrows heavily, as the title suggests, from Oliver Holmes' *On Sacred Ground* (1980), a documentary about the blockade by Yungngora people of oil exploration works near a sacred site at Noonkanbah. It also draws upon numerous other sources, including artworks by Aboriginal and European painters from colonial times. European costumes are used symbolically, sometimes via photographs in which Kennedy – including a performance element in the repertoire of his art – has actors striking comical poses for the camera of photographer Sandy Edwards. Kennedy included these figures – judge, military officer and businessman – in the full-scale reworking of a historical painting that he made for the installation.

In contrast to the studiously disjunctive cutting in the first *November Eleven* tape, Hughes took great care with *November Eleven: On Sacred Land*, to create smooth compositional transitions between disparate archival material. For example, the effect of one generation of children filing into a mission hall (in archival film) becoming another (performing a contemporary post-colonial play in a similar hall) is achieved by matching the screen direction, proportion and composition of the moving figures from one image to the next. Likewise, the screen direction of a hand-shaking oil company executive is matched by that suggested in the still image cut with it from one of the Kennedy/Edwards photo strips. Sounds also emerge seamlessly: preempting the images they are associated with, then merging into the larger composition where they are sustained for a considerable time beyond those images.

The demise of the MFC saw Hughes return – this time as a filmmaker – into the world of the visual arts from which he and the Australian filmmakers' co-ops had originally emerged. In each of the *November Eleven* projects, however, Hughes maintained the single-screen linear status of the videotape so that it could be viewed separately from the gallery exhibit, or even broadcast on television. Here the gallery becomes, firstly, a context-providing venue for a filmmaker's work rather than a site for the integration of video as a wholly interdependent component within a unique spatial creation. In this respect, Hughes' work differs from that of most installation-based video art, including the earlier Kennedy/Parr work – all of which, in the context of the film industry, would be considered avant-garde. Hughes has continued to show his work in art galleries as part of a multiplatform approach to the exhibition of films made primarily for theatrical or television release. These more recent productions do not reflect the influence of the visual art context in the same way as the triptych Hughes produced with Kennedy. Nor are the later works as strident as those lamentations of Australia's historic coup of 1975, when an unelected official sacked an elected government mid-term.

Endnotes

[156] Michael Kirby, 'Whitlam as Internationalist', Whitlam Lecture, 2010, University of Western Sydney, 25 February, p. 2, <http://www.michaelkirby.com.au/images/stories/speeches/2000s/2010_Speeches/2432.Speech–WhitlamLecture–25February2010.pdf>, accessed 19 September 2013.

[157] ibid.

[158] John N Molony, *The Penguin History of Australia: The story of 200 years*, 2nd edn, Penguin, Ringwood, 1988, pp. 358–59.

[159] Stephen Stockwell, 'Beyond Conspiracy Theory: US presidential archives on the Australian press, national security and the Whitlam government', Journalism Education Conference, Griffith University, Academia.edu, Brisbane, 2005, p. 2, <http://www98.griffith.edu.au/dspace/bitstream/handle/10072/2432/32006_1.pdf?sequence=1>, accessed 15 September 2013.

[160] Sir Arthur Tange, 'Reflections looking back: Whitlam and the Central Intelligence Agency', *Defence Policy-Making: A Close-Up View, 1950–1980, 2008*, Canberra Papers on Strategy and Defence, Demetrius at The Australian National University E Press, Canberra, <http://epress.anu.edu.au/sdsc/dpm/mobile_devices/ch02s25.html>, accessed 19 June 2013.

[161] Jenny Hocking, Lionel Murphy: A Political Biography, Cambridge University Press, Oakleigh, Melbourne, 1997, pp. 90–91. A prominent lawyer, senator and member of the ALP's Civil Liberties Committee in the early 1960s, Murphy played a leading role in developing party policy on legal reform.

[162] Jim Stokes, A brief history of the Royal Commission on Intelligence and Security, 2013, National Archives of Australia, <http://www.naa.gov.au/collection/publications/papers–and–podcasts/intelligence–and–security/rcis–historyppaper.aspx>, accessed 15 September 2013.

[163] Hocking, op. cit., p. 163. Hocking provides an informative account of the complex set of circumstances and machinations that conspired upon Murphy at this time.

[164] Stokes, op. cit.

[165] Stockwell, op. cit., p. 8.

[166] A subsequent royal commission found that ASIO's priorities were distorted and that it had improperly

167 Stockwell, op. cit., p. 6.
168 Operation Linebacker II arguably achieved that objective but was widely condemned. It involved up to 120 B-52 Stratofortress planes per night dropping a total of at least 20,000 tonnes of munitions. The raids resulted in over 1,600 civilian deaths. Proponents argued the raids were disciplined and strategic with 'light' loss of life, given their magnitude. *The Washington Post* saw it as 'the most savage and senseless act of war ever visited, over a scant 10 days, by one sovereign people over another'. James Curran, 'Whitlam v Nixon', *The Australian*, 1 August 2012, News Corp Australia, Adelaide, <http://www.theaustralian.com.au/news/features/whitlam–v–nixon/story–e6frg6z6–1226439818865>. Al Hemingway, 'Into the Teeth of the Tiger', *VFW Magazine*, vol. 85, no. 4, 2012, Veterans of Foreign Wars, November/December, <http://digitaledition.qwinc.com/display_article.php?id=1199157>. Rebecca Kesby, 'North Vietnam, 1972: The Christmas bombing of Hanoi', *BBC News Magazine*, 24 December 2012, British Broadcasting Service, <http://www.bbc.co.uk/news/magazine–20719382>, accessed 15 September 2013.
169 Philip Dorling, 'Whitlam radical, Fraser arrogant, Hawke moderate: Secret cables reveal Murdoch insights', *The Sydney Morning Herald*, 20 May 2013, <http://www.smh.com.au/federal–politics/political–news/whitlam–radical–fraser–arrogant–hawke–moderate–secret–cables–reveal–murdoch–insights–20130520–2jvtl.html>, accessed 15 September 2013.
170 Stockwell, op. cit., p. 7.
171 ibid.
172 Kent G Sieg, 'Marshall Green', in Cathal J Nolan (ed.), *Notable U.S. Ambassadors Since 1775: A Biographical Dictionary*, Greenwood, Westport, 1997, p. 122.
173 ibid., p. 120.
174 Stockwell, op. cit., p. 8.
175 ibid., p. 10.
176 Dorling, op. cit.
177 ibid.
178 Stockwell, op. cit., p. 12. According to Bolton, a house owned by Anthony had been let to an officer of the CIA. Geoffrey Bolton, *The Middle Way 1942–1995*, vol. 5, 5 vols, 2nd edn. *The Oxford History of Australia*, Oxford University Press, South Melbourne, 2001, originally published 1996, p. 375.
179 Stockwell, op. cit., p. 5.
180 ibid., p. 12.
181 Clyde Cameron, Jane Lanbrook & Tony Douglas, *The CIA in Australia*, Part 3, 1986, radio broadcast, Watching Brief, Public Radio News Services, Melbourne. The Central Intelligence Agency (CIA) has published extensive documentation of its overt and covert involvement in a number of countries, including Chile. See Kristian C Gustafson, 'CIA Machinations in Chile in 1970: Reexamining the Record', Studies in Intelligence, *Journal of the American Intelligence Profession*, vol. 47, no. 3, 14 April 2007, Center for the Study of Intelligence, CIA, Washington DC, <https://www.cia.gov/library/center-for-the-study-of-intelligence/csi–publications/csi–studies/studies/vol47no3/article03.html>, accessed 19 June 2013. See also Florencia Melgar & Sarah Gilbert, 'The Other 9/11', SBS Interactive, 2013, Special Broadcasting Service, <http://www.sbs.com.au/theother911/>, accessed 16 September 2013.
182 Tange, op. cit.
183 L Britt Snider, 'Oversight of Covert Action', *The Agency & The Hill: CIA's Relationship with Congress, 1946–2004*, vol. 47, no. 3, ch. 9, 14 April 2007, Center for the Study of Intelligence, The Central Intelligence Agency (CIA), Washington DC, 9 May, p. 281, <https://www.cia.gov/library/center-for-the-study-of-intelligence/csi–publications/books–and–monographs/agency–and–the–hill/The%20Agency%20and%20the%20Hill_Book_1May2008.pdf>, accessed 19 June 2013. According to Snider,

this Senate inquiry was the first ever oversight investigation into the CIA's activities in a friendly country.
184 ibid.
185 See Marian Wilkinson, *Allies*, 1983, 16 mm, colour, 94 minutes, Sydney, Distributed by Ronin Films.
186 AFC, Industry Overview, Australian Film Commission, Sydney, 1999, p. 4. Jeffery in Barbara Hall, Fred Harden & Pat Longmore, 'An oral history of the Melbourne Filmmakers Co-operative', in Barbara Creed, John Davies, Freda Freiberg, David Hanan & Kim Montgomery (eds), *Papers and Forums on Independent Film and Asian Cinema*, La Trobe University, Melbourne, ASSA, AFTRS, 1982, p. 146. At the outset, even the Experimental Film and Television Fund had been constructed primarily as a means to support the establishment of a commercial feature film industry. See ACA, Interim Report: Film Committee, Australia Council for the Arts, Interim, Sydney, 1969. Under the administration of the Australia Council and the AFI, however, the EFTF had played an important part in developing a range of media-art practices and activities. See Ken Berryman, 'Allowing young filmmakers to spread their wings: The educational role of the Experimental Film and Television Fund', thesis (MEd), Centre for the Study of Education Communication and Media, La Trobe University, Melbourne, 1985.
187 Colin Golvan, 'The trouble with Australian films', *Farrago*, 9 July 1976, p. 21.
188 John Hughes, Discussion paper sent to selected independent filmmakers, Melbourne & Sydney, 1978.
189 MFC, Last Ditch Resistance Screening: *Menace*, flyer, John Hughes, MFC, 1977.
190 See Ina Bertrand, 'Filmmmakers' Co-Ops', in Ina Bertrand (ed.), *Cinema in Australia: a Documentary History*, University of New South Wales Press, Sydney, 1989, pp. 373–377 and John Hughes, *Traps*, interview conducted by John Cumming, Melbourne, 29 November 2000. Hughes and Kennedy met at Preston Institute of Technology (PIT) when a colleague of Kennedy and co-op filmmaker Rod Bishop invited Hughes to show *Menace* to art students there. PIT later became a campus of RMIT University. According to Berryman, Bert Deling also taught at Preston in the late 1970s. See Berryman, op. cit.
191 For many years after the demise of the co-op, Nigel Buesst ran the Independent Filmmakers Association and published *The Filmmakers Handbook*, a practical digest of organisations, facilities, resources and reference material. This was a survival kit for Melbourne's independent and student filmmakers that kept something of the filmmakers' co-op spirit alive in Melbourne throughout the 1980s.
192 It is probably for this reason that only Kennedy is cited as producer of this first collaboration.
193 For example, articles in a file created by John Hughes in 1979 and labelled Brecht/Benjamin included: John Fekete, 'Benjamin's Ambivalence', *Telos*, no. 55, Spring 1978, pp. 192–198; Sandor Radnoti, 'Benjamin's Politics', *Telos*, vol. 11, no. 3, Fall 1978, pp. 63–81; Colin MacCabe, 'Realism and the Cinema', *Screen*, vol. 15, no. 2, Summer 1974, pp. 7–27; Bertolt Brecht, *Brecht on Theatre*, Hill and Wang, NY, 1964; Walter Benjamin, *Illuminations*, translated by Harry Zorn, Pimlico, London, 1999. Originally published Harcourt, 1968, Jonathan Cape, 1970.
194 Paul Stevenson, 'Martin Eslin on Bertolt Brecht', MSC Newsletter, vol. 5, no. 8, October 1979, pp. 3–6.
195 John Willett, *The New Sobriety: Art and Politics in the Weimar Period 1917–33*, Thames and Hudson, London, 1978.
196 ibid., p. 105.
197 ibid., p. 107.
198 John Hughes, *What I Have Written* and *After Mabo*, interview conducted by John Cumming, Melbourne, 3 July 2002.
199 Peter Kennedy, Artist (sculptor), (installation artist), (performance artist) Designer (architect/interior architect/landscape architect), *Design & Art Australia Online*, 2011, <http://www.daao.org.au/bio/peter-kennedy/works/>, accessed 15 September 2013.
200 Much of this sound comes from recordings of radio broadcasts that were made by Hughes on 11 November 1975. Hughes says that he and Kennedy 'went to some trouble to get the best quality recordings they could find', often directly from television broadcasters. Hughes, 2002, op. cit.

[201] John Scott, Hughes' first housemate and the writer of *What I Have Written* (see Chapter 8), was teaching radio drama at Swinburne Institute of Technology where he worked with Moore (ibid.). The title of the radio version 'Now is the time, if ever there was a time, for the people of Australia to rise in anger and start to intervene in the affairs of their own country' came from the speech by Victorian Trades Hall Council secretary John Halfpenny that accompanies protest footage in the video.

[202] In his 1985 investigation of Hawke's role in the labour movement, *Traps*, Hughes would uncover some testimony connecting Hawke and others in journalism and the labour movement to covert activity by organisations such as the CIA (see Chapter 5). Dorling writes that US diplomatic cables now reveal Hawke was a particularly valued source of information who 'conferred regularly with the US consulate in Melbourne'. Philip Dorling, 'The real word about Whitlam', *The Sydney Morning Herald*, 9 April 2013, <http://www.smh.com.au/federal-politics/political-news/the-real-word-about-whitlam-20130408-2hh5k.html>, accessed 10 June 2014.

[203] Connor & Lipsett, together with other artists such as Lye & Cornell, created montage films from discarded or remnant 'found' footage. In the days before domestic video recorders, Connor also filmed images from television news broadcasts. In the early 1980s a genre of video art emerged that employed low-cost video equipment to continue this Dadaist tradition of appropriating and reconfiguring 'found' material, usually drawn from television. See Nicholas Cope, 'Northern Industrial Scratch: the history & contexts of a visual music practice', thesis (PhD), Faculty of Art, Design & Media, University of Sunderland, June 2012, <http://ethos.bl.uk/OrderDetails.do?uin=uk.bl.ethos.576523>, accessed 16 October 2014.

[204] Conner's early films featured in the New American Cinema programs screened to a packed house at the Dendy Cinema in Melbourne in 1968 and are likely to have screened at the MFC. See Peter Mudie, *Ubu films: Sydney underground movies 1965–1970*, UNSW Press, Sydney, 1997; MFC, Alternate Cinema: Australia and USA, flyer for screening, Melbourne Filmmakers Co-op, circa 1972; Bruce Conner & DEVO, Mongoloid, 1978, b&w, 3 minutes, Producer DEVO, Scriptwriter Bruce Conner.

[205] See John Hughes, 'Albie's blind eye to the why', *Nation Review*, 3–9 November 1978, p. 22 and Eva Cockroft, 'Abstract Expression, Weapon of the Cold War', *Artforum*, June 1974, pp. 39–41.

[206] MIMA, MIMA Yearbook vol. 1, 1986, VHS, colour, 56 minutes, Modern Image Makers Association, Melbourne. MIMA reflected the preference of many filmmakers whose work is labelled avant-garde for the term 'experimental.' Usage has seen these generic terms used interchangeably but there is history and ideology behind each of them. The terminology employed by Hughes at the time is used for the purpose of this discussion. In 2000 the first two *November Eleven* tapes, then over twenty years old, were screened in two different Brisbane art galleries. John Hughes, *Traps*, interview conducted by John Cumming, Melbourne, 29 November 2000.

[207] From 1941 to 1969 Ho Chi Minh was the leading figure of the Vietnamese independence movement against attacks by Japanese, British, French, American & allied forces, including those of Australia. See François Sully & Marjorie W. Normand (ed.) *We the Vietnamese – Voices from Vietnam*, Praeger, 1971.

[208] Robin Laurie, 'Some recollections of life in the APG', *The Pram Factory: Australian Theatre History*. The Australian Performing Group at the Pram Factory, 2005, Suzanne Ingleton, <http://www.pramfactory.com/memoirsfolder/Laurie-Robin.html>, accessed 6 February 2013.

[209] Walter Benjamin, 'The Author as Producer', in Peter Demetz (ed.), *Reflections: Essays, Aphorisms, Autobiographical Writings*, Edmund Jephcott (trans.), 1st edn. A Helen and Kurt Wolff Book, Harcourt Brace Jovanovich, Inc., New York, 1978, p. 229.

[210] Jonathan Holmes, 'Istoria', Centre for the Arts, University of Tasmania, Hobart, 1986, p. 2.

[211] Willett, op. cit., p. 218–22.

[212] Paulo Freire, *Pedagogy of Hope*, Bloomsbury, London 1992, p.86.

CHAPTER 4:
Film-Work

FILM-WORK POSTER (CAROL PT, 1981).

Documentary film and the trade union arts movements of the 1940s and 1950s provided the cultural context and aesthetic stimulus for a wide range of work outside the orbit of commercial cinema. Alongside film societies (see Chapter 1) and amateur cine clubs (see Chapter 10), their work prefigured that of the filmmakers' co-ops and access video groups in the late 1960s and early 1970s (see Chapter 1). The filmmaking that emerged around all these movements underpins much of the diversity and innovation of contemporary screen culture in Australia. At those times there was little industrial-scale production or commercial exhibition of local films in Australia. The film society movement was in fact central to the function and survival of film culture in Australia in the post-war period. Through their local film society, ordinary Australians expanded their knowledge and experience of international cinema beyond the Anglo-American monoculture of the commercial cinema chains that otherwise went largely unchallenged. *Film-Work* (1981) is the first of a series of films through which John Hughes explores this history of collective, creative effort in film through scholarship, production, distribution and exhibition.

In 1977 the Sydney-based Crowsfoot Films collective (Garry Lane and Peter Gray) commenced production, without funding, of a documentary about the epic and ill-fated Victorian power workers' strike, *Know Your Friends, Know Your Enemies* (1977).[213] While working at Melbourne State College (MSC), Hughes interviewed Lane and Gray for the national film magazine *Cinema Papers* and helped them find archival footage.[214] Crowsfoot Films continued the tradition of collective, independent, working-class filmmaking in Australia that Hughes had learnt about while making *Menace*. That tradition had its foundations in the Realist Film Association in Melbourne (see Chapter 10), Joris Ivens' work with maritime workers

JOHN HUGHES, KEITH GOW AND GLENYS PAGE ON LOCATION IN 1979 FOR *FILM-WORK*.

in Sydney on *Indonesia Calling* (1946, see Chapter 11), and the Waterside Workers' Federation Film Unit (WWFFU), which followed that collaboration. In these movements, Hughes would find a triptych of film projects that would take thirty years to complete.[215]

During his research for *Menace*, Hughes recognised the WWF and Realist film units as mainstays of oppositional independent filmmaking in post-war Australia and as precursors to the filmmakers' co-operatives and the access video movement that he and his peers were engaged with in the 1960s and 1970s. The social conditions of Australian alternative culture in the immediate post-war years were very different to those of the counterculture generation to which Hughes belonged. In her book about the WWFFU, Lisa Milner describes a vibrant and highly organised working-class cultural movement that was based in a union hall on the Sydney docks during the 1950s.

Sixteen cultural groups were active [...] The busy curriculum was encouraged by the actors, musicians and artists who, returning from World War II, could not find work in their preferred occupation, and went onto the wharves, where casual employment was the norm. Gang 364, filled with these activists, was dubbed 'the Brains Trust'.[216]

Milner demonstrates the significance and scale of film society activity and of documentary and 16 mm film production in Australia in the post-war years. Independent, sponsored and government filmmaking has often been omitted from histories of Australian cinema, which depict the 1950s and early 1960s as a period of inactivity. Milner shows that while Australian filmmakers are known to have made only eight feature films between 1953 and 1958, hundreds of short films were produced in that time and community-based film screenings were conducted on a massive scale. In 1953 *The Motion Picture Directory* claimed the non-theatrical audience for films was six million per year. This represented growth of two million in two years.[217]

From 1953 to 1958 the Waterside Workers' Federation Film Unit (WWFFU) produced, distributed and exhibited eleven documentary films on issues affecting Australian workers. The unit's productions provided an alternative source of media at a time when Cold War propaganda on the mainstream airwaves and newsreels consistently employed anti-union rhetoric. Norma Disher, Keith Gow and Jerome (Jock) Levy formed the unit after working together at the New Theatre in Sydney. Gow was introduced to 16 mm filmmaking by Bob Mathews of the Realist Film Unit that formed around the New Theatre in Melbourne (see Chapter 10).[218] The WWFFU's efforts built on the Sydney waterside workers' first experience of political filmmaking during the production of Joris Ivens' *Indonesia Calling* (1946, see Chapter 11). All of this activity was undertaken in the context of an international mobilisation of the creative arts galvanised in the 1920s by the Berlin-based Workers International Relief (WIR) and in the 1930s by the anti-fascist struggle of the Spanish Civil War.[219] In 1994 McMurchy claimed that 'in total contrast to the conservatism of most sponsored documentaries' the WWFFU produced 'forceful agitprop documentaries' on many issues affecting workers' lives.[220]

Film-Work was the first of Hughes' films to be financed by the feature film industry-oriented Australian Film Commission (AFC). The AFC's Creative Development Branch (CDB) provided finance for short and documentary films. The CDB employed a progressive and somewhat democratic method for selecting projects by means of peer assessment by a panel of three industry professionals, usually experienced filmmakers. Hughes'

FILM-WORK (1981).

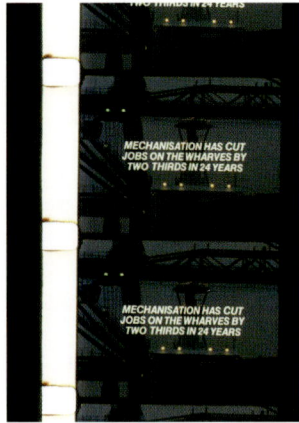 

ABOVE: *FILM-WORK* (1981); **ABOVE RIGHT:** MARGOT NASH TAKING A LIGHT READING FOR THE *FILM-WORK* INTERVIEW WITH JOCK LEVY.

proposal was initially rejected. But, undeterred, he embarked on 'an interesting battle' to have the AFC overturn its decision. Firstly, he wrote a 'de-construction' of the assessors' comments, including a list of the positive statements and 'the resistances', and pointing out errors of fact or logic.[221] A second interview was called in which the most resistant assessor was replaced. Hughes remembers this as an intense meeting to which he took a tape recorder. He recalls the chairperson noting that Hughes' arguments had 'a Jesuit quality to them in their rigor'.[222] Hughes was not permitted to use the recorder but he was able to negotiate a compromise in which he had to 'jump certain hoops'.[223] Such campaigns would become a feature of Hughes' work as producer of his own independent films. Faced with a potential rejection, Hughes maintained a clear, positive and confident attitude about his project as he had originally presented it. While he was persistent, he avoided repetition by actively working on the assessors' understanding of, and responses to, his proposal. He gave priority to reframing and pointing out inconsistencies in those responses. In this Freire-like move he made the process itself problematic, rather than internalising and expanding on problems identified in his own work. Hughes did not defer to the funding authorities – he negotiated with them as an equal power.

Film-Work combines scenes selected from four of the WWF films with production stills from those films and from the *Film-Work* shoot itself. The three WWF filmmakers are interviewed alone in their contemporary working environments and together at the New Theatre. Following on from *Menace*, *Film-Work* asserts that there was an active alternative media in Australia during the early years of the Cold War. Its basis of support was neither commerce nor government but the trade union movement. In the film, Norma Disher stresses the importance of independent communication by trade unionists and celebrates the example of committed militancy that waterside workers set:

[…] the wharfies didn't go home after their meeting. They went out onto the streets with their leaflets and pamphlets and stood on corners and actually talked to people and explained to them *what was going on. […] always it will be the only answer to the media for the workers themselves [to] get out and tell the ordinary people who are also workers – what their case is all about.*

Keith Gow claimed that in the newsreels of the time, workers were depicted as powerless 'rabble' and that this was quite deliberate. The WWFFU wanted to show them as powerful and strong. Hughes would have concurred with this aim. It might have reminded him of Paulo Freire's idea that 'The oppressed must be their own example in the struggle for their redemption'.[224]

By 1957 the WWF union – diminished in membership by mechanisation of the waterfront – could no longer afford to act as the sole supporter of its film unit. *Film-Work* depicts the ACTU as simply abandoning the WWFFU. In her recent study of the WWFFU story, however, Milner found that proposals were floated within the NSW Trades and Labour Council and nationally through the ACTU to convert the unit into a trade union film co-operative.[225] The idea may not have been promoted well by union executives, however, and by 1958 an insufficient number of individual trade unions had made the commitment to help finance such a co-operative.

Hughes also sees the WWFFU as a casualty of what he described in a report to the ACTU Arts Committee as the Menzies government's exclusion of 'everyone but the media monopolies' from broadcast television upon its introduction in 1956.[226] In another version of events the WWFFU might have had airtime on a national broadcast network. They were one of the few full-time production outfits in Australia at that time and were well positioned to take on such a challenge were it offered. Hughes describes the Waterside Workers' Federation films as all but unknown by the time he came across their existence in 1975. In a 1981 flyer he notes, 'These films are part of an Australian cultural heritage largely ignored by both film and labour historians'.[227] Hughes felt they should be remembered and saw ignorance of them as symptomatic of the countercultural emphasis of the independent film movement as it re-emerged in the late sixties.

Hughes believes the labour movement and film culture spheres had become separated by the fragmentation of political activity into discrete social movements such as feminism and environmentalism. On the other hand, he sees *Film-Work* as borrowing feminist strategies. Feminists were recovering 'the concealed or the buried history of women' in films such as Jeni Thornley's *Maidens* (1978). The primary impetus behind *Film-Work* was to reveal a 'hidden history' shared by the labour movement and the independent film movement. In 1993 John Hughes told interviewer Peter Hughes that, rather than archaeology, the aim of *Film-Work* was to create a sense of continuity for the political work that Hughes and other filmmakers and activists were doing within contemporary media culture.[228]

Drawing on an idea from the philosopher Walter Benjamin – a German Jew who witnessed the rise of Nazism – Hughes saw the election of a conservative federal government in 1975 as 'a moment of danger' for independent filmmakers and progressive social reformers in Australia that caused the memory of the WWFFU to 'flash up'. *Film-Work* opens with the passage of text from Benjamin in which these phrases appear. The Australian film industry establishment, through the AFC, soon abandoned the Melbourne Filmmakers Co-operative (MFC) in much the same way as the ACTU had abandoned the WWF's film unit two decades earlier. But what

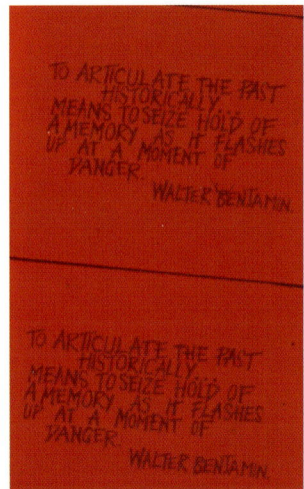

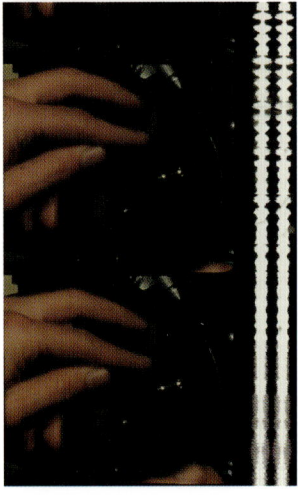

FROM TOP: THE OPENING GRAPHIC IN *FILM-WORK* – A QUOTE FROM WALTER BENJAMIN; LOADING A 16 MM ARRIFLEX ST CAMERA IN *FILM-WORK* (1981).

interested Hughes more than the story of the WWFFU's demise was the story of its survival, the way it was able to function, with trade union support, as a voice of opposition when Australia's Cold War political culture was at its most oppressive.[229]

There is symmetry between the three WWFFU filmmakers and the trio who made *Film-Work*. Margot Nash, the cinematographer of *Film-Work*, was camera assistant on the shoot for *Menace*. With fellow 'Anarcho Surrealist Insurrectionary Feminist' Robin Laurie, she had made the playfully militant film *We Aim to Please* in 1976. John Whitteron was editor and sound recordist for the film and, according to Hughes, also made a particularly significant contribution to the film conceptually.[230] Hughes wrote, produced and directed *Film-Work* and says there were many intense discussions with Whitteron and Nash about the modes of representation within it. He describes their complex and fruitful collaboration as stemming from a shared inexperience and a wonder at the art of filmmaking.[231] As the following discussion shows, this is something Disher, Gow and Levy's recollections mirror.

In *Film-Work*, Norma Disher observes that 'the most useful education in politics' comes 'through cultural forms.' This is a central statement in the film that had resonance for the young makers of *Film-Work* whose practice was primarily concerned with the politics of culture. In a collection of interviews made with nine young independent filmmakers in 1976, Nash said she wanted to understand the social function of images – 'how political processes affect the way films are made and how they are seen'.[232] For his part, Hughes said, 'I see film as inevitably political in the sense that any relationship you have with the world can be seen in political terms'.[233] All nine shared an attitude critical of the hierarchical, male-dominated structures and practices of the mainstream film industry and speak optimistically about the development of alternative independent film culture, especially through women's cinema groups.

In the 1950s social realism was important to filmmakers with progressive political ideas. The WWFFU wanted

KEITH GOW, JOHN WHITTERON AND MARGOT NASH FILMING A SCENE FOR *FILM-WORK* OUTSIDE FILM AUSTRALIA IN SYDNEY.

to convey – with veracity – what life was like for workers, and looked to the realist filmmakers of revolutionary Russia: Sergei Eisenstein and Vsevolod Pudovkin. They also had an eye on the Italian neorealists. Levy, an actor himself, had a particular interest in the human drama of working life. He observes of the wharfies who appear in the WWFFU's *The Hungry Miles* (1955) – a reconstruction of conditions on the waterfront in the Depression years – that they were able to carry out what the filmmakers wanted because they had lived through the period themselves. This was drama imbued with actuality.

After 1968 many political filmmakers were inspired by the formally experimental avant-garde of early twentieth-century Marxist cultural production such as Bertolt Brecht, Dziga Vertov and the constructivists. The highly self-reflexive work of Godard and Gorin's Dziga Vertov Group, such as *British Sounds* (1969), was an important conduit for this influence. This Godardian and constructivist impulse is built into the structure of *Film-Work* – which traces the chronology of the filmmaking process itself – while accommodating a more conventional (or 'realist') arrangement of the WWFFU's story. The second image of the film reveals the red background to the opening

THE WWFFU CAMERA AND PROJECTION VAN IN *FILM-WORK* (1981).

Benjamin quote, to be the top of a card table around which the WWFFU filmmakers and the *Film-Work* crew are gathered. A Polaroid photograph of this gathering is filmed lying on the same table while it develops. In this scene the repeated sound of a Polaroid camera 'stands in' for all cameras, and the action of its instantaneously self-developing image 'stands in' for new technology and for the photographic process itself. Likewise, the artifice of the bold red surface has been exposed. It is a simple table – an object within the documentary *mise-en-scène* – but the plain, smooth, brightly coloured surface continues to assert the visual effect of an abstract, stylised graphic design element that Hughes attributes to the constructivist artist Lissitzky's 'red wedge'. Hughes describes the tension between the constructivist and social realist elements within this image as a 'dialectical moment of implicit critique'.[234]

FILM-WORK (1981).

The photographic record of the film shoot itself – the filming of the very scene we are watching (via the instantaneous Polaroid) – places the present tense events within *Film-Work* into the domain of memory. After the appearance of the Polaroid, another superimposed, handwritten graphic announces 'Sydney, December 1979. Waterside Workers' Federation Film Unit with Film Crew.' This graphic adopts the function of a photo caption while it graphically obscures what it describes. The film crew is Hughes, Nash and Whitteron. The graphic situates in time the making of the film we have begun to watch, while it also identifies the people involved as collective productive entities: the WWFFU and the contemporary film crew. As the graphic fades out, allowing the developed Polaroid image to become clearly visible, Keith Gow's voice announces:

[…] *any film is propaganda of one sort or another. It always contains a point of view, a message of some sort. It can't be otherwise. Every aspect, from the beginning to the end, requires the highest possible degree of selectivity and judgments – thousands and thousands of judgments.*

The reappearance of the hand holding a second photograph further emphasises the materiality and

KEITH GOW AND MARGOT NASH BEHIND THE
CAMERAS IN *FILM-WORK* (1981).

KEITH GOW WITH CLOCKWORK BOLEX 16 MM CAMERA
AND JOHN WHITTERON OPERATING THE NAGRA
SOUND-TAPE RECORDER IN *FILM-WORK*.

constructed nature of the image in this film – this piece of propaganda. From the beginning, what Hughes describes as 'a constructivism in the aesthetics of the film', is evident.[235] Like Godard, Hughes requires the listener-viewer to process text from both the sound and the image tracks.[236] While there is a variation in texture – the printed word and the spoken word work consecutively – the flow of text is continuous. Gow's statement is incorporated in such a way that it works in unison with these effects. It provides a literal illustration of the constructed nature of film and telegraphs the intent of *Film-Work* to be completely frank about the bias at work within it.

Hughes reflected on propaganda again in 1982 when he collaborated with film scholars by contributing a chapter to the book *The Documentary Film in Australia*.[237] 'Propaganda Then and Now' follows from, and refers to, *Film-Work* and develops his long-standing critique of the idea of 'objective' and 'value-free' media. Hughes draws on industrial relations psychologist Alex Carey's work, reiterating Keith Gow's statement in *Film-Work* that 'All film is propaganda.' Hughes argues against the conventional documentary notion of neutrality that asserts, 'This is the antithesis of propaganda and, consequently, most credible'.[238] Hughes celebrates the classic self-reflexive film *Man with a Movie Camera* (1929) by Dziga Vertov, the revolutionary Russian documentarist whose name Godard and Gorin adopted for their radical film collective in 1968. In 1958 Vertov said the goal of that film was 'to acquaint people with the grammar of cinematic means' rather than to hide those means 'as was usually considered mandatory in other films'.[239] In reviewing documentary films historically, Hughes noted that without self-reflexivity the 'propaganda quality of documentary is most evident in retrospect' when the 'ideological mask of objectivity' that 'appears opaque in proximity' becomes transparent in hindsight.[240]

Two of the most wonderful moments of self-reflexivity in Australian filmmaking are the scene in *Dalmas* in which Deling hands over the remaining film stock to the cast and crew (see Chapter 1), and a scene in *Film-Work* where Gow turns a camera upon the crew. As Gow discusses his

JOHN HUGHES CAPTURED BY GOW'S BOLEX CAMERA IN *FILM-WORK* (1981).

first opportunity to use the 'tools of film-making,' six frame (one quarter of a second) flashes of red are cut between shots of equipment being prepared for filming and still images of Gow at work on films in the 1950s. Again, the formal strategy here is Godardian and, together with the use of Polaroid photographs, closely echoes the opening of *Angel City* (1976), a film by the American independent Jon Jost, to which Hughes acknowledges a stylistic debt.

Gow explains that films are 'written with the camera' as he picks up a small clockwork 16 mm Bolex cine camera from his desk. Gow's mentor, Bob Mathews of Realist Films, had advised him to 'Get it running, quickly … because things happen fast.' Gow turns the Bolex on and *Film-Work* cuts to the blurred image from it as he frames a shot of Margot Nash behind the *Film-Work* camera, John Whitteron with the Nagra tape recorder and Hughes with a wry grin on his face. Gow's voice says, 'I think you'd better cut.' The screen goes black. The next scene begins with the camera slate in frame and the sound of the crew starting the shot.

This Pirandellian film-within-a-film scene exemplifies the synthesis of ideas, from two generations of oppositional filmmakers, that makes *Film-Work* a rich text. The image demonstrates what Gow is explaining but in a form which he was unlikely to have employed in a film himself. While it is believable that Gow has taken up the loaded Bolex of his own accord and spontaneously turned it on the crew who are filming him, Hughes explains that this formalist scene is a set up of the younger filmmakers' invention in contrast to the social realism that informs the WWFFU films.[241]

Rather than undercutting the realist filmmakers with its formal strategies, however, *Film-Work* recasts their concerns and ideas about cinema in contemporary terms. It does so through the dynamics of its own text and the relationship it strikes with its viewers. There is formalism in *Film-Work*, but it is not a formalist film as such. The film's primary function is to construct a tradition of oppositional cultural politics that transcends generation and style. It eschews the approach of the unified realist text without weakening its own propagandist intent.

 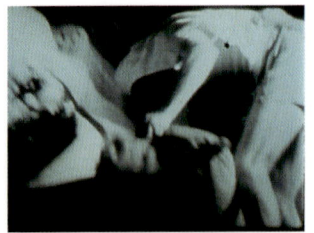 

FROM LEFT: WORKERS RECREATE A STRIKE OF THE DEPRESSION YEARS IN THE WWFFU FILM *THE HUNGRY MILES* (1955); THE HARD MANUAL LABOUR OF DOCK WORK MID-TWENTIETH CENTURY IN *THE HUNGRY MILES*; NORMA DISHER, KEITH GOW AND JOCK LEVY REVIEWING THEIR FILMS ON AN EDITING BENCH IN *FILM-WORK* (1981).

Like all of Hughes' films, *Film-Work* subtly positions and re-positions the viewer in relation to its own status as a documentary text and to the other texts, objects, and subjects represented within it. This is evident in the way interviewees' eye lines are arranged on-screen. Gow, Disher and Levy are interviewed together in a theatre auditorium and in an editing room. As each member of the trio speaks they look off-screen, acutely to the left, towards the editing machine or theatre screen. While this device seems natural and obvious in a film about filmmaking, it is unusual for it to be used in such a sustained way. The eye line of the speakers in these scenes is almost fully perpendicular to that of the viewer, rather than meeting it (as would be the case in a direct address set up in the style of Peter Watkins) or between these extremes (towards an interviewer understood to be just off-camera) as in a conventional interview.

Gow runs the films through a flatbed film-editing machine. The WWF filmmakers discuss specific elements of their films while *Film-Work* cuts to full-screen images of these – occasionally including the frame of the viewing screen. When Gow stops on an image, a freeze frame is sometimes inserted into Hughes' reprint of the original film. The audience of *Film-Work*, then, has the illusion of seeing what the filmmakers are seeing within the mise-en-scène. In this way, the listener-viewer is invited into a material and critical relationship with the WWFFU films through a position of identification with the WWFFU filmmakers.

Graphic arrangements of symbolic colour in the *mise-en-scène* and text on the screen are used in *Film-Work* to present historic struggles as a series of intersections, transformations, appropriations and turning points. Levy discusses the foreign ownership of Australian cinemas while an anti-communist Department of Information (DOI) propaganda film is projected on a theatre screen at the right of frame. On the left, a list of over 50 British- and American-owned 'Australian' cinema companies scrolls up the frame. As Levy goes on to mention that the Communist Party was near to becoming 'a mass party at that time,' Hughes and Whitteron cut to a completely empty frame of red. White margins appear at the top and bottom of frame, so it appears that a communist flag is being revealed, but as Levy's discourse turns to American imperialism, the camera pulls back further to show that this band of red is merely one stripe on the United States flag. Levy then appears leaning on a stage set at the New Theatre. From this indeterminate space – between reality and artifice, public and private, night and day – he explains: 'If you were branded as a socialist or a communist you were finished.' On the cinema screen, the 20th Century Fox Movietone News closing banner reveals the real authors of the DOI propaganda film.

FROM LEFT: GOW 'HOISTED UP BY TWENTY OR THIRTY WHARFIES' AND 'PROTECTED FROM ANYONE WHO WANTED TO STOP' HIM FROM RECORDING A UNION PROTEST'; JOCK LEVY, 'YES, IT'S STILL WITH US'. *FILM-WORK* (1981).

Levy speaks of 'a form of cultural control that the Americans and English had over this country.' He pauses, continuing to look off-screen, as if towards his interlocutor – presumably Hughes.

There is silence …

A superimposed graphic moves across the bottom of frame: "had …"?

It appears as if Levy is engaged in a dialogue with the graphic elements in the film itself, but it also appears that the filmmaker is speaking off-camera. This active, subjective graphic text is also addressed to the viewer by its presence on the screen. The screen cuts to black for one second. In the next scene, Norma Disher discusses the demise of the film unit and her initial confidence that it would re-emerge, declaring: 'Films for me were trade union films.'

In these scenes, *Film-Work* carefully places individual experience within the history of politics and culture. It is this history that Hughes, Nash and Whitteron set out to explore in the film, just as it was the history of trade unionism that the WWFFU filmmakers sought to understand and communicate in films like *November Victory* (1955) and *Hewers of Coal* (1957).

To Hughes, the establishment and development of the Waterside Workers' Federation Film Unit during the height of the Cold War was of particular significance for filmmakers of the future, and for the labour movement.[242] Here was a model of oppositional art as a product of collaboration rather than individualism, in which the trade union provided an appropriate model, or at least organisational umbrella, for collective creative effort with a progressive social purpose. While developing the *Film-Work* project, Hughes worked hard to lever opportunities for the re-engagement of the Australian trade union movement with screen production. In 1979 he helped to organise the Trade Union Film Festival and to establish the Trade Union Film Society in Melbourne. Hughes also prepared a discussion paper on screen production for the ACTU.[243] Here he warned against making high budget films within the commercial film industry, which was controlled by a very few multinational distribution and exhibition companies. He suggested the WWFFU as a successful model to consider and recommended that the ACTU keep abreast with technological and policy change in television, arguing: 'It is crucial that union movement involvement becomes a cornerstone of any public campaign for community television'.[244]

Hughes recalls that John Whitteron went to Leipzig Film Festival with *Film-Work*.[245] This was the first significant international exposure Hughes' work had received. *Film-Work* also screened at the Melbourne, Sydney and Adelaide film festivals and Hughes presented the film himself at tertiary institutions and various special events.[246] With the MFC defunct, Hughes lodged *Film-Work* with the Sydney Filmmakers Co-op for distribution until its demise in 1986. AFI Distribution took over until 2001 when the withdrawal of AFC Cultural Activities funding led to its closure and to all the Sydney Filmmakers Co-operative (SFC) and AFI-held films being returned to the filmmakers.[247] Canberra-based company Ronin Films was able to take on some titles, but Hughes' early films, including *Film-Work,* were out of distribution for a decade until Artfilms' DVD release in 2011 (see Chapter 1).

In 1982 Public Access and Community Television broadcast *Film-Work* as part of Australia's first national public television test transmission.[248] Veteran actor, teacher and leading film buff John Flaus introduced *Film-Work* to the television audience. Hughes recalls that Flaus wore a blue singlet during the studio presentation that Hughes directed:

He was the alternative David Stratton. It was fantastic and he did a beautiful job. It was really good. It was against a blue-screen, I think; so there [were] images of Norma Disher carrying the light through the darkness in the background [...][249]

Fittingly, the first television broadcast of a film by John Hughes was on public television (albeit in a trial form), in a collaboration between independent filmmakers and community television groups.

Hughes also presented *Film-Work* at the inaugural Film and History Conference in 1981 as well as the inaugural conference of the Australian Screen Studies Association (ASSA) at La Trobe University in Melbourne in 1982.[250] He also helped to organise the independent film, video and television stream at the ASSA event.[251] Here, independent film culture was placed firmly within its contemporary international context while attention was also paid to historical and local issues.[252] Film-Work won an ATOM award and was selected as a finalist for a Greater Union Award at the Sydney Film Festival.

Inspired by the WWFFU, and the production workshops model that was evolving in the UK, Hughes directed his energies in the early 1980s into establishing a contemporary production

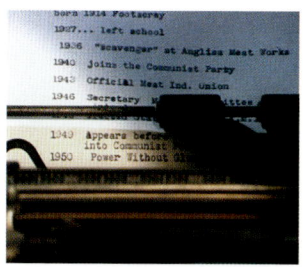  

FROM LEFT: *IS IT WORKING?*; FRANK HARDY TELLS OF THE LENGTHS SEELAF WENT TO TO HELP HIM PUBLISH THE GROUNDBREAKING NOVEL *POWER WITHOUT GLORY* DESPITE THE THREAT OF LEGAL ACTION; NOEL COUNIHAN (ON THE VIDEO MONITOR) AND HIS PORTRAIT OF GEORGE SEELAF IN *IS IT WORKING?* (1984).

unit under the auspices of the trade union movement. By early 1983, with several new projects underway, Hughes initiated the creation of a film unit at the Victorian Trades Hall Council (VTHC). With the help of Geoff Hogg, Director of the Trades Hall Arts Workshop at the time, and with a participation and equity grant fom the Commonwealth Employment Program (CEP), the VTHC Film and Video Unit employed four emerging filmmakers: Penny Robins, Andrew Taylor, Tony Wright and Cath Dyson. They completed projects for different unions and found distribution with the AFI for all of them.

The first project the new team worked on was *Is it Working? George Seelaf for the record* (1984). The Australia Council Community Arts Board's Archival Film Program provided small grants to make oral history recordings, on 16 mm film, of significant living cultural figures. With typical resourcefulness and his CEP-funded trainee team, Hughes was able to go beyond the narrow bounds of archival interviews, creating a fully developed 52-minute documentary film.[253]

Is It Working? includes interviews with Seelaf collaborators: unionist Wally Curran, artist Noel Counihan and writer Frank Hardy. George Seelaf, with whom Hughes had worked at the Trade Union Clinic in 1974, and had interviewed in *Menace*, was a trailblazer for action on health and safety, arts, cultural development and social work within the trade union movement. He was also a champion of the working-class Western suburbs of Melbourne where he pioneered community health and community arts by founding the Footscray Trade Union Clinic and Research Centre in 1964 and Footscray Community Arts Centre in 1974. As secretary of the Australasian Meat Industry Employees' Union from 1947 to 1973, Seelaf conducted successful campaigns for annual leave and improved hours, wages and conditions for meat workers. In a biography for the Australian National University, John Lack writes that under Seelaf's tenure 'the union also became noted for its enlightened opposition to anti-Semitism and rejection of homophobia, and for its support for small farmers in an industry dominated by meat cartels'. He was a member of the central committee of the Communist Party of Australia (CPA) 'but, instinctively pragmatic and ameliorative, he had little enthusiasm for communist theory, and readily defied party ideologues'.[254] Lack cites an ASIO report that Seelaf had declined the offer a high-paid position in private enterprise saying 'my work and my beliefs are my religion'. Hughes was impressed with the fact that Seelaf also refused to accept an Order of Australia because it was to be presented to him by John Kerr, the Governor-General who sacked Whitlam (see Chapter 3).[255]

FROM LEFT: HUGHES SEARCHING THROUGH OUTTAKES OF SEELAF FROM *MENACE* IN *IS IT WORKING?*; JOHN HUGHES MAKING A PHONE CALL TO THE AUSTRALIA COUNCIL IN THE OPENING SCENE OF *IS IT WORKING?* (1984).

Hughes' affectionate study of Seelaf takes the reflexive form of *Film-Work* further – into self-reflexivity. *Is It Working?* begins with Hughes making a phone call to the Australia Council, includes his discussions with University of Melbourne archivist Andrew Reeves, and shows Hughes searching the outtakes from *Menace*. These scenes also prefigure the use of research as a narrative device in *Traps* (1984, see Chapter 5) and *The Archive Project* (2006, see Chapter 10).

With Robins as producer, Hughes also wrote and directed *Changing Schools* (1985), a video made for teachers unions and school organisations, which foregrounds issues of representation by drawing from educational films dating back to 1912. Here, Hughes and Robins take interest in a local film from 1971 that 'mixes up dramatic reconstructions, acted sequences and cinéma vérité observational accounts,' declaring that *A Moment of Brightness*, made for the Teachers Association, 'should be among the classics of trade union film work'.[256] They also discovered a notable and extraordinary exception to the conventional practices and ideologies of the educational film genre in the 1947 production *Australia at School* by Stanley Hawes.[257] They see this film as significant because it engages with issues that aren't prominent again until the 1970s: the democratic participation of parents and the education of girls.

Had it been available at the time, Hughes and Robins might also have included *In My Beginning: A Story of New Education* (1947) by the Realist Film Unit (see Chapter 10), With a title derived from TS Eliot, this film was made collectively with a progressive school in Warrandyte called Koornong to campaign to raise money to keep it running. Established in 1939, Koornong prefigured the student-centred and reflexive 'open classroom' approach to teaching and the democratic participation of students in Victoria's Department of Education community schools during the 1970s. Clive Nield, the school's founder, says in the narration for the film 'Democracy is not a lesson that we can learn from books or teachers, it's a way of living together using reason instead of force to settle problems that arise.'[258]

HUGHES AND UNIVERSITY OF MELBOURNE ARCHIVIST ANDREW REEVES DISCUSSING SEELAF'S LIFE AND WORK IN *IS IT WORKING?* (1984).

The movement towards the democratisation of education in the early 1970s would have been familiar to Hughes. It was allied with the community arts and media movements and with the idea of 'citizens' control of social environments' (see Chapter 2) and it drew upon contemporary thinkers such as Alvin Toffler, Ivan Illich, Erich Fromm and Paulo Freire. In Victoria, a number of alternative school models were explored within the government education system. Articles about alternative education appeared regularly in the popular press and for a few years these ideas entered the mainstream of public discourse. Back in 1973, Hughes and an ABC camera colleague, Canadian Ben Trudeau, created a photographic slide and audiotape educational resource called *School: What are the Alternatives?* With an audience of secondary school students and teachers in mind, the tape included informal discussions with students at a number of Victorian state Department of Education schools. These were 'normal' high schools and 'community' schools. The study guide in the kit carries a quote from Gerry Tickell, a campaigner for the democratisation of schooling since the late 1960s, one of the Department's innovators and the co-ordinator of Swinburne Community School (SCS): 'The school is small enough to allow students and staff to share in the day to day operations' and 'seeks to involve students in the life of the community and to enable them to learn at first hand about the structures and operations of society'.²⁵⁹ I was lucky enough to be a student at SCS in 1973. It occurs to me now that this experience of non-authoritarian progressive education may have made me especially receptive to *Film-Work* when Hughes presented it at Rusden College several years later.

The democratic approach to education, like the approach that Hughes had developed towards filmmaking by the time he made *Film-Work*, is reflexive. Just as the community school 'exposed its day to day operations' *Film-Work* exposes its own process of production. The idea of 'first hand' learning 'about the structures and operations of society' reflects ideas that Paulo Freire articulated about democracy as an ongoing dialectical process – a work in progress – with which education must engage by fostering the practical application of a reflective, critical consciousness. Reflecting on this work in *Pedagogy of Hope*, Freire says that Erich Fromm responded by telling him jocosely: 'An educational practice like that is a kind of historico-sociocultural and political psychoanalysis'.²⁶⁰ In this vein, community schools brought conventional ideas about education and society into question by instituting alternative practices and new sets of social relations. Similarly, *Film-Work* brings different traditions, conventions and generations of social-documentary filmmaking into a productively unstable yet sympathetic dialogue with each other. Later chapters will show that Hughes refined this approach through his work for television into what he came to call a 'critical collaboration with orthodoxy'.

With Penny Robins as producer and Tony Wright as director the VTHCFVU team made *Fair Go!* (1984) – a short film designed to inform youth of their legal rights in the workplace. After the completion of the Commonwealth Employment Program (CEP) grant, Robins and Wright continued the trade union video work, establishing Video Projects, and had Hughes direct a number of short videos, including the follow-up project *How Does it Strike You?* (1985), in which teacher John Kesselschmidt guides a class of students at Footscray Technical School (now Footscray City College) through an industrial dispute role-play game. *Acceptable Risk* (1985) addressed occupational health and safety for the telecommunications union.

The New Education movement of the 1930s and 1940s and the community schools movement of the 1970s developed in parallel and in dialogue with workers' cultural groups, collective and trade union film units, artists' and filmmakers' co-operatives and community-based arts and media movements. The first wave emerged in the wake of World War II and the global struggle against fascism. The second came towards the end of an oppressive Cold War between opposing forms of authoritarianism, amid the convulsions of a First World torn by the scale and ferocity of one of its neocolonial wars upon small countries seeking independence in the Third World (see Chapters 2 & 3). These movements illustrated that, in a democratic society, trade unions, co-operative and collective enterprises, government departments and state-owned corporations are all capable of supporting and hosting the development of initiatives towards practical democracy.

What the Waterside Workers' Federation modelled was filmmaking with a progressive social purpose, built on collectivism rather than individualism, with the moral and material support of a member-based trade union organisation. Hughes created a portrait of that model then

HEWERS OF COAL (1957) IN FILM-WORK (1981).

pursued various initiatives until he finally managed to establish a contemporary equivalent. This activity followed – and was in many ways a direct response to – the collapse of the Melbourne Filmmakers' Co-op under the weight of state patronage in a neoliberal political climate in which the ethic of public service was being supplanted by the ethos of capitalist managerialism. The historical inquiry that underpinned these efforts – and that *Film-Work* embodies – is driven, then, by a sense of urgency and necessity similar to that which drove the WWFFU filmmakers. The story of the making of *Film-Work* and Hughes' subsequent work with the VTHCVU also attenuated and provided examples of the collaboration between filmmakers that characterised much of the independent filmmaking that took place in the 1970s. Hughes' confidence in managing the relationship between filmmaker and funding body demonstrated that a peer evaluation process could be transformed into a dialogic one. *Film-Work* itself provides a unique model of reflexive dialogue within practice between two generations of socially engaged and critically astute artists.

Endnotes

[213] Crowsfoot Films, *Save a Starving Film*, pamphlet, Ultimo, 1979. From 1973 to 1982 Crowsfoot (Peter Gray and Garry Lane) undertook an ambitious slate of 16 mm projects, produced in four states without funding, including *The Battle for Bowen Hills* (1973–1982) and *Know Your Friends, Know Your Enemies* (1977–1982).

[214] Peter Gray & Garry Lane, Crowsfoot Films, interview conducted by John Hughes, 1979. John Hughes, Crowsfoot. Letter to Peter Gray & Garry Lane, MSC Media Arts, Carlton North, 22 November 1979.

[215] *Film-Work* (1981), *The Archive Project* (2006), *Indonesia Calling: Ivens in Australia* (2009).

[216] Lisa Milner, *Fighting films: a history of the Waterside Workers' Federation Film Unit*, Pluto Press, North Melbourne, Vic., 2003, pp. 23–24.

[217] ibid., p. 35.

[218] Deane Williams, *Australian Post-War Documentary Film: an Arc of Mirrors*, Intellect, Bristol, 2008, p. 23.

[219] Vance Kepley Jr, 'The Workers International Relief and the Cinema of the Left 1921–1935', *Cinema Journal*, vol. 23, Autumn, 1983, pp. 7–23.

[220] Megan McMurchy, 'The Documentary', in Scott Murray (ed.), *Australian Cinema*, Allen & Unwin, Sydney, 1994, p. 189.

[221] John Hughes, *Film-Work*, interview conducted by John Cumming, Melbourne, 12 September 2000.

[222] ibid.

[223] ibid.

[224] Paulo Freire, *Pedagogy of the Oppressed*, Penguin, London, 1972, p. 30.

[225] Milner, op. cit., pp. 57–59.

[226] John Hughes, Trade Unions, Film and Television, ACTU Arts Committee, discussion paper, Melbourne, 1979.

[227] John Hughes, *Film-Work* flyer, 1981.

[228] Peter Hughes, 'A way of being engaged with the world: the films of John Hughes', *Metro*, no. 93, Autumn 1993, pp. 46–55.

[229] John Hughes, op. cit.

[230] John Hughes & Michael Renov, 'Conversation with Michael Renov', Visible Evidence IX Conference, Tivoli Theatre, Fortitude Valley Brisbane, from notes taken by John Cumming, 2001.

[231] ibid.

[232] Chris Warner, Cynthia Connop & Ginny Brook, 'Filmmaking in Australia', *Farrago*, Friday 9 July 1976, pp. 11–14. This article provides a snapshot of a late 1970s milieu in which feminist and countercultural political thinking was prevalent.

[233] ibid.

[234] John Hughes, notes on transcript, email to John Cumming, Melbourne, 24 June 2002.

[235] ibid.

[236] See Jean-Luc Godard & Jean-Pierre Gorin, *British Sounds/See You at Mao*, 1969, 16 mm, colour, 51 minutes, Kestrel Productions/London Weekend Television. Hughes had also used this device in *Some Aspects of Australian Racism* (see Chapter 9).

[237] John Hughes, 'Propaganda then and now', in Ross Lansell & Peter Beilby (eds), *The Documentary Film in Australia*, Cinema Papers in association with Film Victoria, North Melbourne, 1982, pp. 142–145.

[238] ibid., p. 143.

[239] Dziga Vertov, 'Love for the living person', edited and translated by Annette Michelson. *Kino-Eye: The Writings of Dziga Vertov*, Pluto Press, Sydney, 1984, pp. 147–157, originally published 1958.

[240] John Hughes, op. cit., p. 143.

[241] John Hughes, *Film-Work*, interview conducted by John Cumming, Melbourne, 12 September 2000.

[242] John Hughes, 'Keith Gow', *Cinema Papers*, January 1988, p. 4.

[243] John Hughes, letter to Mr Schefferle (State Film Centre), Melbourne, 11 October 1979.

[244] John Hughes, Trade Unions, Film and Television, ACTU Arts Committee, discussion paper, Melbourne, 1979, pp. 1–3.

[245] John Hughes, 2000, op. cit.

[246] For example, at an Australian Association of Film and Video Libraries screening at the State Film Centre in Melbourne on 8 December 1981, Hughes gave 'an address on the theme of oppositional film work and the Cold War', Newsletter no. 3, AAFVL (Victorian Branch), Melbourne, 1981.

[247] AFID, *Film-Work* database, Magic List, Australian Film Institute Distribution, Melbourne, 2000.

[248] Open Channel, *Open: Public Television* program schedule, Melbourne, 1982.

[249] John Hughes, 2000, op. cit.

[250] Anne Hutton, *Papers of the First Australian Film and History Conference*, Australian Film and Television School, North Ryde, Canberra, 1981.

[251] Rick Thompson, Conference arrangements, letter to ASSA organisers, La Trobe University, Bundoora, 10 March 1982. David Hanan, letter to John Hughes, Monash University, Clayton, 9 March 1982.

[252] Meaghan Morris, 'Notions of Independence', in Barbara Creed, John Davies, Freda Freiberg, David Hanan & Kim Montgomery (eds), *Papers and Forums on Independent Film and Asian Cinema*, La Trobe University, Melbourne, ASSA, AFTRS, 1982. This keynote paper provided a central theme at ASSA 1982. Melbourne academic Lesley Stern aligned the interests of feminism and the independent sector in the paper 'Women/Filmmaking/Independence'. ASSA, 'Abstracts', 1982, *Welcome to the First Australian Screen Studies Conference*, Australian Screen Studies Association, Victoria. In that vein, the contemporary activities of the Sydney Filmmakers Co-operative were considered and celebrated, while there was eulogy and anger in a lively seminar about the demise of its Melbourne counterpart. Barbara Hall, Fred Harden & Pat Longmore, 'An Oral History of the Melbourne Filmmakers Co-operative', in Creed et al., op. cit., pp. 141–155.

[253] Hughes, John, Is it Working? George Seelaf for the Record, 1984, 16 mm, colour, 48 minutes, Melbourne, Producer John Hughes, Scriptwriter Hughes, John, Camera Tony Wright, Andrew Taylor, Jaems Grant, Sound Cath Dyson, Georgina Guilfoyle, Editor Zbigniew Friedrich. Featuring Noel Counihan, Wally Curran, Frank Hardy, Deb Mills, Andrew Reeves & George Seelaf. Produced with assistance from the Community Arts Board and the Archival Film Project of the Australia Council.

[254] John Lack, 'Seelaf, George (1914–1988)', *Australian Dictionary of Biography*, National Centre of

Biography, Australian National University, <http://adb.anu.edu.au/biography/seelaf-george-14878/text26068>, accessed 28 November 2013.

[255] AFID, *Is It Working?* flyer, AFI Distribution, 1985.

[256] John Hughes & Penny Robins, 'More than meets the eye', films used in *Changing Schools*, Video Projects, Melbourne, 1985.

[257] From 1946 until 1970, Stanley Hawes was producer in chief of the Australian government's film division (see Chapter 10).

[258] Ken Coldicutt, Bob Mathews & Gerhart (Gerry) Harant, *In My Beginning: A story of New Education*, 1947, 16 mm, colour, sound, 17 minutes, Realist Film Unit Melbourne, Scriptwriter Joseph Clive Nield and students of Koornong School, in particular, Mavourneen Box, Souzka Frankel & Jenepher Potts, in John Hughes & Uri Mizrahi, *The Archive Project*, 2006, DVD box set, Distributed by Artfilms. My recollection is that this film re-emerged in the early 1990s, when the Nield family gave film prints to Graeme Cutts, who entrusted them to me for archiving. The 16mm colour print of the film was accompanied by a reel of black and white, 35 mm nitrate film. These were telecined for the Nields at the AFTRS before lodgement with the NFSA.

[259] John Hughes and Ben Trudeau, *School: What are the alternatives?* Education Media Australia, 25 x 35mm slides, audio cassette and study guide, Melbourne, 1973.

[260] Paulo Freire, *Pedagogy of Hope*, Bloomsbury, London 1992, p.96

FROM LEFT: JUDITH (CAROLYN HOWARD), THE FICTIONAL JOURNALIST, MEETS DENIS FRENEY, SUB-EDITOR OF *TRIBUNE* MAGAZINE, COMMUNIST AND INSPIRATIONAL ACTIVIST FOR HUMAN RIGHTS; *TRAPS* (1985).

CHAPTER 5:

Traps

In the 1980s a number of cultural projects that had long been the focus of attention by filmmakers, critics and scholars appeared to be within reach. Independent filmmaking, together with teaching and research in cinema and media, had achieved a degree of institutional acceptance internationally. There was a great deal of discussion and organisation around the idea of a diverse independent media that intersected in various ways with practice in the visual and performing arts and with personal, local, national and global politics. Alternative approaches to narrative and documentary form continued to be explored across the arts, while a concerted engagement with funding bodies saw the development of a professional independent sector within the film industry. Meanwhile, neoliberal economic policies saw direct subsidy of film and television production in Europe and Australasia wound down amid a wave of privatisation of the publicly held assets and services. Terms like 'industry', 'career' and 'market' began to supplant notions of culture, activism and community. *Traps* (1985) is a film that reflects all of these trends and consciously explores a good number of them.[261]

At the AFI's 'Visions of Independence' event in 1982, Ekhart Stein of ZDF television in Germany argued for the creation of small niches of opportunity for innovative independent filmmaking within television.[262] 'Free market' policies, driven by neoliberal ideology, were beginning to move government funding away from direct subsidy of independent films and away from in-house production by state-owned broadcasters. The deregulation and outsourcing that resulted from this would open up the broadcasting industries to independent filmmakers working in mainstream genres. A completely market-driven broadcasting industry, however, was unlikely

FROM LEFT: A COMMERCIAL TELEVISION NETWORK STAND, PART OF THE TALLY ROOM SPECTACLE FOR THE 1985 FEDERAL ELECTION, IN *TRAPS* (1985); INDEPENDENT FILMMAKER PAT FISKE RECORDING SOUND FOR *TRAPS*.

to provide airtime to the range of filmmaking practices represented in the wider independent community that had found support through direct cultural subsidies. When he returned to Australia in 1984, Stein spoke of the shifting sands of an encroaching cultural desert created by commercial global media corporations. Again, his advice was to find oases of opportunity – niches in which to survive.[263] What Stein may not have predicted was that, under such circumstances, terms such as 'independence', 'access' and 'community' begin to lose their ideological function. Rather than serving as markers of ongoing, collective creative intervention upon the social and cultural landscape, these terms begin to be used as labels in branding and market segmentation.

Since the 1973 overthrow of the progressive government of Salvador Allende in Chile (see Chapter 3) – a democratically elected government that had sought to redistribute wealth to the poor – a global program of neoliberal reform has delivered an enormous concentration of wealth and power into the hands of a few leading to 'the erosion of democratic governance', according to an Oxfam report. 'Almost half of the world's wealth is now owned by just one per cent of the population' who are taking an increasingly larger share of national wealth in most recorded countries between 1980 and 2012. In that time the wealthiest one per cent of Australians increased their proportional share of national income by approximately 100 per cent.[264]

In 1980s Britain the government of Margaret Thatcher (an ardent supporter of the tyrant Pinochet) pioneered, in the West, the handover of public assets to large-scale commercial interests that had been rehearsed in Chile after the coup d'état. The principle of public service was substituted for the rule of market economics. Independent filmmakers responded by arranging their film co-operatives and video centres into an industrial sector by forming a national peak body, the Independent Film Association (IFA). The IFA secured a market (and finance) for small-scale local and regional production within the structure of the UK's new television network Channel 4. Likewise, in Australia, Hughes and his peers became particularly active in alliances between filmmakers, academics, funding bodies and trade unions through a series of interventions upon the structure of the cultural environment in which they worked.

ERIKA ADDIS, CINEMATOGRAPHER AND PRODUCER OF *SERIOUS UNDERTAKINGS*, WITH JOHN HUGHES FILMING A SCENE FOR *TRAPS* (1985).

After the demise of their co-operative (see Chapter 4), independent filmmakers in Melbourne found some niches for survival in the remnant infrastructure of media centres, film institutes, technical and teachers colleges and universities. Hughes continued to work at Melbourne College of Education (MCE), directing *Gunana: Homeland of the Mornington Island Woomera Dancers* (1982) for its Media Production Centre.[265] The Sydney Filmmakers Co-operative was still in operation. It was distributing films and its free national broadsheet, *Filmnews*, was the main organ of news and opinion for independent filmmakers across Australia. The Creative Development Fund and the Women's Film Fund of the Australian Film Commission (AFC) were the main sources of direct finance for independent films, while the Cultural Activities branch supported the infrastructure of distribution, exhibition and reception. Productions were mainly in short format or documentary form. Audiences were found largely through non-theatrical release of 16 mm film prints, alongside educational and training films, cinema classics, art cinema and contemporary independent films from abroad. Film festivals, film societies, community

FROM LEFT: 'WE'RE REMINDED THAT OUR COUNTRY WAS BORN IN A PRISON AND RAISED THERE ...' – CAROLYN HOWARD AS JOURNALIST JUDITH; PAUL DAVIES AND CAROLYN HOWARD IN A SCENE FROM *EXITS* USED IN *TRAPS* (1985); JUDITH ON HER WAY TO LEARNING ABOUT THE SYSTEMIC UNDERSIDE OF FASCIST POLITICS – ORGANISED CRIME, ARMS AND DRUGS DEALING, AND INTELLIGENCE NETWORKS.

groups, secondary schools, colleges and universities provided the main sites for exhibition of independent work. Government, non-profit and small commercial agencies were all involved in distribution. The use of video, in both production and distribution, was stimulated by the market ascendance of inexpensive VHS and Beta cassette formats for domestic use.

The reflexive approach had become a prominent trait in films made by the independent filmmakers who gathered with screen studies academics at the Australian Screen Studies Association (ASSA, see Chapter 4) conference of 1982. In this regard, the place of Alexander Kluge, Jean-Marie Straub and Danièle Huillet had become more widely recognised, alongside Godard, through publications such as Martin Walsh's 1970s essays in *The Brechtian Aspect of Radical Cinema*.[266] Helen Grace's *Serious Undertakings* (1982) typified the shift towards the essay-film as a viable form for those independent filmmakers wishing to experiment simultaneously with the conventions and devices of both documentary and dramatic form. While Hughes' *Film-Work* (1981, see Chapter 4) employed reflexive and self-reflexive devices within the documentary genre, Grace had gone a step further by creating a work of hybrid form in the spirit of Laura Mulvey and Peter Wollen's *Riddles of the Sphinx* (1977). In *Serious Undertakings*, actors perform scripted interviews while stage direction and laboratory optical effects are used ironically and reflexively.[267]

Fruitful experimentation was also underway at this time with the combination of dramatic and documentary modes of production by filmmakers of a less academic bent. Peter Tammer, a founder of the Melbourne Filmmakers Co-operative (MFC, see Chapter 1) and the editor of Hughes' *Menace*, had included a very different element of dramatisation to powerful effect in two films. In his prize-winning and at times harrowing documentary *Journey to the End of Night* (1982), a traumatised World War II veteran, Bill Neave, recounts his war experiences in deeply personal, waking-nightmare performances that Tammer orchestrated for dramatic effect.[268] For the feature film *Mallacoota Stampede* (1981), Tammer created a loose fictional premise and snarrative framework that was inseparable from the location and circumstances of production for the film itself.[269] Continuing the spirit of the French new wave that had influenced him and other founders of the MFC in the 1960s, he worked on very low budgets with non-professional cast in a mode that married improvised performance with a very direct documentary camera style.[270] The moments of greatest poignancy in *Mallacoota Stampede* are ones in which the camera records encounters between people that are at once fictional and actual. In 1982 Hughes introduced *Mallacoota Stampede* to his students as 'experimental narrative'.[271] Tammer's film can be situated between dramatic and documentary genres and draws upon realist tendencies in both. In his own filmmaking, Hughes was interested in seeing how far the documentary form could be taken from realism and notions of objectivity without entirely losing its claim to evidence-based authority.

The performance makers Carolyn Howard and Paul Davies introduced the combination of documentary and dramatic forms to Hughes' filmmaking by way of their own film and theatre work and through collaboration with him in the 1980s. Along with several others, including the playwright Hannie Rayson, Howard was a co-founding member of the independent community theatre company, Theatre Works.[272] Davies joined the Theatre Works' artistic directorate after the company staged his first site-specific play *Storming Mont Albert By Tram* in 1982. Howard and Davies provided a significant single influence on the character of Hughes' filmmaking in the early 1980s. They took a collective, ensemble approach to devising and producing creative works. Davies and Howard, together with Pat Laughren, co-directed the 50-minute docudrama *Exits* (1980), in which they played the lead roles. Hughes recalls meeting Davies and Howard in 1980 when they arranged to screen *Exits*, together with Hughes' *November Eleven* (1979), on the fifth anniversary of the sacking of the Whitlam government. This was one of the last events to take place at the Pram Factory, the central institution in Melbourne's alternative theatre scene of the 1970s. Hughes sought the collaboration of Howard and Davies, reusing scenes from *Exits* and creating new dramatic scenes for *November Eleven: Work in Progress* (1981) and later *Traps*. They also performed in several scenes written by Davies for Hughes' 1988 film *All That is Solid* (see Chapter 6). This quartet of films produces a loose intertextual narrative that traces the characters that Howard and Davies created for their 1980 film from youth to early middle age.

The Theatre Works team shared Hughes' interest in ideas pioneered by Erwin Piscator and Bertolt Brecht in the 1930s.[273] In 1978 Willett explained that:

Piscator's aim was to make the theatre into a mixture of lecture hall and debating chamber, where the audience would see a socially relevant play supported by a wealth of documentary material, and so be inspired to argue the issues out.[274]

In cinema, films such as Godard's *Masculin féminin* (1966), Haskell Wexler's *Medium Cool* (1969) and Jost's *Angel City* (1976) had demonstrated that moments of actuality could be used to add authenticity while simultaneously disrupting the realist diegesis of a fiction film.[275] The residue of such Piscatoresque effect can be found in both *Exits* and *Traps*. At an Independent

  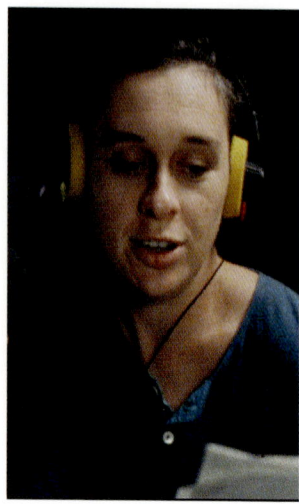

FROM LEFT: '… IT'S A FAIR BET, IF YOU'RE TALKING ABOUT HUNDREDS OF MILLIONS OF DOLLARS WORTH OF TAX AVOIDANCE, THAT THEY'RE NOT UNION OFFICIALS' – FINANCE JOURNALIST MICHAEL GILL; PAUL DAVIES AND CAROLYN HOWARD AS JUDITH AND GEORGE PICK UP A CONVERSATION THEY STARTED IN THEIR OWN FILM *EXITS* (1980) IN *TRAPS* (1985); JUDITH REPORTS ON THE POLITICAL USE OF POLICE TO INTIMIDATE MAINSTREAM JOURNALISTS.

Film Action Committee (IFAC) seminar in 1984, Davies described making *Exits* as like discovering 'a new kind of theatre and film'. He said, 'applying the principles of a news crew to dramatic film' in combination with 'documentary elements' led to a 'conjunction of forces' that produced 'limitless opportunities'.[276] This was the dialectical dynamic of 'documentary theatre for which Piscator coined the term 'epic' and for which Brecht and his collaborators had developed a performance style.[277] Howard and Davies' approach to performance in all their work for the screen is a development and adaptation of their theatrical interpretation of this style.[278]

For a performer in the epic mode, the emphasis is upon the text and its delivery. Rather than being naturalistic, the delivery is demonstrative of social and ideological type. On the stage, the epic actor demonstrates a character in broad, stylised, gestural brush strokes while maintaining their persona as actor and thereby revealing the constructed nature of the performance. The character portrayed is often a historical one, so the actor's demonstration also reveals the process of history as a construct. The performer does not merge with the text through character but rather presents the text as an artefact in its own right. Howard's almost neutral performance style in *Traps* was described in a review by Annette Blonski as 'deliberately casual' and 'an anti-performance'.[279] Howard and Davies employed a minimum of character affect and gesture. They do not wear the psychologically convincing mask of character, nor do they reveal or draw upon their own persona in depth as a source of psychological realism.

On a number of levels, *Traps*, Hughes' second feature length film, reflects the impact that neoliberal or so-called economic rationalist ideology had upon politics and social relations in the late twentieth century. The right-wing coup d'état in Chile showed that – among industrialists, professionals and petit-bourgeoisie – the commercial interests of employers and traders and the privileges the market bestows upon them can be considered more precious than democracy or any of the human rights or services that might be ensured by a democratic state. Thatcher, driven by the same belief in the preeminence of the banker, the investor and the merchant, provided arms and moral support to Pinochet's miltary regime in Chile.

Under pressure from Northern and Western-controlled multinationals and global financial institutions, governments around the world began to privatise state assets. The winding back of the public service and of free access to education and health care were key elements in this conscious degradation of the common wealth. The world's poorest countries have been bound helplessly to this agenda through debt. Concern about this neoliberal push was not confined to those on the political left. There has been a long-standing concern among both traditionally conservative and liberal thinkers about the influence of overseas investors in Australia. On the traditional conservative side, the colourful Liberal prime minister John Gorton characterised Australia's historical posture in seeking overseas capital as that of a puppy keen to please 'on any conditions'. After serving as govenor of the federal Reserve Bank of Australia (RBA) in the 1960s, Nugget Coombs expressed disquiet about entrusting matters of national concern to 'men whose purposes are not ours'.[280] Indeed, something that undid the Whitlam government in Australia was an attempt to circumvent old Anglo-European ties and neocolonial American ties by seeking loans from the Arab world.[281] The Fraser Liberal-Country Party government's dismantling of Whitlam's Medibank, easing of controls on foreign ownership and refusal to implement new resource taxes on the largely foreign-owned mining industry were consistent with the neoliberal agenda. However, while the more socially progressive Hawke and Keating Labor governments of 1983 to 1996 reinstated universal health care (as Medicare) and considerably improved social welfare, they continued the neoliberal agenda with deregulation of the banking sector and the first large-scale privatisation of government-owned corporations.

In *Traps,* Hughes undertakes an inquiry into a perceived betrayal of the left by the federal Labor Party under Hawke's leadership. He does this through stories that journalists can't or won't publish in mainstream media and by exploring the part journalists play in managing them. It ends with Hawke's 1985 re-election. Hughes described the film at the time as 'not so much about political stories as an exploration of the ways in which political stories are constructed'.[282] *Traps* continued a number of threads established in *November Eleven: Work in Progress* (see Chapter 3). Again, the sacking of the Whitlam Labor government provides the primal scene and Howard and Davies provide the fictional thread, with their ensemble approach, performance style and some scenes taken directly from their own film *Exits*. In scenes Hughes shot for *Traps,* Judith and George – Howard and Davies' characters from *Exits* – are found ten years later. Judith secures a government-funded position as a trainee radio journalist through the influence of her old admirer, George. Judith's character conducts a series of documentary interviews with journalists and politicians. She also provides a subjective voice for narration in the film and enables narrative links to a Labor Party national conference and the 1985 federal election tally room. Gwenda Wiseman plays the part of Judith's flatmate, but she does so by playing herself – an artist working on a mural for the Builders Labourers Federation (BLF) at the time the film was being made. She is a documentary subject appearing within the artifice of dramatic scenes rather than within the artifice of documentary interviews. Hughes describes the scenes between Judith and Gwenda as 'the ideal form' of a combination of documentary and fictional

  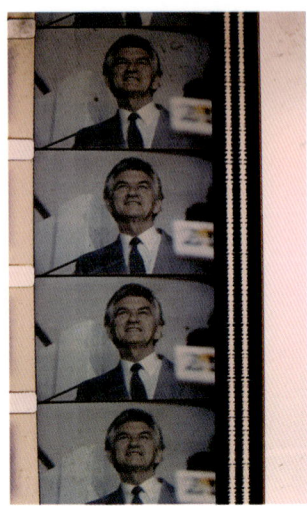

FROM LEFT: 'ONE OF THE MESSAGES IN THE FILM IS TO THINK ABOUT THE RESPONSIBILITY' OF AUSTRALIA'S ALLIANCE WITH THE USA. JOURNALIST MARION WILKINSON AT THE LAUNCH OF HER FILM *ALLIES* (1983) IN *TRAPS* (1985); 'ANOTHER MAN IN THE SHADOWS, ANOTHER SET OF POWER RELATIONS …' – HUMPHREY McQUEEN; REINSTATED AS PRIME MINISTER, HAWKE IS 'THE RIGHT BOSS FOR THE JOB' ACCORDING TO JUDITH IN *TRAPS*.

elements.[283] Without the dramatic device of Judith's character, Wiseman would also have been an interview subject in *Traps*.

In 1983 Hughes received a letter from the AFC rejecting his application for production finance for *Traps* but agreeing to invest A$5000 in development of the project.[284] Hughes immediately used this money to start making the film. Without a predetermined structure, he wanted to get certain events on film, including the tally room for the 1983 federal election and the premiere screening, in Canberra, of Marion Wilkinson's *Allies* (1983), a documentary that examines diplomatic relations between the USA and Australia and the CIA's role in that relationship.[285] Through this approach, Hughes was able to present, for completion finance, a work already in progress. The final film, of 96 minutes, was wholly funded by the AFC.

The vicarious seduction of power through journalism experienced by the character Judith in *Traps* relates, both directly and metaphorically, to the use of politics as entertainment in the media. This is the central theme in *Traps*. Part of the fascination of the film is the way it teases its Australian audience with half-revealed secrets about the power politics of their own nation state. This is information and speculation that, due to our libel laws, remains taboo in the sphere of publication and broadcasting. In one of Judith's interviews, Michael Gill describes the political intimidation he experienced as a journalist investigating the relationship between big business and government in the state of Victoria during the 1970s, including an illegal police raid on his home.

Traps is a film about power. For Hughes it is about political power and the power of the media. He described the film's characters as representative of different approaches to the larger agenda of formal politics: 'The idea was to break open the normal account of the representation of political discourse from journalists and professional media workers in the mainstream'.[286] He was trying

GEORGE (PAUL DAVIES) JOINS JUDITH (CAROLYN HOWARD) AS SHE EDITS INTERVIEWS FOR HER PROGRAM AT COMMUNITY RADIO STATION 3RRR IN *TRAPS* (1985).

to provide a comprehensive description of the political landscape. In parallel with this attempt to locate a unifying narrative of national political life, *Traps* represents a shift towards self-examination on the part of the orthodox left. At its release in 1986, Hughes said: 'I'd like to see people coming away from *Traps* with a tendency to question the assertions of the left just as much as the assertions of the right'.[287] With *Traps*, the temptation to deliver the totalising rhetoric so pronounced in *November Eleven: Work in Progress* is tempered but not entirely dispensed with.

Some of the main strengths and weaknesses of *Traps* stem from Hughes' adoption of characters and scenes from *Exits* and his adaptation of aesthetic cues and characterisations from Alexander Kluge. Howard's Judith, adopted from *Exits* (1980), is developed into the central character of *Traps*. In one scene she rejects 'Cold War logic' that 'doesn't leave any room for criticism' and asks George, 'Why do I have to be on one side or the other?' The critique here came from Davies, Howard and Laughren five years earlier. What they opened to question was the implicit alliance of pro-Soviet leftists with Stalinism. In Hughes' *Menace*, a decade earlier, an adult Mick Counihan had discussed shaking off Stalinism as an adolescent. So this was far from a point of contention or self-critique for the progressive left in the 1980s. In *Traps*, Howard's Judith is adapted to the role

ABOVE: JOHN FLAUS AS A CATHOLIC PRIEST 'IN THE VANGUARD OF THE CRUSADE AGAINST COMMUNISM' IN A SCENE BORROWED FROM PHILLIP NOYCE'S *NEWSFRONT* (1978) AND IN THE CONFESSIONAL WITH CAROLYN HOWARD IN *TRAPS* (1985).

of a female investigator like those played by Alexandra Kluge in a number of her brother's films of the 1960s and 1970s. A feminist perspective is implicit in this move, as are questions about the domination by men of the world of party politics and the media that Judith explores. Blonski notes, however, that where Kluge's heroine in *The Patriot* (1979) 'was eccentric, voluble and prone to conduct alchemical experiments,' Hughes and Howard's Judith is 'relentlessly dour'.[288]

As reviewer Paul Byrnes put it, 'Feature film meets documentary, and sometimes you're not sure which is which'.[289] Like many films in the broad docudrama genre, *Traps* is a documentary with fiction in it. However, these elements are in a dialectical rather than an illustrative relationship to each other. Howard performs the mediating function of the documentary journalist – interviewing, discussing, commentating, providing information and narrating – but she does so as the fictional character Judith. When Judith reads aloud the script she is writing (the script for the narration in *Traps*), questions about the reliability of documentary narration and the issue of an authorial voice are brought into relief. Previously employed by Godard, Straub-Huillet and others, this dramatisation of narration foregrounds it as something that is constructed, performed, recorded and edited.[290] *Traps* could be understood then as two integrated texts (a fictional drama and a documentary) that reflexively keep account of their own construction, while also accounting for, contributing to and interfering with each other. Each is so ruptured by the other that neither can stand alone.

Tim Rowse, among other reviewers, noted the 'density' of image and sound in *Traps*.[291] The fictional, semi-fictional and documentary scenes that were shot for the film are intercut with newsreel footage and scenes from other Australian films. In addition to Davies, Howard and Laughren's *Exits*, Hughes quotes from Phillip Noyce's historical dramatic feature *Newsfront* (1978) and Wilkinson's *Allies*.[292] Iconic still photographs are also introduced through the device

JUDITH (CAROLYN HOWARD) AND GWENDA WISEMAN IN *TRAPS* (1985).

of Gwenda's preparatory work for her trade union mural. The first image she looks at in *Traps* is the same as the last one in the photo sequence that concludes the story-time scene in *November Eleven: Work in Progress*. The collection of such material is typical of conventional historical documentary production in which visual material is scavenged to illustrate interview sound. Hughes and scriptwriter Davies find alternative means to link this material while creating a network of intertextual connections. For example, they open and close *Traps* with scenes in a confessional that bring Judith together with the priest (John Flaus) from *Newsfront* (1978) and weave outtakes from *Allies* into their detective story.

The editing style of *Traps* follows that of *November Eleven: On Sacred Land* (1983). While much of the film is composed of complex montage, this is not disjunctive, nor does the editing draw attention to itself. Hughes and editor Zbigniew Friedrich smooth and soften the transitions between and within the scenes. Even when material is brought together from disparate sources, continuity is maintained from shot to shot. Camera movements and the screen direction of action are matched and sound is bridged between scenes extensively. The music track is edited and rearranged so that instrumental and lyrical phrases are positioned strategically in relation to the images and the other sounds. Usually the lyrics and dialogue can both be discerned, but as Blonski noted in 1986:

The risk of confusion is high, but [Hughes'] experimentation with the relationship between sound and image bears fruit in what is, for Hughes, an uncharacteristic (and welcome) attention to the latter and a desire to play with space and time.[293]

CLOCKWISE FROM LEFT: ELECTION TALLY ROOM; GWENDA WORKS ON A MURAL FOR THE BLF; GWENDA TELLS JUDITH OF A CORPORATE EXECUTIVE'S THREAT TO HAVE HER MURAL ERASED IN *TRAPS* (1985).

While there is virtuosity in this editing, it is certainly difficult to absorb so much information simultaneously. In 1985 David Stratton applauded the film in *Variety*, but noted its 'sometimes frustrating' complexity, while Eisenhuth described it as 'too densely packed, too scrambled.[294] *Traps* requires repeated scrutiny to reveal the density of thematic and dialectical connections within its larger montage structure. A close analysis akin to a deconstruction of each of Hughes and Friedrich's editing decisions would be required to reveal every nuance of the film's articulation.

Traps is built around characters and scenes from *Exits* and adopts that film's naturalistic docudrama style. Unlike *November Eleven: Work in Progress* (see Chapter 3), with its counter-realist studio scenes, *Traps* offers itself for reading as a realist text. This realist aesthetic and the open and polyphonous structure of the film allow unintended discourses to rise above the surface of Hughes' two-dimensional symbolic use of characters. The investigation Judith undertakes is the investigation that the film makes. Therefore, it can also be seen as belonging to Hughes. Judith is a researcher, like Hughes. She provides a vehicle for many of his concerns, dilemmas and interests. In interviews however, Hughes refuses such biographical readings of his work.

[...] if there's a kind of authorial consciousness it's present in the structure of the work and the structure of the method rather than it being articulated in a particular character in the film.[295]

Hughes controls the explicit political narrative through character as type but has little interest in his characters as psychological entities. While the director is concerned with an anti-realist construction of his overt political text, personal political subtexts are generated by the interaction between the realistic characters and the documentary style of filming (after *Exits*). These subtler dynamics and scenarios, in turn, can be read as allegory. Such a reading is attempted here.

In one of the scenes from *Exits*, Judith expresses a desire to 'be in a situation where things are happening to [her] really fast.' She is necessarily ambitious – attracted towards the apparent centres of power in politics and journalism. The gap between what is known and what is published – the terrain of conspiracy theories – has the allure of esoteric knowledge. Like Hughes, she seeks out authoritative experts. One of these experts interviewed in *Traps*, Michael Gill, confronts Judith with a potential Catch-22, in the part a journalist plays within the economy of political power:

The most powerful influence always is that other people control information and unless you have a certain amount of it to ask questions you're never gonna get any further and make the step that you need to make.

Judith believes that in her work on mainstream politics and media, she is engaged in a meaningful process of revelation. Gwenda warns Judith that she may be 'getting trapped into the same sort of box that the politicians are in' and might become 'one of the boys.' In his review of *Traps*, Tim Rowse notes:

Gwenda thinks she is doing something more important: enabling other people to speak through their murals and banners. Traps does not leave us with that as an answer but Gwenda's argument counterpoints Judith's quest fruitfully.[296]

Blonski is less generous, writing that Gwenda implies 'that she, and the union for which she works, occupy a position of pure, untainted political radicalism, by comparison with the defensive position Judith takes on the role that journalists can play'.[297] Drawing on his experience of political art and community media, Hughes wanted 'to incorporate the possibility that cultural workers in other fields were also partaking of the formulation of political debate'.[298] His set up of this debate, however, is such that Gwenda's presentation of the case for alternative political discourse is couched in the rhetoric of an idealised view of the organised labour movement. This was especially contentious at the time because some labour commentators were reporting that the BLF had 'displayed a record of sectarian disunity with every other union in the building industry'.[299] The film eschews this contention however and Gwenda's case becomes pitched in a kind of competition between the two characters.

For Hughes, the characters in *Traps* represent positions on a political spectrum. The film provides a stage upon which seemingly incompatible doctrines can compete. As figures in a

TRAPS (1985).

realist drama, however, the characters of Gwenda and Judith appear to be engaged in a clash of egos. This narrative element of rivalry is not acknowledged, debunked or resolved. A dour and brittle veneer of camaraderie, commitment and critical debate cements a relationship that appears tedious and humourless, cloistered in self-righteousness and doctrine. It is perhaps this awkwardness – the apparent lack of insight in the characters about personal ambitions and doctrinal loyalties – that prompted Susan Dermody and Liz Jacka to see *Traps*, ironically, as a film not entirely 'confident to speak directly about things political'.[300]

Having witnessed something of the milieu the film depicts, I can't help but read *Traps* against the grain of the filmmaker's intent – viewing the realist elements of character and dialogue as social documentation. As the film portrays it, the milieu of politically committed community art and media work appears to be a closed one in which ideological steadfastness is an important virtue. Here, political identity, social and professional relationships and the realpolitik of survival are inseparably fused. This social scenario either reflects or parallels the privatisation of consciousness implicit in the neoliberal privatisation of society that the Thatcher, Reagan and Hawke governments had put into motion by that time. Either it had been internalised, even among leftists, or a parallel sublimation of the private imperative already existed on the orthodox left. *Traps* presents me with an analogy of the independent film and video sector that Hughes and I lobbied for at the time the film was made. Viewed from this perspective the film offers insight into the capacity of that sector to alienate many among a new generation of media artists who were my peers.

Immediately after the 1982 ASSA conference, and drawing upon the focus created within its independent strand, Hughes set about establishing the Independent Film Action Committee as a Melbourne base from which Victorian and national funding bodies could be lobbied. As the youngest member of the IFAC, I imagined that it could stand for the whole spectrum of independent film and video activities. Whilst the IFAC and its partner organisations interstate did lobby effectively on many fronts, the IFAC most efficiently represented the more established arm of the independent filmmaking community. What seemed to me at the time as the most speculative and least sustainable aims were securing equitable wages and conditions for filmmakers and finance for independent work on a more ambitious scale. Unless predicated on the public purse for cultural endeavour being expanded enormously, this worthy intent appeared to be at odds with the ideals of inclusivity, diversity, support for experimentation and what are nowadays referred to as 'emerging' practitioners. Time would tell, however, that in fact this agenda married well with the corporate one of government film agencies.

In keeping with the legislation enabling all federal film institutions, the AFC was intent on honing the broad community of independent filmmakers – whose individual projects would, in most cases only occasionally and partially, be funded by it – into a much smaller professional sector. This industrial sector would be dependent on AFC support at the outset and would somehow find commercial markets in the long term. Importantly, and in line with the rhetoric of industrial and corporate practice, funding bodies were also loading up budgets for films of all types with expensive risk-management costs.

The 'independent sector' that groups like the IFAC gained official recognition for was built upon the surviving institutions and personnel that had emerged from the co-ops and video access centres of the 1970s, and included a number of documentary filmmakers like Hughes. The nature of their work meant that, of all non-commercial producers, these documentary filmmakers had taken leading organisational roles, had the political acumen to lobby bureaucrats effectively and were often well equipped to read – and write – cultural policy.

The confluence of factors described above led to higher production, administration, insurance and reporting costs in funded film budgets. In her 1988 review of the AFC's Creative Development Fund, Megan McMurchy reported that between 1980–1981 and 1987–1988, the Fund's spending capacity had in fact doubled. During the same period, however, the cost per minute of funded projects increased eightfold. Consequently, funding for independent films was becoming much less accessible and the sector became increasingly professional and exclusive. This, and the fact that the independent film sector was becoming defined in increasingly conventional industrial terms, meant that IFAC did not attract and had not effectively accommodated the interests of many among a new 'post-punk' generation of media artists.

Like many of the co-op filmmakers a decade earlier, the emerging media artists and cultural activists of the 1980s who were my contemporaries often came to film through the visual arts. They tended to eschew both orthodox left politics and industrial professionalism. Their effective exclusion from and avoidance of the established modes and paradigms of institutional and political engagement that that IFAC represented reinforced a wilful naiveté about the realpolitik of the film industry for almost an entire generation. By extension, the Australian film industry lost almost an entire generation of potential leadership. In this younger milieu, networks of activity interlaced film with the contemporary avant-garde of music, music video, multimedia

TRAPS (1985).

performance and video art. 'No-budget' production in the Super-8 format was prevalent. Indeed the Super-8 movement is the most noted legacy of this generation of filmmakers. At a time when 16 mm film remained the preferred format for professional production, however, and given that a number of these filmmakers (Bill Mousoulis, Marie Craven, Chris Windmill and Philip Brophy, to name a few) worked in that format when they could, the Super-8 brand that many of this generation of independent filmmakers wore can be seen as a badge of marginalisation within the larger independent film scene of the 1980s. For a short time there was something of a return to the ethos of the Experimental Film and Television Fund (EFTF) – but on a much smaller scale – with the AFC's modest No Frills Fund. It provided costs-only budgets for small projects, usually shot on Super-8 or low-band video. The energy behind this initiative came from a community arts organisation, the Melbourne Fringe Festival. The IFAC supported the idea in principle but it ran counter to the fantasy of establishing a wage earning proletariat of cultural workers.

Publicly owned infrastructure for the exhibition of independent films in Australia was in decline by the time the AFI took up *Traps* for distribution in cinemas in several states.[301] Hughes entered *Traps* in the AFI Awards in both the feature and documentary categories because it was a feature length documentary. The film was then included in the feature program of an AFI touring exhibition, and according to Hughes, the magazine *Cinema Papers* subsequently 'insisted' upon *Traps*' status as a feature.[302] Initially this confusion was advantageous: the film toured nationally, and compared to Hughes' earlier films, *Traps* received a considerable amount of coverage by film reviewers nationally. When Hughes later sought finance from a fund established expressly for first-time feature directors however, this confusion presented a potential problem. It became important for Hughes to stress that *Traps* was devised, financed and produced as a documentary despite having dramatic elements including a central, fictional character and a skeletal overarching narrative. Hughes left Australia for the first time when *Traps* was invited to the Mannheim and Tyneside film festivals. It also screened at the Sundance Film Festival.

After the election of the Hawke federal Labor government in 1983, state subsidy of Australian screen culture continued to shift away from public infrastructure and grant-based funding towards a model of investment based upon commercial enterprise. Exhibition and distribution opportunities became increasingly limited for all independent filmmakers in the mid-1980s, especially after the demise of the co-op in Sydney and the AFI's loss of its Longford Cinema in Melbourne. Critical reception for independent work continued to be piecemeal. The culture that had developed around the idea of an independent film sector in Australia was small, lacked political currency and occurred too late to provide a bulwark against the general tide of economic and cultural policy.

To stay on the road beyond the 1980s then, the independent sector needed to maintain political traction on four fronts. Firstly, a rearguard action was being fought to protect what publicly and community-controlled resources the sector had left. The most important of these was the failed attempt to save the Sydney Filmmakers Co-operative. Secondly, budgets needed to reflect the professional nature of the work and the shift from something called 'culture' towards something called 'industry'. Thirdly, seeing that the days of a directly subsidised sector were numbered, the independents needed to establish a new professional and economic base. Privatisation and outsourcing meant that the mainstream television market would open up to those independent filmmakers who could service it. Finally, new markets were sought that might be opened to independents through a combination of new technology, regulation and indirect subsidy. The introduction of cable television nationally and commercial television services in remote areas had potential to create such markets for local independent work provided appropriate regulatory encouragement was in place. Hughes was involved on each of these fronts and was perhaps the most active and strategic advocate in the Melbourne lobby. During this time he produced *Traps* together with the second and third tapes of the *November Eleven* collaboration with Peter Kennedy (see Chapter 3).

Traps draws upon traditions of film and theatre practice that mix documentary and dramatic modes in different ways. It pays homage to the films *Newsfront* and *Exits* by way of quotation. Through its dense montage, *Traps* investigates the complex forces shaping a Labor Party on its return to government. By infecting the documentary moment with fiction, the film upsets the status of filmed actuality material as evidence. The narrative of *Traps* can be read as a portrait of the cultural left under stress at a time when federal sponsorship of community arts and film culture infrastructure had been receding for a number of years. The year *Traps* was completed – 1985 – was the year that the Sydney Filmmakers Co-operative (SFC) was shut down. The board of the SFC-founded *Filmnews,* together with its dynamic and resourceful editor Tina Kaufman, managed to resist pressure from the AFC to apply a cover price to Australia's screen newspaper for another decade.[303] The days of systematic institutional support for a diverse yet self-identifying independent film and video community in Australia, however, were over.

Endnotes

[261] John Hughes, *Traps*, 1985, 16 mm, colour, 96 minutes, Melbourne/Sydney, Producer John Hughes, Scriptwriters Paul Davies & John Hughes, Camera Katrina Bowels, Erika Addis & Jaems Grant, Sound Laurie Robinson, Jack Holt, John Cruthers, Lou Hubbard & Pat Fiske, Editor Zbigniew Friedrich. Featuring Carolyn Howard, Gwenda Wiseman, Paul Davies, John Flaus, Lesley Stern, Drew Cottle & Peter Summerfield with David Combe, Tony Walker (2JJJ), Michael Gill (*The Age*), Anthony McAdam (*Quadrant*), Denis Freney (*Tribune*), Greg Hywood (*Financial Review*), PP McGuinness (*Financial Review*), Humphrey McQueen, Paul Lyneham (Channel 7), Mark Aarons (ABC), Steven Sewell. Produced with assistance from the CDF of the AFC.

[262] See Stein in Creed, Barbara, John Davies, Freda Freiberg, David Hanan and Kim Montgomery (ed.) *Papers and Forums on Independent Film and Asian Cinema*, ASA (Victoria), AFTRS, Melbourne, 1982.

[263] Eckart Stein, 'Securing working definitions of narrative through discussion of genres of independent filmmaking', *AFI Conference: Independent Narrative Filmmaking and Television Marketing*, Sydney, personal notes taken by John Cumming, 1984.

[264] These are conservative estimates based on reported taxable income. Ricardo Fuentes-Nieva & Nick Galasso, *Working for the Few: Political capture and economic inequality*, briefing paper 178, Oxfam International, London, 2014, <http://www.oxfam.org/sites/www.oxfam.org/files/bp-working-for-few-political-capture-economic-inequality-200114-summ-en.pdf>, accessed 16 October 2014.
Rob Oakeshott, a former lobbyist and conservative National Party parliamentarian at state and federal level has described the political power that a handful of business people now have in Australia: 'Our key decisions for the future are now being outsourced at a level never before seen. Parliamentary democracy is going through its own sort of privatisation'. As one of a number of independent members of federal parliament holding the balance of power during the Labor government of Julia Gillard (2010-2013) Oakeshott witnessed how charm, money and manipulation of the media 'sent many necessary policy reforms to the doghouse' before the 'select few' resumed 'their happy place of command and control'. Rob Oakeshott, 'Capitalist punishment', The Saturday Paper, 2014, Melbourne, 9 August, p.15.

[265] John Hughes, *Gunana: Homeland of the Mornington Island Woomera Dancers*, 1982, U-matic colour, 29 minutes, Melbourne, Producer Melbourne College of Education Media Production Centre. This professional documentary was produced on Super- 8 film. Like 16 mm in the 1930s, Super-8 was introduced in the 1960s as an amateur format. During the early 1980s, independent filmmakers and some commercial producers turning to the miniature celluloid format.

[266] Martin Walsh, *The Brechtian aspect of radical cinema*, BFI Pub., London, 1981

[267] Helen Grace, *Serious Undertakings*, 1982, 16 mm, colour and b&w, 28 minutes, Sydney, Producer Erica Addis, Camera Erica Addis, Sound John Cruthers. Produced with assistance from the Women's Film Fund. Distributed by Ronin Films.
Laura Mulvey and Peter Wollen, *Riddles of the Sphinx*, 1977, 16 mm, colour, 92 minutes, BFI, London.

[268] Peter Tammer, *Journey to the End of Night*, 1982, 16 mm, colour, 70 minutes, Melbourne.

[269] Peter Tammer, *Mallacoota Stampede*, 1981, 16 mm, colour, 60 minutes, Melbourne.

[270] Tammer told me that the budget was inadequate and that, together with related problems in production, this meant he was unable to film all of the scenes in the original script.

[271] John Hughes, *Contemporary Cinema*, course outline, Melbourne State College, 4 June 1982.

[272] Davies, also a television scriptwriter, was known at the time for his work on the seminal Australian television series *Homicide* (1964–1976).

[273] Robin Laurie also cites Piscator and Brecht (together with Buster Keaton, George Wallace and Meyerhold) as key influences on the theatre workers who assembled around La Mama in the 1960s in Robin Laurie, 'Some recollections of life in the APG', *The Pram Factory: Australian Theatre History*. The

Australian Performing Group at the Pram Factory, 2005, Suzanne Ingleton, <http://www.pramfactory.com/memoirsfolder/Laurie–Robin.html>, accessed 6 February 2013. Laurie also directed and collaborated on Theatre Works' first site-specific play *The Go Anywhere Show* in 1981.

[274] John Willett, *The New Sobriety: Art and Politics in the Weimar Period 1917–33*, Thames & Hudson, London, 1978.

[275] Jean-Luc Godard, *Masculin féminin/Masculine Feminine*, 1966, 35 mm, b&w, 103 minutes, Paris; Haskell Wexler, *Medium Cool*, 1969, 35 mm colour, 111 minutes, Chicago; Jon Jost, *Angel City*, 1976, 16 mm, colour, 76 minutes, Los Angeles.

[276] Paul Davies, 'Alternative Working Structures', *IFAC Production Matters Seminar*, Melbourne, personal notes taken by John Cumming, 1984.

[277] John Willett, 'Epic Theatre', in Alan Bullock & Stephen Trombley (eds), *The New Fontana Dictionary of Modern Thought*, 4th edn, Harper Collins, London, 2000, p. 277.

[278] In addition to *Exits* and Hughes' films, Howard and Davies appear in a health and safety film. The style of performance in each of these appears to be largely independent of the three directors' influence. Kim Dalton, *The Myth of the Careless Worker*, 1983, video, colour, 29 minutes, Open Channel, Melbourne.

[279] Annette Blonski, 'End game', *Cinema Papers*, May 1986, p. 85.

[280] Geoffrey Bolton, The Middle Way 1942–1995, vol. 5, 5 vols, 2nd edn. *The Oxford History of Australia*, Oxford University Press, South Melbourne, 2001. Originally published 1996, p. 180.

[281] See Chapter 3 for a discussion of the demise of the Whitlam government.

[282] Ken Linnett, 'Taming of the Left in Australia', film review, *The Melbourne Times*, 5 March 1986, p. 10.

[283] John Hughes, *Traps*, interview conducted by John Cumming, Melbourne, 29 November 2000.

[284] Hughes notes with some amusement that the letter was dated the 11 November 1982.

[285] Marian Wilkinson, *Allies*, 1983, 16 mm, colour, 94 minutes, Sydney, Producer Sylvie Le Clezio. John Hughes, *Traps*, AFC, Development Finance application, 1983.

[286] Hughes, interview conducted by John Cumming, op. cit.

[287] Hughes in Linnett, op. cit.

[288] Alexander Kluge, *The Patriot/Die Patriotin* (The Female Patriot), 1979, 35 mm, b&w and colour, 121 minutes, Kairos-Film, Germany, Producers Alexander Kluge & Willi Segler (ZDF), Scriptwriters Christel Buschmann, Alexander Kluge & Willi Segler, Editor Beate Mainka-Jellinghaus. Blonski, op. cit.

[289] Paul Byrnes, 'Traps', film review, *Sydney Morning Herald*, 13 March 1986.

[290] See, for example, Jean-Luc Godard and Jean-Pierre Gorin's *British Sounds* (1969), Kestrel Productions/London Weekend Television and *Tous va bien* (1972) and Jean-Marie Straub & Danièle Huillet, *Introduction to an accompaniment to a cinematographic scene by Arnold Schoenberg* (1976).

[291] Tim Rowse, '*Traps*: A sympathetic joke on its audience', *Filmnews*, February/March 1986, p. 15.

[292] Phil Noyce, *Newsfront*, 1978, 35 mm, colour, 110 minutes, Palm Beach Pictures, Producers Phil Noyce & Bob Ellis, Scriptwriter David Elfick, Executive Producers Chris Haywood, Wendy Hughes, Bill Hunter & Gerard Kennedy, Camera Vincent Monton. Wilkinson, op. cit.

[293] Blonski, op. cit.

[294] David Stratton, 'Traps', *Variety*, 26 June 1985, p. 20. Susie Eisenhuth, 'A documentary that tries to say too much', film review, *Sun-Herald*, 16 March 1986.

[295] Hughes, interview conducted by John Cumming, op. cit.

[296] Rowse, op. cit.

[297] Blonski, op. cit.

[298] Hughes, op. cit.

[399] Palmada, 'BLF de-registration is a danger to the union movement', *Tribune*, 12 March 1986, p. 4.

[300] Susan Dermody & Elizabeth Jacka, *The Screening of Australia: Anatomy of a National Cinema*, vol. 2, 2 vols, 1st edn, Currency Press, Sydney, 1988, p. 242.

[301] The AFI had given up control of the Longford Cinema in Melbourne and exhibited with private operators outside Sydney and Hobart. It continued to screen some films, including documentaries like *Traps* theatrically throughout the mid-1980s. AFID, 'Traps', advertisement, *Tribune*, 12 March 1986, p. 10.

[302] John Hughes, *What I Have Written* and *After Mabo*, interview conducted by John Cumming, Melbourne, 3 July 2002.

[303] Tina Kaufman edited *Filmnews* for seventeen of its twenty years in print. The legacy of *Filmnews* has continued in the form of *RealTime* to which Kaufman contributes. *RealTime* is a free national contemporary arts newspaper. *RealTime* <http://www.realtimearts.net>, accessed 16 October 2014.

CHAPTER 6:
All That is Solid

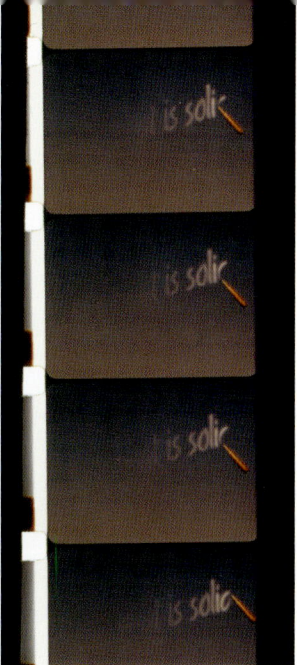

All That is Solid (1988) is a unique experimental television documentary produced through a funding program that was equally innovative. This chapter examines the background to both, surveys the film's varied critical reception and delves into questions about the nature of cinematography and performance on screen that Hughes' first film for television raises.

By the mid-1980s John Hughes recognised that the creative and political trajectory of his work was not compatible with the emergent commercial imperatives of major funding bodies. Rather than resigning himself to this circumstance, Hughes sought to both influence funding policy and locate alternative avenues of support for documentary filmmaking. These efforts led to initiatives such as the Australian Film Commission (AFC)/Australian Broadcasting Corporation (ABC) Documentary Fellowship, a program providing a chance for a handful of leading independent documentary filmmakers to make a film for television while working outside the conventional restraints broadcasters customarily imposed on the documentary form. This eased the transition from directly subsidised production and helped transform the institutionally recognised independent sector into the commissioned documentary arm of the mainstream television industry that it was to become. *All That is Solid*, the film that Hughes made under this program, pushed beyond the conventions of television on many fronts.[304] The film provides a focus for this chapter on collaborative creative processes and the function of dramatisation within essay-film form.

Some of the most productive moments in the history of documentary filmmaking have been sustained through the creation of employment – rather than commissions – for filmmakers.[305] Hughes pursued such employment both personally and in principle. He had created jobs

HOWARD AND DAVIES ON THEIR WAY TO WORK IN *ALL THAT IS SOLID* (1988).

for other filmmakers on a small scale through the VTHC initiative. Considering the dense, labour-intensive nature of creations such as *Traps* (1985, see Chapter 5), it is understandable that Hughes saw some proper terms of employment – at least during the time of production – as something worth striving for. Such work could not be sustained indefinitely without the bare minimum of professional circumstances. Furthermore, Hughes' generation of filmmakers was approaching 40 years of age and – while at the height of their professional power – growing weary of the struggle to maintain a subsistence income.

In June 1985 Hughes wrote to the AFC asking that they consider initiating research into the economic situation of independent filmmakers. Hughes proposed a study along the lines of that commissioned by the Australia Council and the ANU in 1983 that found that artists subsidised the arts by four times the amount that the government funding agencies did.

He wrote:

In the documentary arena the establishment of the fellowship scheme potentially sets up a very interesting precedent –, that of independent film makers with jobs. (Personally, I think it's a very important precedent, one that I have been keen to pursue in the form of resident artists projects).[306]

A few months later Hughes and David Bradbury were the two pre-eminent filmmakers who received the fellowship he refers to in this letter.[307] For Hughes, the fellowship effectively attenuated the liberal conditions of production financing that independent filmmakers had enjoyed in the 1970s and early 1980s.

It is rare for an independent filmmaker to secure production finance without the need to present a project proposal to their backers. Such creative freedom, offered together with assured exposure to a mainstream broadcast television audience, is probably without precedent in Australia and unlikely to be repeated. The AFC's annual Documentary Fellowships, co-sponsored

CLOCKWISE FROM TOP: ONE OF THE OBJECTS HUGHES GAVE HIS INTERVIEWEES; JAEMS GRANT AND JOHN HUGHES; HUGHES' DAUGHTER EVA HALL WITH CAROLYN HOWARD AND PAUL DAVIES – HOMELESS UNDER THE WESTGATE BRIDGE AS THE OCEANS RISE IN *ALL THAT IS SOLID* (1988).

FROM TOP: SENATOR JO VALENTINE; ACTORS LOUISE SMITH, JOHN HOWARD AND MARK ROGERS IN *ALL THAT IS SOLID* (1988); POET CHRISTOPHER BARNETT CONTRIBUTED WRITING TO *ALL THAT IS SOLID* (STILL FROM VIDEO BY THE AUTHOR).

by the ABC through a guaranteed television presale, did both these things. With a value of A$125,000, the fellowship would allow each filmmaker to 'make a major documentary of their own choice'.[308] McMurchy declared 'The ground has been broken to show more interesting films than the usual TV documentaries'.[309] The ABC would soon impose controls on the scheme, but not before 1986 when Hughes became a recipient.

Before the announcement of the 1986 Documentary Fellowships, Hughes and Peter Kennedy had agreed to work together on a major bicentennial project.[310] The result, curated by Nancy Underhill and substantially financed by the Australian Bicentennial Authority, was *The Stars Disordered*, a gallery exhibition including a video of the 16 mm film *All That is Solid* (1988). The exhibition catalogue includes interviews with Hughes and Kennedy, and colour plate pages of film stills and paintings, with captions including quotes from poet and playwright Chris Barnett's contribution to the script of the film. There is also a short story by Sylvia Lawson and an essay by David Malouf.[311] When Hughes received the Documentary Fellowship, he decided to use it as the resource base for this collaboration. In his painting, Kennedy was working intensively with the motifs of stars and hearts. In a similar vein, Hughes had begun to toy with angels and bullets: objects that could be used metaphorically in a film.

Hughes gathered together a large group of collaborators for *All That is Solid*. The Documentary Fellowship allowed him to pay people for their input at the earliest stage. Paul Davies and Carolyn Howard joined Hughes again, together with actor/director Nicos Lathouris and actors Mark Rogers and Louise Smith. Musician and theatre maker Eric Gradman, who composed the music for the project, is acknowledged together with Davies and Barnett for additional writing. While little of his original writing exists in the completed film, Barnett has told me that Hughes was an unusually genuine and respectful filmmaker in this collaboration.

As with earlier projects, Hughes began recording material while developing the work conceptually.

He interviewed 'non-fiction characters … who saw themselves as having something to say about Australia's future'.[312] For the fictional and performance-based scenes, as for those in *Traps*, Hughes made up a small team based on a conventional documentary crew but including an art director and assistant director who also acted as production manager. For *All That is Solid* a costume designer and make-up artist were included. All were former associates of Hughes with connections going back to the Pram Factory or *Dalmas* (1973) or the Melbourne Filmmakers Co-operative (MFC).

Having the time to do research was one of the privileges of the year-long fellowship, as was the freedom from fundraising work that it brought.[313] Hughes read widely and listened to the radio. He assembled a list of possible interviewees for an exploration of the future. The final collections of non-fiction characters in the film represent a marketplace in which ideas 'are competing like some kind of commodity'.[314] Hughes noted in a 1988 interview with his partner Carole Sklan that just as the bicentenary provided examples of battles to 'occupy the past,' there were 'constant battles' underway to occupy the future.[315] These often involved what he called 'the ghastly threat inherent in the magical thinking of the radical right.' The following year he told Ron Banks that the premise he developed for *All That is Solid* was that the future is 'immobilised by different sections of the community'.[316]

Eric Gradman referred Hughes to Marshall Berman's 1982 book *All That Is Solid Melts Into Air* in which *The Communist Manifesto* is described as 'the first great modernist work of art'.[317] A scholar of the leading nineteenth-century modernists, Berman argues that Marx and Engels' manifesto has a place not only in the literature of political and economic modernisation, but also in that of 'modernism in art, culture and sensibility'.[318] In essence, Berman identifies a dialectical poetics in Marx that 'expresses some of modernist culture's deepest insights' and 'dramatises some of its deepest inner contradictions'.[319] Chris Barnett's poetry is also imbued with this sensibility. Paraphrasing Marx and Engels, Berman writes, 'To be modern is to live a life of paradox and contradiction'.[320] It was from this section of

NICOS LATHOURIS FORAGES IN A POST-INDUSTRIAL AUSTRALIA IN *ALL THAT IS SOLID* (1988).

FROM TOP: WIND MACHINE AND ANGELS – LOUISE SMITH IN *ALL THAT IS SOLID* (1988); MAGGIE CAMERON, 'THE ANCIENT MEDEA WANTS TO KILL JASON'S NEW LOVER AND HIS CHILDREN. THE MODERN *MEDEA* JUST WANTS TO WIPE THE SMILE OFF YOUR FACE'.

the manifesto – which he returns to several times – that Berman drew the title for his book, and Hughes the title for his film. Other important book references for Hughes were Baudrillard's *Critique of the Political Economy of the Sign*, Guattari's *Molecular Revolutions*, and Paul Virilio's *Speed and Politics*.[321]

Hughes turned to Walter Benjamin for the opening quotation of *All That is Solid*. This aphoristic reflection upon Paul Klee's painting *Angelus Novus* is taken from 'Theses on the Philosophy of History' and lies just two pages after the paragraph that Hughes quotes at the outset of *Film-Work* (1981, see Chapter 4). The street and the arcade are significant sites in both Benjamin and Berman's view of modernity. They have a prominent place in the spatial and symbolic world of *All That is Solid*. For the pre-title scene of *All That is Solid*, Hughes has Louise Smith and Mark Rogers stage the *Angelus Novus* while reciting Benjamin's description of it. The Angel of History is looking upon the 'wreckage' of the past while the storm of progress 'irresistibly propels him into the future, to which his back is turned'.[322] Rogers narrates in the guise of a manic showman. The film's title is an animated photomontage that introduces the whole of David Byrne's popular alternative pop song 'In the Future' – a litany of contradictory futurist scenarios with a strong brass section that sets the tone of Gradman's score for the film.

Rather than forming a linear narrative exposition, the dramatic elements in *All That is Solid* consist of fragmentary images gathered into settings in which personal and global histories and archetypal themes are collapsed together. These tableaus each have a singularity about them as performances or presentations. Smith continues to portray Benjamin's angel, but in contemporary garb – as a shoplifter in a leather jacket. She drops a photograph in the hub of Melbourne's nineteenth-century Block Arcade, while saxophonist Ann Fitzgerald, in the guise of a busker, provides Gradman's score. Maggie Cameron plays an actress – a woman betrayed by her husband – who is preparing for the part of Euripides' *Medea* and finds the photograph in which men browse in a bombed-out library.[323]

The most effective of Mark Rogers' performance scenes, and the polemic centre of the film, is based on a text written by Chris Barnett that Hughes said was 'mixed up with Hugh Stretton's *Political Essays*'.[324] Wearing a neat cheap suit, Rogers sits in the void of a dark studio on an institutional vinyl chair. On the desk in front of him sit two dice and a red plastic coffee cup. The sheets of paper he holds and glances at regularly appear to be a script, but are only props, like those of a television newsreader. The text has been memorised. The cinematographer, Jaems Grant, performs a series of 360-degree Dutch tilts and simultaneously tracks his camera around Rogers who follows it awkwardly, making his address directly into the lens. The ironic monologue ends with the line: 'We warmly welcome developments as they are thought out at the top where the sacrifices are immense but the rewards are many.' The action, determined here by the camera, reinforces the puppet-like stature of Rogers' character and the sense that he is at the mercy of larger forces.

Throughout the film Rogers performs a cipher-like character apparently immersed in, trying desperately to embrace, or simply performing (as an actor/worker) the contemporary ethos of global capitalism. Smith coaches Rogers in a rundown inner-city studio. Here he rehearses another speech in which, as critic John Slavin wrote, he 'narcissistically enumerates his many attributes.' But even as 'self-stroking,' the character's performance is devoid of personal conviction. The desperate propriety of Rogers' performances suggest that, in the 'state of social dysfunction' that Slavin attributes them to, the will to succeed is indivisible from the will to survive.[325]

Carolyn Howard and Paul Davies play the main dramatised scenes in *All That is Solid*, allowing the film to act as a sequel to the story of the characters George and Judith in *Exits* (1980) and *Traps*. While literal narrative connections are not made with earlier texts, as they are in *Traps*, the serial of these 'everyman' and 'everywoman' vignettes constitutes an ongoing soap opera across Hughes' 1980s oeuvre. The characters argue about having children and the future and speak

FROM TOP: MARK ROGERS; LOUISE SMITH AND ROGERS; CAROLYN HOWARD AND PAUL DAVIES IN *ALL THAT IS SOLID* (1988).

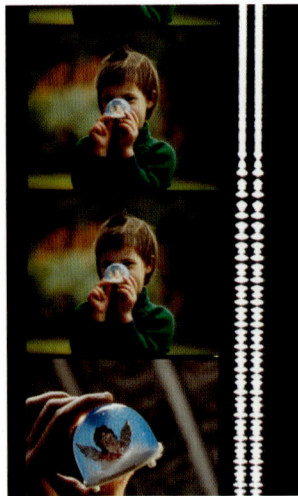

FROM TOP: EVA HALL WITH SNOW DOME; TED WHEELWRIGHT (TOP) AND REV. KLIMIONOK ('NUCLEAR WAR AND THE SALVATION OF THE RIGHTEOUS') IN *ALL THAT IS SOLID* (1988).

in overblown leftist clichés: 'Look at it as another pair of hands, another enemy for the landlord', George tells Judith. In what Slavin called 'a cloyingly idealised pastoral scene', they later confer on the organisation of their domestic lives – along democratic lines.[326] Finally, they find themselves materially destitute – living under a bridge with their growing child as the sea level rises.

The nine interviews in *All That is Solid* were recorded in various locations around Australia by a number of camera operators using Video-8. Video-8, and later Hi-8, were economical, miniature video formats based around small cassettes of 8 mm gauge magnetic tape. These formats provided the platform for the first video cameras that could compete with Super-8 cartridge film equipment in size and weight. Like Super-8, Video-8 and Hi-8 also triggered a proliferation of cameras from cheap palm-sized automatics to expensive units that were fitted out as professional broadcast cameras. Hughes hoped that the grainy texture of the Video-8 material, in contrast to the scenes shot on 16 mm film, would help create the idea of a parody of television within his film. The use of low-band video material of this kind for key scenes in a broadcast television documentary was unusual in the 1980s and one of the innovations that the terms of the Documentary Fellowship allowed.

Rather than presenting his interviewees with questions, Hughes presents them with a collection of small objects: an angel in a snowstorm paperweight, a dice, a small globe, a bullet and figurines of Mickey Mouse and a bridal couple. Hughes hoped to solicit a range of positions and 'create a sense of turbulence, disintegration and difference' from a critical perspective, which is neither 'certain, or singular, [or] closed off'.[327] In theory, the specific array of meanings is not to be determined by the filmmaker, but is open-ended and subject to the forces set into motion by the mechanism itself. The symbolically prompted performances in these interviews, however, demonstrate that such devices do not necessarily function dialectically or generate intellectual adventure. Innovative processes will not always lead to innovative results but such experimentation is vital.

JOHN HUGHES AND JANE CASTLE WITH VIDEO-8 CAMCORDER WORKING ON *ALL THAT IS SOLID*.

Educationalist Bill Cope sits in darkness next to a slide projector, describing the 'fragmented' and 'localised' visions of the future that are at play in contemporary social discourse. In essence, Cope paraphrases Berman. From the right wing of neoliberal politics, Katharine West arrives at a similar observation, concluding that the 'intellectual life' of Australia 'tends to go into little convenient groups and stereotypes.' She blames an egalitarian social ethos in which 'the laggards and the unproductive win.' Boris Frankel, author of *Post Industrial Utopians*, describes the future as 'being planned for us' by political and industrial power-holders who are 'loading the dice.' Another author, Roberta Perkins, looks forward to a society where 'we completely eliminate gender.' Freda Glynn, director of the Central Australian Aboriginal Media Association (CAAMA), is reminded by the dice of the corrosive effect of the culture of cheating in white society. Echoing a central theme in *November Eleven* (1979, see Chapter 3), Australian Democrat Senator Jo Valentine declares that Australia provides 'the eyes and ears of the American military command' through bases such as Pine Gap. Academic Andrew Mack agrees that an informed public debate has not been allowed on Australia's status as a nuclear target. Writer Craig McGregor says that he does not believe in an 'apocalyptic future.' He sees 'inequality and exploitation' continuing alongside 'creative lives that will slowly change the superstructure.' Meanwhile, the Reverend Reginald Klimionok sees nuclear war as an essential and integral chapter in the salvation of the righteous.

FROM LEFT: KATHARINE WEST TELLS MARK ROGERS THAT IN 'THIS RIGGED RACE … INEVITABLY THE LAGGARDS AND THE UNPRODUCTIVE WIN'; AN INTERVIEW ABOUT GENDER FLUIDITY APPEARS ON A MONITOR BURIED IN A FABRIC SHOP; 'THE BOSSES ARE RAKING IN THE PROFITS,' NEWSPAPER VENDOR IN *ALL THAT IS SOLID* (1988).

Overall, given that Hughes' interview subjects are all practised social commentators and/or ideologues, the strategy of props as prompts is largely redundant. The interviewees have internalised their own scripts and sometimes begin to sound pompous. There are, however, some moments where the subjects stumble about within their own discourse. After losing herself momentarily in the enormity of world historical thinking, West stumbles back upon her script. Almost as if in a trance of revelation, she looks directly at the camera and forecasts with gravity '1990 – our cabinet will be predominantly non-parliamentarian.' This rare moment of spontaneity contains one of the few unprepared but incisive political observations in the film.

The interviews in *All That is Solid* are interlaced with each other and with the other material that makes up the film. The fictional and actual worlds are carefully fused. For example, in a shop in the arcade, a television set plays the interview with Roberta Perkins. In another interview, the interviewer is actor Mark Rogers – in costume. Ted Wheelwright presents a vision of corporate brainwashing. This bleak prospect frames Rogers' hollow sales-pitch-of-the-self-performance that appears to be impelled more by fear than neediness. In such combinations, the performance scenes are more than illustrative. These scenes are reflexive in nature and encourage the viewer to perceive the interviews in the film as performances.

Ultimately Rogers delivers his rehearsed speech with manic evangelical conviction in a shopping mall. Here the filmmakers insert a performance of their own devising into the world of actuality (as street theatre) and then film it as part of a larger documentary mise-en-scène. This actuality setting includes the seemingly antiquated sloganeering of a vendor of socialist newspapers, busking Morris dancers and a group of spectators who have gathered around Rogers and his street theatre set. Rogers skips around the frame of a children's swing from which hangs a video monitor. The monitor plays images and sounds of Rev. Klimionok and a large congregation of his proselytes locked in a repetitive recitation of the Pentecostal song 'I believe in miracles'.

This pining song continues into a scene where an estranged father (Nicos Lathouris) visits his young son and recalls a dream in which he and the boy dig out from pack ice something that the child recognises as a heart. Hughes wrote this scene as a response to some of Peter Kennedy's early heart drawings that he felt 'seemed to seek a kind of utopian yearning for unity and

ABOVE: YANI AND NICO LATHOURIS IN *ALL THAT IS SOLID* (1988).

wholeness'.[328] The penultimate scene of the film, when the child watches his father drive away, has a poignancy that goes beyond such symbolic formulae. In this fictional interlude, questions about the nature of relationships, emotional responsibility and masculinity are briefly glimpsed. But the grand narrative preoccupations soon take hold again with a cut to Wheelwright recalling that it was a 'very small boy' who saw that the emperor had no clothes. This montage tends to reduce the powerful image of personal separation from the preceding scene into a polemic rhetorical metaphor.

In 2002 Hughes recalled that the AFC/ABC Documentary Fellowship placed him in a privileged position. 'I'm given a budget for a film and wages for a year – unheard of – and the only kind of brief is to do something called "innovate" – with the form'. Hughes felt this necessitated addressing 'on as many levels as I could' the question, 'What are the outside edges of what we understand documentary to be and how can they be pushed?'[329] Given that Hughes and many of his peers had been experimenting with documentary form for many years, this is a somewhat rhetorical question. Yet it does suggest that Hughes was very conscious of the challenge that such unprecedented freedom presented for producing innovative work for a national broadcast audience.

In line with the conception of *All That is Solid* as a parody of television conventions, it is structured according to a commercial television hour: seven-minute sequences (consisting of three scenes in the case of television drama) are followed by a certain number of advertisements of either fifteen, thirty or sixty seconds duration. In this schema the interviews serve as the commercial breaks and the interviewees can be seen as sponsors whose ideas are on offer in an ideological marketplace. Hughes also had in mind the experience of a viewer rapidly changing television channels. He admits, 'No one in their right mind would recognise that what they were watching was a parody of television'. So the gesture is an abstract and invisible one. The focus is on the expectations that were associated with the documentary form in broadcast television and to 'turning them on their head' in an arbitrary and literal way.[330]

John Slavin and Adrian Martin have provided the two most considered and incisive reviews of *All That is Solid*. In a brief review for *Filmnews* in 1988, Martin considered the film 'an almost

FROM TOP: 'THE FUTURE IS CURRENTLY BEING PLANNED FOR US ... LIMITING THE FUTURE OPTIONS' – BORIS FRANKEL; 'CAPITALISM IS A CASINO' – TED WHEELWRIGHT IN *ALL THAT IS SOLID* (1988).

total failure', while in his 1989 review Slavin celebrates it as a success. He finds depth, density and dialectical relationships between elements in the film:

Within the mosaic of its various abbreviated threads, its narratives, it suggests a pattern of rich relationships which seem, after a second or third viewing, to be inexhaustible.[331]

On the other hand, Martin writes:

When we think of the montage film the example of Alexander Kluge suggests heterogeneity and surprise, an enlarging of the conceptual space between separate blocks. Hughes, by contrast, dampens down and locks in his material. His poetic metaphors [...] are worse than banal – they're over homogenising, determining.[332]

As he did with *Traps*, Hughes intricately knits together the components of the film. For a viewer with Martin's sensibility, this closes 'the gaps between documentary and fiction' – gaps that, in Kluge's films, 'produce an enormous amount of perplexing not immediately calculable experiential and emotional material'.[333] Slavin does not seek such dialectical gaps in the denotation of Hughes' film, but neither does he claim to find them. Slavin celebrates the interconnectedness as creating further 'rich relationships.' He is satisfied with the 'sudden shifts of perspective' and how the film 'successfully incorporates the swift shift of emphasis from one apparently disconnected action to another'.[334]

Slavin praises Hughes' refusal to 'deliver a definitive statement,' but ignores the fact that this absence depends and is built upon an otherwise and ultimately unified text. The conceptual preoccupations of *All That is Solid* engage Slavin, while for Martin the superstructure created from them predetermines and limits the expressive potential of something he has described elsewhere as 'the suggestive power of plastic editing'.[335] Martin notes the limitation inherent in Hughes' formulaic devices, especially when it comes to the 'interviews'. He writes of the symbolic objects: 'As spurs-to-thought for the featured individual/experts interviewed, they elicit only confirmed, standard, self-important responses'.³³⁶

We don't learn much from *All That is Solid* about its interviewees. This can affect the weight their observations carry and contribute to the air of self-importance that Martin sees the film imbuing them with. Ted Wheelwright, for example, was an important figure in the critical understanding of global economics for over two decades. In a 2007 obituary, Frank Sitwell described Wheelwright as having taught and written about 'globalisation' decades before the term had currency.

He warned of its dangers: dependence on foreign investment, economic inequality, environmental degradation, the power of transnational corporations and the undermining of national sovereignty. ³³⁷

In her biography of Lionel Murphy, Attorney-General in the Whitlam government, Jenny Hocking shows that from 1957 when his 'seminal' book *Ownership and Control of Australian Companies* was published, Wheelwright's research influenced policymakers and legal reformers including Murphy.³³⁸ Like Whitlam, – Wheelwright was an airman in World War II. He was awarded the Distinguished Flying Cross and went on to study economics to learn 'what caused war, and why his father – a steelworker – had been out of work for five years during the Depression'.³³⁹ At the time of the American war in Vietnam, he led a demonstration of Veterans Against the War, 'proudly wearing his medals'.³⁴⁰ Yet the vast scope of subject matter and the constraint of the formalised 'interviews' in *All That is Solid* prohibit any exploration of the evidence, ideas or life experience behind Wheelwright's opinions. Where the ambitious scope of other Hughes' films leads to density, here it leads to a kind of thinness.

Both Slavin and Martin recognised *All That is Solid* as an engagement with postmodernism by 'an artist of the left' (Slavin) or '1970s politico' (Martin), but as Martin notes 'it never mentions the word.' Where Slavin finds moments of 'splendid post-modern parody,' Martin finds 'token appropriation of post modern irony.' Martin sees

FROM TOP: SLIM WHITTLE AS A MARXIST EVANGELIST IN *ALL THAT IS SOLID*; 'I CAN'T SEE HOW WE'RE GOING TO TEACH OUR CHILDREN ANY DIFFERENT BECAUSE YOUR CULTURE IS SO STRONG.' FREDA GLYNN TALKS ABOUT THE INFECTIOUS NATURE OF EUROPEAN CULTURE, IN WHICH LYING AND RIP OFFS ARE CONSIDERED CLEVER AND REWARDED, IN *ALL THAT IS SOLID* (1988).

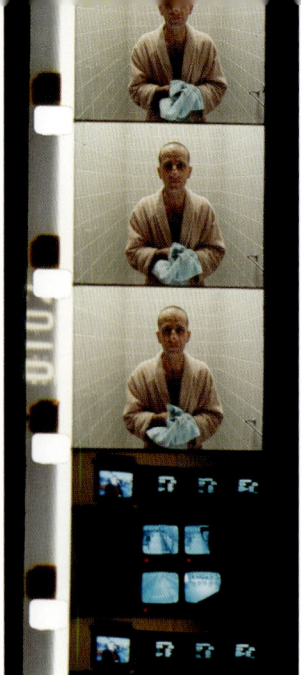

ABOVE: NICO AND YANI LATHOURIS IN *ALL THAT IS SOLID* (1988).

All That is Solid as the 'male counterpart to *Landslides*' (1986), an essay film by Sydney feminist filmmakers of Hughes' generation. He finds in it 'the newly emergent left utopianism that puts a value (at last) in personal/collective dreaming, storytelling, imagining' and consequently, attention to 'modest struggles on many levels, at many moments – subtle shifts in the social ensemble, cracks opening up, lines of flight'.[341]

Where Martin found that Hughes had locked in his material, Hughes regrets that he did not have more control of it. Regarding the parody of television within the structure of the film, Hughes says: 'If the film had been better planned and better executed then it would have been absolutely accessible and available'.[342] *All That is Solid* was a process-oriented project in which Hughes employed collaborators and built his film around the opinions of other authors. Together with the somewhat mannered style of staging and dramatisation, this tends to reinforce the sense of Hughes' directorial and editorial position as an impersonal screen. While the film and many of the strategies employed within it are playful and poetic, these qualities are not wholly effective or sustained. The interviews and dramatised performances are sometimes either too earnest or timid and tend to weigh the film down, or close it off. This is a difficulty that haunted a number of politically and theoretically informed experimental documentary or essay films of the 1980s and 1990s – especially those in which an attempt was made to merge documentary and dramatic form.

In his critique, Martin addresses Hughes' approach to montage and to staging the interviews but not the script, direction of actors or the performances themselves. *Traps*, *All That is Solid*, *One Way Street* and Grace's *Serious Undertakings* all make similar demands on performers. At times these films are weighed down by the theatricality of their scripted monologues and an intellectual over-earnestness – even where such earnestness is presented as a subject of parody, as it is in Grace's film. They belong to what Barrett Hodsdon describes as a 'deconstructive genre' of post-1968 'counter-cinema' essay films that attempted to translate to film a 'Brechtian' style of performance.[343] Among the first Anglophone filmmakers to enter this terrain were British film theorists Laura Mulvey and Peter Wollen. Later, Isaac Julian and Todd Haynes also adopted a reflexive, direct-address style of performance. Haynes' filmmaking is most successfully self-reflexive in *The Karen Carpenter Story* (1987), a film in which no human performers appear. Here, a number of televisual modes of address are deployed and Barbie dolls are used to visually represent the characters and to generate an excruciatingly effective pathos. In Haynes' *Poison* (1991), however, the theatrical performances of actors self-consciously performing texts in highly stylised sets and parodic to-camera interviews seem to me to be excruciatingly portentous and contrived. Yet, in 1974 when Mulvey sat and read from her thesis for the camera in *Penthesilea, Queen of the Amazons*, the earnestness and self-consciousness is not that of an actor, but that of the young intellectual's own nervousness before the task she has given herself: the performance of her own ideas – more so than the performance of herself. While Mulvey and Wollen's film may display the 'earnest theoretical over-determination' that Hodsdon has identified in British examples of the deconstructive essay film, there is a certain visceral sense of risk and urgency in Mulvey's enterprise before the camera. Therefore, the scene is unequivocally one of actuality. And this, it seems to me, is where the difference lies.

Brecht's use of reflexive effects in the theatre was aimed at drawing attention to the material relations between an audience, the performer and the work in performance – the actuality of the theatrical construction on the stage before an audience. What Godard did when employing the cinematic equivalent of this idea was to replace the stage with 'photographed reality' and to treat every scene, no matter how fictional it may be, as an actuality before his camera.[344] This is also why Vertov – the seminal dialectician of documentary film – was so important to Godard. Both filmmakers are anchored in the tradition of actuality (and re-enacted actuality) pioneered by the Lumière brothers and sustained most consistently in the documentary tradition. Howard and Davies also understood this when they made the transition from Brechtian theatre to Brechtian film in *Exits*. Together with Laughren *they filmed it like a newsreel*. In essence, this approach is true to Robert Bresson's idea of 'cinematography'.[345] For Bresson and the new wave filmmakers who followed after him, the coin of the art was life, not drama.

John Hughes recently observed this process at work when writing about Joris Ivens' *Indonesia Calling* (1946, see Chapter 11). He identifies 'the material specificity' of certain scenes involving 'actuals' – non-actors re-enacting events from their own experience. He calls upon Kracauer's idea of cinematography's capacity for the 'redemption of physical reality' to describe a phenomena in which the audience is at once moved by the authenticity of these portrayals and by the 'theatricality of their staging' which 'evokes an allegorical reading'.[346] In *Film-Work* (1980, see Chapter 4), the WWFFU filmmakers noted a similar effect in their re-enacted documentaries and it is evident in much of Hughes' own use of actual subjects starting with *Nowhere Game* (1972, see Chapter 1).

Globally, many of the directors of the 1960s – most famously Godard, Marker, Kluge, Straub-Huillet, Dušan Makavejev, Vera Chytilová and Nagisa Oshima – managed to work quite seamlessly between contrivance and actuality with non-actors and with professional performers in both naturalistic and highly stylised settings. Many of the essay films of Hughes' generation, however, while influenced by this earlier work, do not make the transition to working with actors so comfortably. It is as if, rather than replacing the stage with the camera, the camera is placed in front of the stage. The highly contrived set ups and interview scenes in Todd Haynes *Poison* (to take an extreme example) owe more to Hollywood and the tradition of Thomas Edison's Black Maria studio than they do to any practice of actuality filmmaking. Here, rather than the filmed naturalistic theatre that Vertov rallied against, we have an equally ham-fisted filmed Brechtian theatre.[347]

When cinematography gives way entirely to staged theatricality the camera's capacity as a poetic tool – used with unwavering attention to the actuality before it – is lost. It becomes a device for recording 'takes' that can easily be repeated for it. This is one way in which the gap that Martin identified (between documentary and fiction) is closed in *All That is Solid*. Whilst it refuses 'naturalism', with its use of props, the film drifts into symbolism. Yet, as Godard warned – 'there is nothing symbolic about reality'.[348] And the actors in *All That is Solid* are asked to act: they are given responsibility for representing themselves or for trying precisely not to represent themselves – to perform a kind of Brechtian non-acting for the camera. This sometimes generates a strain in the performances that threatens to overwhelm the text.

In practical terms, how is a critically distanced yet cohesive triangulation of performer, audience and text effectively constructed? The answer appears to lie in the negotiations that filmmakers undertake with the conventions of realist screen direction and performance. In these negotiations, spaces are created that liberate the performer from self-consciousness. For Godard, who often works with professional actors, this has meant rather than requiring his cast to act, putting them in a situation to which they must react. This also means refusing psychological drama whilst holding to narrative: refusing the creation of realist characters and tightly prescribing the mise-en-scène within which the actors can work. Simultaneously, the being of the film is surrendered to the persona of the performers who form its ensemble at any given moment. For Jon Jost it meant, in *Angel City* (1976) for instance, creating (with actor Bob Glaudini) Frank Goya – a laconic pop culture caricature, whose self-consciousness is integral to his engagement of the audience. Hughes and Mark Rogers achieve something similar with the manic salesman character in *All That is Solid* and the stylised interview set-up meshes well with Katharine West's brittleness. Elsewhere, I think there is a lack of such effective engagement with the energising potential of actuality and persona and/or a reticence in the direction of actors and non-actors that leads some performances within *All That is Solid* and, later, *One Way Street* (1992, Chapter 7) to appear distractingly earnest, self-conscious, forced or theatrical.

The visual design of *All That is Solid* is subject to a tension that is related to the performative one discussed above. The graphic arrangement of objects and shapes in the frame within *All That is Solid* continues the pronounced spatial, compositional design sense noted in *Film-Work*. The reality that the superimposed elements of screen design intersect with here, however, is often a wholly staged or constructed one, and the relationship between the subjects and their settings is often metaphoric rather than concrete. Bill Cope's monologues, for example, are intercut with the view from the front of a commuter train as it hurtles through the tunnels and stations of Melbourne's underground rail loop. Cope sits in darkness next to a slide projector that emits a tunnel-like cone of light while he describes the narrow one-tracked visions of the future on offer in contemporary discourse. There is a viscerality to this combination of shots, offering a sense that Cope might be in the tunnel or his projector might be projecting its image. In either case, the audience is drawn with him into the darkness and into the abstractions he describes. While such montage has the capacity to generate a poetic dimension within a film, its potential is undercut here by the premeditated (if not actually scripted) text of Hughes' interviewee. The set up of the scene appears to require Cope to conduct a (staged) performance of his self rather than to react to questions, in the conventional realist interview, or to a dramatic situation that activates the performer's volition.

In 2003 Hughes said his intention in *All That is Solid* was to 'play with ideas about personal or private life within [a] documentary discourse about Australia's future'. He also claimed a junction of personal life and 'documentary discourse,' noting that the actors are 'couples in life as well as in the film'.[349] This is arcane knowledge, however; inaccessible to the audience and never referred to in the film where private life and documentary discourse are strictly separated. The personal is depicted scantly, and only in fictional form, while only the public sphere is treated as actuality. While a number of Hughes' friends and one of his own young daughters appear in the film, this is not a work that is personal in any way that an audience could readily identify. There is no such reticence, however, on the part of the producers of much of the modernist cultural discourse with which *All That is Solid* seeks engagement. In his book of the same title, Berman calls upon his own personal recollections while several of Benjamin's essays include detail of private life and experience.[350]

So *All That is Solid* has some reflexive elements but is not a self-reflexive work like those upon which it draws. As Martin concludes in his 1988 review, there is a lack

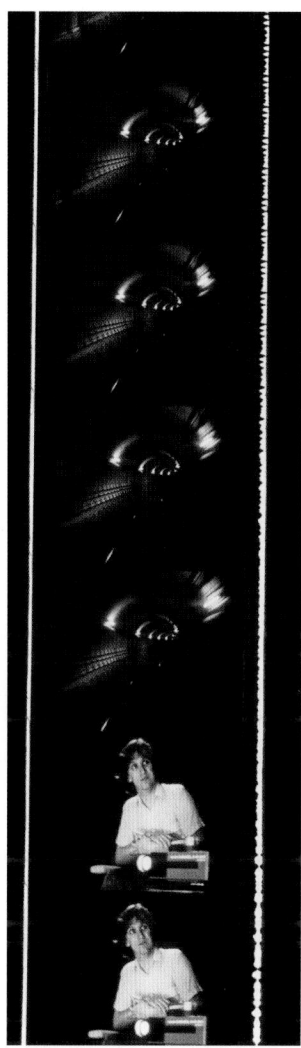

BILL COPE IN *ALL THAT IS SOLID* (1988).

FROM LEFT: BRUSHING HISTORY AGAINST THE GRAIN, THE ANGEL OF HISTORY LOOKS BACK UPON THE SINGULAR CATASTROPHE THAT IS THE CARNAGE OF ALL THE VICTORIES OF RULERS PAST AND PRESENT – MARK ROGERS WITH LOUISE SMITH AS THE EMPATHETIC ANGEL OF HISTORY, OF BENJAMIN, AFTER KLEE; INVITATION TO 1988 PREVIEW SCREENING OF *ALL THAT IS SOLID*.

of reflexive practice 'of self doubt or self interrogation on the film's part'. While Hughes wanted to 'create a sense of turbulence and disintegration', for Martin 'Nothing spills over or bursts out of *All That is Solid* – condemning it finally to a kind of stiffly arch-modernist disingenuousness'.[351] Even when Hughes was working directly on the constructivist notion of the artist as impersonal screen, in *Film-Work,* for example, there was a grounded, intimate and personal quality to the work. But in *All That is Solid* many scenes – whether documentary or dramatic in form – appear to be suspended in an unreal, imagistic realm presaged and reverberating with the hysterically futuristic, out-of-body sound of Byrne's song. *All That is Solid* is a unique and interesting, multi-dimensioned experiment but it is also, in this regard, an adventure into abstraction. There are echoes of its world of disembodied ideas and stranded performers in Hughes' later work, but there is also a gradual return to concrete material relations with both historical and contemporary subjects, and the engagingly diffident voice of the filmmaker begins to be heard more clearly again.

All That is Solid was a finalist for both AFI and Sydney Film Festival Greater Union Awards, deservedly won a award for innovation from ATOM and was commended at the Chicago Film Festival. Through the Documentary Fellowship, this film – Hughes' first for broadcast on mainstream television – was uniquely free of the constraints on content and form that production for broadcast usually entails. Hughes says the Fellowship opened Australian state-owned broadcasters to independent filmmakers.[352] The liberal terms of this entrée to television, however, would not apply in any ongoing or systematic relationship between broadcasters and the wider field of independent production. According to Peter Hughes, the ABC executives ensured they had more creative control in subsequent rounds of the program.[353] Even within the recognised genre of documentary, there would not be an ongoing commitment to work as challenging in form or content as *All That is Solid*.

Endnotes

[304] John Hughes, *All That is Solid*, 1988, 16 mm/Hi-8 video, colour, 54 minutes, Melbourne, Producer John Hughes, Scriptwriters Paul M Davies, Chris Barnett, John Hughes, Camera Jaems Grant, Sound Lloyd Carrick, Editors Jill Holt, Zbigniew Friedrich. Featuring Margaret Cameron, Paul Davis, Mitchell Faircloth, Eva Hall, Carolyn Howard, Nico Lathouris, Yani Lathouris, Mark Rogers, Louise Smith with Bill Cope, Boris Frankel, Freda Glynn, Reginald Klimionok, Andrew Mack, Craig McGregor, Roberta Perkins, Jo Valentine, Katherine West, Ted Wheelwright. Produced with assistance from the AFC-ABC Fellowship, Australian Bicentennial Authority.

[305] Examples from early last century include the WWFFU (see Chapter 4), Film Australia and its antecedents (see Chapter 10) and Grierson's film units at the Empire Marketing Board and the GPO in Britain and at the Canadian Film Board. Locally, the Victorian Department of Education's Film Unit known as the Audio-Visual Education Centre (AVEC) – later absorbed into the Audio-Visual Resources Branch (AVRB) – provided a base for innovative and socially committed filmmakers, notably Ivan Gaal. MIF, 'Ivan Gaal', Melbourne Independent Filmmakers, Bill Mousoulis (ed.) Innersense, Melbourne, March 2009, <http://www.innersense.com.au/mif/gaal.html>, accessed 20 February 2013.

[306] John Hughes & Open Channel, artists' subsidy of the arts, letter to Murray Brown (Cultural Activities Officer AFC) cc'd to John Cumming, IFAC, Melbourne, 3 June 1985.

[307] AFC, '1986 Documentary Fellowship Announced', media release, Australian Film Commission, 17 December 1985.

[308] ibid.

[309] Diana Plater, 'Documentaries find a new mentor – Aunty', *Sydney Morning Herald*, Monday 21 November 1988, p. 13.

[310] The Australian Bicentenary of 1988 marked the 200th anniversary of the arrival of the first fleet of convict ships at Sydney Cove (on 26 January 1788) and the beginning of the European colonisation of Australia.

[311] John Hughes, Peter Kennedy, Sylvia Lawson, David Malouf & Nancy Underhill, *The Stars Disordered*, Nancy Underhill (ed.), Brisbane, University Art Museum, University of Queensland, 1988.

[312] John Hughes, *All That is Solid*, interview conducted by John Cumming, Melbourne, 17 January 2002.

[313] ibid.

[314] ibid.

[315] Carole Sklan, 'Interview with John Hughes', in *The Stars Disordered*, Hughes et al., op. cit., pp. 12–13.

[316] Ron Banks, 'Film-maker's solid vision of the future', interview with John Hughes, *The West Australian*, 1989, p. 18.

[317] Marshall Berman, *All That is Solid Melts into Air: The Experience of Modernity*, 1st edn, Simon & Schuster, New York, 1982, p. 13.
Karl Marx & Friedrich Engels, 'The Communist Manifesto', in Robert C Tucker (ed.), *The Marx-Engels Reader*, Samuel Moore (trans.), 2nd edn, Norton, London, 1978, pp. 331–362.

[318] Berman, ibid., p. 88.

319 ibid., p. 89.
320 ibid., p. 31.
321 Jean Baudrillard, *For a critique of the political economy of the sign*, Charles Levin (trans.), St Louis, Missouri, Telos Press, 1981.
Félix Guattari, *Molecular revolution: psychiatry and politics*, Rosemary Sheed (trans.), Harmondsworth, Penguin, 1984.
Paul Virilio, *Speed and politics: an essay on dromology*, Mark Polizzotti (trans.), NY, Columbia UP, 1986.
322 Walter Benjamin, *Illuminations*, translated by Harry Zorn, Pimlico, London, 1999. Originally published Harcourt, 1968. Jonathan Cape, 1970, p. 249.
323 *Ruins of the Holland House Library, London, 1940* (photographer unknown) cited by Hughes in John Hughes et al., *The Stars Disordered*, op. cit., p. 10.
324 Sklan, op. cit.
325 John Slavin, 'The Hole in the Doughnut', *The Age Monthly Review*, May, 1989, p. 12.
326 ibid.
327 Hughes in Sklan, op. cit.
328 Hughes in Sklan, op. cit.
329 John Hughes, *All That is Solid*, interview conducted by John Cumming, Melbourne, 17 January 2002.
330 ibid.
331 Slavin, op. cit.
332 Martin, op. cit.
333 ibid.
334 Slavin, op. cit.
335 Adrian Martin, 'Collage and Montage in Contemporary Australian Experimental Film and Video, and its Origins', in Arthur McIntyre (ed.), *Contemporary Australian Collage*, Craftsman House, Roseville, 1990, p. 54. While Martin may have had something of the same complaint of *Traps*, he did acknowledge its 'scrutiny of the editing and doctoring process of film'.
336 Martin, 1998, op. cit.
337 Frank Stilwell, Obituary: Ted Wheelwright, 1921–2007, The University of Sydney News, 2007, <http://sydney.edu.au/news/84.html?newsstoryid=1868>, accessed 21 December 2013.
338 Jenny Hocking, *Lionel Murphy: A Political Biography*, Cambridge University Press, Oakleigh, Melbourne, 1997, p. 70.
339 Sitwell, op. cit.
340 ibid.
341 Martin, op. cit.
342 Hughes, op. cit.
343 Barrett Hodsdon, *Straight Roads and Crossed Lines: The Quest for Film Culture in Australia from the 1960s?* Bernt Porridge Group, Shelton Park, 2001, p. 28.
344 Gene Youngblood, 'Jean-Luc Godard: No Difference between Life and Cinema', in David Sterritt (ed.), *Jean-Luc Godard Interviews*, UP Mississippi, 1998, pp. 9–49. Originally published Los Angeles Free Press, 1968, p. 29.
345 Robert Bresson, *Notes on Cinematography*, translated by Jonathan Griffin, Urizen Books, New York, 1997. Originally published *Notes sur le cinématographe*, 1975.
346 Siegfried Kracauer, *Theory of film: the redemption of physical reality*, Oxford University Press, 1960, quoted in John Hughes, 'After Indonesia Calling', PhD exegesis, School of Media and Communication, College of Design and Social Context, RMIT University, Melbourne, November 2012, p. 206.
347 See, for example, the inter-titles at the beginning of *Man with a Movie Camera/Chelovek s kinoapparatom*, Dziga Vertov, 1929, 35 mm, b&w, 68 minutes, Kino International Corporation, USSR.

[348] Quoted in Youngblood, op. cit., p. 39.
[349] John Hughes, *All That is Solid*, interview conducted by John Cumming, Melbourne, 17 January 2002.
[350] See, for example, 'In the Forest of Symbols: Some Notes on Modernism in New York' in Berman, op. cit., pp. 287–248 and 'Unpacking My Library,' 'Hashish in Marseilles' and 'Thought Figures' in Walter Benjamin, *Selected Writings 1927–1934*, translated by Rodney Livingston et al., vol. 2, 2 vols, Harvard UP, Massachusetts, 1999, pp. 486–493, 673–379 and 723–727.
[351] Hughes in Sklan, op. cit., Adrian Martin, 'All That is Solid', *Filmnews*, August 1988, p. 8.
[352] Sarah Gibson sold *Born to Shop* (1991) to the ABC as a made-for-television version of her AFC-funded experimental documentary *In The Beginning There was Shopping* (1991). For a discussion on *Born to Shop* and *In The Beginning There was Shopping*, see Sarah Gibson, 'The Process of Innovation', in National Centre for Australian Studies (ed.), *The Big Picture: Documentary Filmmaking in Australia*. Papers from the 2nd Australian Documentary Conference, NCAS Monash University, Clayton, 1991, pp. 74–83.

After his fellowship project, *The Last Day's Work* (1987) Brian McKenzie went on, as Hughes would later do, to work as a television executive (commissioning editor at the ABC) before returning to filmmaking. McKenzie's life as an independent filmmaker parallels Hughes' in a number of ways. He has created a unique oeuvre of modest but extraordinarily powerful documentary films and, like Hughes, also ventured into dramatic feature filmmaking.
[353] Peter Hughes, 'The Documentary Project and Postmodernity', thesis (PhD), School of Arts and Media, La Trobe University, Bundoora, 1997, p. 150. See also Peter Hughes, 'Innovation or audience: the choice for documentary? An examination of the Australian Documentary Fellowship Scheme, 1984–1989', Screening the Past, no. 4, 1998, 15 September, <http://tlweb.latrobe.edu.au/humanities/screeningthepast/firstrelease/fir998/PHfr4.html>, accessed 16 August 2013.

ONE WAY STREET: FRAGMENTS FOR WALTER BENJAMIN (1992.)

CHAPTER 7:

One Way Street

Through a discussion of *One Way Street*, a film about the Jewish German philosopher Walter Benjamin (1892–1940), this chapter revisits the question of performance and explores the development of a unique audio-visual poetic dimension to John Hughes' films. In all his work, the creative dimension is inextricably linked to research.

My motivation in making work is to have the opportunity to study something to try to understand something.[355]

In the documentary films that follow *All That is Solid* (1988), John Hughes explores film-form along two parallel trajectories. Firstly, there will be a continued emphasis on performer-based theatrical mise-en-scène. Chapter 6 outlined the view that, while it raises intriguing possibilities, this approach can undermine the material function of the camera and of the human subject that are deployed so deftly in Hughes' early films. This approach also places enormous demands on the performer – professional actors and non-professionals alike. It is not until *What I Have Written* (1996, see Chapter 8) that Hughes will get to work with actors in a fully dramatic mode of production. The second trajectory, however, has its origins in Hughes' early work and particularly in the as yet unreleased *Some Aspects of Australian Racism* (1973, see Chapter 9). This approach leads towards more concentrated work on montage and screen design. In *One Way Street: Fragments for Walter Benjamin* (1992) a more communicative conceptual density is achieved through layering and collage within the frame.[356]

One Way Street is the first of Hughes' films that is truly international in its scope and appeal. Benjamin's writing has and continues to be an important reference point in Hughes' thinking. Quotes from Benjamin open *Film-Work* and *All That is Solid*.

FROM LEFT: A GRAPHIC SCREEN DESIGN; ENVIRONMENTAL SCULPTOR DANI KARAVAN IN *ONE WAY STREET* (1992).

While produced independently of broadcasters, this project marks Hughes' move into an effective relationship of what he calls 'critical collaboration' with the conventions of television, and in this case specifically, of the biopic.[357] The film incorporates dramatisations which are not quite formally resolved together with a realisation of the potential of digital editing technology as a tool for screen design that is truly groundbreaking.

With the approach of the fiftieth anniversary of Benjamin's death, Hughes contemplated a fitting tribute. At first he considered creating a live global experimental television event using satellite links and prerecorded material. This would have been a real innovation for Australian broadcasting, but it seems satellites could be arranged for sport but not for art or philosophy. In 1989 it became apparent that Peter Sainsbury (a producer from the UK, and at the time, Director of Film Development at the AFC) was keen to promote intellectually and artistically challenging work within mainstream forms of filmmaking. Hughes seized the opportunity and secured development finance for a television documentary about Benjamin. Taking to the research for this project with fervour, he read all of the available English language editions of Benjamin's work and publications by the English language scholars he wanted to interview for the film. By this time, Hughes had completed the undergraduate degree he had started decades earlier at La Trobe University and had taken up a lectureship in film and television in the Visual Arts Department at Monash University. He also enrolled in a Master of Arts degree by coursework at Monash and his work on Benjamin formed the basis of a thesis. A research tour in Europe and America became something of a pilgrimage for Hughes. While in Berlin and Paris he filmed around the addresses in which Benjamin had lived. In the cemetery of Portbou in Spain, where Benjamin had died while fleeing Nazism, Hughes found a crowd of people and media crews attending the launch of a major work by environmental sculptor Dani Karavan. Hughes' footage of this tribute is included in the final film. Upon returning to Melbourne, Hughes wrote up his research using his Hi-8 video recordings of the initial interviews.

Of the intricate negotiations to secure production finance for *One Way Street*, Hughes told Raffaele Caputo in 1993, 'The bureaucracy goes through its own transformations, and at any

FROM LEFT: ELIZABETH YOUNG-BRUEHL IN *ONE WAY STREET* (1992); WAYNE FEMERI, PAUL DAVIES AND JOHN HUGHES ON SET.

particular moment there are different regimes in play'.[358] When the Australian Film Commission (AFC) rejected his production proposal, saying they liked it but that it was 'not a priority', he embarked on 'a process of explaining' why it *was* a priority to release the film on the centenary of Benjamin's birth in 1992.[359] He arranged to meet with Sainsbury and project officer Gary Warner in their Sydney office and presented a systematic agenda for the meeting. According to Hughes, this meeting established the following: firstly, that the AFC would like to see the film made; and secondly, that from their point of view, a presale agreement with a television broadcaster was not necessary to secure funding from them. Hughes believes this strategy worked because, despite the fact that a television presale had effectively become a precondition for government financing of documentary films in Australia, Sainsbury and Warner felt strongly about the principle of the AFC's independence from television.

It was a tentative opening, but Hughes had pursued it and secured another window of opportunity for federal production finance independently of commercial arrangements. Ironically, ABC television executives later initiated a presale agreement for *One Way Street*. This came as a surprise to Hughes. He currently supposes that the AFC finance attracted the national broadcaster's offer. In any case, rather than having to seek his first sale to television, Hughes was in the much stronger position of having one sought from him.

It has been the case with many documentaries, and most of Hughes' projects, that aspects of research, scripting, filming and (to a lesser extent) editing often occur concurrently or as part of the same process. With production finance in place for the Benjamin film, Hughes repeated some of his research journey with sound recordist Gretchen Thornburn and Erika Addis, the leading cinematographer among Australian feminist filmmakers during the 1980s.[360] Addis used a professional Hi-8 video camera that Hughes hired from fellow documentary filmmaker Pat Fiske.[361] On the last day of filming in Paris, Hughes was hit by a motorcycle, which destroyed the camera and severely damaged his knee. He spent many days in hospital and some material for *One Way Street* had to be gathered remotely.[362]

PAUL DAVIES ON LOCATION WITH THE CREW OF *ONE WAY STREET*.

On Hughes' return to Melbourne, Paul Davies joined him as co-writer for the third time on stylised material for dramatic reconstruction scenes.[363] Hughes values the collaboration with Davies highly and says that ideas tend to emerge in a dialogue between them. An informal script was drawn from a computer database that Hughes had compiled with text and still images from the interviews and collages he had recorded during his research. The presentation of material from this database could be arranged in various ways and Hughes adapted it as a tool for a script editor and in scheduling the production.

For dramatised scenes in *One Way Street*, Nick Lathouris, Maggie Cameron, Mark Rogers and Louise Smith again made up the core performance ensemble. Together they developed a method of collaboration and a hybrid form of performance. Unlike *All That is Solid*, this was not a process-oriented project. For Hughes, the 'mode of performance' in *One Way Street* needed to be consistent with the particular stylisation and sensibility that Nicolette Freeman's cinematography brought to these scenes. Editor Uri Mizrahi, an Israeli Australian, helped Hughes to understand and articulate the Jewish aspects of Benjamin's experience.[364]

In a review of *One Way Street*, Humphrey McQueen noted the way Hughes 'jigsawed his screen with multiple comments and images', in tribute to the 'key device' of fragmentation and montage in Benjamin's writing. McQueen contrasted this 'political' choice with the conventional form of television biopics in which 'Ideas are reduced to their biographies. The lives of artists and philosophers are plundered for their gossip quota'.[365] In 2011 Hughes said:

I didn't want to go into making an entirely abstract work about the ideas of Benjamin. I thought it was 'fair enough' to try to write it into something that also had this biographical moment, but … how do you recess the wonderful romantic myth of the figure of Benjamin and bring the ideas to the foreground? Once you establish that question, you can then try and ask it each time a decision needs to be made about the work.[366]

MARK ROGERS AND LOUISE SMITH IN THE BERLIN SCENE OF *ONE WAY STREET* (1992).

Hughes believes *One Way Street* succeeds in deploying some of the strategies of the biopic form while displacing others. He sees the textual strategies in the film as draft ideas about the biopic genre and the conformity that tends to surround its use. The aim, he says, was 'to create a readable image but one that required an interpreting spectator'.[367] He was striving for a poetic rather than a literal quality and chose to create tableaus that were stark and allegorical rather than naturalistic. Cameron's performances include quotations, while some of Lathouris' scenes are distinctly constructivist, or 'serial' in form, with their bold, mechanical repetition of gesture. This style was carried through in studio sets that revealed their constructed quality. Hughes thinks, however, that he should have come up with a solution that did not involve costume because it introduces a naturalistic element that threatens the stylisation of all the other design and performance elements in the film.

The first quotation that Cameron presents, from the memoirs of Lisa Fittko, is about helping Benjamin escape from France. Hughes recalls directing Cameron to perform this as if entertaining a dinner party after a few drinks. Cameron also presents quotes from Benjamin's writing and, in a third mode of performance,

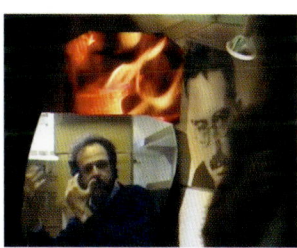

ABOVE TOP: *NEW GERMAN CRITIQUE* EDITOR ANSON RABINBACH IN A *ONE WAY STREET* SCREEN DESIGN; **ABOVE:** NICO LATHOURIS AND MAGGIE CAMERON IN A DRAMATISED SCENE OF *ONE WAY STREET*.

FROM LEFT: BENJAMIN ESCAPES GERMANY WITH PAUL KLEE'S *ANGELUS NOVUS*; MICHAEL JENNINGS, AUTHOR OF *DIALECTICAL IMAGES* IN *ONE WAY STREET* (1992).

plays a fictional acquaintance of Benjamin to present information and photographs from his personal life.

When I asked Hughes about the elegiac tone and emotional resonance of his film he described Benjamin's life as a very moving story and the insights of his work as very powerful. Hughes then moves directly to a discussion of the role of music in his films, explaining that he often gets 'foundational ideas' from music and saying 'ideas and choices about music are a very early part of the creative process for me'.[368] At the time *One Way Street* was conceived he was 'dedicated' to the work of Steve Reich. Later he found Laurie Anderson's song 'The Dream Before: Homage to Walter Benjamin'. Hughes used Reich's music for the sequence in the film that he finds the most moving: the sequence in which Lathouris, as Benjamin, cuts Klee's *Angelis Novus* from its frame and escapes from his apartment building. The Anderson song is used in the first and last scenes of the film. It includes the same passage about the *Angelis Novus* from Benjamin's 'Theses on the Philosophy of History' as Hughes used at the beginning of *All That is Solid*. These lyrics accompany the suicide scene that ends *One Way Street*.

One Way Street provoked substantial and thoughtful responses from a number of writers. Writing for *Photofile* in 1994, Adrian Martin sees the film as a 'nightmare project' because of the range of 'potentially cold and unforgiving' responses he anticipates it will get from audiences both familiar and unfamiliar with Benjamin.[369] He acknowledges the wisdom behind the 'mosaic construction' of the film but warns of the difficulty of the essay film genre that simultaneously attempts to be an act of art and criticism. Its 'self-conscious, routinely referential and analytical position' is distinguished from the 'innocence and discovery' of 'true, original works of experimental cinema' such as the 1920s avant-garde films that Hughes incorporates into *One Way Street*. Martin characterises the difference in the modes of creativity of Benjamin and Hughes as 'between those who make culture in a visionary or powerful way' and cultural workers 'who stand on the cusp between independent production and the academy'.[370] This is a delineation that can be lost in commentary that emphasises the Benjaminian qualities in Hughes' work.

FROM LEFT: SUSAN BUCK-MORSS; GRAPHIC QUOTATION IN *ONE WAY STREET* (1992).

Martin's review also revisits the question – first raised in reference to *All That is Solid* (1988, see Chapter 6) – of the discomfort he sees in Hughes' work with the purely personal.[371] While conceding that Hughes is right to avoid losing the political 'inside the ideological ruse of the personal', he thinks the film fails to evoke 'the grating poverty' of Benjamin's 'nomadic, freelance existence'.[372] Martin may be disconcerted by an affinity, implied by the film, between Benjamin and the modern-day academic commentators of the Benjamin industry who speak from a situation of very distinct material and social conditions. McQueen saw in this a trend to incorporate Benjamin 'into the academic world he never managed to join in life'.[373] Martin, however, notes a 'somewhat distanced and questioning manner' in the interview sequences, where each subject is 'posed strictly within their official academic role'.[374] This distance is often achieved – consciously or otherwise – in the framing that Hughes tends to employ when interviewing experts. Typically, this is a medium shot, usually taken in an office or workplace, and often from what appears to be a slightly elevated camera position. This set up is used for several of the interviews in *One Way Street*.

The contemporary interviews in *One Way Street* are free of obvious contrivance – unlike the dramatised scenes in this film or the interview scenes in *All That is Solid* (see Chapter 6). Martin describes the interview with Susan Buck-Morss as offering 'one of the most arresting moments of the film'.[375] Ross Gibson, who worked as script editor on *One Way Street*, saw a 'gratifying sense of domesticity' and a 'downhome love of Benjamin's ideas' in these scenes.[376] Anna Dzenis wrote in *Metro Magazine* of the enthusiasm conveyed by the interviewees, while Jane Freeman writing in the *Melbourne Times* described the academics in the film as 'one of its greatest strengths' and as radiating 'an engagement with Benjamin that is emotional and personal'.[377] She attributes this to the time Hughes and his subjects took over the interviews. As Gibson explains, Elizabeth Young-Bruehl's 'slow burn intelligence is allowed to find its rhythm, a rhythm which one rarely sees on television and which for that very reason is quite compelling'.[378]

One Way Street creates a tangible sense of the threat and calamity of Nazism. This is achieved through text and montage that is kept in good balance, never overwhelming the film itself or becoming overstated or clichéd. The human disaster resonates as if from the periphery of the film's focus – one fragile life and a whole culture of sensibility and intellect that Nazism threatens to smother. The film conveys both the material and the spiritual dimensions of this terrible resonance.

One Way Street premiered theatrically in Melbourne alongside *Thread of Voice* (1993), a new film by the stoically experimental sound poetry performance collective Arf-Arf.[379] Hughes' video was later included in the national tour of a major collaborative art gallery exhibition and lecture series *What John Berger Saw*, dedicated to the ideas of the art historian and writer.[380] This film can be seen as a transitional work in Hughes' relationship with the 'market'. It was initially financed independently of television, but engaged articulately with the conventions and possibilities of the technology and visual language of contemporary television.

In a paper for the 1993 Film and History Conference, historian Tony Barta describes Ross Gibson's *Camera Natura* (1985, 32 minutes), David Perry's *The Refracting Glasses* (1993, 109 minutes) and Hughes' *One Way Street* as 'path breaking and original'.[381] He describes these 16 mm films as having a 'truly cinematic treatment of the associative process' that is 'closer to the rhetoric of the poem, the instant of an image, than it is to an essay.' *One Way Street* was also well received on the film and media-art festival circuit. I first saw the film at Experimenta, a festival of experimental video/computer art in Melbourne, in 1993. It seemed ironic that this television documentary (albeit an unusually innovative one) employed video editing with more imagination and experimental flair than any of the 'cutting edge' video art at that event.[382] In the article, 'Life as a Project of Montage,' Gibson provides a historical context and an interpretation of Benjamin's work. Gibson sees the film as 'an enactment of a *way of being engaged with the world*' that is 'attuned to the way Benjamin chose to be both immersed in

JOHN HUGHES AND CINEMATOGRAPHER NICOLETTE FREEMAN SET UP A SHOT WITH A 16 MM FILM CAMERA.

PHOTO COLLAGE IN *ONE WAY STREET* (1992).

and detached from the world of experience that he was anatomising' – a description that sheds light on Hughes's adoption of Erwin Kisch's 'impersonal screen'.[383] Other phrases from Gibson's piece might also be applied to a description of John Hughes' wider body of work. He described Benjamin's life as 'a project of montage, a methodical, continuous experiment of conjunction' in which 'images, ideas, texts, traditions and procedures' were 'jammed together'.

Like Stan Hughes' 1956 shop window displays, all independent filmmaking up until the 1980s could be seen as straddling private experience and public discourse. Indeed, much independent artistic practice within the history of European Australia has had some of this element of the amateur about it. Such practice depends upon a degree of volunteerism and personal commitment that was not essential to work undertaken in an institutional or commercial context.

Independent filmmaking in the 1990s existed for the most part in the cultural domains of either mainstream state-owned television, in visual art oriented 'new media' production or in the marginal practices of self-funding artists. There were some isolated windows of opportunity to work between these spheres but federal funding for filmmaking was increasingly tied to 'market' demand through commercial devices such as the television presale. While the market participants were most often agencies of government, such as the ABC or SBS television stations, this further subsidy was expressed in the terms of a commercial arrangement. Most documentary producers were now largely dependent on the patronage of television. With typical acumen, however, Hughes continued to find niches of opportunity for public investment in his modestly budgeted projects without editorial input or interference by broadcasters or other commercial interests. Through an AFC scheme for first-time feature directors, he became one of a handful of filmmakers to produce a feature film wholly financed by that funding body, with *What I Have Written*.

Following the shift of federal film funding responsibilities to the Australian Film Commission (AFC) in the late 1970s, producers led by John Cruthers, together with AFC Creative Development Branch (CDB) staff led by Vicki Molloy, had sought in vain to extend the scope of CDB-style funding to include feature films. For all the activity and energy around independent film in the 1980s, however, the opportunity for the feature film equivalent of Grace and Addis' *Serious Undertakings* (1982) had not eventuated.[386] In 1990s Australia, promising, emerging filmmakers were no longer being programmatically supported through a gamut of production experience as Hughes and many of his peers had been throughout the preceding two decades. With budgets now in the hundreds of thousands of dollars each, the AFC and state film corporations were funding a small number of short films at professional standard. There was no significant market for them.

It soon became apparent that for the price of a handful of short films, a one-million-dollar feature film could be made and launched into the general market. With the backing of the AFC's Peter Sainsbury, a number of unconventional, low-budget feature films began to emerge. Ross Gibson's *Dead to the World* (1991) and Susan Dermody's *Breathing Under Water* (1992) were both directed by filmmakers who had made innovative short films and, as writers and academics, had been active in independent film culture for many years.[387] Tracey Moffatt's *beDevil* (1993) retained the short film format within a feature film presentation and explored a range of narrative modes and visual styles.[388] With *What I Have Written,* Hughes joined this stable of first-time narrative feature filmmakers.

In 1992 Hughes read, and was captivated by, a short story in the literary journal *Scripsi*. The story formed a novella within John Scott's novel *What I Have Written*.[389] Hughes and Scott have had a long association. They shared a house as teenagers and Scott had created the soundtrack used in the first *November Eleven* (see Chapter 3). The same year he dedicated a poem, and in 2001 a book, to Hughes.[390] Hughes commissioned Scott to write a screenplay adaptation of his novel. It was with this screenplay that Hughes secured development finance from the AFC for the film *What I Have Written*.

The novella contained within *What I Have Written* is the work of one of Scott's fictional characters, a jealous and obsessive academic in a university visual arts department. Hughes believes his experience at the time he read the novel, lecturing in the Visual Arts Department at Monash University, triggered his understanding and engagement with the book and led him to make it into a film. While he found aspects of that particular institutional environment 'vivid and engaging,' he also saw in academic life 'a kind of darkness' in the potential for office politics to get mixed up with scholarly and ideological differences.[391]

Scott's novel is in three parts, each representing the point of view of one of the central characters. The first is the novella ascribed to writer and academic Christopher Houghton. It chronicles the demise of his love for his wife, Sorel, while on sabbatical in France. It also details the erotic correspondence he receives from Frances, a woman they met in Paris. The second is Sorel's account. Sometime after their return from France, Christopher has a stroke and goes into a coma. Later, Jeremy, Christopher's best friend and colleague, presents Sorel with the novella.

what I have written

CHAPTER 8:

What I Have Written

WHAT I HAVE WRITTEN.

John Hughes has described the role of the central character in his dramatic feature film *What I Have Written* (1995) in strictly formal terms. She plays the part of a detective – and the film 'is about texts and their readings, and their unknowability'.[384] Reading this, I wondered at the gap between my experience of the film and the director's account of it. Was Hughes unaware of his film's emotional dimensions? Or was he simply being disingenuous?

One genre that proponents of independent screen culture have long sought to establish is the low-budget experimental feature. This would augment and draw upon other innovative non-feature practices of independent film and video. Precedents include Giorgio Mangiamele's *Clay* (1965), Deling's *Dalmas* (1973, see Chapter 1) and Dave Jones' *Yackety Yack* (1974).[385] These last two films, rather than seeking to override the viewer's critical faculties through the efficacy of their narrative drive, had sought to engage their audience in a dialectic about the conventions of traditional feature filmmaking.

The 1990s saw a brief return to experimental narrative feature filmmaking in Australia with a clutch of films, including John Hughes' *What I Have Written,* a film that in more subtle ways marries formal and thematic concerns. For this film Hughes got to work with actors – still at times in a stylised mode of representation – but within the broadly realist context of the dramatic feature.

2000, originally published as conference papers in 1999, p. 190.

[381] Tony Barta, 'Making it Strange: Camera Natura, One Way Street and The Refracting Glasses as Realism, Surrealism and the Poetics of History in Film', in John Benson, Ken Berryman & Wayne Levy (eds), *Screening the Past: The Sixth Australian History and Film Conference Papers*, Melbourne, La Trobe University, 1993, pp. 205–210.

[382] John Cumming, 'Perplexities: Experimenta 1992', *Artlink*, vol. 13, no. 1, March–May 1993, pp. 61–62.

[383] Gibson, op. cit., p. 18. Peter Hughes adopted this phrase the following year as a title for the most thorough study yet to be published of Hughes' oeuvre. Peter Hughes, 'A way of being engaged with the world: the films of John Hughes', *Metro*, no. 93, Autumn 1993, pp. 46–55.

Endnotes

[355] John Hughes, 'Back Story Update with John Hughes', recording by John Cumming of interview conducted by Amanda Kerley & William Head, *Generation Next* Documentary Conference, Open Channel & Cinema Nova, Carlton, Australia, 13 October 2011.
[356] John Hughes, *One Way Street: Fragments for Walter Benjamin*, 1992, 16 mm, colour, 58 minutes, Melbourne, Producer John Hughes, Scriptwriters Paul Davies & John Hughes, Camera Nicolette Freeman, Erika Addis, Editor Uri Mizrahi. Featuring Nick Lathouris, Maggie Cameron, Mark Rogers, Louise Smith. Produced with assistance from the AFC & ABC. Distributed by Artfilms.
[357] Peter Hughes, '*After Mabo*', in Geoff Mayer and Keith Beattie (ed.), *The Cinema of Australia and New Zealand*, 24 Frames, Wallflower Press, London, 2007, p. 178.
[358] Raffaele Caputo & John Hughes, 'John Hughes interviewed by Raffaele Caputo', *Cinema Papers*, October 1993, pp. 35–37.
[359] ibid.
[360] Addis photographed and produced *Serious Undertakings* (see Chapter 5).
[361] Hi-8 is a miniature videotape format that in the early 1990s came to occupy a similar status in relation to fully professional broadcast formats as Super-8 had occupied in relation to 16 mm film during the early 1980s.
[362] A local cameraperson in Riga recorded an interview with the daughter of Benjamin's lover, Asja Lacis, using a list of questions that Hughes sent by fax. John Welshman, an art historian and Monash colleague, interviewed Benjaminist Valery Podorogawho in Russia. John Hughes, *One Way Street*, interview conducted by John Cumming, Melbourne, 15 March 2002.
[363] Davies also co-wrote *Traps* and *All That is Solid*.
[364] John Hughes, *One Way Street*, interview conducted by John Cumming, Melbourne, 15 March 2002.
[365] Humphrey McQueen, 'Walter Benjamin: a life in scraps, quotes & fragments', ABC Radio 24 Hours magazine, 1992, p. 50.
[366] John Hughes, *Back Story Update*, op. cit.
[367] Hughes, *One Way Street*, interview, op. cit.
[368] ibid.
[369] Adrian Martin, 'Poetic Politics: A Response to John Hughes' One Way Street', *Photofile*, vol. 43, November 1994, pp. 24–26.
[370] ibid., p. 26.
[371] John Hughes, *All That is Solid*, 1988, 16 mm/Hi-8 video, colour, 54 minutes, Melbourne, Producer John Hughes, Scriptwriters Paul M Davies, Chris Barnett, John Hughes.
[372] Martin, op. cit.
[373] McQueen, op. cit.
[374] Martin, op. cit.
[375] ibid.
[376] Ross Gibson, 'Life as a Project of Montage', *Filmnews*, November 1992, pp. 17–18.
[377] Jane Freeman, 'Subversion – TV gets serious', *Melbourne Times*, 2 December 1992. Anna Dzenis, 'One Way Street: Fragments for Walter Benjamin', *Cinema Papers*, October 1993, pp. 33–35.
[378] Gibson, op. cit.
[379] Arf-Arf (Marcus Bergner, Michael Buckley, Frank Lovece, Marisa Stirpe), *Thread of Voice*, 1993, 16 mm, colour, 20 minutes, Melbourne, Associate Producer Marie Craven, Line Producer Roslyn Walker, Camera Robin Plunkett, Sound Ray Boseley & Leesa Marie Spencer. Produced with assistance from the Australian Film Commission.
[380] Nikos Papastergiadis (ed.), *What John Berger Saw*, ANU Canberra School of Art Gallery, Canberra,

FROM TOP: JACEK KOMAN AS JEREMY; MEMORY OR FANTASY IN *WHAT I HAVE WRITTEN* (1995); THE FINAL SCRIPT WITH HUGHES' VISUAL ICONS FOR EACH SCENE.

The third section is Jeremy's account of his love for Sorel, his encouragement of Christopher's infidelity and his invention of the novella in Christopher's name.

Scott's screen adaptation is close to his original novel in most respects. While in the book there is no way for Sorel to know the real author of 'Christopher's novella', in the screenplay this is possible and she makes an active intervention, conducting a thorough investigation that eventually reveals Jeremy's jealousy and deceit. Hughes explained to Paul Kalina that Scott created 'dense and intelligent structures' in the screen adaptation, intercutting the three sections of the novel.[392] While Scott provided both the narrative structure of the film and the ideas and themes that permeate it, Hughes was responsible for the conception and management of the film's formal and visual style. He describes his work on the screenplay as that of 'designer'.[393] Hughes wanted to create a different mode of representation for each of the three narrative accounts in *What I Have Written*.

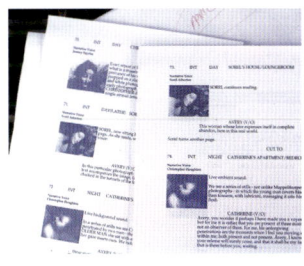

KOMAN ON JEREMY'S COUCH IN *WHAT I HAVE WRITTEN* (1995).

Building on his work with images in the scripting of *One Way Street* (1992, see Chapter 7), he created small graphic icons to indicate, on every page of the treatment, the visual world of each scene.

Through the affinity between Scott and Hughes, *What I Have Written* reflects many of the recurring elements of Hughes' documentary films. The university setting is familiar to both men, but there is a deeper thematic and formal correlation. A concern with representation (and differing modes of representation) is central to Scott's novel and all Hughes' work. There is a Brechtian quality to the reworking and retelling of a history in the story. The text within the text, a trope familiar in Hughes' films, is present in the novel in the form of the novella. The manipulation of information to serve a personal cause in Scott's book parallels the creative and critical concern with political propaganda in Hughes' work. Rivalry between friends and peers is a propelling dynamic in the drama of the novel, as it was in *Traps* (1985, see Chapter 5). Likewise, research is the driving action of the protagonists (Sorel and Judith) in both stories, and is a core activity for Hughes in his work and in his brief self-portrayal in *Is It Working?* (1985, see Chapter 4).

MARTIN JACOBS AS CHRISTOPHER, AND JACEK KOMAN AS JEREMY IN A PUBLICITY STILL FOR *WHAT I HAVE WRITTEN* (1995).

The characters in Scott's novel are also typical for a John Hughes' film. Jeremy and Christopher are academics and writers. Intellectuals are dominant in Hughes' films but there is usually an artist present too. In *What I Have Written*, Sorel, with her singing and her practical love, represents difference itself in a world dominated by academic mystification and the fantasies and delusions of men. Hughes' documentary films have included a range of portrayals of artists at work: Hansen in *Cybernetic Synergy*, Gwenda in *Traps*, Maggie Cameron in *All That is Solid* and Dani Karavan in *One Way Street*. They provide insights and responses that are distinct from those of the journalists, public intellectuals, eminent scholars and curators that the films focus on. In *What I Have Written*, Christopher, the character that the narrative revolves around, is both artist and academic. As the absent author, he occupies a position similar to the one Hughes had leant towards in his documentary filmmaking up to this time.

In response to Scott's scene breakdown, and Hughes' innovative treatment presentation, Peter Sainsbury, at the AFC, arranged development finance for *What I Have Written*. This enabled Hughes to hire script editor Annette Blonski to work with Scott on the full screenplay. After Sainsbury left the AFC, he became, at Hughes' invitation, co-producer of the project. Sainsbury

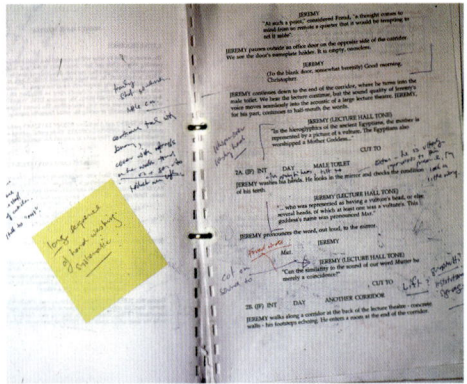 

FROM LEFT: MARKED-UP PRODUCTION SCRIPT; CINEMATOGRAPHER DION BEEBE SHOOTING TEST FOOTAGE WITH A SUPER-8 FILM CAMERA FOR *WHAT I HAVE WRITTEN*.

had a long list of producing credits in the UK, notably as executive producer of *Radio On* (1979), Christopher Petit's definitive independent road movie of the late seventies.[394] Together, they were able to secure production finance entirely from the AFC. The film was financed after Sainsbury's tenure at the film commission, but the precedent he set there of supporting innovative feature projects is likely to have played a part in opening opportunities for projects such as *What I Have Written*.

Hughes believes that there are more similarities than differences between documentary production and narrative feature filmmaking. While the A$1.5 million budget was very low for a feature film, Hughes had more and better resources than for any previous project. Priority was given to a four-week preparation period with the cast. Hughes learnt a great deal from the actors during this work. He described the process of 'workshops rather than limited and instrumentally designed rehearsals' as an outstanding feature of the project.[395]

Hughes says his reference points from the outset were Chris Marker's *La Jetee* (1962), Bill Henson's photographs, Nicolas Roeg's *Bad Timing* (1980) and Todd Haynes' *Poison* (1991). Hughes explains that *La Jetee*:

[…] proposes a very complex set of ideas about memory and the image, the recovery of memory and the past and the future, in which the meaning of moments recalled is in a constant state of transition … an indeterminacy, present and non-present characters becoming quite different people.[396]

When he heard that Sarah Stollman, the production designer of *Poison* was living in Melbourne, Hughes promptly recruited her to work alongside local cinematographer Dion Beebe on the visual design of the film. In 2002 Stollman described the process of working on the film with Hughes and Beebe as one of 'making a piece of art' and said that *What I Have Written* was 'probably the most satisfying film I have designed, on that level. … I was so involved in every layer and the concepts

GILLIAN JONES IN *WHAT I HAVE WRITTEN* (1995).

were so strong intellectually.'[397] Hughes wanted to combine the effect of the monochrome still images that make up *La Jetee* with the compositional quality and subtle tonal treatment of Bill Henson's photographs. This effect, 'on a cusp of black-and-white and colour, or a cusp of the image stilled and the image moving,' was to be used for the novella sequences in *What I Have Written*. For the scenes in which Sorel investigates the mystery of the novella, Hughes had in mind a look of documentary realism and for Jeremy's scenes, 'a more saturated, almost surreal' visual quality.[398] Initially, he had imagined creating these effects by shooting black-and-white stills, low-band videotape and 16 mm film on a very low budget. Finally, however, the three distinct treatments of the image were all achieved by using colour 16 mm film shot in the Super-16 format for enlargement to 35 mm theatrical prints. Hughes and Beebe worked with laboratory optical supervisor Ian Sheath to achieve the different quality of image by way of laboratory printing processes using both colour and monochrome 35 mm printing stocks.[399]

In 1996, *What I Have Written* won an award for best film at Mystfest in Italy and was nominated for a Golden Bear Award at the Berlin International Film Festival and a Bronze Horse Award at the Stockholm International Film Festival. Because it is a feature film that achieved a commercial cinema release, *What I Have Written* received more press coverage than all of Hughes' documentary films combined. Much of this coverage, however, is in the form of short newspaper reviews. As with the documentary work, only a small number of substantial critical pieces about this film have been published. Lesley Stern's response to *What I Have Written*, in *Cinema Papers*, provides the most evocative description of the film and the play of image and meaning within it. She describes the way shifts of colour create a sense of movement in the still image sequences

WHAT I HAVE WRITTEN (1995).

as the story 'enmeshes the imaginary and the real'. Stern was unimpressed with Scott's novel and found some of its portentousness seeping into the language in the film. She felt that Scott, Hughes and Blonski, however, had transformed the material for the film. Drawing on an idea of French philosopher, Gilles Deleuze, she concludes:

I was absorbed – in a way I find very rare in Australian cinema – by the thought of cinema, by being caught up in the act of cinema thinking. When Deleuze uses this phrase, he is indicating not a particular kind of cerebral cinema, but a propensity for the cinema to enact, in the way that no other medium can, certain ways of conceptualizing and apprehending the world. It is not that philosophy illuminates the cinema, but that the cinema philosophises. At its most exciting, the cinema can generate new relationships that turn upside down all our predictable ways of conceiving time and presence. It does this not through representing ideas, but through an enactment, through apprehending the senses, through the matter of cinema. What I Have Written *does this sensationally through conjuring, out of thin air, something that matters.*[400]

At the outset of her *Metro Magazine* review of *What I Have Written*, Anna Dzenis takes up Hughes' interest in issues of representation. From within this schema she extracts an interpretation that is at once analytic and personal. She writes of the novella sequence, which is composed of expressionistic still images depicting the 'disintegration of the couple – separated in frames' amid Gothic architecture:

The heart of the film lies in this evocation, these spaces, spaces of uncertainty, spaces between images and their resonance, words and their narration, a work of art and its reading, people and their fantasies, their quest for passionate love and connection. The poignancy and tragedy comes when we realise that the wildest fantasies were, in the end, no one's possibility – never to be a reality in this or anyone's world. It is this fact of disconnection, this deep sense of impossibility, that the film makes one feel profoundly.[401]

ANGIE MILIKEN AS SOREL, AND JACEK KOMAN AS JEREMY IN *WHAT I HAVE WRITTEN* (1995).

Presented with this closing passage from Dzenis' piece, Hughes said, she 'very accurately goes to the central question of the film'. He also noted that Dzenis does this 'from the point of view of someone who is feeling the loss that is available in a real embodied encounter with what criticism calls indeterminacy'.[402]

Both Dzenis and Stern's pieces are significant in the body of critical writing surrounding Hughes' work up to this time because they suggest that, in *What I Have Written,* Hughes achieves a lucid poetic quality. Beyond the 'didactic centre,' Dzenis writes, 'what is most compelling is not what is told or shown but what one is allowed to feel and experience'. As I have argued in previous chapters, in Hughes' earlier films, attempts at such poetics through dramatisation sometimes lack energy and veracity. The emotional and the personal also often seem to be proscribed from or didactically co-opted within the documentary and essay-style work. In *What I Have Written,* Hughes explores the construction of emotionally resonant sequences and threads in a much more concentrated way. The film brings into relief the 'fact of disconnection' that for Dzenis is an emotional discovery. Hughes, however, prefers to discuss this disconnection as an intellectual concept – 'indeterminacy' – upon which theoretical authority – 'criticism' – can be brought to bear.

MILIKEN AND HUGHES PREPARE A SCENE FOR *WHAT I HAVE WRITTEN*.

There is no attempt by Hughes to impose a Brechtian style of performance on the screen with *What I Have Written*. Like Scott's script, the actors' performances are largely naturalistic. The mannered style that Jacek Koman applies to the deceitful Jeremy appears to stem from the actor's work of inhabiting the character rather than from the application of a formal device.

In *What I Have Written*, Sorel is at the emotional and moral centre of the story. The other characters project their failings and wants onto her. With Scott's script, actor Angie Miliken, whose performance is the most naturalistic in style, clearly conveys the unpretentious equanimity of this character. Sorel is neither selfless nor dependent. For her, love is an ethical matter rather than a narcissistic pursuit. She is not a victim; rather, she presents a profoundly optimistic perspective as she negotiates and researches the basis of her faith in her partner. In the presence of her comatose husband, unable to ascertain the extent of his apparent infidelity, she wrestles with conflicting impulses of anger, forgiveness and remorse.

As Scott, Hughes and Miliken construct, direct and perform it, Sorel's private quest is not to fulfil an impossible fantasy, close an existential gap in her being or establish a passionate intensity in her most intimate relationship. Her concern is for rectitude of sentiment. She wants to know how she should feel and what she should think. Sorel's quest is for emotional justice – within herself, for her and her partner. When interviewing Hughes for *Cinema Papers*, Paul Kalina sets out to discuss the film in the terms of conventional film criticism most familiar to mainstream filmmakers. He attempts to engage Hughes in a discussion of the psychology of the characters as if they were real people. In his responses, however, Hughes moves immediately to the question of representation. In doing so, he is attempting to draw attention to the central concerns of the film and to subvert the critical paradigm, but his response can also be read as resisting engagement with the personal dimension of the story's characters. As Adrian Martin observed, this response is 'somewhat dry'.[403] When I asked Hughes about the seemingly disingenuous response to Paul Kalina's questions about the central character, he refers to my description of Sorel's 'journey' as evidence of a realist dimension to the work that evokes this kind of engagement with the film:

The work of the director is precisely to evoke this dimension and make it available to the spectator: in performance, in action, in camera framing, in moves, in art direction, in cutting and so on. I've just wanted to talk about other, different things; it doesn't mean I'm not attentive to these issues of the emotional dimensions of the film. The film could not be made without insights and positions on these questions, of course.[404]

While Hughes has little interest in discussing the interpersonal dynamics and psychology of his fictional characters, he is interested in generating discourse about their representational effect. In the context of a culture for the production and reception of dramatic feature films in which the psychology of individual characters is absolutely privileged and endlessly dissected or recited, such resistance and intervention from a director ought, perhaps, be a welcome provocation.

Hughes' return to employment in tertiary education in the early 1990s was brief. With a feature film in production, he left Monash University at the end of his first contract there. Inspired by the experience of making *What I Have Written*, Hughes spent 1996 trying to gain funding for other stories by John Scott. These were also unconventional projects that would be difficult to finance. The budget for *What I Have Written* had provided Hughes with a modest income during development and production of that film. He had to borrow money in order to develop the new projects. Hughes did this by taking out a producer's loan from the state funding body Film Victoria. This loan would have to be repaid from the budget of future projects and Hughes decided to limit such debt to one year of speculative work on dramatic feature film concepts. Before that year was over, however, he was swept up in a new documentary project and in a significant turn of political events.

Endnotes

[384] Paul Kalina, '*What I Have Written*', *Cinema Papers*, February 1996, pp. 8–10.
[385] Bert Deling, *Dalmas*, 1973, 16 mm, colour, 103 minutes, Apogee Films, Melbourne.
Dave Jones, Yackety Yack, 1974, 16 mm, b&w, 86 minutes, Melbourne.
[386] Helen Grace, *Serious Undertakings*, 1982, 16 mm, colour and b&w, 28 minutes, Ronin Films, Producer

Erika Addis, Sydney.

[387] Ross Gibson, *Dead to the World*, 1991, 35 mm, colour, Huzzah Productions, Producer John Cruthers, Australia.

Susan Dermody, *Breathing Under Water*, 1992, 78 minutes, Periscope Productions, Sydney.

[388] Tracey Moffatt, *beDevil*, 1993, 35 mm, colour, Sydney, Producer Tracey Moffatt. Produced with assistance from the AFC.

[389] John A Scott, *What I Have Written*, McPhee Gribble, Ringwood, 1993.

[390] John Scott, 'The Celebration (11 September 1973)', *From the Flooded City*, Makar Press, Brisbane, 1981, p. 19.

John Scott, *The Architect*, Penguin, Ringwood, 2001.

[391] John Hughes, *What I Have Written* and *After Mabo*, interview conducted by John Cumming, Melbourne, 3 July 2002.

[392] Kalina, op. cit., p. 9.

[393] Hughes, op. cit.

[394] Christopher Petit, *Radio On*, 1979, colour, Bristol, Producer Keith Griffiths, Executive Producer Renée Gundelach & Peter Sainsbury. Featuring David Beames, Lisa Kreuzer, Sandy Ratcliff, Andrew Byatt, Sue Jones-Davies. Produced with assistance from the BFI.

Sainsbury was a founder of The Other Cinema, which distributed films including Godard's *British Sounds* (1969) in England. He was also a former BFI executive and co-producer of Peter Greenaway's *A Zed & Two Noughts* (1986), 35 mm, colour, 115 minutes, Producers Kees Kasander and Peter Sainsbury, UK, distributed by Artificial Eye, BFI, Umbrella. See Sylvia Harvey, 'The Other Cinema – a History, 1970–77', *Screen*, vol. 26, no. 6, November–December 1985, pp. 40–57.

[395] Kalina, op. cit., p. 10.

[396] ibid., p. 10. Lesley Stern has also made a comparison in similar terms with *Last Year at Marienbad* (Alain Resnais, 1961) but Hughes says there was no conscious reference to the Resnais film. Lesley Stern, 'Severed Intensities: Conjuring John Hughes' What I Have Written', *Cinema Papers*, February 1996, pp. 12–13. Hughes, op. cit.

[397] Mandi Bialek-Wester, 'Interview with Sarah Stollman', *Senses of Cinema*, no. 23, 2002, November–December, <http://sensesofcinema.com/2002/23/stollman/>, accessed 23 February 2013.

[398] John Hughes, Dion Beebe, Ian Sheath & Dominic Case, 'The Film of the Book', *Cinema Papers*, February 1996, pp. 27–28.

[399] ibid.

[400] Stern, op. cit., p. 13.

[401] Anna Dzenis, 'John Hughes' What I Have Written', *Metro*, no. 107, 1996, p. 24.

[402] John Hughes, *What I Have Written* and *After Mabo*, interview conducted by John Cumming, Melbourne, 3 July 2002.

[403] Adrian Martin, '*The Confessional*, *What I Have Written* and the "Art Film"', *The Week In Film,* ABC Radio National, 13 July 1996.

[404] John Hughes, email to John Cumming, Melbourne, 23 February 2010.

A SCENE FROM *AFTER MABO* (1997) INCORPORATING IMAGES FROM *SOME ASPECTS OF AUSTRALIAN RACISM* (1973).

CHAPTER 9:

Some Aspects of Australian Racism

Contemporary Australia is a post-colonial nation divided – by all objective measures – along cultural and racial lines. It is one of the richest countries on Earth and yet many of its Aboriginal and Torres Strait Islander citizens live in Third World conditions. Both Indigenous and non-Indigenous independent filmmakers have traced this social terrain, sometimes collaboratively. John Hughes' contribution to this body of work spans four decades and begins with *Some Aspects of Australian Racism* (1973).[405] Following some advice he received from the prominent young Aboriginal activist Gary Foley while devising that film, Hughes' focus in these projects has primarily been upon the perceptions and representational practices of non-Indigenous culture. *Moments Like These* (1989) traces the representation of Indigenous people in Australian cinema. *After Mabo* (1997) examines a national struggle over Indigenous land rights and functioned as a partisan work of advocacy at a critical historic moment in that struggle. *River of Dreams* (1998) shows how the imperatives of large-scale commercial investment overwhelm consideration for culture and environment.

With each generation of aspiring filmmakers there are some from non-Indigenous backgrounds who hit upon the idea of making a film that addresses the situation of Aboriginal and Torres Strait Islander people. The impulse here is often complex. An awareness of the apparent social issues

FROM LEFT: A SHOT FROM ALESSANDRO CAVADINI'S *NINGALA A-NA* (1972) IN *AFTER MABO* (1997); *SOME ASPECTS OF AUSTRALIAN RACISM* (1973).

can emerge almost simultaneously with an interest in documentary filmmaking. Also, in this divided society, such a project can be imagined as a bridge – a means to learn about an 'other' from whom these young filmmakers' lives have often been largely if not completely segregated. Meanwhile, the commercial media generally avoid, trivialise, dehumanise and sensationalise Indigenous issues. This has the dual effect of engendering 'white' ignorance and missionary zeal – two things Aboriginal and Torres Strait Islander communities are well-practised at having to deal with. These films 'about' Indigenous people rarely get off the ground. When John Hughes embarked on such a project in his early twenties he acquired some exposure to Indigenous perspectives, but he admits to having some element of the naiveté characterised here.

What distinguished Hughes' approach in the early 1970s is that he sought the advice of Aboriginal activists. Then, rather than feeling rebuffed by the response he received, he listened, adjusted his perspective and persisted in finding a way to work through the issues that arose. A film was made which did quite effectively navigate the pitfalls inherent in such an exercise. Yet Hughes shelved it in a polemic gesture that now appears less potent than the film itself. Hughes has maintained and developed the ethic that he established in this early stage of his filmmaking through a number of films that deal with the colonial legacy of contemporary Australia.

Early in 1966 the Conciliation and Arbitration Commission spared the British Vesteys company the expense of a 1965 equal wages claim by Gurindji stockmen and house servants at their remote Wave Hill cattle station in the Northern Territory. An extended strike ensued and with support from non-Indigenous people, including trade unionists and author Frank Hardy (see Chapter 4), became a national campaign for land rights with marches in the south led by activists including Gary Foley. This campaign led to prime minister Gough Whitlam transferring leasehold title to Gurindji spokesman Vincent Lingiari in a historic ceremony at Daguragu (Wattie Creek, see Chapter 11) in 1975 and to the Aboriginal Land Rights Act (Northern Territory) of 1976.[406]

Hughes says that he first met Aboriginal people and became interested in their struggle as a child on a church youth group bus tour to Alice Springs. He also recalls hearing speeches as a teenager

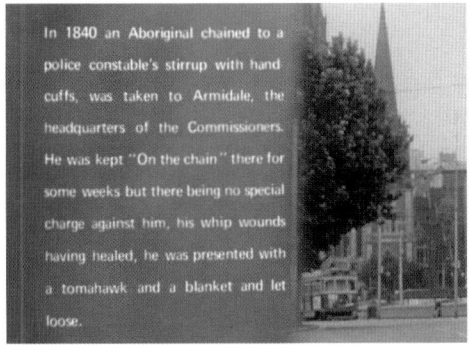 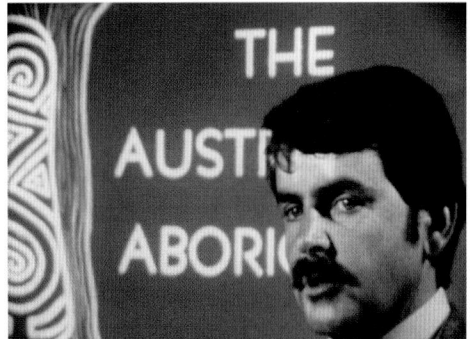

FROM LEFT: A WALL IN THE LEFT FOREGROUND PROVIDES A NEUTRAL BACKGROUND THAT ANTICIPATES THE PLACEMENT OF GRAPHIC TEXT IN THE SCREEN DESIGN OF *SOME ASPECTS OF AUSTRALIAN RACISM*; WALTER McVITTY IN *SOME ASPECTS OF AUSTRALIAN RACISM* (1973).

at Emerald Hill about Aboriginal advancement and the Gurindji Wave Hill dispute. A few years later, in the early 1970s, Hughes read some of CD Rowley's study of the impact of colonisation on Aboriginal societies.[407] Inspired to make 'a film concerning urban Aboriginal experience', he was awarded A$2500 from the General Production Fund of the Film, Radio and Television Board (FRTB) of the Australia Council to make what became his only unreleased film *Some Aspects of Australian Racism*.[408] During his research for this project, Hughes met the Indigenous activists Bruce McGuinness and Gary Foley at the Aboriginal Advancement League.[409] Hughes recalls Foley telling him that films on such topics should be made by Aboriginal people and that, as a white filmmaker, Hughes should focus on white Australian racism.[410] This was around the time that McGuinness became possibly the first Aboriginal filmmaker with his short *Blackfire* (1972).[411]

Some Aspects of Australian Racism (1973)

Hughes' surviving version of *Some Aspects of Australian Racism* is a 16 mm print that has the appearance of a completed film, but for the absence of a title and credits. Its focus is consistent with the advice Foley and McGuinness gave. In the first section, pastoral images of domesticated farmland are accompanied by the voices of Aboriginal community leaders describing their personal experience of racism. Printed texts depicting colonial attitudes and contemporary political debate are superimposed over these images. While many of these elements are didactic in themselves, their rich combination and flow in the film lead to a density of image, sound and text that generates dialectal connections and is quite demanding to follow.

The middle section of the film depicts an impersonal urban environment. Commuters make their way along city streets and workmen climb around a building under construction. In voice-over, Lorna Lippmann, an officer of the Centre for Research into Aboriginal Affairs at Monash University, declares, 'If you look at any of the institutions of our society you'll find that they are racist'. Here, the graphics become a design element within the screen space and the camera shot. The camera shot composition often anticipates the placement of the superimposed text.

FROM TOP: THE TRACKING SHOT FROM THE UNRELEASED *SOME ASPECTS OF AUSTRALIAN RACISM* (1973) USED IN *AFTER MABO*; 'ALL THE MEDIA SEEMED TO BE IN THE HANDS OF OUR ENEMIES.' A NEWS CAMERA BEHIND A COMMONWEALTH POLICE CORDON; GARY FOLEY AND BOB MAZA AT THE 1972 ABORIGINAL EMBASSY IN SCENES FROM ALESSANDRO CAVADINI'S *NINGLA A-NA* (1972) USED IN *AFTER MABO* (1997).

This approach to screen design forecasts the dense layering of text and image in Hughes' later works from *Traps* (1985, see Chapter 5) through to *Indonesia Calling* (2009, see Chapter 11).

The final section of *Some Aspects of Australian Racism* is concerned with overtly racist educational material, much of which was produced in England in the 1930s and some of which was still being used in Australian schools forty years later. Walter McVitty, lecturer in children's literature at Melbourne College of Education, reads and discusses some wildly erroneous passages while images from mid-twentieth century educational magic lantern slides are projected over his face and across the screen behind him. In a graceful, disciplined and quite elaborate two-minute dolly shot through a classroom, non-Aboriginal children read selected passages from these texts on cue. Hughes says Godard's *British Sounds* inspired this tracking shot which found its way into *After Mabo* over twenty years later. Hughes returned to the subject of racism before *After* Mabo, however, when he wrote and directed *Moments Like These* in 1989.

Despite taking Foley's advice and concentrating *Some Aspects of Australian Racism* on his own culture, Hughes did not feel comfortable continuing with a project that was still in some ways 'about' Aboriginal people. He eventually resolved to make a polemic gesture. He edited the 16 mm film, laid up and mixed the sound and had a laboratory create a print with superimposed graphics, including the historical quotes. He says he used just some of the money from the Australia Council, kept a print himself and returned the remaining money together with the other print to the Council with a report saying: 'I cannot make the film I have been funded to make. We don't need any more films about Aboriginal people by white filmmakers'.[412] For *After Mabo* (1996), Hughes had a telecine video copy made from his 16 mm print of *Some Aspects of Australian Racism*. To date, the film remains unreleased and will not be found in any library or other collection.

BOB MAZA IN *MOMENTS LIKE THESE*.

Moments Like These (1989)

After the release of *All That is Solid* (1988, see Chapter 6), Hughes was commissioned to write the tender for a series of videotapes co-produced by Open Channel and the Townsville Aboriginal and Islander Media Association (TAIMA) for the federal Department of Employment, Education and Training. Hughes wrote and directed the first of these. Like *Changing Schools* (1985, see Chapter 4), *Moments Like These* was research-based and drew upon a vast resource of archival film. The film presents an analysis of the way Indigenous people have been represented throughout the history of Australian cinema. For this project, Hughes commenced a very productive and continuing collaboration with the editor Uri Mizrahi.

Moments Like These incorporates clips from Baldwin Spencer's anthropological films of the early 1900s, newsreels and significant dramatic features by Australian filmmakers such as Charles Chauvel's *Uncivilised* (1936) and *Jedda* (1955) and Ned Lander's *Wrong Side of the Road* (1981).[413] Two films that Hughes would revisit in later work were the British production *Bitter*

FROM LEFT: *AFTER MABO* SCREEN COLLAGE; PAUL KEATING, LABOR PRIME MINISTER OF AUSTRALIA 1991–1996, IN *AFTER MABO* (1997).

Springs (1950) and *Ningla A-Na* (1972), a seventy-two minute Australian documentary about the establishment of the Aboriginal Embassy in Canberra and the police action surrounding it.[414]

Presented directly to camera by veteran Indigenous actor Bob Maza, Hughes' script for *Moments Like These* sounds like personal testimony. Sitting in an old movie theatre, Maza looks to the screen as he introduces clips that exemplify the issues of representation and cultural reception that he discusses. As Peter Hughes pointed out in 1993, this 'mode of address' places non-Indigenous viewers in the 'uncomfortable' position of being spoken to as if they too were Aboriginal or Torres Strait Islander Australians.[415] This reversal brings conventional assumptions into relief and throws light on the layers of misapprehension about Aboriginal people imbedded in non-Indigenous culture. This twenty-seven minute video may be the first film to deal explicitly with the representation of 'Aboriginality' in Australian film. In contrast to the multitude of issues, voices, perspectives and modes of address that characterise *All That is Solid*, John Hughes uses this more contained project to find an effective mode of address and an elegant formal solution to a single thematic problem.

After Mabo (1997)

Hughes' next examination of Australian racism, *After Mabo*, chronicles one chapter in the long-running and nationwide struggle over the land rights of Aboriginal and Torres Strait Islander people. The film was a partisan response to arguments, scare tactics and media campaigns that government, sections of the mining industry and agribusiness had launched to garner support for hobbling Indigenous land rights legislation in Australia. It was to function as a partisan work of advocacy at a critical historic moment in that struggle. By the 1990s Aboriginal communities had equipped themselves and mainstream institutions, including the film and television industries, with protocols to minimise the scope and impact of inappropriate and ill-devised projects. Simultaneously, these communities have nurtured a cohort of professionals –

FROM LEFT: 'THEY HAD THE PERCEPTION THAT THEY WERE FROM THE FUTURE AND WE WERE FROM THE PAST.' – RICHARD FRANKLAND SPEAKS AT A PARLIAMENTARY HEARING ON NATIVE TITLE; NATIONAL INDIGENOUS WORKING GROUP MEETING IN CANBERRA IN *AFTER MABO* (1997).

including filmmakers – of their own. *After Mabo* is the result of collaboration initiated by Richard Frankland, an Indigenous filmmaker and community leader.

The Hawke Labor government's proposed 'Land Rights' legislation of 1983 was the compromised result of decades of campaigning by Indigenous Australians to secure title to land.[416] It promised inalienable freehold title of Aboriginal land (on an equal footing with other Australians), full legal protection of sacred sites, Aboriginal control over mining on Aboriginal land, access to 'mining royalty equivalents' and compensation for lost land.[417] None of these promises would become law. A vigorous campaign by mining and agribusiness interests was driven zealously by the then Premier of Western Australia and National President of the Australian Labor Party, Brian Burke.[418] Burke's case exemplifies the political and financial resources of those who oppose the comparatively meagre land rights lobby. Burke had an unrivalled capacity to draw money and votes to the Labor Party. He was also a central subject of the 1992 'WA Inc.' Royal Commission that identified an outstanding history of 'improper conduct'.[419]

For ten years, alongside the political campaign for land rights, four Meriam people from the Murray Islands, led by Eddie Mabo, pursued legal avenues to challenge the myth of terra nullius (the idea that the Australian continent belonged to no one prior to European occupation). It was this campaign that led, through the 1992 Mabo decision of the High Court, to some recognition of the land ownership rights of Indigenous Australians beyond the Northern Territory.[420] The legislative response of the Keating Labor government to that ruling was to create a special form of land title for Aboriginal land – one that ensured the primacy of non-Aboriginal interests in Crown land. This was the Native Title Act of 1993.[421] Gary Foley expressed the view of many of the more skeptical Indigenous campaigners when he described the Act as 'a fraud and a farce' that would not give 'land justice' to Aboriginal Australians.[422] The Act certainly was far from what the Hawke government had promised a decade earlier.

Elected in March 1996, the Liberal-National Party coalition government, led by John Howard, gave high priority to further watering down the legislation governing land claims by Indigenous

FROM LEFT: JOHN HOWARD, LIBERAL PRIME MINISTER OF AUSTRALIA 1996–2007; NOEL PEARSON, CHAIR CAPE YORK LAND COUNCIL, AND HOWARD AT THE 1997 ABORIGINAL RECONCILIATION CONVENTION IN *AFTER MABO* (1997).

Australians. The outcome would further favour pastoral leaseholders and mining corporations. Leaders from Aboriginal and Torres Strait Islander communities established a National Indigenous Working Group (NIWG) to coordinate a response to this attack. Richard Frankland, CEO of Victoria's Mirimbiak Nations Aboriginal Corporation, a musician, singer-songwriter and filmmaker, was keen to get NIWG endorsement for an advocacy film about the amendment issue, but had no time to produce and direct it himself. Frankland asked Hughes, who had recently worked as script editor on Frankland's award-winning short *No Way to Forget* (1995), to take on the project.[423] Hughes says Frankland rang him from one of the first NIWG meetings in Canberra asking that he write a treatment in a matter of hours. Events were moving quickly. Hughes was soon video recording NIWG meetings while seeking finance and a television release for the project.

As he did with *Some Aspects of Australian Racism* in the early 1970s, Hughes faced the dilemma of how a non-Indigenous person worked on stories involving Aboriginal issues. This was resolved firstly through a kind of contract between Hughes, Frankland and Mirimbiak in which Mirimbiak had ownership and control of the project. Hughes, trading as Early Works, managed the project, making an initial application for funding through Mirimbiak and then dealing with the Australian Film Commission (AFC) as a third contractual entity directly. Debra Annear, a non-Indigenous production manager who had worked on *No Way to Forget*, co-produced the project with Hughes: recording sound in Broome, managing legal clearances for a myriad of elements within the film and attending to AFC and SBS cost reporting requirements.

It was October 1996 when Hughes began attending NIWG meetings as an observer, while cameraperson Peter Zakharov recorded events under his direction. During this time Hughes was 'trying to work out' how to make the film.

One of the things I learnt at one of those early meetings was the way that the Aboriginal leadership worked with various lawyers and advisers who were also present. [...] all the discussion would take place among the Indigenous leadership there, who would debate points.

They'd come to an agreement about a position on a certain point and then often they'd say: 'OK, well we'll go and have a smoke and get the technicians to write that up.' So, the technicians would be these extremely bright, smart, well-educated, non-Indigenous lawyers. [They] *would then go into the back of the room, with their portable computers and come up with a form of words which they would debate, then they'd bring the form of words back to the meeting and pass them round. Everyone would read them and there'd be radical critiques of what had been written – extremely well informed, legalistic critiques of the form of words that had been presented to them – and the technicians would be sent away to do it again.*[424]

Hughes decided that his job was to be the 'technician', the person who makes the film for the group who had, in a way, commissioned him. He wanted to try to take on board whatever Indigenous community input he received from Frankland.

Together, Frankland and Hughes recognised that it would not be desirable, nor politically possible, to use a central character to represent the different kinds of authority at work in the NIWG. Regardless of what they said, such a character would be seen to be *representing* Aboriginal people. Other elements that had to be absorbed from Frankland's project brief were 'specificity of place,' a nationwide scope and a broad historical perspective.[425] All these requirements matched with Hughes' experience and interests.

The national significance and immediacy of the events covered, and the strong Indigenous involvement, meant that Hughes did not have to battle for priority treatment by funding bodies as he had in the case of *One Way Street*.[426] Finance was negotiated with two former Independent Film Action Committee (IFAC, see Chapter 5) associates: David Tiley (AFC project officer) and Claire Jager who commissioned the project on behalf of SBS television. The AFC made a positive decision in mid-December of 1996. On 23 December 1996 the High Court found in favour of the Wik peoples in their claim that native title co-existed with pastoral leasehold in Cape York Peninsula. In January 1997 Hughes recorded 16 videotapes at the Wik summit of Indigenous leaders in Cairns.[427]

In March 1997 the National Farmers' Federation (NFF) launched a major advertising campaign declaring that the High Court decision – which only related to leaseholds on Crown land – had created 'uncertainty for farmers'. In *After Mabo,* Marcia Langton describes the 'atmosphere of hysteria' that led many Australians to believe that freehold land could be subject to Indigenous land claims. Much of the media commentary surrounding the Wik decision fanned this hysteria. Patrick Dodson, chair of the Council for Aboriginal Reconciliation, describes a choice in Australian race relations at this juncture between 'foundations in justice' and a direction based on expediency and vested interest.

In May 1997 prime minister Howard released his Cabinet's controversial and wide-ranging Ten-Point Plan of amendments to the Native Title Act. The plan greatly reduced Indigenous participation in decisions about the use of their ancestral land.[428] The dramatic climax of *After Mabo*, of this episode in Australian history, and of the so-called 'history wars', came at the Aboriginal Reconciliation Convention in Melbourne later that month. Many delegates quietly

FROM LEFT: NOEL PEARSON AND PATRICK DODSON, CHAIR, COUNCIL FOR ABORIGINAL RECONCILIATION; GALARRWUY YUNUPINGU, CHAIR OF THE NORTHERN LAND COUNCIL IN *AFTER MABO* (1997).

stood and turned their backs as Howard banged the podium and railed against what he saw as a 'black arm band' view of Australian history.

The publicity material for *After Mabo* includes a line, devised by Hughes, describing the project as 'an instance of reconciliation through collaboration'.[429] Hughes originally hoped to negotiate 'an explicit structure of Indigenous contribution' from autonomous, regional Indigenous media groups across the country.[430] There is a reflection here of the original conception of the Walter Benjamin project (*One Way Street*, see Chapter 7) as a live global television event. These ideas stemmed from Hughes' long-standing interest in the raw possibilities of the medium itself and the social arrangement of information it can facilitate. They go beyond the scope of conventional demarcations and processes between and within television production and programming. These ideas also carry a degree of logistical complexity that may be routine in the case of a major sporting event, for example, but they go beyond the remit and capacity of a commissioned producer with a limited budget and rudimentary administrative infrastructure. The result is that such innovation is rarely even thought about and the development of the social potential of the media lags well behind the development of technical capacity.

If *After Mabo* fails to meet Hughes' original hope for it as a formal experiment in the social mode of production, its content offers unique glimpses of collaborative political processes within Australia's Indigenous community. This is what Hughes had promised at the outset and recognised in the first material he shot for the project. He wrote in a letter at the time:

Already there is a real sense of a strong, resourceful democratic organisation of energetic and committed people working together co-operatively with openness and purpose.[431]

The film also documents some of the behind-the-scenes operation of mainstream politicians and media: the 'consultative' meetings and photo opportunities. The observational documentary style of these core scenes is familiar to television viewers and is at the centre of what Hughes describes as a 'critical collaboration with orthodoxy' in *After Mabo*.[432]

FROM LEFT: JOHN DUDU, KARAJARRA ELDER IN *RIVER OF DREAMS* (1998); A SHOT OF MICHAEL PATE FROM EALING STUDIO'S *BITTER SPRINGS* (1951) FORMS PART OF A SCREEN DESIGN IN *AFTER MABO* (1997).

As with *One Way Street* (1992, see Chapter 7), screen design is central to the formal arrangement of this film. Images appear within images, expanding, contracting, freezing and enveloping each other. In an incisive chapter devoted to *After Mabo* in *The Cinema of Australia and New Zealand*, Peter Hughes discusses this dialectic of televisual form that 'constantly works to foreground the enunciation' which the purely observational documentary usually conceals.

[*After Mabo*] *challenges the realism and transparency of the image, and thus its ability to unproblematically present events ... The fragmentary nature of the documentary problematises the claim to a single mediated truth, and dissolves continuities of time and space which commonly provide for the audience a position of knowledge and certainty about the events portrayed.*[433]

Peter Hughes refers to a fragmentation that stems from an intense juxtaposition of sound upon image, image upon image and sound upon sound in *After Mabo*. The assemblage occurs through both shot-to-shot montage and collage-within-the-frame. This painstaking work of temporal and spatial design, whilst exploding the realist effect, also invites the audience to engage in the examination and creation of meaning within the film. There is a substantial dimension of technology and craft behind this dialectical approach to screen design in John Hughes' films. In 1973 Hughes built texts into the images of *Some Aspects of Australian Racism* through A, B and C roll laboratory printing with celluloid negative film. This process was used at the time for superimposing titles and captions in films. In 1992 the visual layers for *One Way Street* could be combined digitally but also required a specialist facility and a many-staged, tape-based process.[434] Digital videotape allowed copying and layering of the image over multiple generations with minimal loss of picture resolution.

By 1997 entirely digital editing systems made it possible for Hughes and Mizrahi to create multiple layered effects for *After Mabo* immediately and directly on the editing screen. Hughes had begun to imagine this particular dimension from the outset of the project, describing 'a screen design that has certain characteristics of a web page or CD ROM, in which there are

ABOVE: LAND, WATER AND NEWS MEDIA ARE MERGED IN THE SCREEN DESIGNS OF *RIVER OF DREAMS* (1998).

graphics and simultaneous events on the screen'.[435] The result is a densely woven visual fabric containing observational documentary and broadcast news material, clips from news broadcasts and a scene from the 1950 feature film *Bitter Springs* in which a stockman (played by Chipps Rafferty) and a trooper (Michael Pate) argue about Aboriginal land rights. As with other films by Hughes, the density of visual, aural and textual material means there are threads that can only be grasped through repeated viewings.

While deliberately and openly partisan, the observational scenes within *After Mabo* give considerable airtime to conservative leaders, who appear to be as relaxed and candid as politicians are ever likely to be in front of a camera. What they provide is material that gives nuance to the argument the film is making. While surrounded by distinguished Indigenous leaders in the gardens of the prime minister's residence, Howard and NFF leader Donald McGauchie discuss how 'we' have learnt to 'integrate the Australian Natives with the English trees'. The metaphoric value of this statement is unlikely to have been lost on either of these white politicians or their Indigenous guests. Similarly, Liberal senator and Minister for Aboriginal Affairs, John Herron, displays an attitude that is at least patronising, if not calculated to belittle. In showing a delegation of Indigenous leaders some artworks in his office, Herron tells of a contemporary Indigenous artist's apparent misunderstanding of a traditional Aboriginal surgical technique which Dr Herron had explained to them. Such asides rarely figure in televisual treatment of national issues. In Hughes and Mizrahi's hands, however, these apparently incidental fragments provide profound insights into the attitudes of white leadership at a moment in Australian history that was critical for the fate of its Indigenous people.

In *After Mabo*, Hughes also pays careful attention to the choice of words in public pronouncements by conservative leaders and the media. These often reveal an abiding mistrust of Indigenous leaders and disdain for their cause. The High Court decision in favour of Eddie Mabo was a 'day of shame' according to former Liberal leader John Hewson. Following the WIK decision, McGauchie felt it necessary to emphasise 'we're not accepting anything on trust'. According to

Victorian Liberal premier Jeff Kennett, the WIK decision 'has left the Australian community at the edge of an abyss'. Graphics emphasise a similarly belligerent use of language in a commercial television news report that Aboriginal people had 'targeted' and 'set their sights' on a popular national park threatening to make parts of it 'off limits to the public' with a 'Mabo-style' land claim.

Whilst the language of mistrust and disdain may not be conscious, the language of fear employed by conservative politicians is described by Indigenous leader and academic Marcia Langton as a deliberate political strategy to 'put an imagined enemy in the minds of the public'. For their part, a number of Indigenous leaders clearly identify the right wing of politics as the source of the attack on native title. *After Mabo* depicts a hardening of attitudes on the right throughout the 1990s – from the NFF supporting Keating's response to the Mabo ruling, under the leadership of Rick Farley in 1993, to the stand McGauchie took in 1997.

In discussing Hughes' use – in the spirit of Walter Benjamin – of verbal, textual and pictorial quotation, Peter Hughes explores an analogy between the arrangement and animation of on-screen text in *After Mabo* with the aesthetic of proprietary presentation software such as PowerPoint. Whereas PowerPoint is 'particularly suited to an instrumental, instructional mode of thinking', Peter says that John 'uses such a style of quotation in a manner which can be seen as subversive of such an instrumental mode' and points to the influence of 'visual arts practice' throughout Hughes' work. [436]

After Mabo was screened by SBS television on 25 November 1997 on the eve of the federal parliamentary debate on the Government's 10-Point Plan. In 1998 the Howard amendments to the Native Title Act were finally passed. In 2000 the United Nations Committee on the Elimination of Racial Discrimination expressed concern that the amendments reduced the rights of Indigenous people in Australia.[437]

River of Dreams (1998)

At some point in the making of *After Mabo,* Hughes thought, 'I need a positive story to conclude this. There needs to be some moment of hope'.[438] Howard's amendments to the Native Title Act removed a requirement for developers and governments to negotiate with probable native title-holders before proceeding with development.[439] Hughes learnt, however, that some developers found the experience of speaking with Aboriginal people in order to reach agreement 'a very positive experience.'[440] Hughes went to Broome to follow up one such story as a possible closing sequence. While in Broome he came across the idea for his next project that would be about proposals to dam the Fitzroy River for irrigation-intensive cotton farming.

By early 1998 Hughes and co-producer Donna Cameron had done a research trip and recorded some material for the project that would become *River of Dreams* (1998).[441] Development finance for this preliminary work came from the state film finance agencies Screen West and Film Victoria. SBSi had commissioned *After Mabo* and, by this time, had also agreed to a presale

FROM LEFT: NOEL PEARSON; NINGALI LAWFORD DELVES INTO WHITE PERCEPTIONS OF COUNTRY IN *RIVER OF DREAMS* (1998).

deal for *River of Dreams*. The presale triggered additional finance under the Film Finance Corporation's (FFC) Documentary Accord scheme and an overall budget of around A$230,000, which was modest given that the project involved a lot of travelling, following events over a long period of time. Hughes' personal finances were exhausted before shooting was completed, and he had to take up a full-time job he was offered at SBSi earlier than planned, so he was not able to be as closely involved with the editing as he had been in the previous projects that Mizrahi had cut for him. Nonetheless, with *River of Dreams* the pair accomplished a further development in their sophisticated multiple image screen design work. Like *After Mabo*, *River of Dreams* is distributed on DVD by Canberra-based Ronin Films. Dr Merrilyn Fitzpatrick founded Ronin with her husband, film historian and filmmaker Andrew Pike OAM in 1974. It is the only commercial company that has been distributing selected Australian independent films since the co-op days.

The multi-layered imagery is woven together in patterns that build upon and reflect the patterns in landscape shots that underpin many of the montage sequences. This creation of patterns from country is also a reflection upon the traditional style of paintings by Aboriginal artists that are also shown in the film. Images are sometimes repeated in a display styled on a filmstrip running along the bottom of the screen with every second frame mirroring the one next to it. This pattern-work is at once abstract and figurative – decorative and significant. A recording of the Sydney Symphony Orchestra's performance of the renowned Australian composer Peter Sculthorpe's composition *Earth Cry* supports it.[442]

A range of texts and voices is used in *River of Dreams*. The multi-talented Western Australian Aboriginal performer Ningali Lawford appears in a presenter-like role, but only as necessary. She addresses the camera/audience directly with an analysis of the Europeans' 'totalising' and god-like view of land. Whilst these are performances of a scripted text, they blend among the interviews with a relaxed and confident delivery. There is an appeal to 'common sense' by a man who has witnessed the gradual degeneration of the Ord River and the surrounding country that was poisoned by insecticides and other chemicals in run-off from channel-irrigated cotton farms.

NINGALI LAWFORD IN *RIVER OF DREAMS* (1998).

River of Dreams won a United Nations award for television environmental reporting, two ATOM awards and was selected for screening by the 2000 Banff Television Festival in Canada.

In 1998 Hughes also directed *Take Five* – a series of thirteen, five-minute documentaries examining works of art in various Australian galleries with Betty Churcher – the highly esteemed scholar, historian and former director of the National Gallery of Australia – as writer and presenter. A decade-long collaboration on short television programs ensued.[443] By the end of the year, Hughes was appointed commissioning editor (Documentary) at SBSi, a subsidiary of SBS Television that functioned with a significant degree of autonomy and innovation as a commissioning agency. Here, he was involved in setting up co-financing schemes around special programs of work. *Unfinished Business*, about Aboriginal people who had been taken from their parents as children, was one that became a theme for a whole week of SBS TV. Hughes says *After Mabo* had caused 'a bit of a stir' and attention for SBS in 1996.[444] Subsequently, *Unfinished Business* was seen as 'very brave' and led SBS managing director Nigel Milan to approach Hughes to produce an Australian version of the American series *Five Hundred Nations,* which had rated well.[445] Perhaps recalling Gary Foley's advice 20 years earlier, Hughes says that he told Milan, 'I can't really do it, we must ask Aboriginal filmmakers to do it.'[446] Overnight, Hughes had to evaluate *Five Hundred Nations* and come up with a concept. His discussion paper explained that in Australia it was not possible to do a history of Indigenous cultures in the same way that *Five Hundred Nations* had treated the North American experience. Hughes says Milan agreed that such a project would have to be controlled by Aboriginal filmmakers. Initially, Hughes and Rachel Perkins were to be co-executive producers, but eventually producer Darren Dale and director Beck Cole joined Perkins as co-producer and co-director. In 2002 it was this team of Indigenous filmmakers who undertook production, over the following six years, of the epic and groundbreaking documentary series *First Australians* (2008). To undertake initial work on *First Australians* and to pursue other projects of his own, Hughes resigned from SBSi in December 2001. In four years at SBSi, Hughes had a hand in an enormous number of documentary projects and had made a significant impression on the landscape of Australian television.[447]

In 2003 Hughes discussed changes in documentary film culture over the past thirty years with Rachel Maher and Megan Spencer, relative newcomers to documentary filmmaking at the time. He says:

[…] *instead of trying to work out ways of organising together, people* [have] *become more and more isolated because they see themselves as competitors, rather than part of a culture that wants to negotiate with the mainstream decision-making institutions.*[448]

Spencer agreed saying that there was little sense of community among contemporary independent documentary producers at that time and that all were very much 'focused on television'. For a number of years, in an effort to reconnect documentary filmmakers, Hughes initiated and administered the ironically titled 'TOF list': Television Outworkers Forum. Otherwise known as the Australian Documentary Filmmakers Policy Forum, TOF was a free, subscription-based, membership-moderated, electronic mailing list newsletter. On the forum's web page, Hughes described TOF as dedicated to research, strategy and action in support of independent editorial voices in the Australian documentary film industry, where independent filmmakers may contribute to policy development concerning the terms of trade that govern their work, issues of creative control and structural change in documentary financing.[449] Hughes saw TOF as an opportunity to stand up and be counted and he modelled a willingness to do so by signing his own posts and using them to advocate for the 'creative' end of the documentary spectrum.

By describing himself and his peers as outworkers, Hughes was reflecting on his experience as an executive at SBSi. There he saw the enormous potential of thematic programming, together with a shift by television executives from a reactive to a proactive relationship with independent filmmakers. Programmers were becoming more prescriptive and proscriptive about the projects they supported. Hughes describes this as leading to 'a tension between TV as a distribution media for independent film' and independent filmmakers as the makers of predetermined program material.[450]

At the Melbourne Filmmakers Co-operative (MFC) in the 1970s, and to a lesser extent at the Independent Film Action Committee in the 1980s, there was a broad community of independent filmmakers, community media activists, film buffs, students and academics who were engaged in an organised way with the politics of screen culture. At that time, film-funding bodies were more publicly accessible. There was a sense of their function within the broader public sphere and they could be held to account by a wide community of interest. In the twenty-first century, it is primarily as a professional maker of documentary films for mainstream television that Hughes can identify a peer group. TOF tended to provide for a dialogue between this more narrow strata of experienced stakeholders who share inside knowledge of public funding institutions that have a very limited public interface and operate in a mode of commercial-in-confidence more often than in one of public service. The recent shift of TOF discussion to social media has not necessarily enhanced the public profile of this forum.

Some Aspects of Australian Racism stands as a reminder of the intensity of institutional racism that characterised Australian society a mere generation ago. As a film, it reflects the influence of Godard and the idea of developing a rich dialectic between sound, image and text. That film provides an early example of Hughes' unique approach to screen design and the layering and compositing of photographic and graphic elements within the frame. This technique would play an important part in Hughes' conceptual and aesthetic articulation of complex issues of Indigenous land care and land rights in both *River of Dreams* and in *After Mabo*, a work that records an important moment in the history of the land rights movement and a historical struggle for the spiritual identity of a nation.

Endnotes

[405] John Hughes, *Some Aspects of Australian Racism*, 1973 (unreleased), 16 mm, b&w, 12 minutes, Melbourne, Producer John Hughes, Scriptwriter John Hughes. Featuring Dan Atkinson, Geraldine Briggs, David Anderson, Bert Peters, Lorna Lippmann, Walter McVitty. Produced with assistance from the Interim Council for the Australian Film and Television School.

[406] National Archives of Australia, *The Wave Hill 'walk-off'*, Fact sheet 224, 2014, < http://www.naa.gov.au/collection/fact-sheets/fs224.aspx>, accessed 16 October 2014. Dr Coral Dow and Dr John Gardiner-Garden, 'Overview of Indigenous Affairs: Part 1: 1901 to 1991', Publications, Parliament of Australia, < http://www.aph.gov.au/about_parliament/parliamentary_departments/parliamentary_library/pubs/bn/1011/indigenousaffairs1>, accessed 16 October 2014. See also James Miller, *Koori: A Will to Win*, 1 vol., 2nd edn, Angus & Robertson, North Ryde, 1985.

[407] See CD Rowley, *The Destruction of Aboriginal Society*, ANUP, Canberra, 1970.

[408] ACA, Annual Report, Australia Council for the Arts (calendar year), Sydney, 1974, p. 134.

[409] John Hughes, The Melbourne Filmmakers Co-op, interview conducted by John Cumming, Melbourne, 20 September 2001. In the early 1970s the Australia Council had also begun to support training and the development of film production by Aboriginal people through its Aboriginal Arts Board. Bruce McGuinness was producing *That's Life* with Koori Films in 1973 together with films on Aboriginal football and the National Aboriginal Arts Seminar. ACA, Annual Report, Australia Council for the Arts (calendar year), Sydney, 1974, p. 110. See Gary Foley, 'Advice for white Indigenous activists in Australia' in Decolonising Activism, Deactivating Colonialism, Maysar Forum Discussion, Fitzroy, Melbourne, 31 August 2010, <http://www.youtube.com/watch?v=uEGsBV9VGTQ>, accessed 18 December 2013.

[410] Hughes would take up this issue with Foley again some years later in an interview. See John Hughes,

'*Jimmie Blacksmith* ... a star is shorn', *Nation Review*, 1–7 September 1978, p. 21.

411   Liz McNiven, 'A Short History of Indigenous Filmmaking', Australian Screen, National Film and Sound Archive of Australia, <http://aso.gov.au/titles/collections/indigenous-filmmaking/>, accessed 23 December 2013.

412   John Hughes, The Melbourne Filmmakers Co-op, interview conducted by John Cumming, Melbourne, 20 September 2001. To date, the only public evidence of this film is an entry in the Australia Council for the Arts annual report of 1974/5 that reads: 'John Hughes (Vic) Documentary on racism in Australian society A$2500,' ACA, Annual Report, Australia Council for the Arts (July to June), Sydney, 1974/1975.

413   Charles Chauvel, *Uncivilised*, 1936, 77 minutes, Expeditionary Films, Australia, Producer Charles Chauvel, Camera Tasman Higgins, Sound Denis Box, Music Lindley Evans, Editor Frank Coffey, Assistant Editor Mona Donaldson. Featuring Margot Rhys, Dennis Hoey & Ashton Jarry. Harry Weipa & Booya (uncredited). Distributed by Umbrella Entertainment. Charles Chauvel, *Jedda*, 1955, 35 mm, colour, 101 minutes, Charles Chauvel Productions, Producer Charles Chauvel, Scriptwriters Elsa Chauvel, Charles Chauvel, Camera Carl Kayser, Editors Alex Ezard, Jack Gardiner, Pam Bosworth. Featuring Ngarla Kunoth, Robert Tudawali. Distributed by Columbia Pictures (Aust.), British Lion (UK). Ned Lander, *Wrong Side of the Road*, 1981, 79 minutes, Producers Ned Lander & Graeme Isaac, Scriptwriters Ned Lander & Graeme Isaac, Camera Louis Irving, Music No Fixed Address & Us Mob, Editor John Scott. Featuring Ronnie Ansell, Veronica Rankine, Peter Butler, Les Graham, Chris Haywood & Bart Willoughby. Distributed by National Film and Sound Archive.

414   Ralph Smart, *Bitter Springs*, 1951, b&w, 89 minutes, Ealing Studios UK. Alessandro Cavadini, *Ningla A-Na*, 1972, 72 minutes, Australia, Smart Street Films, <http://www.smartstreetfilms.com.au>.

415   Peter Hughes, 'A way of being engaged with the world: the films of John Hughes', *Metro*, no. 93, Autumn 1993, p. 54.

416   Gary Foley, 'How Bob Hawke killed land rights', *Tracker,* 2013, NSW Aboriginal Land Council, 28 February, accessed 22 December 2013.

417   The Hon. Clyde Holding MP Minister for Aboriginal Affairs, *Aboriginal land rights – National legislation*, First Hawke Ministry Cabinet Submissions, Social Policy Committee, Sub. 619 – Decisions 2893/SP and 2913, A13977, National Archives of Australia, 19 December 1983 – 7 March 1984, <http://recordsearch.naa.gov.au/SearchNRetrieve/Interface/DetailsReports/ItemDetail.aspx?Barcode=31424610>, accessed 22 December 2013.

418   Stuart Rintoul, 'Miners and Brian Burke sank land rights hope', *The Australian,* 2013, News Limited, 1 January, <http://www.theaustralian.com.au/in-depth/cabinet-papers/miners-and-brian-burke-sank-land-rights-hope/story-fngr9pxq-1226545827125>, accessed 22 December 2013.

419   Jailed twice and acquitted on appeal once, Burke continued to wield extraordinary influence. As recently as 2007 he was employed as a lobbyist for developers and major mining companies including Australand, Precious Metals Australia, Fortesque Metals Group and Kimberley Diamond Company. Justice Geoffrey Kennedy, Sir Ronald Wilson & Mr Peter Brinsden, 'WA Inc. Royal Commission', 1992, Government of Western Australia, Department of the Premier and Cabinet, State Law Publisher, <http://www.slp.wa.gov.au/publications/publications.nsf/inquiries+and+commissions>, accessed 22 December 2013. David Cohen, 'The Strife of Brian', *The Age*, 2007, Melbourne, 28 February, <http://www.theage.com.au/articles/2007/02/27/1172338625209.html>. Alan Ramsey, 'A role in the fall of a Labor mate conveniently omitted from the eulogies', *Sydney Morning Herald*, 2005, Fairfax Media, July 20, accessed 22 December 2013.

420   Australian Bureau of Statistics, 'The Mabo Case and the Native Title Act', *Year Book 1995*, vol. ABS Catalogue 1301.0, 1 January 1995, <http://www.abs.gov.au/Ausstats/abs@.nsf/Previousproducts/1301.0Feature Article21995>, accessed 22 December 2013.

421   Commonwealth of Australia, 'Native Title Act 1993', Act No. 110 of 1993, *National Native Title Tribunal*,

422 Gary Foley, 'The Contrarian: White Myth-Making and a State of Denial', *Tracker*, 2004, NSW Aboriginal Land Council, 4 April, <http://tracker.org.au/2012/04/the-contrarian-white-myth-making-and-a-state-of-denial/>. This article summarises a more detailed essay by Foley which also contains an extensive list of primary references in Gary Foley, 'The Road to Native Title: The Aboriginal Rights Movement and the ALP 1973–1996', The Koori History Website, Melbourne, July 2001, <http://www.kooriweb.org/foley/essays/essays_page.html>, accessed 23 December 2013.

423 Richard Frankland, *No Way to Forget*, 1995, 16 mm, b&w and colour, 11 minutes, From Sand To Celluloid, Producer John Foss. Featuring David Ngoombujarra. Produced with assistance from the Indigenous Branch of the Australian Film Commission, the Australian state film agencies and SBS Independent. Distributed by Golden Seahorse Productions, NFSA Film Australia Collection.

424 John Hughes, *What I Have Written* and *After Mabo*, interview conducted by John Cumming, Melbourne, 3 July 2002.

425 ibid.

426 In a letter to the AFC project officer, Hughes suggests that the AFC might be required to 'innovate with its own orthodoxy in facilitating the needs of the project'. John Hughes, *After Mabo*, letter to David Tiley (AFC), Melbourne, 16 December 1996. However, he acknowledges that models for the involvement of non-Indigenous production companies in Indigenous production had already been established and tested by the AFC and that the head of the AFC's Indigenous Branch. Headed by Wal Saunders, the Branch had these matters well in hand. This letter also confirms that the AFC was already accommodating the 'urgency of the project'.

427 John Hughes, *After Mabo*, progress report letter to Richard Frankland, Jacqui Geia, John Foss, Mirimbiak Nations Aboriginal Corporation & Debra Annear, Melbourne, 27 January 1997.

428 Commonwealth of Australia, *Native Title Amendment Act 1998,* Australian Government ComLaw, No. C2004A00354, Act No. 97, 1998, Canberra, 27 July, accessed 23 December 2013.

429 SBS Television, *The Cutting Edge*: *After Mabo*, program publicity, 6 November 1997. John Hughes, *After Mabo*, letter to Richard Frankland, Melbourne, 2 October 1997.

430 John Hughes, *After Mabo*, progress report letter to Richard Frankland, Jacqui Geia, John Foss, Mirimbiak Nations Aboriginal Corporation & Debra Annear, Melbourne, 17 February 1997, p. 2.

431 John Hughes, *After Mabo*, letter to John Foss, Otis Sherwell & Julia Mongta, 7 October 1996.

432 John Hughes quoted in Peter Hughes, *After Mabo*, in Geoff Mayer and Keith Beattie (ed.), *The Cinema of Australia and New Zealand*, 24 Frames, Wallflower Press, London, 2007, p. 178.

433 Peter Hughes, ibid.

434 John Hughes, *One Way Street*, synopsis, 1992.

435 John Hughes, *After Mabo*, progress report letter to Richard Frankland, Jacqui Geia, John Foss, Mirimbiak Nations Aboriginal Corporation & Debra Annear, Melbourne, 17 February 1997.

436 Peter Hughes, op. cit., p. 181.

437 United Nations CERD, Summary Record of the 1393rd Meeting, Geneva, 21 March 2000, <http://www.unhchr.ch/tbs/doc.nsf CERD/C/SR.1393>, accessed 24 February 2013.

438 John Hughes, *What I Have Written* and *After Mabo*, interview conducted by John Cumming, Melbourne, 3 July 2002.

439 Hughes cites Sue Jackson, *When history meets the new native title era at the negotiating table, A case study in reconciling land use in Broome, Western Australia: A discussion paper*, NARU, Australian National University, Darwin, NT, 1996.

440 ibid.

441 John Hughes, *River of Dreams*, 1998, SP Betacam, colour, 52 minutes, Early Works, Australia,

Producers Donna Cameron & John Hughes, Scriptwriters Donna Cameron & John Hughes. Produced with assistance from the SBS Independent. Distributed by SBS and Ronin Films.

[442] Peter Sculthorp, 'Earth Cry', conducted by Stuart Challender, CD, recorded 1989, ABC Classics CD no. 426 4812, Australian Broadcasting Commission, Sydney Symphony Orchestra, 1986.

[443] John Hughes, *Take Five*, 1998, Scriptwriter Betty Churcher, Producer John Lewis, 13 parts of 5 mins, ABC TV Arts, Australia. Betty Churcher. Notebooks, MUP, Miegunyah Press, Carlton, 2011, p. 37. When offered the opportunity to create a series of short television segments about art, Churcher 'had no idea how difficult it would be to write [and] craft five minutes of enjoyable information without overkill and without becoming trivial'. She attributes much of the solution of this dilemma to 'the wonderful producer-director John Hughes' saying, 'It was JH's idea to call the first series *Take Five* and to use Dave Brubeck's *Take Five* music'. Hughes recalls *Take Five* as popular and 'a wonderfully instructive work experience'. John Hughes, Melbourne Independent Filmmakers, Bill Mousoulis (ed.) Innersense, Australia, 2010, <http://www.innersense.com.au/mif/hughes.html>, accessed 23 August 2013.

[444] John Hughes, SBSi and after, interview conducted by John Cumming, Melbourne, 9 February 2004.

[445] Santa Barbara Studios & Tig Productions, 1995, Producer WT Morgan & John Pohl, 8-part television series, 500 Nations, USA.

[446] Hughes, op. cit.

[447] For a more thorough discussion of this broadcast series, see Belinda Smaill, 'SBS Documentary and Unfinished Business', *Metro*, no. 126, 2001, pp. 34–40.

[448] Rachel Maher, John Hughes & Megan Spencer, 'Fearless Traditions: Australian documentary culture at the crossroads', *Spinach7*, Winter/Spring 2003, pp. 54–55.

[449] TOF, Television outworkers forum, John Hughes (ed.) Australian Documentary Filmmakers Policy Forum, Melbourne, 2010, <http://lists.culture2.org/cgi–bin/mailman/list info/tof>, accessed 29 June 2010.

[450] Hughes, op. cit.

CHAPTER 10:

The Archive Project

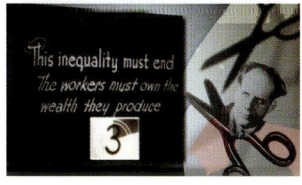

ABOVE: THE 'ONE + ONE' SEQUENCE OF COLLAGES IN *THE ARCHIVE PROJECT* (2006) INVOKES BOTH EISENSTEIN AND GODARD WHILST ELUCIDATING THE VISUAL DIALECTICS OF THE REALISTS' *A PLACE TO LIVE* (1946).

This chapter looks back to the 1940s and forward to a time when filmmaking and web page design begin to merge. It spans the intellectual and creative austerity of the early Cold War period to an overload of information during the War on Terror. In these six decades the apparatus of state-sanctioned surveillance has shifted from being an invisible but invasive presence to a saturating one. Consideration is given here to how Hughes' historical subjects managed to persist alongside the story of his own survival as a critically engaged filmmaker in the early twenty-first century.

As an academic at Monash University in the 1990s, John Hughes encouraged fellow film historian Deane Williams to pursue a PhD research project that considered the role of the Realist Film Association in Australian post-war documentary film.[451] Williams wrote of his research that Hughes had sent him 'on what I thought was a wild goose chase but I now suspect was a deliberate strategy to encourage me to read Australian film differently'.[452] This interest in an alternative view of Australian film history was the motivation for Hughes' own contributions to that field. It is also a motivating idea behind this book.

From the time of researching *Menace* (1976), Hughes had been interested in the idea of a film about the Realist Film movement as a companion piece to *Film-Work* (1981, Chapter 4). *The Archive Project* (2006) extends these earlier investigations of Cold War history in an almost comprehensive celebration of a milieu of fervent discourse and cultural activity the legacies of which include the Melbourne International Film Festival (MIFF).[453] It also joins a larger group of films with a strong historical and biographical focus and a somewhat elegiac tone. With this ninety-eight minute film, Hughes also made an intervention in contemporary audio-visual culture by pushing against the trend to contain documentary filmmaking within the fifty-minute format of the non-commercial television hour. At the same time, the density of the composite screen designs in this film threatens to break out of the non-interactive format. Indeed, the project in some ways led to Hughes' involvement in the design of the *Moving History* website (2007), which traces a parallel history of government film production. There is a renewed emphasis on the activities of the secret service in both these projects, reflecting contemporary concern about the massively expanded function, power and remit of such organisations in the twenty-first century. Hughes' *Archive Project* has a degree of Orwellian relevance he might not have anticipated when thinking about the project in 1984.

The Realist Film Unit (RFU) was established in 1945. Its core members were Ken Coldicutt, Bob Mathews, Gerry Harant, and a little later, Betty Lacey. Williams, drawing on an account in Amirah Inglis' book on Australians in the Spanish Civil War tells how, in the 1930s, Ken Coldicutt travelled the east coast of Australia screening films to raise money for and awareness of the anti-fascist struggle of the Spanish Civil War.[454] The Realist Film Association (RFA) began with screenings at the New Theatre in Melbourne. The intention of the founders was to make films, yet they may have also conducted the first formal film scholarship in Australia. The Realists held seminars on film analysis and theory, published *Realist Film News* and operated a library and bookshop.[455] The Realists sought alliances with the trade union movement and the New Theatre in both Melbourne and Sydney.[456] They also had close connections with the Communist Party of Australia (CPA), yet Mathews and Coldicutt each had different and troubled relationships with the Party. According to Coldicutt, they were never paid by the CPA for the cost of the one campaign film *Prices and the People* (1946) that the Party commissioned from the RFA. The RFU also made *In My Beginning* with the progressive school Koornong (1947, see Chapter 4).[457]

From 2002 until 2006 Hughes dedicated the time available around other endeavours to his Realist Film project. There had been little interest from broadcasters, so Hughes turned his idea into a multiplatform archive project to be worked on from many fronts. In 2002 he arranged to become an artist in residence at the Australian Centre for the Moving Image (ACMI) in its inaugural year of operation at the Federation Square contemporary arts complex in the centre of Melbourne. There was no wage, but as with Video Projects at Trades Hall Council in the 1980s, he had some institutional backing, an email address, and a shared computer. He also stood to earn an artist's fee for creating an installation and curating a screening program: *Independent Voice: Australian political documentary from the 1940s to the 1980s* (2005). Hughes also entered into collaboration with the National Film and Sound Archive (NFSA, then known as Screen Sound), an organisation that knew of the historical import of the work. The ACMI residency went through a number of changes, as did the management of ACMI and with it, curatorial policy. There was a period when Hughes' archive project was to become part of a larger show to celebrate the 150th anniversary of the Eight Hour Day movement in Australia. Instead, the project was exhibited as a three-month installation in '2006 Contemporary Commonwealth' mounted by ACMI and the National Gallery of Victoria at ACMI's large gallery space at Federation Square, nearby to major venues for the 2006 Commonwealth Games.[458]

THE *INDEPENDENT VOICE* INSTALLATION AT THE AUSTRALIAN CENTRE FOR THE MOVING IMAGE, 2006.

With the *Independent Voice* screening, curated and presented at ACMI as part of the Melbourne Cinémathèque program, Hughes set out to demonstrate that 'determinedly independent filmmaking has a long history in Australia'.[459] The program included Realist films from the NFSA. *These Are Our Children* (1946) and *A Place to Live* (1946) were some of the films produced by the RFU for the Brotherhood of St Laurence, as part of a campaign against poverty in inner city Melbourne. Jack Fitzsimons worked with the Realists on *A Place to Live* and produced two other films for the Brotherhood. He was a member of the Victorian Amateur Cine Society, winning their 1946 Members Cup for *Gaol Does Not Cure*. This suggests that 'hobbyist' filmmaking at that time could deal with serious social issues.[460] The RFU project *They Chose Peace* (1952) traces the story of the Youth Carnival for Peace and Friendship held in Sydney in March 1952 against substantial interference from authorities.[461] It was during the making of this film that Bob Mathews literally handed a young Keith Gow a 16 mm Bolex camera to start filming (see Chapter 4). The program also included Hughes' *November Eleven* (1979, see Chapter 3) and three films by collectives: Davies, Howard and Laughren's *Exits* (1980, see Chapter 5), Laurie and Nash's *We Aim to Please* (1976, see Chapter 4) and *Beginnings* (1970, see Chapter 1), the seminal Melbourne anti-war film made by some of the founders of the journal *Cinema Papers*.

The installation included video projections varying in scale across two gallery spaces, glass cases displaying artefacts. Hughes used long strands of rich red ceiling-to-floor drapes to evoke both the flags and banners of political street processions and cinema curtains. A smaller screen set in the larger space, adjacent to a very large screen displaying *They Chose Peace*, displayed ASIO

AN EARLY 1950s PEACE MARCH AND BOB MATHEWS IN *THE ARCHIVE PROJECT* (2006).

surveillance film of people arriving and leaving a Communist Party meeting at the New Theatre, which in the 1950s was located a city block away from the ACMI gallery. Hughes explains:

If spectators were to turn their gaze in the direction of the street, 15 degrees from the screen displaying these 'uncanny' scenes, they would be approximately where that secret camera was hidden some 40 years earlier. This would be evident to those who noted the text specifying where and when the surveillance footage was made, or who recognised the landmark streetscape of Flinders Street between Swanston and Russell Streets. The installation was an ironic 'situational' play with past, present and place, sound and image, nostalgia and politics.[462]

The installation's sound treatment drew on commissioned music by Melbourne composer Martin Friedel, and mixed between the original sounds of the films displayed, with new soundtracks purpose-built for the installation.

Over three decades Hughes had discovered and gathered various documents and film trims from the Realists' films. He had also collected interviews that other historians had recorded with the RFU's late founders. Graeme Cutts provided the only known interview footage of Ken Coldicutt.[463] Hughes had lent historian Deane Williams his Hi-8 video camera to record a research interview with Bob Mathews in the 1990s, knowing that in time this footage would be a useful resource. After some work with development investment from the Australian Film Commission (AFC) and Film Victoria, the Australian Broadcasting Corporation (ABC) documentary division initially rejected *The Archive Project*. ABC TV Arts and Entertainment eventually commissioned it, however, as a half-hour item for the Sunday Arts program. With a television presale, Hughes

FROM LEFT: BOB MATHEWS; MARGARET WALKER IN *THE ARCHIVE PROJECT* (2006).

was able to secure additional production investment from Film Victoria. In-kind contributions came from ACMI, the NFSA and the Melbourne post-production house Music and Effects. The major investor was Hughes' production company, Early Works. This meant that with a budget equivalent to that of a modest 30-minute documentary, Hughes could afford to do the necessary production work and to get Mizrahi on board to edit what was to become a feature documentary. The co-producer of *The Archive Project* film, Philippa Campey, had worked with Hughes at SBSi as the documentary co-coordinator in Melbourne (2000–2002), and was line producer for two of the Hughes/Churcher television art history programs *Take Five*, *The Art of War* (2005) and *Hidden Treasures* (2006).[464]

In his 2003 'Notes on Treatment', Hughes writes of a 'hybrid diary compilation', and has the form of Jost's *Speaking Directly* (1974) and Godard's contribution to *Far From Vietnam* (1967) in mind.[465] While 'The treatment does not foreground the first person narrator, but rather the Realists' stories, their films and their historical context', Hughes proposed to parallel the history of the RFU films with those of his own films which he used as a source of archival material, making his own filmography part of the 'archive' in the title of this film.[466] Whilst they would function as archival material in a conventional manner, Hughes would also introduce his films in a self-reflexive way in the opening scenes of the new work. Indeed, scenes with Keith Gow from *Film-Work* are used to introduce Realist filmmaker Bob Mathews and include a freeze frame of Hughes produced when Gow turns his Bolex camera on the *Film-Work* crew (see Chapter 4).

In his narration for *The Archive Project*, Hughes explains how he recognised scenes from a number of Realist films in a previously unidentified reel of 16 mm trims at the NFSA in Canberra. Hughes' voice-over takes us through this material, noting images that 'evoke social conditions of the mid forties in Australia', the Peace Congress in Melbourne and anti-war graffiti from the early 1950s. Hughes also identifies practices that echo his own approach to filmmaking in 'shots of silent scripted drama' and 'new experiments with screen design'. At this point, against images of

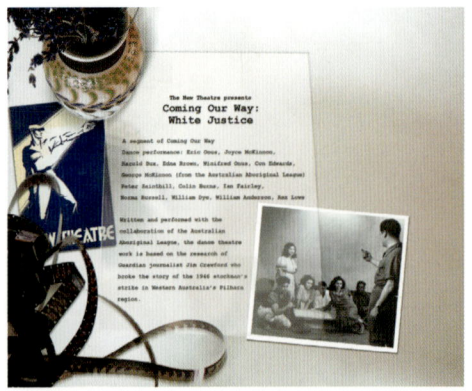 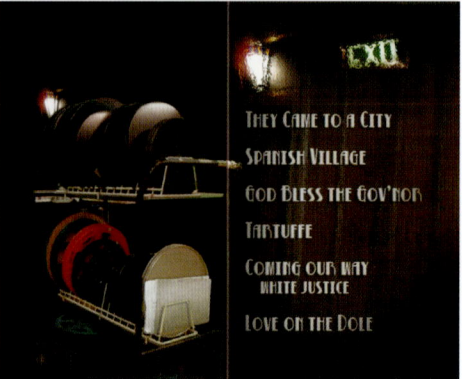

FROM LEFT: INTRODUCTORY PAGE FOR A THREE-MINUTE RFU FILM PROMOTING *COMING OUR WAY: WHITE JUSTICE* – A CO-PRODUCTION OF THE NEW THEATRE AND THE AUSTRALIAN ABORIGINAL LEAGUE ABOUT THE 1948 STOCKMEN'S STRIKE IN THE PILBARA REGION OF WESTERN AUSTRALIA; MENU PAGE FOR THE DVD CONTAINING THE RESTORED RFU FILMS FROM *THE ARCHIVE PROJECT* (2006) DVD BOX SET.

The Slums Are Still With Us (1947), the beautifully modulated voice and considerable intellect of John Flaus invokes Kluge ('My camera sees what is unseen by the society. Look at the invisible ones.') and Virginia Wolf, before expounding a theory that realism is the everyday – the taken for granted, like rediscovering childhood wonder, before the loss of 'innocence' to 'social function'.[467] Drawing on his prodigious knowledge of film history, Flaus then proposes that the unresolved narrative structure of the Realists' *These Are Our Children* was unique for its time. Hughes and Mizhari integrate shots of Flaus' talking head into their screen design amid the sprocket holes of archival material. His own wondrous, methodical attitude and his gentle commentary here marry well with Hughes' narration for the film.

It was something of a breakthrough for Hughes to lend his own voice to one of his films. He accurately describes his narration as 'recessed … minimal, ironic' in its reference to his own encounters with the history at hand.[468] Yet this understated personal narrative does help to articulate the idea that all the film's materials are elements in a process of historical construction. In 2011, at a seminar for emerging documentary filmmakers, Amanda Kerley asked Hughes how he represented the process of investigation in his filmmaking. Hughes explained that the 'treatment solution' that the material for a project called for was often different and that with each film he usually tries to do something that is 'different, formally, to the dominant method of speaking in documentary' – because it is more interesting to do so.[469] He explained that with *The Archive Project,* the first person narrator provided a way to get a 'through line' to the story and provided the best way to make a claim about how it related to the present. Hughes had resisted using the first person narrator for many years. He told Kerley that 'Once upon a time' it was an innovation to speak in an autobiographical voice, giving Mike Rubbo's 1974 *Waiting For Fidel* as an example of work that displaced the 'voice of god' that had been the dominant form of documentary narration for decades. As the practice became mainstream it was commonplace, Hughes explained, for journalists to employ first person narration until it was normalised into the voice of celebrity and lost any capacity for criticism. Mike Moore then took that figure back and turned it into a comic send-up of the celebrity. The position that Hughes settled for as 'tolerable'

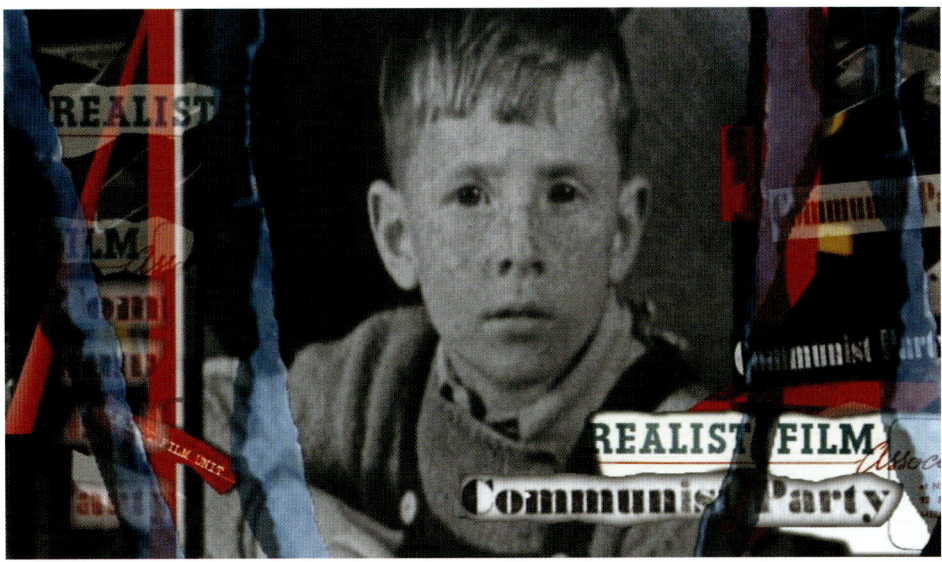

SCREEN DESIGN COMBINING PRINT AND FILM MATERIAL OF THE REALIST FILM ASSOCIATION IN *THE ARCHIVE PROJECT* (2006).

was something he called the 'recessed narrator', which put the material the film was dealing with, rather than personality, into the foreground.[470]

The question of narration also came up with regard to the Realist films within *The Archive Project* film. Due to the poor quality of many of the old optical sound prints, Hughes proposed to create new soundtracks for some of the surviving RFU films. The resultant 'new works' would be 'more technically sophisticated and contemporary' and thus more accessible for audiences of today.[471] To this end, Hughes had already re-recorded voice-overs for *They Chose Peace* and *Prices and the People* with actors Deborah Mailman and Bryan Brown and had organised for Martin Friedel, who composed music for *One Way Street*, to compose and produce music for *The Archive Project*. These restored versions were used for the Independent Voice installation and screening program and were ultimately included in *The Archive Box*, a three-disc DVD set that also included Hughes' documentary feature, and a selection of 'oral history' films that recount the cultural milieu of the RFA, including the New Theatre, the Margaret Walker Dance Group and an account by Philip Adams of his time projecting films for the Association in the mid-1950s. There is also a collection of supporting facsimile documents. The DVDs have richly illustrated menus and two of the discs include indexes of people and topics that link to specific films in the collection.

Hughes' decision to revise the soundtracks to other filmmakers' works was a creative risk and arguably an ethical one too. The result is both respectful and surprisingly harmonious and fresh. The measured use of shots showing Mailman and Brown working at the microphones augments the spectacle of historical construction through montage that is *The Archive Project*. These scenes foreground the reconstructed nature of the sound in the same way that similar

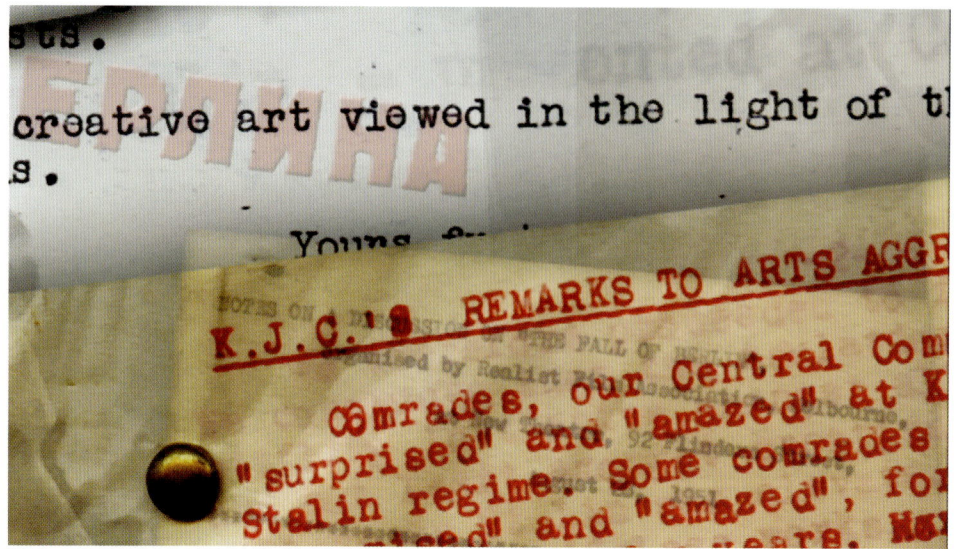

THE TEXTURE OF AN ARCHIVE COLOURS THE SCREEN DESIGN OF *THE ARCHIVE PROJECT* (2006).

scenes in Godard and Gorin's *Tout va bien* (1972) and Straub and Huillet's *Introduction to an accompaniment to a cinematographic scene by Arnold Schoenberg* (1976) had done.[472] In Hughes' film, however, the reflexive effect is achieved most efficiently in the sensitive transition from original to remake in the new sound mix.

The range and quantity of visual material that has been brought together in *The Archive Project* made the film an ideal vehicle for Hughes and Mizrahi to further refine their work on screen design. Hughes' accumulated Realist archive is framed, arranged, layered and mixed together intricately. This concentration on design within the frame, as collage, has always been married with a tendency towards montage. Such bricolage is unusual in Australian filmmaking. More than any previous film by Hughes, *The Archive Project* is a work of montage, yet the use of frames within the frame allows for extended and seemingly uninterrupted passages of archival material.

In sophistication of design and technique *The Archive Project* displays the development that has taken place through *After Mabo* (1997) and *River of Dreams* (1998).[473] Hughes' pre-production notes provide a perfectly accurate description of the finished film:

Stylistically the film must both sustain the integrity of the Social Realism of the original work, and present the films very firmly grounded in the present. The screen design idea proposed achieves this by creating an 'aesthetic of disruption'; it will not feel seamless. Textures, formats and styles will tend to clash rather than be smoothed over.[474]

The Archive Project was made using standard definition broadcast video technology but does employ the widescreen format that became the standard for television in the 2000s. Hughes'

RARE FOOTAGE OF KEN COLDICUTT FROM GRAEME CUTTS' RESTORED 1970s J-FORMAT REEL TO REEL VIDEO IN *THE ARCHIVE PROJECT* (2006).

proposal anticipates how this 16:9 aspect ratio for *The Archive Project* provides a canvas of redundant space left by archival images in the more narrow 4:3 format, allowing for a range of collage techniques to be employed. Hughes' notes continue:

By these means the film can maintain the integrity of the original material, while illustrating context and commentary simultaneously. This will produce a unique form of editing and style; a 'simultaneity' of past and present […] Screen design will anticipate scenes, and sustain the continuance of cut scenes alongside those that follow. That is, we will see elements of still-to-come scenes present in collage with the dominant sequence. One of the affects of this strategy will be a frequent clash of textures, genres and styles, not only during the course of the film as it cites its various sources, but simultaneously in collage as the narrative unfolds.[475]

Hughes and Mizrahi made great use of the 1950s black-and-white ASIO surveillance footage and surveillance photographs of the protagonists of the RFA story as they went about their daily business, unaware of the camera's telephoto gaze. These images of surveillance take on a range of qualities – from ironic to tragic – as an illustrative background or humorous counterpoint to the narrative supplied by words in voice-overs, interviews, and text on screen and archival sound. These ostensibly objective recordings of banal events – roadside comings and goings – also provide the ideal foil for Hughes' ongoing cinematic discourse on the politics of representation.

Historian Tony Barta observed a paradox in the use of words in films of the early 1990s by Ross Gibson, David Perry and John Hughes.

A PHOTOGRAPH FROM 1950 OF ELIZABETH COLDICUTT FILMING WITH A 16 MM CAMERA IN *THE ARCHIVE PROJECT* (2006).

… Film as a reflective medium now can be re-empowered only by the word, so that we listen for images in the words of the storyteller, [and] rely on them for our escape from the redundant and misleading picture on the screen, that misrepresentation of the past by naturalist replication which it was film's forte to achieve.[476]

In *The Archive Project*, the relentless use of words further multiplies the imagery in just this way. Barta's observations of Ross Gibson's *Camera Natura* (1985), David Perry's *The Refracting Glasses* (1993) and John Hughes' *One Way Street* (1992, see Chapter 7) sit well with *The Archive Project*.[477] For him, the earlier films carried a 'deep historical mourning' whilst being 'playful'. They reflect both the 'losses of patterned meaning' that an orthodox Marxist world-view provided and a 'recovery of human hope'.[478] *The Archive Project* is also imbued with something of the elegiac tone of *One Way Street*, particularly with regard to the quiet tragedy that emerges from Graeme Cutts' video interview with Ken Coldicutt. The quality of these restored scenes, particularly the sound quality, is remarkably good and they provide some of the most poignant and haunting material in the film. By this stage of the film we've already heard a lot about Coldicutt, notably from Williams' interview with an elderly Bob Mathews. Reference has been made to some breakdown in their relationship, but the archival material from the 1940s and 1950s has provided the image of a young, dynamic powerhouse of a man. In Cutts' interview, Coldicutt seems to have been wearied by his encounters with Cold War power politics. Hughes and Mizrahi emphasise this quality by slowing down images of Coldicutt's face while asynchronously overlaying the sound of his testimony.

FROM LEFT: ELIZABETH COLDICUTT IN A SCREEN DESIGN INCLUDING 16 MM FRAMES FROM THE REALIST FILM UNIT'S *THESE ARE OUR CHILDREN* (1948), *THE ARCHIVE PROJECT* (2006) DVD BOX SET.

Coldicutt speaks frankly and forcefully of his experiences in the post-war decades: his falling out with and ultimate contempt for officials of the Communist Party and his treatment by the right through blacklisting from government employment and federal attempts to coerce him into spying upon members of a legal and legitimate political party.

Ken's widow, Elizabeth Coldicutt (neé Lacy), who was also an active RFU/RFA member, provides one of the few contemporary interviews conducted for *The Archive Project*. She describes her sacking from a job at the State Film Centre because of her use of its mailing list in a campaign against the Victorian government's attempts to register and control the screening of films through The Cinematograph Films Bill of 1948. According to the film, this was a Bill explicitly aimed at gagging the RFU. While the whole of the Coldicutts' story can only be alluded to, Hughes provides archival documentation, in abundance and in minutiae, of the depth and persistence of

FROM LEFT: A SHOT OF KEITH GOW WORKING AT FILM AUSTRALIA, FROM *FILM-WORK* (1981), REFRAMED IN *THE ARCHIVE PROJECT* (2006); A MENU SCREEN FROM *THE ARCHIVE PROJECT* DVD BOX SET; 16 MM FRAMES FROM THE REALIST FILM UNIT'S *THESE ARE OUR CHILDREN* (1948).

the surveillance and interference that they received from Australian authorities. The combination of artefacts and testimony is overwhelming – both emotionally and as evidence. The ASIO archives illustrate a tragic and absurd hounding of a film association and a group of individuals. They serve as a profound warning about the arbitrary abuse of power by politicians and agents of the state at times when a self-perpetuating perception of a threat to national security is created.

Hughes began to plan *The Archive Project* in earnest in 2002 when the Australian government introduced a broad slate of legislation that increased the already substantial power and reach of the state's security apparatus to unprecedented levels. These included the capacity to detain citizens for up to 48 hours without access to communication or legal advice, while effectively outlawing the steps necessary for a citizenry to publicly hold authorities to account. By the time the film was completed in 2005, the security state was even more emboldened. The *Anti-Terrorism Act 2005* placed unprecedented police power into the hands of intelligence officers and politicians. Howard's Liberal–National Coalition government had control of both houses of parliament and was enacting further legislation, driven by a desire to curb the power of student organisations and trade unions and to maximise the opportunity to extend the state's coercive powers afforded by the perceived threat of terrorism.

Feature length documentaries had already become a rarity on ABC television by 2007. *The Archive Project* was given a prime-time slot on the national broadcaster's main channel at 9.30 pm on 25 January, the night before the Australia Day public holiday. The 90-minute format allows for adequate immersion in the world of the Realists and their tormentors, but there is a sense of abbreviation towards the end of the film. In the closing passages, Hughes and Mizrahi, despite an enormous effort at compression, do not have the luxury either to complete the story in the epic way that it deserves, or to continue and resolve the play with film form that is established so startlingly in the Eisensteinian montage of attractions that constitutes the opening scenes. The Constructivist impulse towards reportage is as much in evidence in here as it was in *Film-Work* (1981, see Chapter 4). With its storehouse of archival materials *The Archive Project* is reminiscent of Tretiakoff's concept of a 'biography of things'. Through the archival video interviews, the film also allows a proximity to the human dimension of the political story it tells.[479]

FROM LEFT: A FILM EDITOR'S VIEWER IN A DVD MENU SCREEN FROM *THE ARCHIVE PROJECT* (2006) DVD BOX SET.

Most importantly, Hughes and Mizrahi use the longer form to include extended excerpts from the RFU films, avoiding the tendency towards concision that plagues most documentaries that deal with time-based art. Hughes holds to an editorial resolve, treating the original films with proper respect for their feel, content and form. The normal televisual routine is to pre-digest such material into predictable, snappy clips and to use this archival chaff primarily as a source for illustrative pillow imagery on which to lay interview sound or narration. Another tendency of television documentary that *The Archive Project* bucks is the habit of selecting archival material that smuggly confirms rather than challenges popular contemporary preconceptions of (and mainstream propaganda from) the past.

In 2006 Hughes' work won nominations from the AFI and awards from the Film Critics Circle of Australia, Australian Teachers of Media (ATOM), the NSW Premier's History Awards and the Film and History Association of Australia and New Zealand. These honours represent the esteem of professional peers in the fields of film, history and education. Finally, Hughes' entire effort as a filmmaker was recognised in 2006 with Film Australia's Stanley Hawes Award for Achievement in Documentary, the most prestigious award in Australian documentary film. Yet, even as a leading filmmaker on the cusp of such public decoration, it took enormous perseverance on Hughes' part to see *The Archive Project* through to completion. He did so, in part, by continuing – like most active Australian artists – to subsidise cultural production with a significant commitment of

Program, Early Works, ABC TV Arts, Producers John Hughes & Philippa Campey, Scriptwriter Betty Churcher, Executive Producer Anna Grieve, Camera Joel Peterson, Sound Mark Tarpey, Steve Best, Music Paul Grabowsky, Editor Uri Mizrahi. Featuring Betty Churcher.
Campey established her own production company in 2004 through which she has produced a number of significant projects. See Philippa Campey, Filmcamp, 2012, <http://www.filmcamp.com.au/>, accessed 23 February 2013.

465 Joris Ivens, William Klein, Claude Lelouch, Jean-Luc Godard, Chris Marker, Alain Resnais & Agnès Varda, *Far from Vietnam/Loin du Vietnam*, 1967, 35 mm, colour, 115 minutes, Slon, Paris.
466 John Hughes, Notes on Treatment, *The Archive Project* Proposal, 2003.
467 The descriptions of Flaus' voice and intellect are from Patricia Edgar who gives a wonderful account of their pioneering work together with film studies at La Trobe University in the early 1970s. Patricia Edgar, 'The John Flaus I Know', John Flaus Dossier, *Senses of Cinema*, issue 72, October 2014, <http://sensesofcinema.com/2014/john-flaus-dossier/the-john-flaus-i-know/>, accessed 16 November 2014.
468 John Hughes, *The Archive Project*, synopsis and proposal, funding application, Melbourne, 2003.
469 John Hughes, 'Back Story Update with John Hughes', recording by John Cumming of interview conducted by Amanda Kerley & William Head, *Generation Next Documentary Conference*, Open Channel, Cinema Nova, Carlton, Australia, 13 October 2011.
470 Michael Rubbo, *Waiting for Fidel*, 1974, 16 mm, colour, 58 minutes, Producers Tom Daly, Colin Low & Michael Rubbo, Editor Michael Rubbo. Hughes, op. cit.
471 John Hughes, *The Archive Project*, synopsis and proposal, funding application, Melbourne, 2003.
472 Jean-Luc Godard & Jean Pierre Gorin, *Tout va bien*, 1972, 35 mm, colour, 51 minutes.
Jean-Marie Straub & Danièle Huillet, *Introduction to an accompaniment to a cinematographic scene by Arnold Schoenberg*, 1976, 17 minutes.
473 See Chapter 9 for a discussion of these films.
474 John Hughes, Notes on Treatment, *The Archive Project* proposal, 2003.
475 ibid.
476 Tony Barta, 'Making it Strange: Camera Natura, One Way Street and The Refracting Glasses as Realism, Surrealism and the Poetics of History in Film', in John Benson, Ken Berryman & Wayne Levy (eds), *Screening the Past: The Sixth Australian History and Film Conference Papers*, Melbourne, La Trobe University, 1993, p. 209.
477 Ross Gibson, *Camera Natura*, 1985, 16 mm, colour, 32 minutes, Australia, Producer John Cruthers, Scriptwriter John Cruthers, Camera Ray Argall, Music Gary Warner, Editor Ian Allen. Produced with assistance from the CDB/AFC. Distributed by Ronin Films.
David Perry, *The Refracting Glasses*, 1993, 109 minutes, Sydney, Camera Simon Smith. Featuring David Perry, Leon Teague, Tommy Thoms, Taylor Owynns & Alia Karihaloo.
478 Barta, op. cit.
479 John Willett, *The New Sobriety: Art and Politics in the Weimar Period 1917–33*, Thames and Hudson, London, 1978, p. 107.
480 John Hughes, *The Archive Project*, synopsis and proposal, funding application, Melbourne, 2003.
481 John Hughes, SBSi and after, interview conducted by John Cumming, Melbourne, 9 February 2004.
482 John Hughes, 'Moving History' A place to think, online multimedia, Film Australia, ABC, Executive Producers Anna Grieve & Ian Allen, 2007, <http://www.abc.net.au/aplacetothink/? – watch>, accessed 2 February 2013.
483 Peter Weir, *Whatever Happened to Green Valley?* 1973, 16 mm, 55 minutes, Film Australia, Sydney.
484 Richard Mason & Jack Lee, *From the Tropics to the Snow*, 1962, colour, 28 minutes, Commonwealth Film Unit, Producer Jack S Allan, Scriptwriters John Morris, Cedric Flower & Pat Flower.

Endnotes

[451] Deane Williams, *Australian Post-War Documentary Film: an Arc of Mirrors*, Intellect, Bristol, 2008. Hughes' research and his collection of Realist Film Unit/Association material underpinned the first chapter of Williams' book.

[452] Deane Williams, 'An arc of mirrors: remaking Australian post-war documentary films', PhD thesis, Cinema Studies, La Trobe University, Bundoora, 2000.

[453] John Hughes & Uri Mizrahi, *The Archive Project*, 2006, colour and b&w, 98 minutes, Early Works, Melbourne, Producers Philippa Campey & John Hughes, Scriptwriter John Hughes, Editor Uri Mizrahi. Produced with assistance from the NFSA, AFC, Film Victoria, ABC TV Arts and Music and Effects.

[454] Deane Williams, 2008, op. cit., p. 32.

[455] John Hughes, *The Archive Project*, synopsis and production proposal, funding application, Melbourne, 2003. Graham Shirley & Brian Adams, *Australian Cinema: The First Eighty Years*, 2nd edn, Angus & Robertson, Sydney, 1989. Originally published 1983, p. 176.

[456] Ray Clarke, a founder of the Sydney RFA, told Lisa Milner that the association's role was to screen films 'to the party and branches'. Lisa Milner, *Fighting films: a history of the Waterside Workers' Federation Film Unit*, Pluto Press, North Melbourne, Vic., 2003, p. 31. The available research suggests that this was not the view of the Melbourne RFA founders.

[457] Realist Film Unit, *Prices and the People*, 1948, 16 mm, b&w, 18 minutes, RFU, Melbourne, Scriptwriters Bob Mathews & Jim Crawford, Camera Bob Mathews & Keith Gow, Narrator Ken Otway in John Hughes & Uri Mizrahi, *The Archive Project*, 2006, DVD box set. Distributed by Artfilms.
Ken Coldicutt, Bob Mathews & Gerhart (Gerry) Harant, *In My Beginning: A Story of New Education*, 1947, 16 mm, colour, sound, 17 minutes, Realist Film Unit Melbourne, Scriptwriter JC (Clive) Nield and students of Koornong School, in particular, Mavourneen Box, Souzka Frankel & Jenepher Potts, in Hughes & Uri Mizrahi, op. cit.

[458] C Green, *2006 Contemporary Commonwealth*, NGV, Melbourne, 2006.

[459] Melbourne Cinémathèque, 'Independent Voice: Australian political documentary from the 1940s to the 1980s', Melbourne Cinémathèque program notes, 13 July 2005.

[460] Ken Coldicutt & John (Jack) G Fitzsimmons, *A Place To Live*, 1946, 16 mm, b&w, silent, 13 minutes, Brotherhood of St Laurence, Melbourne, Producers Fr Gerard Tucker and Realist Film Unit, in John Hughes & Uri Mizrahi, *The Archive Project*, 2006, DVD box set. Distributed by Artfilms.
Ken Coldicutt, *These Are Our Children*, 1946, 16 mm, b&w, silent, 12 minutes, Brotherhood of St Laurence, Melbourne, Producers Fr Gerard Tucker & Realist Film Unit, in Hughes & Uri Mizrahi, op. cit.
John (Jack) G Fitzsimons, *Gaol Does Not Cure*, b&w, 1946, 16 mm, silent, Victorian Amateur Cine Society, Melbourne, held by NFSA.

[461] Bob Mathews, *They Chose Peace: Youth Carnival for Peace and Friendship*, 1952, 16 mm, b&w, 28 minutes, Sydney, Realist Films, Camera Bob Mathews, Keith Gow & David Muir in Hughes & Uri Mizrahi, op. cit.

[462] John Hughes, Notes on *The Archive Project*, email to John Cumming, Melbourne, 30 June 2010.

[463] Cutts' video material existed in the form of two half-inch J-format video reels that he had recorded in the 1970s and that required restoration by the NFSA through a process that includes baking the videotape in an oven before transferring the image and sound to a digital format.

[464] John Hughes, *The Art of War*, 2005, colour, 4 x 26 minutes, Film Australia National Interest Program, Early Works and SBS Independent, Australia, Producers John Hughes, Betty Churcher, Scriptwriter Betty Churcher, Executive Producer Anna Grieve, Camera Joel Peterson, Sound Mark Tarpey, Music Paul Grabowsky, Editor Uri Mizrahi. Featuring Betty Churcher. Produced with assistance from the Australian War Memorial. John Hughes, *Hidden Treasures*, 2006, 10 x 5 minutes, Film Australia National Interest

films are documentaries; however, some include dramatised sequences. *Whatever Happened to Green Valley* (1973) is a community-based project directed by Peter Weir, the now famous (Hollywood) director, which includes scenes created by residents of a housing estate.[483] Each element in *Moving History* has a text overview and other supporting material such as photos, audio and video clips including radio, television and oral history interviews and other text material such as obituaries, reviews and press clippings.

One element in the 'Graphic History' is a sequence called Security. This storyboard documents the monitoring and interference with Film Australia's operations. It begins with an ABC radio interview ('Double Take', 1983) with Stanley Hawes, producer in chief of the Film Division from 1946 until the early 1970s. He discusses the removal of members of his staff, without consultation, and explains that he was 'given to understand' that he was regarded as a security risk himself. The next frame of the 'Graphic History' links to a pdf format display of a copy of a memorandum between the Attorney-General's Department and ASIO concerning suspicions that Hawes was a communist. The composition of the drawings in this sequence is based on frames from the Commonwealth Film Unit classic *From the Tropics to the Snow* (1962) in which the figure of Hawes is represented in dramatised scenes.[484] The comments on the '1960s' web page, where the whole of that film could be viewed, describe it as an example of 'the emergence of a more adventurous period'. The film division was required to produce travelogue films for the purposes of promoting Australia to potential migrants and tourists abroad. *From the Tropics to the Snow* is a self-reflexive satirical pastiche of that genre.

Hughes wrote and designed the *Moving History* website at the conceptual level in collaboration with Film Australia's executive producer Anna Grieve, prescribing the key elements for the ABC's online creative and technical team to work on. The graphics, design and website authoring were delivered by ABC Online staff. This was a commissioned work rather than independent work and the Film Australia films are not independent films. We have seen, however, how the stories of individuals in Hughes' trilogy of films about post-war Australian documentary filmmaking have intersected with the Film Australia narrative, as Hughes' own story does at this juncture. Furthermore, this work by Hughes on a website evolves logically from the highly developed screen designs in his filmmaking and feeds into the conception of his next film.

As much as a writer can emphasise their import, the work of the RFU and the work of Hughes' *Archive Project* can easily be lost or passed over. The RFU's films were confined to small halls; Hughes' film about them was originally destined to appear in an arts program on a Sunday afternoon. The RFU filmmakers were hounded and undermined in their professional lives. For Hughes, like any contemporary independent filmmaker whose work has a different orientation to that of the commercial market – and in an environment where what is heard and seen is increasingly managed by the terms of that market – the limited exposure the films receive may barely seem worth the effort of production. Perhaps, in the case of both Hughes and the RFU, the work is about holding open small spaces of difference, small gaps through which alternative perspectives might be glimpsed.

voluntary effort. Even with his professional standing, knowledge and contacts within the film and television industry – and after enormous effort – it was only possible to secure the most basic finance the project required. He told me that at the time the film was completed, he felt for the first time that it might be his last. That it continues to be so difficult for a filmmaker of Hughes' stature to do this work does not bode well for other, less experienced independent producers – especially those who might seek to be as adventurous in their filmmaking.

The Realists, like Hughes, exemplify the independent filmmaker as educator, organiser and cultural activist. They initiated film scholarship in Australia and, as Hughes notes, laid the foundations for the film society movement and for Australia's first, and some of the world's earliest, international film festivals.[480] Hughes saw *The Archive Project* as especially relevant to young activists who were 'developing their own networks of communication that do not involve the mainstream media'.[481] The collective compilation DVD/web-based project *Time To Go John* was a good example of this digital activism and one that Hughes became involved with in 2004. In this effort, a number of filmmakers joined to create a work that questioned the policies and record of the Howard Liberal-National government. Young filmmakers like those in that collective are a small but important audience for *The Archive Project* beyond its life on broadcast television. Such cultural producers stand to gain from this film a greater understanding – and, importantly, an audio-visual one – of the historical context of their oppositional practice.

Moving History website (2007)

In 2006 Hughes undertook another archival project, writing and designing the conceptual framework of the *Moving History* (2007) website for Film Australia and the ABC.[482] This work compiles a history of Film Australia, the federal government film production company that began as the production arm of the Australian National Film Board (ANFB) in the mid-1940s, became the Films Division of the Department of Information, later became the Commonwealth Film Unit and then Film Australia. The project draws on the archives of Film Australia, the National Film and Sound Archive and on other sources that Hughes identified, including his own archives and the National Archives of Australia's collection of declassified national security files.

The first element in this website is a graphic history of the organisation, arranged as sequences of cartoon frames, in the style of a graphic novel. The sequence, called Origins, begins with a graphic representation of a frame from the opening scene of *Film-Work* (1981, see Chapter 4) in which Keith Gow arrives for work at the Film Australia studios with his motorcycle and sidecar. Clicking on this frame opens a video stream of the actual sequence from the film. Other frames include thought bubbles and captions tracing the antecedence and history of the formation of the Australian National Film Board. It tells a story of bureaucratic competition that fundamentally compromised the hopeful intentions of 'Nugget' Coombs and the Department of Post-war Reconstruction he led and from which the ANFB idea emerged. Each of the other elements in the website is dedicated to a decade of Film Australia activity, with sequences from significant films that were produced by Australia's Commonwealth film production body. Most of these

CHAPTER 11:

Indonesia Calling and *Love & Fury*

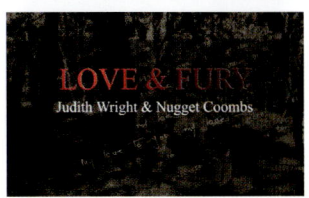

FROM TOP: HUGHES' FILM REVISITS THE TITLE DESIGN OF IVENS' 1946 FILM IN *INDONESIA CALLING: JORIS IVENS IN AUSTRALIA* (2009); *LOVE & FURY* (2013).

Joris Ivens' film *Indonesia Calling* (1946) is a seminal work of underground political filmmaking in Australia. It traces a groundbreaking multicultural, trade union campaign in support of the political independence of the former Dutch East Indies. John Hughes' *Indonesia Calling: Joris Ivens in Australia* (2009) brings original historical research to the investigation of this early independent documentary and uses that story to tease out a number of other threads that resonate with Hughes' earlier films.[485] These include a painful colonial history and the suppression of communism during the Cold War – through a coup d'état and mass executions in Indonesia and through covert witch-hunts and blacklisting in Australia. Hughes also revisits the biopic with this project, and together with Mizrahi, develops the art of documentary screen design to the verge of digital interactivity.

Joris Ivens' *Indonesia Calling* is an exemplar of independent activist documentary filmmaking.[486] It emerged from the spontaneous response of a diverse community of people to an immediate political situation of global significance. The film was made without support or approval from state or commercial interests, on a miniscule budget, with a shooting ratio of little more than 1:1 and with volunteer labour. Solidarity between working people of different races, cultures and nations is at the heart of the production and women made key technical and creative contributions. *Indonesia Calling: Joris Ivens in Australia* (Hughes, 2009) is a documentary about the Ivens' film and those who made it. Hughes' film, which I will refer to by its subtitle, completes a triptych of works about post-war, independent documentary filmmaking in Australia. The main events in this story precede those in *The Archive Project* (2006, see Chapter 10) and *Film-Work* (1981, see Chapter 4).

GRAEME CUTTS IN *INDONESIA CALLING: JORIS IVENS IN AUSTRALIA* (2009).

Like *Menace* (1976), *Film-Work, The Archive Project* and *One Way Street* (1992), the story told in *Joris Ivens in Australia* begins amidst the progressive cultural and political movements of the interwar years. This was a period of intense ideological struggle between left and right, culminating after the Great Depression in a global campaign – led most vigorously by those associated with the communist movement – against the rise of fascism. Ivens' involvement in this milieu and his celebrated engagement with the avant-garde established him as a major figure in the development of documentary filmmaking in its first generation.

In his voice-over narration for *Joris Ivens in Australia*, Hughes describes *Indonesia Calling* as 'a film about a special bond forged between Australians and Indonesians after the war [that] spoke out at a time of great conflict and great hope.' He also speaks of Ivens' film as having lasting implications for Australian documentary. Historian Graeme Cutts did the first substantial English language scholarship on *Indonesia Calling*. In an interview in Hughes' film, Cutts points out that not only the film, but Ivens' stay in Australia was significant. In June 1945 Ivens advised the Australian government regarding the establishment and staffing of the Films Division of the Australian National Film Board, an agency of government that later became Film Australia. As Deane Williams has argued, Australian film history prior to Cutts' writing about *Indonesia Calling* had privileged John Grierson and overlooked Ivens' influence on the development of government film agencies in Australia.

Ivens served in the Dutch military during World War I then studied photochemistry in Berlin during the turbulent years of the Weimar Republic that followed the failed communist revolution of 1919. In 1920s Germany the creative arts were mobilised by communists and the liberal left

FROM LEFT: SCREEN COLLAGE OF JORIS IVENS AND SHIP WORKERS IN SYDNEY, 'IT WASN'T JUST A "POLICING" ACTION BUT AN ATTACK ON THE INDONESIAN PEOPLE'; A TELEVISION INTERVIEW WITH IVENS IN *INDONESIA CALLING: JORIS IVENS IN AUSTRALIA* (2009).

to support the Soviet experiment in Russia and working-class struggles elsewhere. Ivens also developed an affinity with working-class movements while training in German photographic factories.[487] The Berlin-based Workers International Relief (WIR) was established at the behest of Soviet premier Vladimir Lenin with the support of Albert Einstein, George Bernard Shaw, George Grosz and other progressive artists and thinkers. Its purpose was to stimulate the working-class arts movement globally. Film, a propaganda tool that Lenin supported strongly, was central to the WIR's work. In Australia, the Realist Film Association (RFA, see Chapter 10) and the Waterside Workers' Federation Film Unit filmmakers (WWFFU, see Chapter 4) engaged with this network to access the Soviet classics and other progressive films.

It was against the background of this emerging international network in the late 1920s that Ivens engaged with the kind of film culture activity that would be echoed in Australia by the Realist, WWFFU and Co-op filmmakers in the decades that followed. A founder of Der Nederlandsche Filmliga (the Dutch Film League), Ivens was active within both the political and the artistic avant-garde of the modern world against a social background of conservatism and censorship.[488] As Malin Wahlberg notes, the Filmliga manifesto of 1927 was pitched in opposition to commercial film culture and 'advocated for international support of experimental film' with its promise of 'a visual poetry, directly appealing to a viewer's imagination and desire'.[489] Ivens' lyrical short films *The Bridge* (1928) and *Rain* (1929) were soon recognised as classic works of cinematography and montage.[490] He made films for trade unions, the Communist Party of the Netherlands (Communistische Partij Nederland) and for companies across Europe.[491] Ivens also worked in the Soviet Union on the invitation of the great revolutionary filmmaker Vsevolod Pudovkin.

Frustrated by Soviet studio bureaucracy, Ivens arranged to be sent to the USA in 1933. Like many of the subjects of Hughes' films about the Cold War period, Ivens was active in the international anti-fascist movement that was galvanised by the Spanish Civil War in the late 1930s.[492] Ivens joined with left cultural luminaries in New York, including Lillian Hellman and Ernest Hemingway, to raise money for ambulances and went to Spain to film *Spanish Earth* (1937).[493] Ivens attempted a similar project about the Chinese fight against Japanese invasion

INDONESIA CALLING (1946).

but was denied access to the front line and Mao's Red Army. Back in the USA, he struggled with another studio bureaucracy to develop films in support of the war effort but managed to produce the acclaimed 'New Deal' documentary *Power and the Land* (1941).[494]

Towards the end of the war Ivens took up an appointment as the first Netherlands Indies film commissioner. He may have imagined that this position would provide a studio base and an unfettered opportunity to mentor and collaborate with like-minded artists. The Dutch East Indies government-in-exile was resident in Australia during the Japanese occupation of the Netherlands East Indies. Ivens was enthusiastic about his task, a film about the liberation of Indonesia from the Japanese, and the peaceful, gradual handover of power to the Indonesian people. In his narration for *Joris Ivens in Australia* Hughes explains that some Indonesians, however, had greeted the Japanese invasion of their islands as liberation from the Dutch, and under Japanese military supervision, independence leader Sukarno was able to act as head of state. Japan's sudden capitulation, after the American use of nuclear weapons against it, allowed the Indonesian leaders, under irresistible pressure from their youth movement, to declare independence long before the Dutch could return. Independence leaders across Asia hoped America would use its post-war superpower status to see 'sovereign rights and self-government restored to those who have been forcibly deprived of them' as promised by Roosevelt and Churchill in the Atlantic Charter.[495] Robbed of the opportunity to act as self-appointed liberators, however, the Dutch secured initial support from allied forces in conducting 'police actions' against the local 'insurgency' that had sprung up spontaneously around the former territories that they wanted to reclaim.[496] Ivens' plans to work for a colonial power in the interests of a colonised people were dashed.

In Australia, events began to unfold in September 1945 when Indonesian seamen walked off Dutch 'mercy' ships after discovering weapons amongst the cargo. The Waterside Workers' Federation and the Seamen's Union of Australia joined the ban on Dutch ships bound for Indonesia. Chinese and Indian seamen also walked off these ships in solidarity. It soon became apparent to the Dutch secret service and Australian security services that a film was being made about the anti-colonialist waterfront activity in Sydney.[497] Ivens, suspected as a Soviet agent and denied a re-entry visa to the US, came under intense scrutiny. The film was *Indonesia Calling*.

The Dutch colonial leadership had already relocated to Indonesia without Ivens, denying the opportunity for him to meet the undertakings of his contract. Late in November 1945, Ivens made a very public resignation from the Netherlands Indies administration that Hughes says garnered international press for the cause of the Indonesian Republic. All the members of his documentary film unit – the American cinematographer Marion Michelle, two Canadians, an Indonesian and an Australian – also resigned.[498] Catherine Duncan, the Australian playwright, actress, radio scriptwriter, communist and member of the New Theatre League took a position as a founding member of staff in the Film Division of the Australian National Film Board and became the first woman in Australia to write and direct documentary films. Hughes had already explored and written about Duncan and her work in the Film Division in *Moving History* (2007, see Chapter 10).[499]

The limited resources and clandestine means employed to make the original film are now legendary. *Indonesia Calling* was a very independent production. Staff at Supreme Sound in Sydney protected its client from demands by the Commonwealth Police to see the film.[500] Film stock was in very short supply in the late war years. According to Drew Cottle and Angela Keys, however, Kodak was under pressure from the secret services and refused to supply film stock.[501] The producer of the film, Edmund Allison, claimed that Marion Michelle shot most of the footage secretly, on the 1920s clockwork Kinamo camera that Ivens had used to make *Rain*.[502] Ivens himself described hiding a camera in a lunchbox to get shots of the sailors going on strike.[503] There was a hiatus of six months before the last scene was filmed while Ivens recuperated from illness. The last of twenty versions of Duncan's narration script were then recorded in a studio hired for one hour

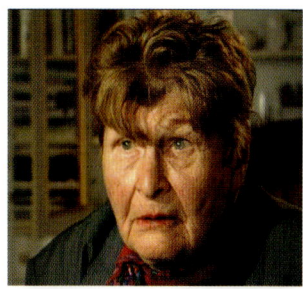

FROM TOP: CINEMATOGRAPHER MARION MICHELLE; CATHERINE DUNCAN – AUSTRALIA'S FIRST FEMALE DOCUMENTARY WRITER-DIRECTOR – IN *INDONESIA CALLING: JORIS IVENS IN AUSTRALIA* (2009).

FROM TOP: BEN CHIFLEY, PRIME MINISTER OF AUSTRALIA 1945–1949; CATHERINE DUNCAN AND CLIPPINGS FROM HER ASIO FILE IN *INDONESIA CALLING: JORIS IVENS IN AUSTRALIA* (2009).

with Duncan's radio colleague, the famous actor Peter Finch.[504]

Hughes draws on an evocative description, from Duncan's diary, of an extended cast and crew screening of *Indonesia Calling* at the sound studio in Sydney. The film had to be screened repeatedly to accommodate the crowd of expatriate Indonesians who came to see it, affirming the volunteer filmmakers' efforts. Local workers and other supporters kept screening the film in a small cinema three times a day for a week.[505] When an export ban was imposed on the film, Allison, in the indefatigable spirit of the independent producer, decided, 'We had to fight it'. The British and American governments, the conservative opposition and media all supported the Dutch in the Indonesian conflict throughout 1947 and most of 1948. Yet, upon its return in the 1946 election, the Chifley Labor government lifted the ban and subsequently referred the Indonesian conflict to the United Nations Security Council. Hughes describes this as a rare moment of foreign policy 'independent of the great powers.' In *Joris Ivens in Australia,* linguist Rabin Hardjadibrata recalls his elation upon seeing *Indonesia Calling* in the early years of the Republic and his surprise that it came from a country widely known as 'White Australia'.

Brussells-based journalist and film writer Ian Mundell has described *Indonesia Calling* as an 'odd' film in which the re-enactment scenes are painstakingly executed but result in something 'unreal'.[506] It may well be that due to the clandestine circumstances of shooting, Ivens' direction of these scenes was limited or delegated to others like English director Harry Watt who was in Australia shooting a feature film at the time. In any case, these scenes have an almost Brechtian effect, as the subjects enthusiastically demonstrate their story for the camera. The very means of production of the film are evident in its almost self-reflexive dramatic tenor. Most importantly, *Indonesia Calling* is a poetic film. As Cutts says in Hughes' film, 'you get this feeling of a rhythm, that is poetic'. That poetry and rhythm would have been very much under Ivens' control in the direction he gave Duncan in her writing and Michelle in her camerawork

AXEL POIGNANT IN *INDONESIA CALLING: JORIS IVENS IN AUSTRALIA* (2009).

and that he brought to the editing and sound. In the PhD thesis about *Indonesia Calling* that John Hughes completed in 2012, he described 'an "essayistic" poetic voice' that 'emerges from within the very delinquent mode of production' of Ivens' film.[507]

Joris Ivens in Australia describes the complex set of political and diplomatic manoeuvres that were triggered by the trade union action and the Ivens' film. Drawing on security files, and picking up a theme explored in *Menace* (1976, see Chapter 2) and *The Archive Project* (2006, see Chapter 10), Hughes traces the repercussions of association with a project that attracted the attention of security services from at least three nations. A 1960 record declares Axel Poignant to be a security risk, citing his purchase in 1938 of a subscription to the West Australian *Workers' Star* magazine and suspicion of association with 'the communist film *Indonesia Calling*'. The first film commissioner and the first producer in chief of the Australian National Film Board's Film Division were also suspect. Stanley Hawes had a file kept on him from 1946 to 1971 and was never allowed permanency in the Australian public service. Catherine Duncan was characterised as particularly wicked. Finally, Hughes notes a 1950s security report to the Menzies government that suggests that if it were to pursue its policy of handing over government film production to private enterprise, staff with adverse security reports should be the first to be sacked.

Despite the primary Australian focus of *Joris Ivens in Australia,* the film pays respectful attention to the Indonesian side of the *Indonesia Calling* story. This is evident in the credentials of the cast of interviewees. The press kit for the film explains that Australian author Charlotte Maramis married an 'Indonesian freedom fighter who played a key role in fighting for the rights of the

JOESOEF ISAK IN *INDONESIA CALLING: JORIS IVENS IN AUSTRALIA* (2009).

Indonesian seamen in Australia'.[508] She then lived through, and wrote about, the early years of Indonesia's independence. Author and historian Joesoef Isak, who grew up during both the Dutch and Japanese occupation of Indonesia, 'was a strong advocate of free speech during President Suharto's authoritarian New Order administration, and imprisoned from 1967–1977 without trial or charge in Indonesia'.[509] Australian Professor Joe Isaac, an expert in foreign policy and industrial relations, also grew up in the Netherlands East Indies, and joined the first Australian Department of Foreign Affairs delegation to Indonesia early in 1946. Hardjadibrata attended Dutch schools before the Japanese occupation of Indonesia and saw *Indonesia Calling* as a teenager in 1947.[510] Like the people in *Menace*, these subjects have been chosen for the authority of their personal experience, as much as for their professional knowledge.

At the centre of the *Indonesia Calling* story is the struggle of the people for liberation from oppression. A momentary glimpse of that utopian possibility is captured in both films. In Ivens' film there are passionate solidarity speeches by hopeful young Indonesian independence activists. A poignant image by the Dutch anti-colonial photojournalist Cas Oorthuys appears repeatedly in Hughes' documentary. It shows an Indonesian boy smiling broadly as he runs through a street. A partly unfurled map under his arm reveals the Indonesian archipelago, and in the bottom right hand corner of its frame, the tip of Australia's landform. Poetically, these images encapsulate the elated spirit of the will to liberation. What they do not convey is the bitter division and violence that characterised the independence movement and the emerging republic. Both the division and the violence have roots in Indonesia's colonial history.

By the end of World War II, Indonesian society had been traumatised and corrupted by centuries of colonial subjugation, exploitation and brutality, during which hundreds of thousands died.[511] Recent scholarship on the history of violence in Indonesia describes a repressive Dutch government apparatus that forcefully imposed social divisions along racial and religious lines and fostered 'entrepreneurs in violence'.[512] Criminal gangs, militias and army units that had to raise their own funds all preyed on local populations to firmly establish a colonial culture in which

FROM LEFT: THE BORDER OF A COLONIAL STAMP FRAMES ARCHIVAL FOOTAGE; A STILL OF JAN MALAKA IN *INDONESIA CALLING: JORIS IVENS IN AUSTRALIA* (2009).

'power and crime were synonymous'.⁵¹³ These groups were active in support of various factions in the independence movement. The violence of the Republic's early years, however, like that of the Dutch colonial era that engendered it, has remained largely absent from the historical record as it is from the necessarily concise account in Hughes' film.⁵¹⁴

The Indonesian narrative within *Joris Ivens in Australia* skips from the inauguration of President Sukarno in 1949 to the mass murders by counter-revolutionary anti-communist militias and the Indonesian military following Suharto's 1965 coup d'état. The latter events stand in for all of the violence of the Republic in the intervening years.⁵¹⁵ This particular compression of the Indonesian narrative makes sense if we understand the protagonists of *Indonesia Calling* and of the independence struggle itself to be predominantly communist. Sukarno's declaration of independence and the bloody coup that brought Suharto to power are also events of post-war Indonesian history most recognisable to foreign audiences. After the declaration and the struggle with the Dutch, the events of 1965 and 1966 are the most relevant to the story of *Indonesia Calling*. Given that the Indonesians involved with the 1946 film included trade unionists and political prisoners brought to Australia by the Dutch, it is likely that many of them were members or supporters of the Indonesian Communist Party (PKI). Hughes' narration turns to elegy as he notes that these people were likely to have been killed following the military coup.⁵¹⁶ Reflecting on the scenes that Ivens staged with Indonesian workers in Sydney, Hughes wrote:

*It is impossible to watch these scenes, with their finely fashioned portraits and in the knowledge of the Indonesian coup of 1965–6, supported by American power and Australian acquiescence and silence, the Suharto regime to follow, the 800,000 'communists' murdered by militia and military, without an overwhelming sense of grief.*⁵¹⁷

Henk Nordholt identifies Indonesia's isolation from the international arena alongside a colonial legacy of the 'strong state' and a deeply rooted culture of political violence as factors that 'devastated the democratic experiment'.⁵¹⁸ Yet until 1965, unlike their Australian counterparts,

Indonesian communists were able to participate in government. As the largest communist party in the non-communist world, the PKI enjoyed an alliance with Sukarno that became more beneficial – and more risky – as his autocracy became more entrenched.

Hughes' narration identifies the Indonesian military, anti-communist militias and Western covert action as the key forces behind Suharto's anti-communist coup. The common thread of covert Cold War political intervention weaves the Indonesian story together with the Australian experience of Ivens and his team as it does with other films in Hughes' oeuvre. The left in Indonesia had always faced other enemies, however, including wealthy rural landlords, militant religious movements, organised crime and rival political parties. From the outset, it was also at odds with much of the conservative nationalist leadership that executed PKI leaders in 1948 after a rebellion amidst the conflict with the Dutch.[519]

To the extent that all films are propaganda, they also contain an element of fantasy. Both the *Indonesia Calling* films consciously provide a utopian and poetic portrayal. The Indonesian independence movement and Australian working-class politics appear in a simplified form in both these films. The vision of Australian society presented in the 1946 film was one of union solidarity transcending nationality, race, culture and religion. In the twenty-first century, this transformational image of mid-twentieth century 'white Australia' confounds the conservative historical stereotypes that continue to dominate mainstream media representations of post-war Australia. Ivens' counter-image may in some small way have helped to engender the popular and institutional imagination of contemporary Australia as a multicultural society. Likewise, as a counterpoint to the prevalence of representations that reflect fear, xenophobia, parochialism and self-interest as defining national characteristics, Hughes' re-circulation of these progressive images might also help a society to redefine itself. In an overview of Ivens' work, Mundell describes the early 'militant' films, including *Spanish Earth,* as 'a complete cinematic response to a political issue, combining elements of documentary argument,

LEFT: MERDEKA! (FREEDOM!) SHIP WORKERS RALLY IN IVEN'S 1946 FILM *INDONESIA CALLING.* **ABOVE:** REPUBLICAN POSTAGE STAMPS SUPPLANT THOSE OF THE DUTCH IN *INDONESIA CALLING: JORIS IVENS IN AUSTRALIA* (2009).

FROM LEFT: STANLEY HAWES; SARDJONO AT WORK IN MELBOURNE, IN A NEWSPAPER ARTICLE AND IN AN ASIO FILE IN *INDONESIA CALLING: JORIS IVENS IN AUSTRALIA* (2009).

reportage, montage of pre-existing footage and fiction'.[520] In broad terms, Hughes and the other filmmakers whose work is discussed in this book share this eclectic approach. Effective communication, rather than purity of aesthetic form, or an ideological commitment to a particular technique of documentary filmmaking, is the foremost concern in this work. As Mundell observed of Ivens: 'If he had lived to see the digital age, it is unlikely that he would have been content to press record and wait for something to happen'.[521] While Ivens would probably have rejected the term 'fiction' to describe his use of reconstruction, he was willing to experiment and gave a great deal of thought to developing documentary methodology. His films usually involved the preparation of scenarios and always had some commentary that was scripted with a great deal of craft. There was no place on the screen for the professional actor in this realist approach because it was important to 'become one with the people you are filming', to earn their trust and to ensure that they understand the filming process.[522] This is the realism that the Realist and WWF filmmakers of *The Archive Project* and *Film-Work* adopted.

As they did with *The Archive Project,* Hughes and Mizrahi draw a wide array of archival visual material together into dense, yet elegant screen designs. As he has done since *Some Aspects of Australian Racism* (1973, see Chapter 9), Hughes lays spoken word over graphic text. Simple superimposed titles were used in the 1970s film while the 2009 work employs digital collages of printed artefacts. Clippings from newspapers, letters and security service files are layered upon each other. These multi-layered and multi-panelled compositions exploit the creative potential that the widescreen digital format affords the filmmaker. They also invite a non-linear use of the film in media such as DVD through pausing, searching among and reading from individual frames within the film.

One frame that is held for ten seconds accompanies archival sound of Catherine Duncan introducing the Indonesian activist Sardjono who worked on the original film. This collage contains about a hundred words of text, a formal portrait photograph from a newspaper clipping and an archival photograph of Sardjono at work in the offices of the Netherlands administration in Australia. A security file clipping is given prominence and might be read (or simply taken in) by the viewer as visual evidence and background to the story told in voice-over. The user who stops the film at this frame, however, can read of Sardjono's nomination by the Dutch

ARCHIVAL IMAGES OF CATHERINE DUNCAN AND JORIS IVENS IN *INDONESIA CALLING: JORIS IVENS IN AUSTRALIA* (2009).

Communist Party and his election in 1934 to the Netherlands Parliament, whilst held in a Dutch prison in Indonesia. There is also some text from an appeal by Sardjono to 'progressive people around the world' that was transmitted by telegraph cable in 1945 and places the Indonesian situation within the context of global developments.

This frame holds supplementary information that cannot be conveyed at length within the 90-minute running time of the film. By pausing on it, these background components become retrievable. This possibility is anticipated by Hughes and Mizrahi's screen collage since A*fter Mabo* (1997, see Chapter 9) and Hughes' 2007 *Moving History* website project (see Chapter 10). Indeed, as he embarked on *Joris Ivens in Australia*, Hughes investigated the possibility of incorporating 'action frames' in the new film. Action frames would be frames within the body of a film that acted like DVD menu icons. These hotlinks would allow a viewer to click to additional content, enabling in-depth and tangential exploration of material that the filmmaker would normally need to exclude. Within the current architecture of DVD technology, Hughes and Mizrahi were only able to hint at this idea through their densely composed screen designs.

Hughes' collaboration with Uri Mizrahi is the longest running and most important to his body of work. Mizrahi has edited all of Hughes' films since *Moments Like These* in 1989. Hughes acknowledged the extent of Mizrahi's contribution to *The Archive Project* with a credit as co-director. In *Joris Ivens in Australia* he is acknowledged for 'Editor, Graphics and Design'. Hughes says that it is a collaborative process and it is difficult to delineate what they each contribute to the conception and design of the collages and montage that make up their work together.

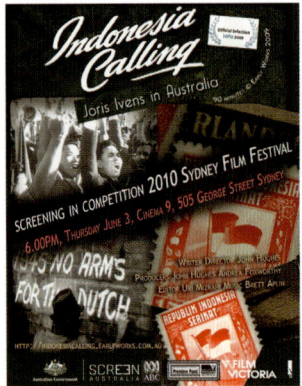 

FROM LEFT: POSTER FOR A SYDNEY FILM FESTIVAL SCREENING; IVENS' GRAVE IN THE CEMETERY OF MONTPARNASSE IN *INDONESIA CALLING: JORIS IVENS IN AUSTRALIA* (2009).

Unlike the working relationship of some directors and editors, theirs is a very interactive one and Hughes is nearly always present while Mizrahi is working. As editor, Hughes says, Mizrahi also contributes a great deal to story structure, especially on a project like *Joris Ivens in Australia*, which weaves together much diverse material and many different narrative threads.

As with each of Hughes' post-war documentary portraits, there is an elegiac quality and a moment of eulogy. In *Joris Ivens in Australia* this happens with shots of Ivens' grave in the cemetery of Montparnasse and television news coverage of his funeral in 1989, less than twenty minutes into the film. The placement of the scene at this early point in the film is interesting because its emotional weight is preemptive. It is as if Hughes is drawing our attention to the conventional function of such scenes in biopics through which the audience grieves, somewhere near the end of a film, for the person they have come to know during the preceding 40 or 80 minutes. The more familiar the audience is expected to be with the subject, the earlier such a scene might appear. The newsreel footage that Hughes uses shows floral tributes from the great film institutions, from the Netherlands and Chinese governments, but also from 'Chinese students whom Joris defended recently'. Those present at the funeral included the Dutch documentary filmmaker Johan van der Keuken, veteran directors Costa-Gavras and Nagisa Oshima, and famous Dutch writer Jan Blokker. In this case, Ivens is a figure unfamiliar to most television viewers and this sequence conveys the message that he is, nonetheless, famous. Hughes described this to me, half-jokingly, as the 'product endorsement' scene.[524]

Indonesia Calling: Joris Ivens in Australia draws on a range of sources for its motion picture imagery. In addition to the various archival sources, Hughes obtained outtakes of Indonesian footage from fellow documentary filmmaker Steve Thomas' documentary *Hope* (2007).[523] Hughes shot most of the original contemporary material himself. In this model of digital image gathering with low-cost camera equipment, it is no longer necessary to engage in a lengthy process of preparation before filming to minimise crew and equipment costs. Conventional film production on celluloid film was usually undertaken in four distinct phases: development, pre-production, production and post-production. The artisanal nature of independent production, especially in documentary, often saw these distinctions blurred. With digital filmmaking, the first three phases have largely become merged, while post-production can start at almost any point in the process. This flexibility means that when Hughes has an interview, and the budget allows, he hires a cameraperson who is available and nearby at the time. So seven different camera people shot the interviews for *Joris Ivens in Australia*.

Before 2008 Hughes secured development investment from the AFC to go to Amsterdam where he recorded material there with a low cost HD/DV CAM video camera. After the project was rejected by ABC TV Documentaries Hughes was able to successfully apply to the one fund in Australia that would provide finance for documentaries without the need for a television presale. This was the Film Finance Corporation (FFC) Innovation Fund, which later became Screen Australia's Special Documentary Fund. Having secured support from this quarter, Hughes went back to the ABC, but this time to their TV Arts and Entertainment programming department. As with *The Archive Project*, they invested in a 30-minute documentary. Hughes explains that, in the end, they got a 90-minute film for their money but that this arrangement with the ABC was mutually beneficial and he was grateful that the Arts programmers did not hold him to the promise of a short version. The ABC presale triggered access to further money from Film Victoria's Documentary Production Fund.

A development in the funding landscape that Hughes says was critical to financing *Joris Ivens in Australia* was the re-engagement of film festivals as investors in Australian films – as was the Melbourne Film Festival through the Unifed fund in the 1960s (see Chapter 1). The Adelaide Arts Festival led this trend in the mid-2000s and Hughes became involved, through the Australian Directors Guild (ADG), in encouraging a similar fund for the Melbourne International Film Festival (MIFF Premiere Fund), to be open to documentary films. The Premiere Fund contributed the final component of the budget on the promise that *Joris Ivens in Australia* would have its world premiere at MIFF. Each of these sources provided tens rather than hundreds of thousands of dollars for the film, but by stitching them all together there was just enough money to make the film and for Hughes to pay himself and others for work on it. Hughes sees the festival funds as making a positive intervention in the support of documentaries because they are not wedded to television forms. What they want are feature length documentaries for theatrical screening and this has the potential to encourage some re-diversification of documentary practice. In addition to being selected for a number of major festivals and awards locally, *Joris Ivens in Australia* was included in the official selection of IDFA – the prestigious International Documentary Film Festival in Amsterdam.

Hughes admits that *Joris Ivens in Australia* was a really difficult film to make and that for a while he had decided it should be his last. In addition to the complex nature of the work itself, there were all the usual problems of low-budget filmmaking, including 'two or three years intensive work that you'd be lucky to be paid for and the stress that is generated by the need to complete the work whilst also making sure you can pay those who help to get it to that stage'.[525] And a low budget doesn't mean freedom from the machinations of financing. On the contrary, a small budget project like *Joris Ivens in Australia* can have quite a complex mix of financing underpinning it. In Australia this means engaging in an exacting and exhausting process of answering to the needs of a number of government agencies and pseudo-commercial corporations. As Hughes says, this is simply an 'appalling' process to go through.[526] These negotiations require a lot of technical work and have led to the producer role becoming dominant in Australian documentary production of the early twenty-first century.

As Hughes' reflections on producing *Joris Ivens in Australia* demonstrated, the combination of subsidy and independence that he and his peers enjoyed in the 1970s is largely unavailable to independent filmmakers today. By 2011, Screen Australia was insisting that 'less experienced filmmakers' engage in partnerships with 'eligible experienced colleagues'.[527] To be eligible for financial assistance in documentary development, for example, producers were required to have 'at least three broadcast documentary credits'.[528] On this measure, Hughes would have been ineligible for the first 23 years of his filmmaking and teams of enterprising young filmmakers like those who made *Film-Work* can be required to supplicate to established producers for an indefinite number of years before being given full authorship of a subsidised production. By 2014 these terms had been relaxed slightly, but the commercial imperatives to which legislators continue to keep funding bodies in lockstep stifles their capacity to effectively engage with significant quarters of the creative community. Many professionals who have been making films for decades have been in this position for a number of years now. Meanwhile, promising projects by young filmmakers can be used as 'cash cows' by struggling (or empire-building) producers for whom market-based, presale financing can create a temptation to inflate budgets and protract the development phase. Only those directors who have developed truly equitable relationships with 'recognised' producers and those who are already well established as director-producers (like Hughes), or as wholly independent producer/director teams, can hope to find a degree of creative independence and editorial freedom in this context. As a result, truly innovative projects are often forced outside the gate-keeping systems that characterise Australia's publicly subsidised screen production industry.[529]

In the five years since completing *Indonesia Calling: Joris Ivens in Australia* Hughes has found support to produce just one of several projects he has been working on. For a time it seemed that the long-planned-for fourth film on the history of independent filmmaking in Australia might get off the ground. By 2011, from an enormous amount of research material gathered with help from filmmakers around Australia, Hughes and Sydney counterpart Tom Zubrycki had competed a ten-page treatment and sixty-two page development proposal for *A Filmmakers' Cinema: 20 years of the Filmmakers' cooperatives*.[600] A sense of urgency came to this project with the deaths in 2009 of Sue Ford and Solrun Hoaas and in 2011 of Esben Storm – all exemplary artists with connections to the co-ops whose combined work and experience encompassed a vast gamut of cinematic possibilities in experimental, feature, documentary and ethnographic filmmaking. With development funds from Screen NSW and Film Victoria in early 2011, Hughes and Zubrycki filmed a number of interviews with filmmakers, including one with SFC founder Albie Thoms shortly before his death in 2012. There was an expression of interest from the ABC, but production finance from conventional film funding sources has yet to be found. Hughes says that research and development on this project has occupied 2014 and will continue in 2015. He describes it as 'a substantial academic research project with online components'.

Hughes is resigned to the fact that the time may have past when support can been found for a documentary about Australia's involvement in the United States-led 2003 invasion of Iraq – another project he had been developing over recent years. During his work on these projects, Hughes was completing his 2012 PhD thesis, 'After *Indonesia Calling*' at RMIT University. This research revolved around Joris Ivens' *Indonesia Calling*, and extends the original historical research Hughes conducted for the *Archive Project* (2006, see Chapter 10) into Australian security organisations' interest in independent cinema during and the Cold War.[601] It also builds on his research into the origins of Australian government film production in the early post-war years for *Moving History* (see Chapter 10) and explores government policy surrounding its demise in 2006–8, 'when funding regimes for Australian film were reconstituted'. As part of this project, Hughes produced a video drawing on material from *Joris Ivens in Australia*. One of Hughes' concerns in this work was 'the essayistic poetic voice' that 'emerges from within the very delinquent mode of production' of Ivens' film. Within eighteen months of submitting his PhD the quality of Dr John Hughes' original research was recognised with two honorary positions: Honorary Fellow with the Faculty of Victorian College of the Arts and Melbourne Conservatorium of Music at the University of Melbourne and Adjunct Professor in the School of Media and Communication in the College of Design and Social Context, RMIT University.

Love & Fury (2013)

John Hughes' latest film at the time of writing brings together a number of the political themes of his earlier work and revisits the idea of dramatisation within documentary form. Inspired by a 2009 *Monthly* essay by Fiona Capp, *Love & Fury: Judith Wright & 'Nugget' Coombs* is a moving half-hour documentary about a discreet and intimate relationship that brought together the stories of these two towering figures of Australian literary and public life.[602] As an interviewee in the film, Capp proposes that 'Judith's concerns about environmental issues influenced Nugget' and 'his concern for land rights influenced her'. The film includes an interview with Professor Tim Rowse, Coombs' biographer and himself a prolific scholar on economic, political and social justice in Australia. He explains how in 1970 Wright 'gave a speech in which she talked about the necessity for the politics of the environment to be an alliance between a scientifically informed and politically committed elite and an emotionally aroused public'. The narration continues this theme: 'feeling, she said, always sways public opinion far more than reason'. Rowse says he thinks Coombs would have shared this view. Just as Hughes was not content to make films that only filmmakers would watch, just as he wanted to reach audiences of the scale television could reach, so too did Wright believe that the environment would not be saved by behind-the-scenes factual presentations by scientists to politicians alone. If all media messages are 'propaganda of one form or another' (as Keith Gow suggested – see Chapter 4) environmentalists, like capitalists, would have to achieve popular communication. Perhaps what Wright had in mind however, more than simple persuasion, were utopian transformational imaginings and the creation – at a societal level – of hope and rectitude of sentiment in relation to the land, the sky and the sea.

A PERSONAL PHOTOGRAPH OF NUGGET COOMBS AND JUDITH WRIGHT TAKEN IN 1989 IN *LOVE & FURY* (2013).

Rowse speaks of how Coombs testified before the 1971 royal commission into proposed drilling for oil in the now World Heritage listed Great Barrier Reef. Dr Coombs, the former Governor of the Reserve Bank, brought new economic concepts of intergenerational equity and responsibility to this question. Meanwhile, Wright, a pioneer of Australian environmentalism in the early 1960s investigating the same question, had started work on her eleventh book *The Coral Battleground*.[603] Brought together as lovers in 1972 amid the electrified atmosphere of the arrival of Whitlam's Labor government and often apart, their love and thoughts were shared through their letters to each other. At fifty-seven and sixty-six years of age respectively, Wright and Coombs each had their own reasons for keeping their relationship discreet. Concerned about the impact of public attention on their families and their work, and mindful of the belligerence to which such attention might be put, the lovers made a pact to keep their relationship a secret outside their closest circle.

Wright's great literary achievements and Dr Coombs' prodigious work as a senior public servant who influenced the policies of seven prime ministers are only a backdrop here. When he retired from the Reserve Bank in 1967, Coombs was appointed by Harold Holt to establish and chair both the Australia Council (see Chapter 1) and the Australian Council for Aboriginal Affairs.[604] The Holt, Gorton and McMahon Liberal governments refused to include land rights on their agenda. In 1972 Whitlam, however, responded positively to calls from Aboriginal and Torres Strait Islander people and is likely to have taken Coombs' advice before declaring 'We will legislate to give Aborigines land rights'.

FROM LEFT: THE BURNING LETTERS; TIM ROWSE IN *LOVE & FURY* (2013).

Love & Fury includes an account by Coombs of the historic 1975 ceremony at Daguragu (Wattie Creek). In writing Whitlam's speech, Coombs conceived the idea that the Prime Minister could pour soil into the hand of Gurindji spokesman Vincent Lingiari. This was a reversal of the 1835 exchange between John Batman and Wurundjeri elders at Merri Creek for possession of what is now Melbourne and its surrounds. An event that Bill Stanner had told him about.[605] Hughes includes an image of one of many paintings of this event that were made over forty years or more later. By that time documentary photography had emerged but painting was still being used to create propagandist interpretations of historical events for public exhibition on a grand scale. Early photographs could be reproduced but did not facilitate the manipulation of the image to the extent painting did. Nor could past events be photographed without re-staging them. It would soon fall to cinema to take on the victor's work in the creative reinterpretation of history.

Whitlam handed over the deeds to traditional lands in a shed, but Fairfax News photographer Mervyn Bishop (who happened to be Aboriginal) persuaded he and Lingiari to repeat the exchange for his camera outdoors where the red soil and blue sky contrasted brilliantly.[606] *Love & Fury* incorporates black and white 16 mm television newsreel footage of this photo opportunity together with photographs in some of which Coombs can be seen beaming from behind Whitlam at an historic moment and the creation of an iconic image of reconciliation. After the constitutional coup d'état of 1975 (see Chapter 3) and the return of a Liberal-National Party coalition, Coombs ended his long career in government and took up a fellowship at the ANU, where he could continue to work closely with and in the interests of Aboriginal and Torres Strait Islander people. In 1978 Coombs published the book *Kulinma: listening to Aboriginal Australians*.[607] He and Wright continued to support the campaign for land rights and formed a committee with other influential non-Indigenous Australians to join the campaign for a treaty. In an archival interview Wright says that a treaty could put Indigenous people 'into a situation where they were dealing on equal terms with the federal government'. In 1981 Eddie Mabo spoke to Coombs and gained support for his land rights case under existing law. Hughes told me he was pleased that the film 'brings to light the role of historian and activist Nonie Sharp in facilitating this historic "secret" meeting' that took place during the 1981 Townsville 'Land Rights and the Future of Australian Race Relations' conference. Mabo's case took eleven more years to prosecute. In 1985 Wright published the book *We call for a treaty*.[608]

In 1992, two weeks after the High Court decision in Eddie Mabo's favour (see Chapter 9), mindful of the powerful enemies their work was no doubt making and spending extended periods living in isolation with failing hearing, Wright was seized by an imperative to burn Nugget's letters – correspondence which Coombs had come to see as a kind of life's work. Late that year they agreed to have their remaining letters released to the National Library of Australia three years after they and Coombs' wife had died. Hughes threads the film around the events that the missing, subsequent and surviving correspondence chronicled.

Sylvia Lawson is a distinguished essayist and critic who has campaigned for Australian filmmaking and independent media since the early 1960s. In a review of *Love & Fury*, she says that Wright's decision to forego poetry in order to concentrate her energy on the wider battles for land rights and the environment was seen by some in the literary world as heresy. That view, says Lawson, 'that art and politics are inherently at odds – is still lurking around. It is at the heart of cultural conservatism; and John Hughes's film-making, from the 1970s to the present, confounds its proponents.' She continues:

His cinema is at once crowded, detailed, elegant and absolutely lucid; at the same time, it is shot through with political and historical understandings.[609]

Love & Fury was developed with investment from Film Victoria and ABC TV Arts. Produced in association with the ABC, with production investment triggered from Screen Australia, the film was to fit a half-hour timeslot in an ABC Arts program. In publicity notes for the film, Hughes describes the 'sometimes painful task' of editing the film to half the length of a 58-minute rough-cut he and Mizrahi had at the end of 2012 'discarding precious stories and ideas and trimming important historical material to within an inch of their lives' while maintaining coherency.[610]

Perhaps the most remarkable aspect of *Love & Fury* is the quality of the production. The 'high production value' Hughes and co-producer Philippa Campey achieve does not come from having an extravagant budget. On the contrary, it comes from painstaking efficiency, a very careful targeting of limited resources, sensitive creative decision-making and a very real affection for their subjects. Good use is made of spectacular stock shots of Australian landscapes such that the only substantial location scenes are interviews and much of the budget is directed towards work with performers and musicians.

With *Love & Fury* Hughes draws very precisely upon cinematography's capacity for the 'redemption of physical reality'. As noted in Chapter 6, Hughes had called upon Kracauer's theorisation of that phenomenon in his PhD writing on Joris Ivens' *Indonesia Calling* (see Chapter 11) – scholarly work that he was completing in parallel with the development and production of *Love & Fury*. The careful orchestration of actuality is most apparent in the employment – for bespoke voice-overs, narration and music – of outstanding professionals who are, crucially, in a position to draw from personal experience that is directly relevant to the matter at hand. This is not a case of psychological dramatic technique or Stanislavskian 'method' acting – in which a performer conjures pertinent emotional memory – it is a matter of something akin to a collage of feeling within the mise-en-scène.

PAUL ENGLISH AND HELEN MORSE IN *LOVE & FURY* (2013).

Radio broadcaster Ramona Koval reads Hughes' narration for *Love & Fury*. Koval's specialisations – as a literary journalist and editor of Australian essays – mean that she has an intimate knowledge of the material. Having conducted the last broadcast interview with Wright in 1999, she also has an emotional connection to her. Furthermore, Koval, like Hughes, Coombs and Wright has been an active contributor to the cultural arena in many voluntary capacities beyond her 'day job'. These include being a judge of the Walkley Awards for Journalism and for literary awards. She has been a board member and advisor to literary festivals and has written in many genres, including novels, in her own right. Before all of this she was a microbiologist and geneticist, so she also has an educated understanding of the natural world – something that parallels Wright's passionate concern for the environment. Koval was a staff elected director of the ABC Board from 2002 - a position created by Whitlam's government in 1975 and abolished by Howard's in 2006. Hughes' own assessment of his choice of narrator is understated. The film most certainly 'benefits from her warmth and familiarity with the material'.[611] Film reviewer for *The Australian*, Geordie Williamson, described Koval's narration as having 'a welcome minimalism'.[612] Indeed, there is a very tangible immediacy and authenticity to the narration such that it really sounds as if Koval is speaking her own mind. This is something that Hughes' script is sure to have allowed her to do as his script for *Moments Like These* had allowed Bob Maza to do twenty-five years earlier (see Chapter 9). For a listener-viewer it is an unusual luxury to enjoy a narration that carries so much emotional and intellectual authority.

Two fine veteran actors, Helen Morse and Paul English, provide readings from Wright and Coombs' writings with, as Williamson observes, 'the kind of elegant restraint that enlarges the spirit of the letters rather than drowning them in the actor's ego'.[613] There is tenderness in these exchanges scripted by the very characters they perform. As self-described 'partners in life as well as art' they were able to embody the role of the elderly and stately couple with aplomb.[614] Hughes filmed their voice-over recording sessions for inclusion within the film's montage as he did with the re-voicing sessions in *The Archive Project* (see Chapter 10). Whilst this does the Constructivist job of drawing attention to the constructed and edited nature of the televisual work, it might appear at first to be a stylistic contrivance. In fact, these scenes bring further layers of authentic actuality to the film. Firstly there is the pleasure the actors are having – with the rich vocabulary and textual material of the letters, with their craft and with each other. This is heightened by the fact that personal letters are in their very nature scripts for performance of the self by others – brought to life, in a virtual way, by their intended readers. Unintended readers can thus inhabit letters as heartfelt and well crafted as those in *Love & Fury* with equal veracity – particularly if they are accomplished actors.

The sound recording session introduces another dynamic in that the actors are standing side by side as they would to record a radio play. And in the case of both radio plays and voice-over recordings, the actors' work involves reading from a script rather than speaking lines memorised for a conventional scripted performance on stage or screen. The viewer is also conscious of the fact that this is a performance that we are not usually meant to see. We are being given a peephole into the actor's work, just as the letters allow us to peer into the intimate exchanges of others. A quartet of realities and personas is dialectically at play then within these scenes.

There is a delightful moment when sixty-five year old Morse reads Wright's response to plans that Coombs has suggested for a trip they would take together to Alice Springs. Part of this exchange is read over shots from Solrun Hoaas's poetic short portrait film *At Edge* (1981).[615] With her distinctive hand-held camerawork, Hoaas follows Wright – also in her mid-sixties at the time – as she wanders through open scrub land, gently touching trees and plants. As the reading continues, Hughes cuts to a medium two-shot of the actors in the studio. Morse sways slightly and glances in the direction of English with a tiny grin as she reads that she 'ought to book into a motel for decency's sake but won't anyway'. A reverse shot follows of the pair. Morse glances up conspiratorially then looks briefly again towards English with a slight and cheeky smile almost as if pretending to hide something from her self – or the unknown imagined witnesses she has just spoken of.

The subtle feelings that show on English's face in this scene are in response to Wright's words. He is both reading these from the page and hearing them from his own lover, Morse. He is at once a Coombs' foil to Morse's evocation of Wright and English the actor – a sensitive and intelligent reader of Wright's text. There is no eye contact between the actors in these shots. Each of them is immersed in the letter they are reading. I complained in Chapter 6 that a similar private relationship among the cast in *All That Is Solid* was arcane knowledge but in these studio scenes in *Love & Fury* there is a tangible affection.

Whether or not we know of the personal relationship that these performances might draw upon, it seems that it was an actuality available to the actors, the film's director and viscerally to the listener-viewers.

Composer Brett Aplin arranged a version of the 1938 pop and jazz standard *You go to my head* and produced two versions with Melbourne jazz singers Hetty Kate and 'Olympia' (Olivier Bartley) as the theme song for *Love & Fury*. Aplin provides a range of other music for the film. That such craft and care should be taken for the music track of a half-hour television arts program is admirable. It also means that the musical sound is unique to the film and the relationship it profiles. Aplin is able to reflect, through his musical contribution, the emotional resonance the film, its characters and stories have for himself, Hughes and the other artists involved. The listener-viewer's experience of the film then, is more singular than it would be had all the music been acquired from already-published sources that would carry associations of their own.

For a film in which human feelings play a central role, all of these choices and all of this care bear fruit. In Hughes' oeuvre, *Love and Fury* is a relatively simple film, but it rewards repeated viewing.

Endnotes

[485] John Hughes, *Indonesia Calling: Joris Ivens in Australia*, 2009, Digital Betacam, colour and b&w, 90 minutes, Early Works, Australia, Producers John Hughes & Andrea Foxworthy, Scriptwriter John Hughes, Editor Uri Mizrahi. Featuring Graeme Cutts, Andre Stufkens, Susan Geldho, Joesoef Isak, Charlotte Maramis, John Daniell, Maggie Keane, Jan Lingard, Professor Joe Isaac, Arthur Gar Lock Chang & Rabin Hardjadibrata. Produced with assistance from the Australian Broadcasting Corporation, the Melbourne International Film Festival (MIFF) Premiere Fund, Film Victoria & Screen Australia. Distributed by Artfilms.

[486] Joris Ivens, *Indonesia Calling*, 1946, 35 mm, b&w, 22 minutes, Australasia Production, Sydney, Producer The Waterfront Unions of Australia, Scriptwriter Katherine Duncan, Executive Producer Peter Finch, Camera Marion Michelle.

[487] Joris Ivens, *Joris Ivens and China*, New World Press, Beijing, 1983, p. 135.
Kees Bakker, Inventory of the Joris Ivens Archives, European Foundation Joris Ivens Nijmegen, 1999, p. 3.

[488] Ian Mundell, 'Joris Ivens', *Senses of Cinema*, no. 37, October–December 2005, Senses of Cinema, Brussels, <http://sensesofcinema.com/2005/great-directors/ivens/>, accessed 24 February 2013.

[489] Malin Wahlberg, 'Wonders of cinematic abstraction: J. C. Mol and the aesthetic experience of science film', *Screen*, vol. 47, no. 3, 2006, pp. 273–289, <http://screen.oxfordjournals.org/content/47/3/273.full>, accessed 4 September 2013.

[490] Joris Ivens, *The Bridge* (*De Brug*) 1928, 35 mm, b&w, 14 minutes, Rotterdam, Camera Joris Ivens, Editor Joris Ivens.
Joris Ivens, *Rain* (*Regen*), 1929, 35 mm, b&w, 15 minutes, The Netherlands, Prod. Joris Ivens, Camera Joris Ivens, Sound version prepared 1932 by Helen van Dongen, Editor Joris Ivens.

[491] Joris Ivens, 1983, op. cit., p. 136–137.

[492] Dorothee Verdaasdonk, 'Ivens, Joris', *Film Reference*, <http://www.filmreference.com/Directors-Ha-Ji/Ivens-Joris.html>, accessed 24 February 2013.

[493] Joris Ivens, *Spanish Earth*, 1937, 35 mm, b&w, 52 minutes, Contemporary Historians, Inc., New York, Scriptwriters Joris Ivens & Ernest Hemingway, Camera John Ferno, Sound Irving Reis, Editor Helen Van Dongen.

[494] Joris Ivens, *The Power and the Land*, 1940, 35 mm, b&w, 33 minutes, US Film Service, commissioned by Rural Electrification Administration (REA), US Ministry of Agriculture, USA, Scriptwriters Edwin Locke,

Joris Ivens & Stephen Vincent Benét, Executive Producer William P Adams, Camera Floyd Crosby, Arthur Ornitz, Editor Helen van Dongen. Mundell, op. cit.

[495] Joshua Kurlantzick, *The Ideal Man: The Tragedy of Jim Thompson and the American Way of War*, Wiley, Hoboken, New Jersey, 2011, p. 48.

NATO, *The Atlantic Charter*, President of the United States, FD Roosevelt, Prime Minister of HM Government in the United Kingdom, W Churchill, North Atlantic Treaty Organisation, 1941, <http://www.nato.int/cps/en/natolive/official_texts_16912.htm>, accessed 12 February 2013.

[496] Robert Cribb & Colin Brown, 'Towards Cataclysm, 1959–65', *Modern Indonesia: A history since 1945*, Longman, London, 1995, pp. 82–96.

[497] John Hughes, 'Indonesia Calling: Joris Ivens in Australia', *Senses of Cinema*, no. 51, 2009.

[498] Graeme Cutts, 'Indonesia Calling and Joris Ivens', in Albert Moran & Tom O'Reagan (eds), *An Australian Film Reader*, Currency Press, Sydney, 1985, p. 353. Note that in that publication, Cutts' name is incorrectly spelt 'Graham'.

[499] John Hughes, 'Moving History' *A place to think*, online multimedia, Film Australia, ABC, Executive Producers Anna Grieve & Ian Allen, 2007, <http://www.abc.net.au/aplacetothink/? – watch>, accessed 2 February 2013.

[500] Cutts, op. cit., p. 358.

[501] Drew Cottle & Angela Keys, 'From Colonial Film Commissioner to Political Pariah: Joris Ivens and the Making of Indonesia Calling', *Senses of Cinema*, no. 41, 2006.

[502] Designed by Prof. Emanuel Goldberg, for hand-held use outside the studio – and especially for the amateur – the Kinamo was the smallest 35 mm cine camera. Ivens had worked on the Kinamo production line while in Dresden in the early 1920s, admired Goldberg and demonstrated with his own films that this camera could be used to create art at a professional level. Such cameras freed a generation of artists from the constraints of commerce and the studio. Michael K Buckland, 'The Kinamo movie camera, Emanuel Goldberg and Joris Ivens', *Film History*, vol. 20, no. 1, 2008, pp. 49–59.

[503] Joris Ivens, 1983, op. cit., p. 91.

[504] Finch had starred in Charles Chauvel's *The Rats of Tobruk* (1944).

[505] Cottle & Keys, op. cit.

[506] Mundell, op. cit.

[507] John Hughes, 'After *Indonesia Calling*', PhD exegesis, School of Media and Communication, College of Design and Social Context, RMIT University, Melbourne, November 2012, p. 178.

[508] John Hughes, '*Indonesia Calling: Joris Ivens In Australia*', Early Works, press kit, 9 July 2009, Melbourne, <http://earlyworks.com.au/the-stacks/post/press-kit-indonesia-calling-joris-ivens-in-australia/>, accessed 24 February 2013, p. 8.

[509] ibid.

[510] ibid.

[511] The 1873–1904 war, aimed at deepening the imprint of Dutch authority across the archipelago, saw military expeditions in a dozen provinces. Over 100,000 people (12,500 Dutch soldiers and 15% of the population) died in Aceh alone. Henk Schulte Nordholt, 'A genealogy of violence', in Freek Colombijn & J Thomas Lindblad (eds), *Roots of violence in Indonesia*, Institute of South East Asian Studies, Singapore, 2002, pp. 36–37.

[512] ibid., pp. 33–62.

[513] ibid.

[514] William Frederick, 'Shadows of an unseen hand. Some patterns of violence in the Indonesian revolution, 1945–1949', in Freek Colombijn & J Thomas Lindblad (eds), *Roots of violence in Indonesia*, Institute of South East Asian Studies, Singapore, 2002, p. 147. Hughes points to Benedict Anderson's classic detailed account of the Indonesian liberation movement. Benedict Anderson, *Java in a time of revolution:*

occupation and resistance, 1944–46, Cornell UP, Ithica 1972.

[515] Some reviewers of *Joris Ivens in Australia* have even conflated the main protagonists and events across these two decades. Patricia Aufderheide, *IDFA, Ivens, Oranges and More,* The Centre for Social Media, Washington, DC, 2009, <http://www.centerforsocialmedia.org/blog/making–your–media–matter/idfa–ivens–oranges–and–more>, accessed 17 September 2013.

[516] Hughes told me that he printed frames from *Indonesia Calling* of people in the original film and took these with him when he met people in hope of tracing some of them, but his attempts to trace the Indonesian activists in Ivens' film produced no leads. He says many would also have died in the 1948 struggle and reprisals around the Madiun uprising.

[517] Hughes, 'After Indonesia Calling', PhD exegesis, op. cit., p. 206.

[518] Nordholt, op. cit., p. 43.

[519] Cribb & Brown, op. cit., p. 31.

[520] Mundell, op. cit.

[521] ibid.

[522] Joris Ivens, 1983, op. cit., p. 84.

[523] Steve Thomas, *Hope*, 2007, colour, 104 minutes, Scriptwriters Sue Brooks & Steve Thomas. Distributed by Gil Scrine Films.

[524] John Hughes, notes on draft, email to John Cumming, Melbourne, 23 February 2010.

[525] ibid.

[526] ibid.

[527] Screen Australia, Development Programs, Industry Support, Sydney, 2011, <http://www.screenaustralia.gov.au/industry_support/Development.asp>, accessed 21 February 2011.

[528] Screen Australia, Documentaries Development, Industry Support, Sydney, 2012, <http://www.screenaustralia.gov.au/funding/documentary/development.aspx>, accessed 23 February 2013.

[529] See, for example, Stephen Thomas' record of his own experience and that of a number of other experienced documentary filmmakers in Stephen Thomas, 'Hope – Towards an ethical framework of collaborative practice in documentary filmmaking', MA thesis, School of Film and Television, The University of Melbourne (VCA). Melbourne, December 2010, <https://minerva-access.unimelb.edu.au/handle/11343/36279> accessed 16 October 2014.

[600] John Hughes & Tom Zubryki, *A Filmmakers' Cinema: 20 years of the Filmmakers' cooperatives*, Treatment and Development Proposal, Melbourne and Sydney, 2011.

[601] John Hughes, 'After Indonesia Calling', PhD thesis exegesis, School of Media and Communication, College of Design and Social Context, RMIT University, Melbourne, November 2012]

[602] Fiona Capp, 'In the Garden: Judith Wright & Nugget Coombs', *The Monthly*, June 2009. John Hughes, *Love & Fury*: Judith Wright & 'Nugget' Coombs, 2013, colour, 28 minutes, Early Works & ABC TV, Producers Philippa Campey & John Hughes, Scriptwriters Penelope Chai & John Hughes, Executive Producer Katrina Sedgwick, Music Brett Aplin, Editor Uri Mizrahi. Featuring Ramona Koval (narrator), with Helen Morse & Paul English, produced with assistance from the Screen Australia, ABC1 Artscape, 10 pm Tuesday 23 April.

[603] Judith Wright,*The coral battleground*, Thomas Nelson, West Melbourne, 1977.

[604] National Museum of Australia, 'HC Coombs', *Collaborating for Indigenous Rights*, < http://indigenousrights.net.au/people/pagination/hc_coombs>, accessed 16 October 2014.

[605] Dr Herbert C Coombs, Kulinma: listening to Aboriginal Australians, Australian National University Press, Canberra, 1978, p. 182. This event was described by William Buckley - who had lived with the Wathaurung Aboriginal community for 32 years - as a 'hoax of the white man, to possess the inheritance' of a people who had 'no chiefs claiming or possessing any superior right over the soil' and who probably saw the exchange as acknowledgement of a shared belonging. Buckley, William in *Batman's treaty*, State Library of Victoria, <http://ergo.slv.vic.gov.au/explore-history/colonial-melbourne/pioneers/batmans-

treaty>, accessed 16 October 2014.
[606] Mervyn Bishop in 'Mervyn Bishop', *Photography Collection Handbook*, Art Gallery of New South Wales, 2007, <http://www.artgallery.nsw.gov.au/collection/works/58.2000/>, accessed 16 October 2014. Bishop, Mervyn, Prime Minister Gough Whitlam pours soil into the hand of traditional land owner Vincent Lingiari, type C photograph, National Portrait Gallery, http://www.portrait.gov.au, accessed 16 October 2014.
[607] Coombs, op. cit.
[608] Wright, Judith, *We call for a treaty*, Collins/Fontana, Sydney, 1985.
[609] Sylvia Lawson, 'Such a bloody wonderful place', *Inside Story*, Swinburne Institute for Social Research, Hawthorn, 28 April 2013, <http://insidestory.org.au/such-a-bloody-wonderful-place>, accessed 16 October 2014.
[610] John Hughes, February 2013, 'Program makers' personal statement', *Love & Fury: Judith Wright & 'Nugget' Coombs*, Delivery Materials (publicity), Early Works, <http://earlyworks.com.au/wp-content/uploads/2014/03/Love___Fury_Press_Kit__EPK_.pdf>, accessed 16 October 2014. Judith Wright, *We call for a treaty*, Collins/Fontana, Sydney, 1985.
[611] ibid.
[612] Geordie Williamson, 'Love blooms in the afternoon', *The Australian*, April 20 2013, <http://www.theaustralian.com.au/arts/review/love-blooms-in-the-afternoon/story-fn9n8gph-1226623732167>, accessed 16 October, 2014.
[613] ibid.
[614] Helen Morse and Paul English, The Power of Love, 2013, fortyfivedownstairs poetry readings, <http://www.fortyfivedownstairs.com/events/the-power-of-love>, accessed 16 October 2014.
[615] Solrun Hoaas, At Edge, 1981, 16mm, colour, 21 minutes, Distributed by Ronin Films, <http://www.roninfilms.com.au>

CONCLUSION

John Hughes' films have kept a vigil on the intellectual trends of his generation while paying tribute to earlier generations of progressive political artists. They have coordinates in the history of twentieth-century art, and represent a sustained approach to a critical practice in filmmaking, the continuity of which is unique in contemporary Australian cinema. These intellectual and artistic interests are at the centre of Hughes' capacity to continually move forward and engage the enthusiasm and confidence of others. Hughes' numerous and often repeated collaborations with some of Australia's leading artists, intellectuals, film scholars and social activists testify to the knowledge, curiosity, integrity and skill he brings to these collaborations.

Hughes' almost barometric relationship to the zeitgeist means that he has populated his films with contemporary intellectual authority. These films have helped establish a place for the voice of sophisticated cultural scholarship on Australian screens. I have argued, however, that the expert's presence has sometimes helped to mask a clear and acknowledged authorial voice. Especially in the work of the 1980s, tension is apparent between artistic and intellectual aspirations and between poetic and didactic impulses – tensions that also appear to me to exist between the protagonists and performances in these films. The most sympathetic characters in Hughes' films are artists: John Hansen, in *Cybernetic Synergy*, who left the engineering profession to pursue his experiments in electronic art. Robin Laurie, in *Menace*, is a young performer in the benevolent shadow of the towering intellect of her father, Ted. In *Traps*, Gwenda Wiseman is an artist arguing the virtues of community-based political work with the studious and ambitious young investigative journalist. Maggie Cameron is the actress and woman betrayed, going through the emotion of her part as Medea amid a phalanx of confident soothsayers in *All That is Solid*. Benjamin is the fragile writer, exhumed by admiring experts, in *One Way Street*. In *What I Have Written*, Sorel, the kind-hearted singer, struggles with the delusion and jealousy of romantic and ambitious male academics. In *The Archive Project* something of this tension seems finally to have been resolved. As with *Film-Work*, the artist/intellectuals take centre stage, experts in a purely academic mode are scarce and Hughes, as narrator for the first time, speaks for himself. In *Indonesia Calling* ideas are found at work within the lives and testimony of historical players and witnesses as they are within the richly textured collage and poetic montage of historical materials.

Hughes' work with screen design recalls his father's shop window displays. Starting with the unreleased *Some Aspects of Australian Racism*, Hughes has found ways to simultaneously arrange and layer multiple images and text within the space of a single screen image. He has created structures in which the process of representation itself generates cinema thinking (see Chapter 8) and displaces the usual dependence upon narrative intrigue and extrovert personalities. In the later films, this approach prefigures a hybrid of filmic text that might be both viewed in a linear fashion and browsed in-depth.

Hughes was one of a second wave of co-op filmmakers who brought with them an interest in film as a media for social change and who benefited from the cohesive force of feminism. The most determined and politically astute of these filmmakers were documentarists who, from the mid-1970s, redefined independent film by participating in the transformation of a diverse co-op culture of underground activity into a specialist, professional industrial sector within the legitimate culture industries. To the extent that these filmmakers undertake experimentation with film form, they do so in what Hughes describes as a 'critical collaboration' with the conventional genres, practices and institutions of the mainstream film and television industries. The ramifications of this development for other strands of independent filmmaking warrant investigation elsewhere. What can be said here is that by aligning himself with – and lobbying for – the broader documentary sector, Hughes also helped to sustain one of the few remaining rafts of opportunity for the continued production of independent films at a professional level in Australia.

In a historical frame that emphasises Hughes' development as a documentary filmmaker, the stylistic hybridity of his early filmmaking can be seen as emanating from a desire to push the bounds of conventional documentary propriety. Certainly his work stems from a response to the conventions of television production that he first encountered as a young painter with a day job as a news camera operator. Furthermore, Hughes has located most of his experiments with film form squarely within the documentary tradition. The documentary form, however, is not the only one for the cinematic expression of political perspectives. What Hughes' filmmaking reflects most strongly in its formal play is the eclectic and inclusive influence of the early Melbourne Filmmakers Co-operative culture from which it emerged. Hughes' dramatic feature *What I Have Written* also reflects this diverse aesthetic. In doing so it hints at the variety of form, content and production regime that a sustained commitment to innovation and creative risk-taking could bring to the ongoing subsidy of feature filmmaking in Australia.

From *Menace* to *Joris Ivens in Australia*, Hughes' films have demonstrated a disturbingly consistent tendency in Australian security culture, specifically in the oversight and manipulation of political activity and cultural institutions. At a time when the power and scale of global surveillance, security and media enterprises have increased to unprecedented levels, it would be naive to dismiss these phenomena, or concern about them, as belonging to a bygone era of Cold War paranoia. Hughes' films describe and meticulously document the application of sustained and systematic partisan political policing and state-sponsored persecution of citizens within a First World democracy. They also tell of how the sovereignty of nations of the south and the east, including Australia, are consistently ruptured by political policing from powerful interests in the north. Since the earlier of his films were made, further evidence of the extent and import of these activities in Australia has emerged. This work shows the role independent filmmaking can play in sounding out and drawing attention to such tendencies.

The story of Hughes' filmmaking also demonstrates that local and national governments and government corporations have, nonetheless, provided resources for the production of work that is critical of the status quo, of received opinion and of the government of the day. In a liberal democracy they have an obligation to do so. Since the overthrow of socially and culturally progressive, democratically elected governments by military force (Chile 1973) and by at least questionable constitutional means (Australia 1975) however, liberal democracy has been systematically dismantled on a global scale. Its place has been taken by the ironically labelled neoliberal agenda in which – as we saw in Chapter 5 – there is an ever-increasing concentration of wealth and power into the hands of a few. For public investment in film and television in Australia, this has taken the form of a shift from policies based on public interest, innovation, community engagement and cultural development to ones based on 'the market'. This means divesting control and resources from institutions that are accountable to the citizenry to large-scale commercial interests and to government-owned corporations that are effectively being groomed for handover to the private sector.

Hughes' films are a legacy of his tenacity – a tenacity that is essential to the work of the independent filmmaker. I have tried to illustrate how, throughout numerous transformations in Australian screen culture, Hughes has maintained creative control of his work. In his service as a filmmaker he has chosen to make only the kinds of projects that interest him and for which he can see a public benefit. He has done so largely on his own terms through a remarkably attenuated yet intermittent history of subsidised production. Without diverse avenues for public subsidy, or some equivalent mechanism of support, this creative enterprise would have been severely curtailed. In the late 1990s Hughes' creative interests and those of the television market seemed, momentarily, to merge at their margins. Yet, in the first decades of the twenty-first century, at the very time when his work is being officially and publicly lauded, and through a spectrum of economic circumstances, it is taking longer and becoming more difficult than ever for him to raise the rudimentary finance for his projects.

Meanwhile, the range of work that attracts commercial finance continues to be extremely limited. Hughes' work – and that of the earlier filmmakers his films examine – encompasses a range of alliances for making films beyond the corporate and institutional fence lines. Whilst most of these collaborations – with art galleries, trade unions and non-government organisations – have been short-lived, they have provided vital bridges for the traffic of talent and ideas at times when creative independence in our filmmaking has been otherwise largely forsaken.

The story of Hughes' films shows that, for an independent filmmaker, success means not giving up even at times when opportunities are modest and progress is slow. Exceptional skill alone is not enough to ensure such longevity. Patience and commitment to the work, an understanding of its historical context and importance, together with stratagems in securing the support it requires, are attributes that are critical to the persistence of independent voices in contemporary media. While Hughes has worked primarily within the broad documentary genre, his approach to each of his films is to explore a different possible path in an ongoing project, extending aesthetic, technical and formal boundaries along the way. By continuing to produce and find an audience for such films, Hughes has maintained an effective arm of politically orientated cultural activism within a wider ongoing struggle for openness in Australian society and screen culture.

When the global forces of political, military and economic power leave even national leaders limited volition, the work of artists who train their attention on political issues might lie in creating markers, however modest or marginalised, that attest to a spirit of creativity and resistance. Hughes' films, like the work of the artists and activists he honours within them, will continue to serve that purpose by virtue of the care and attention they manifest. The quality of this work lies not in how well it performs or subverts a set of conventions and expectations, but in its embodiment of ideas that have been shared and lived with, sometimes for decades. The longevity of this work stems from its foundation in history and from the play of critical insight with imaginative, collaborative, technical and aesthetic craft. The care with which such work is made invites an attentive witness.

Appendix I:
Acronyms and Abbreviations

AAFVL	Australian Association of Film and Video Librarians
ABC	Australian Broadcasting Commission (1932–1983), now Corporation
ABT	Australian Broadcasting Tribunal
ACA	Australia Council for the Arts
ACMI	Australian Centre for the Moving Image
ADG	Australian Directors Guild
AFC	Australian Film Commission
AFTS	Australian Film Television School (1976–1985), formerly FTS (1970–1975)
AFTRS	Australian Film Television and Radio School, formerly FTS and AFTS
AIDC	Australian International Documentary Conference
ANU	Australian National University
ASIO	Australian Security Intelligence Organisation
ASPERA	Australian Screen Production Education and Research Association
ASSA	Australian Screen Studies Association (1982–1991)
ATOM	Australian Teachers of Media
BFI	British Film Institute
BLF	Builders Labourers Federation
BMC	British Motor Corporation
CAAMA	Central Australian Aboriginal Media Association
CAF	Cultural Activities Fund of the AFC
CAVRC	Carlton Access Video and Resource Centre
CDB	Creative Development Branch of the AFC
CDF	Creative Development Fund of the AFC
CEBS	Church of England Boys Society
CEP	Commonwealth Employment Program
CIA	The Central Intelligence Agency
CICD	Committee for International Co-operation and Disarmament
CPA	Communist Party of Australia
DOI	Department of Information
EFTF	Experimental Film and Television Fund
EMA	Education Media Australia
FFC	Film Finance Corporation
FRTB	Film, Radio and Television Board of the Australia Council

FTS	Film Television School
IFA	Independent Film Association
IFAC	Independent Film Action Committee
ICFTS	Interim Council for a Film and Television School
IDFA	International Documentary Film Festival Amsterdam
JAFS	Just Another Film Society
LSD	Lysergic acid diethylamide
MAVMC	Melbourne Access Video and Media Co-operative
MCE	Melbourne College of Education, later MSC
MIF	Melbourne Independent Filmmakers
MIFF	Melbourne International Film Festival
MFC	Melbourne Filmmakers Co-operative (or Co-op)
MSC	Melbourne State College, formerly MCE
MOMA	Museum of Modern Art
NFF	National Farmers' Federation
NFF	No Frills Fund
NIWG	National Indigenous Working Group
NLA	National Library of Australia
NLR	New Left Review
NGC	New German Critique
NSW	The state of New South Wales (Australia)
NYFC	New York Film-makers' Co-op
OPEC	Organisation of Petroleum Exporting Countries
PEP	Participation and Equity Program
PIT	Preston Institute of Technology
PKI	(Partai Komunis Indonesia) Indonesian Communist Party
RCTS	Remote Commercial Television Services
REA	Rural Electrification Administration
RFA	Realist Film Association
RFU	Realist Film Unit
SBS	Special Broadcasting Service
SBSi	Special Broadcasting Service Independent
SCS	Swinburne Community School
SFCV	State Film Centre of Victoria
SFC	Sydney Filmmakers Co-operative (or Co-op)
SSAAANZ	Screen Studies Association of Australia and Aotearoa/New Zealand (2010–)
TAIMA	Townsville Aboriginal and Islander Media Association
VCA	Victorian College of the Arts
VFC	Victorian Film Corporation, now Film Victoria

VTHC	Victorian Trades Hall Council
WFF	Women's Film Fund of the AFC
WWF	Waterside Workers' Federation
WWFFU	Waterside Workers' Federation Film Unit

Appendix II: Filmography and Media Works – John Hughes

John Hughes & Martyn Goddard, *Nowhere Game*, 1971, 16 mm, b&w, 24 minutes, Magic Dragon Productions, Melbourne, Scriptwriters John Hughes & Martyn Goddard, Camera John Hughes. *Short Films by John Hughes*, distributed by Artfilms, <http://www.artfilms.com.au>.

John Hughes, *Ted Laurie on American War Crimes*, 1972, 1/2" video, b&w, 25 minutes, Melbourne. Formerly distributed by Melbourne Access Video and Media Co-operative.

John Hughes, *Some Aspects of Australian Racism*, 1973 – unreleased, 16 mm, b&w, 12 minutes, Melbourne, Producer John Hughes, Scriptwriter John Hughes. Featuring Dan Atkinson, Geraldine Briggs, David Anderson, Bert Peters, Lorna Lippmann, Walter McVitty. Produced with assistance from the Interim Council for the Australian Film and Television School.

John Hughes & Ben Trudeau, *School: What are the alternatives?* 25 x 35 mm slides and audio cassette, Education Media Australia, Melbourne, 1973.

John Hughes, *Cybernetic Synergy: The Kinetic Art of John Hansen*, 1974, 16 mm, colour, 19 minutes, Melbourne, Producer John Hughes, Scriptwriter John Hughes, Camera John Hughes, Editor John Hughes. Produced with assistance from the Experimental Film and Television Fund, Film and Television Board, Australia Council for the Arts. *Short Films by John Hughes*, distributed by Artfilms, <http://www.artfilms.com.au>.

John Hughes, *Abortion a woman's decision*, 1974 (location unknown), video & 16 mm, b&w, 30 minutes, Melbourne, Scriptwriter John Hughes, Camera John Hughes, Editor John Hughes.

John Hughes, *The CIA and Fascism in Australia,* 1974, U-matic, 60 minutes, Melbourne. Featuring Senator Bill Brown, Dr Bill Richards at Melbourne University. Formerly distributed by Melbourne Access Video and Media Co-operative.

John Hughes, *Menace,* 1976, 16 mm, 96 minutes, Melbourne, Producer John Hughes, Scriptwriter John Hughes, Camera Rod Bishop, Margot Nash, Gordon Glenn, Sound Lloyd Carrick, Editor Peter Tammer. Featuring Dorothy Gibson, Lloyd Edmunds, Pat Counihan, Ralph Gibson, George Lees, Noel Counihan, George Seelaf (OA), Bon Laurie, Ted Laurie (QC), Stella Lees, Robyn Laurie, Mick Counihan. Produced with assistance from the Film, Radio & TV Board of the Australia Council/AFC. *Film-Work/Menace* distributed by Artfilms, <http://www.artfilms.com.au>.

John Hughes & Andrew Scollo, *November Eleven,* 1979, U-matic, colour, 18 minutes, Melbourne, Producer Peter Kennedy, Scriptwriter Peter Kennedy, Sound Robert Moore, John Scott. *Short Films by John Hughes*, distributed by Artfilms, <http://www.artfilms.com.au>.

John Hughes, *Film-Work,* 1981, 16 mm, colour, 46 minutes, WWFFU, Australia, Producer John Hughes, Scriptwriter John Hughes, Executive Producers Norma Disher, Keith Gow & Jock

Levy, Camera Margot Nash, Glenys Page, Sound John Whitteron, Editors John Whitteron, Chris Warner, Viv Carroll. Featuring Norma Disher, Keith Gow, Jock Levy. Produced with assistance from the AFC. *Film-Work/Menace* distributed by Artfilms, <http://www.artfilms.com.au>.

John Hughes, *November Eleven: An Australian History – Work In Progress – Part 2,* 1981, 1" video, colour, 19 minutes, Melbourne, Producer John Hughes, Scriptwriter John Hughes. Featuring Carolyn Howard & Paul Davies.

John Hughes, *Gunana: Homeland of the Mornington Island Woomera Dancers*, 1982, U-matic colour, 29 minutes, Media Production Centre, Melbourne College of Education, Producer Philip Johnson, Executive Producers Brian Sheedy, Brian Walsh, Camera John Hughes, Sound Dennis Claringbold, Music Jimmy Cliff, No Fixed Address, Editors John Hughes, Lisa Dethridge, Sasha Trikojus. Featuring Woomera Dancers, Kenny Jacobs. Made in collaboration with the people of Mornington Island.

John Hughes, *November Eleven: On Sacred Land,* 1983, 1" video, colour, 18 minutes, Melbourne, Producers Peter Kennedy & John Hughes, Scriptwriters John Hughes & Peter Kennedy, Sound John Hughes, Editors Sasha Trikojus & John Hughes. Produced with assistance from the Visual Arts Board, Australia Council.

John Hughes, *CF (Cystic Fibrosis),* 1983, 16 mm, colour, 24 minutes, Melbourne, Camera Jaems Grant. Produced with assistance from Film Victoria.

John Hughes, *How Does it Strike You?* 1985, 1" video, colour, 23 minutes, Video Projects, Melbourne, Producer Penny Robins. Produced with assistance from the Trade Union Information and Resource Centre of the VTHC, the Bureau of Youth Affairs, Department of Employment and Industrial Affairs and PEP.

John Hughes, *Acceptable Risk,* 1985, video, colour, Video Projects, Melbourne. Produced with assistance from the Australian Post and Telecommunications Union.

John Hughes, *Traps,* 1985, 16 mm, colour, 96 minutes, Melbourne/Sydney, Producer John Hughes, Scriptwriters Paul Davies & John Hughes, Camera Katrina Bowels, Erika Addis & Jaems Grant, Sound Laurie Robinson, Jack Holt, John Cruthers, Lou Hubbard & Pat Fiske, Editor Zbigniew Friedrich. Featuring Carolyn Howard, Gwenda Wiseman, Paul Davies, John Flaus, Lesley Stern, Drew Cottle & Peter Summerfield with David Combe, Tony Walker (2JJJ), Michael Gill (*The Age*), Anthony McAdam (*Quadrant*), Denis Freney (*Tribune*), Greg Hywood (*Financial Review*), PP McGuinness (*Financial Review*), Humphrey McQueen, Paul Lyneham (Channel 7), Mark Aarons (ABC), Steven Sewell. Produced with assistance from the CDF of the AFC. Distributed by Artfilms, <http://www.artfilms.com.au>.

John Hughes, *Is It Working? George Seelaf for the Record,* 1984, 16 mm, colour, 48 minutes, Melbourne, Producer John Hughes, Scriptwriter John Hughes, Camera Tony Wright, Andrew Taylor, Jaems Grant, Sound Cath Dyson, Georgina Guilfoyle, Editor Zbigniew Friedrich. Featuring Noel Counihan, Wally Curran, Frank Hardy, Deb Mills, Andrew Reeves & George Seelaf. Produced with assistance from the Community Arts Board and the Archival Film Project of the Australia Council.

John Hughes, *Changing Schools,* 1985, 1" video, 18 minutes, Education Image, Melbourne, Producer Penny Robins, Executive Producer Greg Day & Ron Theile. Produced with assistance from the Victorian Council of School Organisations, Victoria's 150th Education

Committee and the Teachers Federation of Victoria.

John Hughes, *All That is Solid,* 1988, 16 mm, Hi-8 video, colour, 54 minutes, Melbourne, Producer John Hughes, Scriptwriters Paul M Davies Chris Barnett, John Hughes, Camera Jaems Grant, Sound Lloyd Carrick, Editors Jill Holt, Zbigniew Friedrich. Featuring Margaret Cameron, Paul Davis, Mitchell Faircloth, Eva Hall, Carolyn Howard, Nico Lathouris, Yani Lathouris, Mark Rogers, Louise Smith with Bill Cope, Boris Frankel, Freda Glynn, Reginald Klimionok, Andrew Mack, Craig McGregor, Roberta Perkins, Jo Valentine, Katherine West, Ted Wheelwright. Produced with assistance from the AFC-ABC Documentary Fellowship and the Australian Bicentennial Authority. Distributed by Artfilms, <http://www.artfilms.com.au>.

John Hughes, *Moments Like These,* 1989, colour, 27 minutes, Open Channel, TAIMA, Melbourne, Producer John Hughes, Scriptwriter Tony Wright, Camera Jaems Grant. Featuring Bob Maza. Produced with assistance from the Department of Employment, Education & Training.

John Hughes, *The Golden Mountain,* 1990, colour, 29 minutes, SBS, Sydney, Scriptwriters Philip Howe & John Hughes, Camera Jaems Grant & Andrew Scott, Sound Sonia Leber & David Wright, Editor Philip Howe. Featuring Chandrabhanu, Ambika Docherty, Arun Munoz, Tina Young, Radhika & Shanti Moorthy. Produced by SBS TV.

John Hughes, *One Way Street: Fragments for Walter Benjamin,* 1992, 16 mm, colour, 58 minutes, Melbourne, Producer John Hughes, Scriptwriters Paul Davies & John Hughes, Camera Nicolette Freeman, Erika Addis, Editor Uri Mizrahi. Featuring Nico Lathouris, Maggie Cameron, Mark Rogers, Louise Smith. Produced with assistance from the AFC & ABC. Distributed by Artfilms, <http://www.artfilms.com.au>.

John Hughes, *What I Have Written,* 1995, 35 mm, colour, 98 minutes, Early Works, Melbourne, Producers John Hughes & Peter Sainsbury, Scriptwriter John Scott, Camera Dion Beebe. Featuring Martin Jacobs, Gillian Jones, Jacek Koman, Angie Milliken. Produced with assistance from the AFC & ABC. Distributed by Beyond International, Globe and Artfilms, <http://www.artfilms.com.au>.

John Hughes, *After Mabo,* 1997, SP Betacam, colour, 84 minutes, Earlyworks/Mirimbiak Nations Aboriginal Corporation, Melbourne, Producers Debra Annear & John Hughes, Scriptwriter John Hughes, Camera Peter Zakharov, Sound Mark Tarpey, Editor Uri Mizrahi. Featuring Richard Frankland. Produced with assistance from the AFC, SBSI, ATSIC. Distributed by Ronin Films, <http://www.roninfilms.com.au> and Artfilms, <http://www.artfilms.com.au>.

John Hughes, *Take Five,* 1998, 13 x 5 minute series, ABC TV Arts, Australia, Producer John Lewis, Scriptwriter Betty Churcher, featuring Betty Churcher.

John Hughes, *River of Dreams,* 1998, SP Betacam, colour, 52 minutes, Early Works, Australia, Producers Donna Cameron & John Hughes, Scriptwriters Donna Cameron & John Hughes. Produced with assistance from the SBS Independent. Distributed by SBS, Ronin Films, Artfilms. Distributed by Artfilms, <http://www.artfilms.com.au>.

John Hughes, *The Art of War,* 2005, colour, 4 x 26 minutes, Film Australia National Interest Program, Early Works and SBS Independent, Australia, Producers John Hughes, Betty Churcher, Scriptwriter Betty Churcher, Executive Producer Anna Grieve, Camera Joel Peterson, Sound Mark Tarpey, Music Paul Grabowsky, Editor Uri Mizrahi, featuring Betty Churcher. Produced with assistance from the Australian War Memorial.

John Hughes, *Hidden Treasures,* 2006, 10 x 5 minutes, Film Australia National Interest Program, Early Works, ABC TV Arts, Producers John Hughes & Philippa Campey, Scriptwriter Betty Churcher, Executive Producer Anna Grieve, Camera Joel Peterson, Sound Mark Tarpey, Steve Best, Music Paul Grabowsky, Editor Uri Mizrahi, featuring Betty Churcher.

John Hughes & Uri Mizrahi, *The Archive Project,* 2006, colour and b&w, 98 minutes, Early Works, Melbourne, Producers Philippa Campey & John Hughes, Scriptwriter John Hughes, Editor Uri Mizrahi. Produced with assistance from the NFSA, AFC, Film Victoria, ABC TV Arts and Music and Effects. Distributed by Artfilms, <http://www.artfilms.com.au>.

John Hughes, 'Moving History' *A place to think*, online multimedia, Film Australia, ABC, Executive Producers Anna Grieve & Ian Allen, 2007, <http://www.abc.net.au/aplacetothink/?- watch>, accessed 2 February 2013.

John Hughes, *An Unstoppable Force – Betty Churcher with John Olsen,* 2008, colour, 26 minutes, Film Australia National Interest Program, Early Works, Producers Betty Churcher & John Hughes, Scriptwriter Betty Churcher. Distributed by ABC TV.

John Hughes, *Indonesia Calling: Joris Ivens in Australia,* 2009, Digital Betacam, colour and b&w, 90 minutes, Early Works, Australia, Producers John Hughes & Andrea Foxworthy, Scriptwriter John Hughes, Editor Uri Mizrahi. Featuring Graeme Cutts, Andre Stufkens, Susan Geldho, Joesoef Isak, Charlotte Maramis, John Daniell, Maggie Keane, Jan Lingard, Professor Joe Isaac, Arthur Gar Lock Chang & Rabin Hardjadibrata. Produced with assistance from ABC TV, MIFF Premiere Fund, Film Victoria & Screen Australia. Distributed by Artfilms, <http://www.artfilms.com.au>.

John Hughes, *Love & Fury: Judith Wright & 'Nugget' Coombs,* 2013, colour, 28 minutes, Early Works & ABC TV, Producers Philippa Campey & John Hughes, Scriptwriters Penelope Chai & John Hughes, Executive Producer Katrina Sedgwick, Music Brett Aplin, Editor Uri Mizrahi. Featuring Ramona Koval (narrator), with Helen Morse & Paul English, produced with assistance from the Screen Australia, ABC1 Artscape, 10 pm Tuesday 23 April.

Appendix III:
Bibliography – John Hughes

John Hughes, 'Community Use of Video', *Learning Exchange*, March 1973, pp. 14–15.

John Hughes, Stuart Longmuir, Rod Harris, Gary Lewis & Danny O'Sullivan, *Submission to the Film and Television Board of the Australia Council for the Arts for the establishment of a Community Video Exchange*, Video Exchange group, Melbourne, 1973.

John Hughes, 'What to do with a Greek bearing gifts', *Learning Exchange*, December 1974, pp. 4–7.

John Hughes, 'Melbourne Film Maker's Co-op', in Charles Merewether and Ann Stephen (ed.), *The Great Divide*, 1977, pp. 66–68.

John Hughes, 'Albie's blind eye to the why', *Nation Review*, 3–9 November 1978, p. 22.

John Hughes, 'Jimmie Blacksmith … a star is shorn', *Nation Review*, 1–7 September 1978, p. 21.

John Hughes, 'Propaganda then and now', in Ross Lansell & Peter Beilby (eds), *The Documentary Film in Australia*, *Cinema Papers* in association with Film Victoria, North Melbourne, 1982, pp. 142–145.

John Hughes, 'Unanimity and Disagreement', *Filmnews*, January/February 1983, p. 7.

John Hughes, 'Independent Film Action in Victoria', *Filmnews*, July 1983, p. 1.

John Hughes & Tom Zubrycki, 'Kemira: Diary of a strike', *Filmnews*, October 1984, pp. 12–14.

John Hughes & Brett Levy, 'The Waterside Workers' Federation Film Unit, 1953–1958: An Interview with Norma Disher, Keith Gow and Jerome Levy', in Tom O'Regan & Albert Moran (eds), *An Australian Film Reader*, Currency Press, Sydney, 1985, pp. 365–373.

John Hughes & Kim Dalton, *New Windows/Old Landscapes/Blue Sky*, Open Channel, submission to the Australian Broadcasting Tribunal on remote commercial television services, Fitzroy, 1985.

John Hughes & Penny Robins, 'More than meets the eye', *Films Used in Changing Schools*, Video Projects, Melbourne, 1985.

John Hughes, 'Screened from Access: The Public and Television', *Arena*, no. 80, 1987, pp. 68–74.

John Hughes, 'Keith Gow', *Cinema Papers*, January 1988, p. 4.

John Hughes, 'Book Review: Modernism Relocated: towards a cultural studies of visual modernity', *Metro*, no. 104, 1995, pp. 79–81.

John Hughes, Dion Beebe, Ian Sheath & Dominic Case, 'The Film of the Book', *Cinema Papers*, February 1996, pp. 27–28.

John Hughes, 'Indonesia Calling: Joris Ivens and Australia', *Ivens Magazine*, no. 13, 2007, European Foundation Joris Ivens, Nijmegen NL, December, pp. 26–29, <http://www.ivens.nl/upload/10304_Acr212.tmp.pdf>, accessed 3 February 2013.

John Hughes, 'Moving History' *A place to think*, online multimedia, Film Australia, ABC, Executive Producer Anna Grieve & Ian Allen, 2007, <http://www.abc.net.au/aplacetothink/?-watch>, accessed 2 February 2013.

John Hughes, 'Indonesia Calling: Joris Ivens in Australia', *Senses of Cinema*, no. 51, 2009.

John Hughes, *John Hughes*, Melbourne Independent Filmmakers, Bill Mousoulis (ed.) Innersense, Australia, 2010, <http://www.innersense.com.au/mif/hughes.html>, accessed 23 August 2013.

Hughes, John, 'After Indonesia Calling', thesis (PhD) exegesis, School of Media and Communication, College of Design and Social Context, RMIT University, Melbourne, November 2012.

Hughes, John, *The Archive Project (book): The Realist Film Unit in Cold War Australia*, Early Works & ATOM, Melbourne, 2013.

Appendix IV: References

AAFVL, *Newsletter No. 3*, Australian Association of Film and Video Libraries (Victorian Branch), Melbourne, 1981.

ACA, *Interim Report: Film Committee*, Australia Council for the Arts, Interim, Sydney, 1969.

ACA, *Annual Report*, Australia Council for the Arts (calendar year), Sydney, 1974.

ACA, *Annual Report*, Australia Council for the Arts (July to June), Sydney, 1974/1975.

AFC, '1986 Documentary Fellowship Announced', media release, Australian Film Commission, Sydney, 17 December 1985.

AFC, *Industry Overview*, Australian Film Commission, Sydney, 1999.

AFID, *Is It Working?* flyer, AFI Distribution, 1985.

AFID, 'Traps', advertisement, *Tribune*, 12 March 1986, p. 10.

AFID, Film-Work, database, Magic List, Australian Film Institute Distribution, Melbourne, 2000.

Anderson, Benedict, *Java in a time of revolution: occupation and resistance*, 1944–1946, Cornell UP, Ithaca, 1972.

Arf-Arf (Marcus Bergner, Michael Buckley, Frank Lovece, Marisa Stirpe), *Thread of Voice*, 1993, 16 mm, colour, 20 minutes, Melbourne, Associate Producer Marie Craven, Line Producer Roslyn Walker, Camera Robin Plunkett, Sound Ray Boseley & Leesa Marie Spencer. Produced with assistance from the Australian Film Commission.

Artfilms, *Kit Guyat Films: President Johnson's Visit, Balmain and The Phallic Forest*, Kit Guyatt Films, Doczy, Kriszta (ed.) Contemporary Arts Media, 2012, <http://www.artfilms.com.au/Detail.aspx?ItemID=4927>, accessed 10 January 2013.

ASSA, 'Abstracts', 1982, *Welcome to the First Australian Screen Studies Conference*, Australian Screen Studies Association (Victoria).

Athenaeum, 'Advertisement', *The Sun*, Saturday 20 July 1974, p. 19.

Aufderheide, Patricia, *IDFA, Ivens, Oranges and More*, Future of Public Media, The Centre for Social Media, Washington, DC, 2009, <http://www.centerforsocialmedia.org/blogs/future_of_public_media/idfa_ivens_oranges_and_more/>, accessed 24 February 2013.

Australian Bureau of Statistics, 'The Mabo Case and the Native Title Act', *Year Book 1995*, vol. ABS Catalogue No. 1301.0, 1 January 1995, <http://www.abs.gov.au/Ausstats/abs@.nsf/Previousproducts/1301.0Feature Article21995>, accessed 22 December 2013.

Author not attributed, 'Prime Minister Condemns Peace Convention', *The Canberra Times*, Thursday 17 September 1953, p. 1.

Author not attributed, 'Tim Burstall: Film writer, producer, director', *Obituaries*, 2004, Milesago: Australasian Music & Popular Culture 1964–1975, <http://www.milesago.com/Obits/frames7.htm>, accessed 7 January 2013.

Author not attributed, 'Mike Leyland dies, aged 68', *Perth Now*, 14 September 2009, News Limited, <http://www.perthnow.com.au/news/mike-leyland-dies-aged-68/story-e6frg12c-1225772917208>, accessed 14 February 2013.

Bailey, Genevieve & Benj Binks, *Doco3000*, Melbourne, 2013, <https://www.facebook.com/Doco3000>, accessed 14 February 2013.

Bakker, Kees, *Inventory of the Joris Ivens Archives*, European Foundation, Joris Ivens Nijmegen, 1999.

Balsaitas, Jonas, 'Biography', *Charles Nodrum Gallery*, 2012, Melbourne, <http://www.charlesnodrumgallery.com.au/artist–biography.asp?idArtistInfo=383&idArtist=1088>, accessed 9 January 2013.

Balsaitis, Jonas, *Image of a Point Seen Through* 1970, acrylic on canvas. Modern Australian Painting. Distributed by Charles Nodrum Gallery.

Banks, Ron, 'Film-maker's solid vision of the future', interview with John Hughes, *The West Australian*, 1989, p. 18.

Barta, Tony, 'Making it Strange: Camera Natura, One Way Street and The Refracting Glasses as Realism, Surrealism and the Poetics of History in Film', in Benson, John, Ken Berryman & Wayne Levy (eds), Screening the Past: The Sixth Australian History and Film Conference Papers, Melbourne, La Trobe University, 1993, pp. 205–210.

Baudrillard, Jean, *For a critique of the political economy of the sign*, Charles Levin (trans.), St. Louis, Missouri, Telos Press, 1981.

Benjamin, Walter, 'The Author as Producer', in Demetz, Peter (ed.), *Reflections: Essays, Aphorisms, Autobiographical Writings*, Edmund Jephcott (trans.), 1st edn, A Helen and Kurt Wolff Book, Harcourt Brace Jovanovich, Inc., New York, 1978, pp. 220–238. Originally published Paris, 1934. Der Autor Als Produzent in Versuche uber Brecht, 1966.

Benjamin, Walter, *Illuminations*, translated by Zorn, Harry, Pimlico, London, 1999. Originally published Harcourt, 1968, Jonathan Cape, 1970.

Benjamin, Walter, *Selected Writings 1927–1934*, translated by Rodney Livingston et al., vol. 2, 2 vols, Harvard UP, Massachusetts, 1999.

Berman, Marshall, *All That is Solid Melts into Air: The Experience of Modernity*, 1st edn, Simon & Schuster, New York, 1982.

Berryman, Ken, 'Allowing young filmmakers to spread their wings': The Educational Role of the Experimental Film and Television Fund', thesis (MEd), Centre for the Study of Education, Communication and Media, La Trobe University, Melbourne, 1985.

Bertrand, Ina, 'Filmmakers' Co-Ops', in Bertrand, Ina (ed.), *Cinema in Australia: a Documentary History*, University of New South Wales Press, Sydney, 1989, pp. 373–377.

Bertrand, Ina & William D Routt, *The Story of the Kelly Gang*, The Moving Image, ATOM, St Kilda, 2007.

Bialek-Wester, Mandi, 'Interview with Sarah Stollman', *Senses of Cinema*, no. 23, 2002, November–December, <http://sensesofcinema.com/2002/23/stollman/>, accessed 23 February 2013.

Bishop, Mervyn, in 'Mervyn Bishop', *Photography Collection Handbook*, Art Gallery of New South Wales, 2007, < http://www.artgallery.nsw.gov.au/collection/works/58.2000/>, accessed 16 October 2014.

Bishop, Mervyn, *Prime Minister Gough Whitlam pours soil into the hand of traditional land owner Vincent Lingiari*, type C photograph, National Portrait Gallery, http://www.portrait.gov.

au, accessed 16 October 2014.

Bishop, Rod, Gordon Glenn, Scott Murray & Andrew Pecze, *Beginnings*, 1970, 16 mm, b&w, 58 minutes.

Blonski, Annette, 'End game', *Cinema Papers*, May 1986, p. 85.

Blonski, Annette, 'At the Government's Pleasure: Independent Cinema', in Blonski, Annette, Barbara Creed & Freda Freiberg (eds), *Don't Shoot Darling!* Greenhouse, Melbourne, 1987, pp. 40–60.

Blonski, Annette, Barbara Creed & Freda Freiberg, *Don't Shoot Darling! Women's Independent Filmmaking in Australia*, Greenhouse, Melbourne, 1987.

Bolton, Geoffrey, *The Middle Way 1942–1995*, vol. 5, 5 vols, 2nd edn, The Oxford History of Australia, Oxford University Press, South Melbourne, 2001. Originally published 1996.

Brealey, Gil, 'SAFC 40th Anniversary Speech', *Australian International Documentary Conference (AIDC)*, no. 27, February 2012, Adelaide Studios, <http://www.safilm.com.au/library/Gil Brealey Speech 40th Anniversary AIDC Opening Night_0.pdf>, accessed 24 February 2013.

Brecht, Bertolt, *Brecht on Theatre*, Hill and Wang, NY, 1964.

Brennan, Richard, 'Tim Burstall', *Screen Australia*, 2004, Australian Film Commission (AFC) archive, <http://afcarchive.screenaustralia.gov.au/newsandevents/afcnews/feature/tim_burstall/newspage_113.aspx>, accessed 8 January 2013.

Bresson, Robert, *Notes on Cinematography*, translated by Griffin, Jonathan, Urizen Books, New York, 1997. Originally published Notes sur le cinématographe, 1975.

Buckland, Michael K, 'The Kinamo movie camera, Emanuel Goldberg and Joris Ivens', Film History, vol. 20, no. 1, 2008, pp. 49–59, <http://connection.ebscohost.com/c/articles/32046653/kinamo–movie–camera–emanuel–goldberg–joris–ivens>, accessed 21 September 2013.

Buckley, William in 'Batman's treaty', State Library of Victoria, < http://ergo.slv.vic.gov.au/explore-history/colonial-melbourne/pioneers/batmans-treaty>, accessed 16 October 2014.

Burstall, Tim, *Two Thousand Weeks*, 1969, 35 mm, b&w, 88 minutes, Producers David Bilcock Sr & Patrick Ryan, Scriptwriters Burstall, Tim & Patrick Ryan, Camera Robin Copping, Music Don Burrows, Editor David Bilcock Jr. Featuring Mark McManus & Jeanie Drynan.

Byrnes, Paul, 'Traps', film review, *Sydney Morning Herald*, 13 March 1986.

Cameron, Clyde, Jane Lanbrook, Tony Douglas, 'The CIA in Australia Part 3', 1986, radio broadcast, *Watching Brief*, Public Radio News Services, Melbourne.

Campey, Philippa, *Filmcamp*, 2012, <http://www.filmcamp.com.au/>, accessed 23 February 2013.

Cantrill, Arthur & Corinne Cantrill, *Cantrills Filmnotes*, Melbourne, 2011, <http://www.arthurandcorinnecantrill.com/filmnotes.html>, accessed 10 January 2013.

Capp, Fiona 'In the Garden: Judith Wright & Nugget Coombs', *The Monthly*, June 2009.

Caputo, Raffaele & John Hughes, 'John Hughes interviewed by Raffaele Caputo', *Cinema Papers*, October 1993, pp. 35–37.

Cavadini, Alessandro, *Ningla A-Na*, 1972, 72 minutes, Australia, Producer Alessandro Cavadini. Distributed by <http://www.smartstreetfilms.com.au>.

Cavalcanti, Alberto, 'Alberto Cavalcanti: His Advice to Young Producers of Documentary', *Film*

Quarterly, no. 9, 1955, pp. 354–355.

Chauvel, Charles, *Uncivilised*, 1936, 77 minutes, Expeditionary Films, Australia, Producer Charles Chauvel, Camera Tasman Higgins, Sound Denis Box, Music Lindley Evans, Editor Frank Coffey, Assistant Editor Mona Donaldson. Featuring Margot Rhys, Dennis Hoey & Ashton Jarry. Harry Weipa & Booya (uncredited). Distributed by Umbrella Entertainment.

Chauvel, Charles, *Jedda*, 1955, 35 mm, colour, 101 minutes, Charles Chauvel Productions, Producer Charles Chauvel, Scriptwriters Elsa Chauvel, Charles Chauvel, Camera Carl Kayser, Editors Alex Ezard, Jack Gardiner, Pam Bosworth. Featuring Ngarla Kunoth, Robert Tudawali. Distributed by Columbia Pictures (Aust.), British Lion (UK).

Christie, Ian, Jon Jost: a voice from the margins, 1983, Eleventh Hour television program, *Visions*, Large Door, Channel 4 TV, London.

Churcher, Betty, *Notebooks*, MUP, Miegunyah Press, Carlton, 2011.

Cockroft, Eva, 'Abstract Expression, Weapon of the Cold War', *Artforum*, June, 1974, pp. 39–41.

Cohen, David, 'The Strife of Brian', *The Age*, 2007, Melbourne, 28 February, <http://www.theage.com.au/articles/2007/02/27/1172338625209.html>, accessed 22 December 2013.

Coldicutt, Ken & John (Jack) G Fitzsimmons, *A Place To Live*, 1946, 16 mm, b&w, silent, 13 minutes, Brotherhood of St Laurence, Melbourne. Producers Fr Gerard Tucker and Realist Film Unit, in John Hughes & Uri Mizrahi, *The Archive Project*, 2006, DVD box set. Distributed by Artfilms.

Coldicutt, Ken, *These Are Our Children*, 1946, 16 mm, b&w, silent, 12 minutes, Brotherhood of St Laurence, Melbourne, Producers Fr Gerard Tucker and Realist Film Unit, in John Hughes & Uri Mizrahi, *The Archive Project*, 2006, DVD box set. Distributed by Artfilms.

Coldicutt, Ken, Bob Mathews & Gerhart (Gerry) Harant, *In My Beginning: A story of New Education*, 1947, 16 mm, colour, sound, 17 minutes, Realist Film Unit Melbourne, Scriptwriter Joseph Clive Nield and students of Koornong School, in particular, Mavourneen Box, Souzka Frankel & Jenepher Potts, in John Hughes & Uri Mizrahi, *The Archive Project*, 2006, DVD box set. Distributed by Artfilms.

Commonwealth of Australia, 'Native Title Act 1993', Act No. 110 of 1993, *National Native Title Tribunal*, Com Law, <http://www.nntt.gov.au/Information-about-native-title/Pages/The-Native-Title-Act.aspx>, accessed 22 December 2013.

Commonwealth of Australia, 'Native Title Amendment Act 1998', *Australian Government*, vol. C2004A00354, Act No. 97, 1998, ComLaw, Canberra, 27 July, accessed 23 December 2013.

Conner, Bruce & DEVO, *Mongoloid*, 1978, b&w, 3 minutes, Producer DEVO, Scriptwriter Conner, Bruce.

Cook, Peter S, *Red Barrister: A Biography of Ted Laurie QC*, 1st edn, La Trobe University Press, Bundoora, 1994.

Coombs, Dr Herbert C, *The Australia Council for the Arts – Progress and Plans*, UNESCO, Australia Council, Pamphlet File, Canberra, 1969.

Coombs, Dr Herbert C, Kulinma: listening to Aboriginal Australians, Australian National University Press, Canberra, 1978.

Coombs, Dr Herbert C, *Trial balance*, Macmillan, South Melbourne, 1981.

Cope, Nicholas D, 'Northern Industrial Scratch: the history and contexts of a visual music practice', thesis (PhD), Faculty of Art, Design and Media, University of Sunderland, England, June 2012, <http://ethos.bl.uk/OrderDetails.do?uin=uk.bl.ethos.576523>, accessed 16 October 2014. Cottle, Drew & Angela Keys, 'From Colonial Film Commissioner to Political Pariah: Joris Ivens and the Making of Indonesia Calling', *Senses of Cinema*, no. 41, 2006.

Creed, Barbara, John Davies, Freda Freiberg, David Hanan and Kim Montgomery (ed.), *Papers and Forums on Independent Film and Asian Cinema*, Australian Screen Studies Association (Victoria), Australian Film and Television School, Melbourne, 1982.

Cribb, Robert & Colin Brown, 'Towards Cataclysm, 1959–65', *Modern Indonesia: A history since 1945*, Longman, London, 1995, pp. 82–96.

Crowsfoot Films, *Save a Starving Film*, pamphlet, Ultimo, 1979.

Cumming, John, Jane Madsen & James Swinson, *First Time Tragedy, Second Time Farce*, 1989, 16 mm, colour, 75 minutes, Counter Productions (Australia) & Zero One (UK), Executive Producer Russell Porter, Camera John Cumming, John Gulliver, Vicki Hastrich & James Swinson, Sound John Cruthers, Piers Douglas, Andrew Howie, Jane Madsen, Mark Nash & James Swinson, Music Steve Skaith, Editor Jane Madsen. Featuring Bart Willoughby, Robyn Archer, Richard Dooley, Mathew Green, Clare Madsen, Peter Marz, Norman Fisher, Lance Dixon, Gerry Lomas, London Greenpeace, Francis Williams, Robbie Thorpe, Millie Ingram, Marie Bennett, Mac Silva, Ding Li, Helen Hassoura, Dr Andrew Theophanous MP, Alf Bamblett, Sonia Sedmak, Roberto Malara. Produced with assistance from Film Victoria.

Cumming, John, 'From crystals to pixels: new technology in the documentary work of John Hughes' in *Selected papers : Film & history conference, Canberra Australia 2-5 December 2004 : 12th biennial conference of the Film and History Association of Australia and New Zealand* Bertrand, Ina & Marilyn Dooley (eds), National Film and Sound Archive, 2004.

Cumming, John, 'Perplexities: Experimenta 1992', *Artlink*, vol. 13, no. 1, March–May 1993, pp. 61–62.

Cumming, John, 'A long road to the small screen: John Hughes and the independent film and video movement in Australia', thesis (MA), Cinema Studies, La Trobe University, Melbourne, 2004.

Cutts, Graeme, '*Indonesia Calling* and Joris Ivens', in Moran, Albert & Tom O'Reagan (eds), *An Australian film reader*, Currency Press, Sydney, 1985, pp. 350–364.

Cutts, Graeme, 'Interview with Giorgio Mangiamele', *Cinema Papers*, July 1992.

Dalton, Kim, *The Myth of the Careless Worker*, 1983, video, colour, 29 minutes, Open Channel, Melbourne.

Danks, Adrian, 'Arrested Developments or from *The Heroes are Tired to The Tomb of Ligeia*: Some Notes on the Place of the Melbourne University Film Society in 1960s Film Culture', in O'Hanlon, Seamus (ed.), *Go: Melbourne in the Sixties*, Circa, Beaconsfield, 2012, pp. 101–114.

Davies, Paul, 'Alternative Working Structures', IFAC Production Matters Seminar, Melbourne, author's notes, 1984.

Davies, Paul, Carolyn Howard & Pat Laughren, *Exits*, 1980, 16 mm, colour and b&w, 47 minutes, Stringybark Films, Melbourne, Producer Davies, Paul, Scriptwriters Davies, Paul,

Carolyn Howard & Pat Laughren, Executive Producers Davies, Paul, Charlie Dale, Carolyn Howard, Anne Grey & Robert Antoniades, Camera Paul Cavell, Music Lynton Macfadzean, Peter Bostman, Peter Holden. Featuring Monica Bannikoff, Robert Antoniades, Kim Bannikoff, Charlie Dale, Paul Davies, Mary Anne Grey, Carolyn Howard, Pat Laugheran, Kerry O'Rourke. Produced with assistance from the Creative Development Branch, Australian Film Commission.

Delamoir, Jeannette, 'The Explosive Life of an Exploiteer: Franklyn Barrett Tours North Queensland with "The Ten Commandments",' *Australia's Living Archive*, 2011, National Film and Sound Archive, Canberra, <http://www.nfsa.gov.au/research/papers/>.

Deling, Bert, *Dalmas*, 1973, 16 mm, 103 minutes, Apogee Films, Melbourne, Producer Deling, Bert, Camera Sasha Trikojus, Sound Lloyd Carrick. Featuring Peter Whittle, Peter Cummins, Max Gillies, John Duigan, Roger Ward. Produced with assistance from the Australia Council, Experimental Film and Television Fund.

Department of Communications, Information Technology and the Arts, 'Review of Australian Government Film. Funding Support, issues paper', 2006, <http://arts.gov.au/sites/default/files/pdfs/australian–film–review.pdf>, accessed 22 February 2013.

Dermody, Susan, *Breathing Under Water*, 1992, 78 minutes, Periscope Productions, Sydney, Producer McMurchy, Megan, Camera Erika Addis, Sound John Dennison, Music Elizabeth Drake, Editor Diana Priest. Featuring David Argue, Maeve Dermody, Kristoffer Greaves, Anne-Louise Lambert.

Dermody, Susan & Elizabeth Jacka, *The Screening of Australia: Anatomy of a National Cinema*, vol. 2, 2 vols, 1st edn, Currency Press, Sydney, 1988.

Disher, Norma, Keith Gow & Jock Levy, *The Hungry Miles*, 1955, 16 mm, b&w, 25 minutes, Waterside Workers' Federation Film Unit, Sydney. Featuring Leonard Teale.

Dorling, Philip, 'Whitlam radical, Fraser arrogant, Hawke moderate: Secret cables reveal Murdoch insights', *The Sydney Morning Herald*, 20 May 2013, <http://www.smh.com.au/federal–politics/political–news/whitlam–radical–fraser–arrogant–hawke–moderate–secret–cables–reveal–murdoch–insights–20130520–2jvtl.html#ixzz2etxEMd5g>, accessed 15 September 2013.

Dow, Dr Coral and Dr John Gardiner-Garden, 'Overview of Indigenous Affairs: Part 1: 1901 to 1991', *Publications*, Parliament of Australia, < http://www.aph.gov.au/about_parliament/parliamentary_departments/parliamentary_library/pubs/bn/1011/indigenousaffairs1>, accessed 16 October 2014.

Dwoskin, Stephen, 'Film-Related Organizations: Filmmakers Co-op', *Filmwaves*, no. 3, 3 February 1998.

Dylan, Bob, 'Visions of Johanna', Blonde on Blonde, Columbia Records, USA, 1966.

Dzenis, Anna, 'One Way Street: Fragments for Walter Benjamin', *Cinema Papers*, October 1993, pp. 33–35.

Dzenis, Anna, 'John Hughes' What I Have Written', *Metro*, no. 107, 1996, pp. 21–24.

Edgar, Patricia, 'The John Flaus I Know', John Flaus Dossier, *Senses of Cinema*, issue 72, October 2014, <http:// sensesofcinema.com/2014/john-flaus-dossier/the-john-flaus-i-know/>, accessed 16 November 2014.

Eisenhuth, Susie, 'A documentary that tries to say too much', Film review, *Sun-Herald*, 16 March 1986.

Enzensberger, Hans Magnus, 'Constituents of a Theory of the Media', *Raids and Reconstructions: Essays in Politics, Crime & Culture*, Hood, Stuart (trans.), Pluto Press, London, 1976, pp. 20–53. Originally published 'Baukasten zu einer Theorie der Medien', *Kurbuch Verlag*, Berlin, 1970. *New Left Review*, London, 1970.

Fekete, John, 'Benjamin's Ambivalence', *Telos*, no. 55, Spring 1978, pp. 192–198.

Film Victoria, 'Australian Films at the Australian Box Office', 8 June 2011.

Fitzsimons, John (Jack) G, *Gaol Does Not Cure*, b&w, 1946, 16mm, silent, Victorian Amateur Cine Society, Melbourne, held by NFSA.

Foley, Gary, 'The Road to Native Title: The Aboriginal Rights Movement and the ALP 1973–1996', The Koori History Website, Melbourne, July 2001, <http://www.kooriweb.org/foley/essays/essays_page.html>, accessed 23 December 2013.

Foley, Gary, 'White myth-making and a State of Denial', *Tracker*, 2004, NSW Aboriginal Land Council, 4 April, <http://tracker.org.au/2012/04/the-contrarian-white-myth-making-and-a-state-of-denial/>, accessed 22 December 2013.

Foley, Gary, 'How Bob Hawke killed land rights', *Tracker*, 2013, NSW Aboriginal Land Council, 28 February, accessed 22 December 2013.

Frankland, Richard, *No Way to Forget*, 1995, 16 mm, b&w and colour, 11 minutes, From Sand To Celluloid, Producer Foss, John. Featuring David Ngoombujarra. Produced with assistance from the Indigenous Branch of the Australian Film Commission in association with the Australian State Film Agencies and SBS Independent. Distributed by Golden Seahorse Productions, NFSA Film Australia Collection.

Frederick, William, 'Shadows of an unseen hand. Some patterns of violence in the Indoneian revolution, 1945–1949', in Colombijn, Freek & J Thomas Lindblad (eds), *Roots of violence in Indonesia*, Institute of South East Asian Studies, Singapore, 2002, pp. 143–172.

Freire, Paulo, *Pedagogy of the Oppressed*, Penguin, London, 1972.

Freire, Paulo, *Pedagogy of Hope*, Bloomsbury, London, 1992.

French, Lisa & Mark Poole, *Shining a Light: 50 years of the Australian Film Institute*, The Moving Image, Australian Teachers of Media (ATOM), St Kilda, 2009.

Fuentes-Nieva, Ricardo & Nick Galasso, Working for the Few: Political capture and economic inequality, 178 Oxfam briefing paper – summary, Oxfam International, London, 2014, <http://www.oxfam.org/sites/www.oxfam.org/files/bp-working-for-few-political-capture-economic-inequality-200114-summ-en.pdf>, accessed 16 October 2014.

Fuller, Trevor, 'Bruce Pollard and Pinacotheca: psychological content', *Artlink*, vol. 26, no. 4, 2006.

Gerbaz, Alex, 'The legacy of the Experimental Film and Television Fund, 1970–78', National Archives of Australia, Canberra, 2009.

Gibson, Ross, *Camera Natura*, 1985, 16 mm, colour, 32 minutes, Australia, Producer Cruthers, John, Camera Ray Argall, Music Gary Warner, Editor Ian Allen. Produced with assistance from the CDB/AFC. Distributed by Ronin Films.

Gibson, Ross, *Dead to the World*, 1991, 35 mm, colour, Huzzah Productions, Australia,

Producer John Cruthers, Scriptwriter Ross Gibson, Cast, Lynette Curran, John Dole, Tibor Gyapjas, Agnieszka Perepeczko & Richard Roxborough. Produced with assistance from the AFC.

Gibson, Ross, 'Life as a Project of Montage', *Filmnews*, November 1992, pp. 17, 18.

Gibson, Sarah, *Born to Shop*, 1991, colour, 50 minutes, Sydney. Produced with assistance from the AFC-ABC. Distributed by Ronin Films.

Gibson, Sarah, *In The Beginning There was Shopping*, 1991, 16 mm, colour, 59 minutes, Sydney. Produced with assistance from the AFC-ABC Documentary Fellowship.

Gibson, Sarah, 'The Process of Innovation', in National Centre for Australian Studies (ed.), *The Big Picture: Documentary Filmmaking in Australia. Papers from the 2nd Australian Documentary Conference*, NCAS Monash University, Clayton, 1991, pp. 74–83.

Gibson, Sarah & Susan Lambert, *Landslides*, 1986, 16 mm, colour, 75 minutes, Red Heart Pictures, Sydney, Camera Michael Ewers, Jack Lambert, Sound Cameron Allan, Denise Haslem, Editor Ray Thomas. Produced with assistance from the AFC-ABC Documentary Fellowship.

Godard, Jean-Luc, *Masculin féminin/Masculine Feminine*, 1966, 35 mm, b&w, 103 minutes, Paris.

Godard, Jean-Luc & Jean-Pierre Gorin, *British Sounds/See You at Mao*, 1969, 16 mm, colour, 51 minutes, Kestrel Productions/London Weekend Television.

Godard, Jean-Luc & Jean-Pierre Gorin, *Tous va bien*, 1972, 35 mm, colour, 51 minutes.

Goddard, Martyn, 'Westgate Bridge collapse', *ABC News*, Camera John Hughes, 15 October 1970, Melbourne, <http://www.youtube.com/watch?v=UR8eYevYcg8>, accessed 10 January 2013.

Golvan, Colin, 'The trouble with Australian films', *Farrago*, 9 July 1976, p. 21.

Grace, Helen, *Serious Undertakings*, 1982, 16 mm, colour and b&w, 28 minutes, Sydney, Producer Addis, Erica, Camera Erica Addis, Sound John Cruthers. Produced with assistance from the Women's Film Fund. Distributed by Ronin Films, <http://www.roninfilms.com.au>.

Grace, Helen & James Kesteven, 'The Public Wants Features!': Creative Underdevelopment of Australian Independent Film Since the 1960s', in Creed, Barbara, John Davies, Freda Freiberg, David Hanan & Kim Montgomery (eds), *Papers and Forums on Independent Film and Asian Cinema*, Australian Screen Studies Association (Victoria), Australian Film and Television School, La Trobe University, Melbourne, 1982, pp. 16–36.

Gray, Peter & Garry Lane, *The Battle For Bowen Hills*, 1973–82, 16 mm, b&w, 22 minutes, Crowsfoot Films, Producer Gray, Peter.

Gray, Peter & Garry Lane, *Know Your Friends, Know Your Enemies*, 1977–82, 16 mm, colour, 20 minutes, Crowsfoot Films, Producers Gray, Peter & Garry Lane.

Green, C, *2006 Contemporary Commonwealth*, NGV, Melbourne, 2006.

Greenaway, Peter, *A Zed & Two Noughts*, 1986, 35 mm, colour, 115 minutes, UK, Producers Kasander, Kees & Peter Sainsbury, Camera Sacha Vierny, Editor John Wilson. Distributed by Artificial Eye, BFI, Umbrella.

Gustafson, Kristian C, 'CIA Machinations in Chile in 1970: Reexamining the Record', *Studies in Intelligence, Journal of the American Intelligence Profession*, vol. 47, no. 3, 14 April 2007,

Center for the Study of Intelligence, The Central Intelligence Agency (CIA), Washington DC, <https://www.cia.gov/library/center–for–the–study–of–intelligence/csi–publications/csi–studies/studies/vol47no3/article03.html>, accessed 19 June 2013.

Guattari, Félix, *Molecular revolution: psychiatry and politics*, Rosemary Sheed (trans.), Harmondsworth, Penguin, 1984.

Hall, Barbara, 'In Every Street, In Every Head', interview with John Hughes, *Film-maker*, 1977.

Hall, Barbara, Fred Harden & Pat Longmore, 'An Oral History of the Melbourne Filmmakers Co-operative', in Creed, Barbara, John Davies, Freda Freiberg, David Hanan & Kim Montgomery (eds), Papers and Forums on Independent Film and Asian Cinema, La Trobe University, Melbourne, ASSA, AFTRS, 1982, pp. 141–155.

Hanan, David, letter to John Hughes, Monash University, Clayton, 9 March 1982.

Harden, Fred & Corinne Cantrill, 'The Alternative Cinema and the Film Co-ops ... Are the two compatible?' *Cantrills Filmnotes*, no. 12, December 1972, pp. 18–21.

Harvey, Sylvia, 'The Other Cinema – a History, 1970–77', *Screen*, vol. 26, no. 6, November–December 1985, pp. 40–57.

Haynes, Todd, *Superstar: The Karen Carpenter Story*, 1988, 35 mm, colour, 43 minutes, Producers Haynes, Todd & Cynthia Schneider, Scriptwriters Haynes, Todd & Cynthia Schneider, Camera Barry Ellsworth, Editor Todd Haynes. Featuring Merrill Gruver, Michael Edwards, Melissa Brown, Rob LaBelle.

Haynes, Todd, *Poison*, 1991, 35 mm, 85 minutes, Killer Films, Producers Vachon, Christine & James Schamus, Scriptwriter Haynes, Todd. Distributed by Zeitgeist Films.

Hemingway, Al, 'Into the Teeth of the Tiger', *VFW Magazine*, vol. 85, no. 4, 2012, Veterans of Foreign Wars, USA, November/December, <http://digitaledition.qwinc.com/display_article.php?id=1199157>, accessed 19 September 2013.

Hoaas, Solrun At Edge, 1981, 16 mm, colour, 21 minutes, Distributed by Ronin Films, <http://www.roninfilms.com.au>

Hocking, Jenny, *Lionel Murphy: A Political Biography*, Cambridge University Press, Oakleigh, Melbourne, 1997.

Hodsdon, Barrett, *Straight Roads and Crossed Lines: The Quest for Film Culture in Australia from the 1960s?*, Bernt Porridge Group, Shelton Park, 2001.

Hodsdon, Bruce, 'The Carlton Ripple and the Australian Film Revival', *Screening the Past*, no. 23, 26 April 2009, La Trobe University, Melbourne, <http://tlweb.latrobe.edu.au/humanities/screeningthepast/23/carlton-australian-revival.html>, accessed 22 December 2013.

Holding, The Hon. Clyde, MP Minister for Aboriginal Affairs, Aboriginal land rights – National Legislation, First Hawke Ministry, Social Policy Committee, Cabinet Submission 619 – Decisions 2893/SP and 2913, A13977, National Archives of Australia, 19 December 1983 – 7 March 1984, <http://recordsearch.naa.gov.au/SearchNRetrieve/Interface/DetailsReports/ItemDetail.aspx?Barcode=31424610>, accessed 22 December 2013.

Holmes, Jonathan, 'Istoria', Centre for the Arts, University of Tasmania, Hobart, 1986.

Holmes, Oliver, *On Sacred Ground*, 1980, 16 mm, colour, 58 minutes, Film Australia, Scriptwriter Robin Hughes, Camera John Hosking, Editor Louise Anivitti.

Holt, Rt Hon. Harold, *Cultural Activities*, The House of Representatives, Australia, press release,

Canberra, 1967.

Hughes, John, 'Community Use of Video', *Learning Exchange*, March 1973, pp. 14–15.

Hughes, John, 'General Background of the Formation of the Video Exchange', Malcolm Cormack, Rod Harris, John Hughes, Gary Lewis, Stuart Longmuir, Danny O'Sullivan & Alexandra Shive, *Submission to the Film and Television Board of the Australia Council for the Arts for the establishment of a Community Video Exchange – Appendix 1*, Video Exchange, Melbourne, 1973, pp. 7–9.

Hughes, John, 'A Selection of Past and Future Projects', Malcolm Cormack, Rod Harris, John Hughes, Gary Lewis, Stuart Longmuir, Danny O'Sullivan & Alexandra Shive, *Submission to the Film and Television Board of the Australia Council for the Arts for the establishment of a Community Video Exchange – Appendix 2*, Video Exchange, Melbourne, 1973, pp. 9–11.

Hughes, John, *Some Aspects of Australian Racism*, 1973 (unreleased), 16 mm, b&w, 12 minutes, Melbourne, Producer John Hughes, Scriptwriter Hughes, John. Featuring Dan Atkinson, Geraldine Briggs, David Anderson, Bert Peters, Lorna Lippman, Walter McVitty. Produced with assistance from the Interim Council for the Australian Film and Television School.

Hughes, John, *Abortion a woman's decision*, 1974, video & 16 mm, b&w, 30 minutes, Melbourne, Scriptwriter Hughes, John, Camera John Hughes, Editor John Hughes.

Hughes, John, *Cybernetic Synergy: A Film about the Kinetic Work of John Hansen*, 1974, 16 mm, colour, 19 minutes, Melbourne, Producer John Hughes, Scriptwriter Hughes, John, Camera John Hughes, Editor John Hughes. Produced with assistance from the Experimental Film and Television Fund, Film and Television Board, Australia Council for the Arts. Distributed by Artfilms, <http://www.artfilms.com>.

Hughes, John, 'What to do with a Greek bearing gifts', *Learning Exchange*, December 1974, pp. 4–7.

Hughes, John, *Menace*, 1976, 16 mm, 96 minutes, Melbourne, Producer John Hughes, Scriptwriter Hughes, John, Camera Rod Bishop, Margot Nash, Gordon Glenn, Sound Lloyd Carrick, Editor Peter Tammer. Featuring Dorothy Gibson, Lloyd Edmunds, Pat Counihan, Ralph Gibson, George Lees, Noel Counihan, George Seelaf (OA), Bon Laurie, Ted Laurie (QC), Stella Lees, Robyn Laurie, Mick Counihan. Produced with assistance from the Film, Radio & TV Board of the Australia Council/AFC. Distributed by Artfilms, <http://www.artfilms.com.au>.

Hughes, John, *Menace*, program notes, 1977.

Hughes, John, 'Jimmie Blacksmith … a star is shorn', *Nation Review*, 1–7 September 1978, p. 21.

Hughes, John, 'Albie's blind eye to the why', *Nation Review*, 3–9 November 1978, p. 22.

Hughes, John, discussion paper sent to selected independent filmmakers, Melbourne & Sydney, 1978.

Hughes, John, letter to Mr Schefferle (State Film Centre), MSC Media Arts, Melbourne, 11 October 1979.

Hughes, John, *Crowsfoot*, letter to Gray, Peter & Garry Lane, MSC Media Arts, Carlton North, 22 November 1979.

Hughes, John, *Trade Unions, Film and Television*, ACTU Arts Committee, discussion paper, Melbourne, 1979.

Hughes, John, *Film-Work* script, personal archives of John Hughes, Melbourne, 1980.

Hughes, John, *Film-Work*, flyer, 1981.

Hughes, John, *Film-Work*, 1981, 16 mm, colour, 46 minutes, WWFFU, Australia, Producer John Hughes, Scriptwriter Hughes, John, Executive Producers Disher, Norma, Keith Gow & Jock Levy, Camera Margot Nash, Glenys Page, Sound John Whitteron, Editors John Whitteron, Chris Warner, Viv Carroll. Featuring Norma Disher, Keith Gow, Jock Levy. Produced with assistance from the AFC. *Film-Work/Menace* distributed by Artfilms, <http://www.artfilms.com.au>.

Hughes, John, *November Eleven: An Australian History – Work In Progress – Part 2*, 1981, 1" video, colour, 19 minutes, Melbourne, Producer John Hughes, Scriptwriter Hughes, John, featuring Carolyn Howard & Paul Davies.

Hughes, John, *Contemporary Cinema*, course outline, Melbourne State College, 4 June 1982.

Hughes, John, *Gunana: Homeland of the Mornington Island Woomera Dancers*, 1982, U-matic colour, 29 minutes, Media Production Centre Melbourne College of Education, Producer Philip Johnson, Executive Producers Brian Sheedy, Brian Walsh, Camera John Hughes, Sound Dennis Claringbold, Music Jimmy Cliff, No Fixed Address, Editors John Hughes, Lisa Dethridge, Sasha Trikojus. Featuring Woomera Dancers, Kenny Jacobs. Made in collaboration with the people of Mornington Island.

Hughes, John, 'Propaganda then and now', in Lansell, Ross & Peter Beilby (eds), *The Documentary Film in Australia, Cinema Papers* in association with Film Victoria, North Melbourne, 1982, pp. 142–145.

Hughes, John, *Traps*, AFC, Development finance application, 1983.

Hughes, John, *Is it Working? George Seelaf for the Record*, 1984, 16 mm, colour, 48 minutes, Melbourne, Producer John Hughes, Scriptwriter Hughes, John, Camera Tony Wright, Andrew Taylor, Jaems Grant, Sound Cath Dyson, Georgina Guilfoyle, Editor Zbigniew Friedrich. Featuring Noel Counihan, Wally Curran, Frank Hardy, Deb Mills, Andrew Reeves & George Seelaf. Produced with assistance from the Community Arts Board and the Archival Film Project of the Australia Council.

Hughes, John, *Acceptable Risk*, 1985, video, colour, Video Projects, Melbourne. Produced with assistance from the Australian Postal and Telecommunications Union.

Hughes, John, *Changing Schools*, 1985, 1" video, 18 minutes, Education Image, Melbourne, Producer Robins, Penny, Executive Producer Day, Greg & Ron Theile. Produced with assistance from the Victorian Council of School Organisations, Victoria's 150th Education Committee and the Teachers Federation of Victoria.

Hughes, John, *How Does it Strike You?* 1985, 1" video, colour, 23 minutes, Video Projects, Melbourne, Producer Robins, Penny. Produced with assistance from the Trade Union Information and Resource Centre of the Victorian THC, the Bureau of Youth Affairs, Department of Employment and Industrial Affairs and PEP.

Hughes, John, *Traps*, 1985, 16 mm, colour, 96 minutes, Melbourne/Sydney, Producer John Hughes, scriptwriter Paul Davies & John Hughes, Camera Katrina Bowels, Erika Addis &

Jaems Grant, Sound Laurie Robinson, Jack Holt, John Cruthers, Lou Hubbard & Pat Fiske, Editor Zbigniew Friedrich. Featuring Carolyn Howard, Gwenda Wiseman, Paul Davies, John Flaus, Lesley Stern, Drew Cottle & Peter Summerfield with David Combe, Tony Walker (2JJJ), Michael Gill (*The Age*), Anthony McAdam (*Quadrant*), Denis Freney (*Tribune*), Greg Hywood (*Financial Review*), PP McGuinness (*Financial Review*), Humphrey McQueen, Paul Lyneham (Channel 7), Mark Aarons (ABC), Steven Sewell. Produced with assistance from the CDF of the AFC. Distributed by Artfilms, <http://www.artfilms.com.au>.

Hughes, John, 'AFC Regresses', *IFAC Newsletter*, January–April 1986.

Hughes, John, 'Screened from Access: The Public and Television', *Arena*, no. 80, 1987, pp. 68–74.

Hughes, John, *All That is Solid*, 1988, 16 mm/Hi-8 video, colour, 54 minutes, Melbourne, Producer John Hughes, Scriptwriters Chris Barnett, Paul M Davies, John Hughes, Camera Jaems Grant, Sound Lloyd Carrick, Editors Jill Holt, Zbigniew Friedrich. Featuring Margaret Cameron, Paul Davis, Mitchell Faircloth, Eva Hall, Carolyn Howard, Nico Latouris, Yani Lathouris, Mark Rogers, Louise Smith with Bill Cope, Boris Frankel, Freda Glynn, Reginald Klimionok, Andrew Mack, Craig McGregor, Roberta Perkins, Jo Valentine, Katherine West, Ted Wheelwright. Produced with assistance from the AFC-ABC Fellowship, Australian Bicentennial Authority. Distributed by Artfilms, <http://www.artfilms.com.au>.

Hughes, John, 'Keith Gow', *Cinema Papers*, January 1988, p. 4.

Hughes, John, *Moments Like These*, 1989, colour, 27 minutes, Open Channel, TAIMA, Melbourne, Producer John Hughes, Scriptwriter Tony Wright, Camera Jaems Grant. Featuring Bob Maza. Produced with assistance from the Department of Employment, Education & Training.

Hughes, John, *One Way Street*, synopsis, 1992.

Hughes, John, *One Way Street: Fragments for Walter Benjamin*, 1992, 16 mm, colour, 58 minutes, Melbourne, Producer John Hughes, Scriptwriters Paul Davies & John Hughes, Camera Nicolette Freeman, Erika Addis, Editor Uri Mizrahi. Featuring Nico Lathouris, Maggie Cameron, Mark Rogers, Louise Smith. Produced with assistance from the AFC & ABC. Distributed by Artfilms, <http://www.artfilms.com.au>.

Hughes, John, *Opening Lines: What to do with a Greek bearing gifts*, letter to Kaye Griffin (Open Channel), personal archives of John Hughes, East Brunswick, 10 November 1993.

Hughes, John, *What I Have Written*, 1995, 35 mm, colour, 98 minutes, Early Works, Melbourne, Producers John Hughes & Peter Sainsbury, Scriptwriter John Scott, Camera Dion Beebe. Featuring Martin Jacobs, Gillian Jones, Jacek Koman, Angie Milliken. Produced with assistance from the AFC & ABC. Distributed by Beyond International, Globe & Artfilms, <http://www.artfilms.com.au>.

Hughes, John, 'Book Review: Modernism Relocated: towards a cultural studies of visual modernity', *Metro*, no. 104, 1995, pp. 79–81.

Hughes, John, *After Mabo*, letter to David Tiley (AFC), Melbourne, 16 December 1996.

Hughes, John, *After Mabo*, letter to John Foss, Otis Sherwell & Julia Mongta, Melbourne, 7 October 1996.

Hughes, John, *After Mabo*, progress report letter to Richard Frankland, Jacqui Geia, John Foss,

Mirimbiak Nations Aboriginal Corporation & Debra Annear, Melbourne, 27 January 1997.

Hughes, John, *After Mabo*, letter to Frankland, Richard, Melbourne, 2 October 1997.

Hughes, John, *After Mabo*, progress report letter to Frankland, Richard, Jacqui Geia, John Foss, Mirimbiak Nations Aboriginal Corporation & Debra Annear, Melbourne, 17 February 1997.

Hughes, John, *After Mabo*, 1997, SP Betacam, colour, 84 minutes, Early Works/Mirimbiak Nations Aboriginal Corporation, Melbourne, Producers Debra Annear & John Hughes, Scriptwriter John Hughes, Camera Peter Zakharov, Sound Mark Tarpey, Editor Uri Mizrahi. Featuring Richard Frankland. Produced with assistance from the AFC, SBSI, ATSIC. Distributed by Ronin Films, <http://www.roninfilms.com.au> and Artfilms, <http://www.artfilms.com.au>.

Hughes, John, Take Five, 1998, 13 x 5 minute series, *ABC TV Arts*, Australia, Producer John Lewis, Scriptwriter Betty Churcher, featuring Betty Churcher.

Hughes, John, *River of Dreams*, 1998, SP Betacam, colour, 52 minutes, Early Works, Australia, Producers Donna Cameron & John Hughes, Scriptwriters Donna Cameron & John Hughes. Produced with assistance from the SBS Independent. Distributed by Ronin Films, <http://www.roninfilms.com.au> and Artfilms, <http://www.artfilms.com.au>.

Hughes, John, *Film-Work*, interview conducted by John Cumming, Melbourne, 12 September 2000.

Hughes, John, *Nowhere Game*, interview conducted by John Cumming, Melbourne, 1 August 2000.

Hughes, John, *Traps*, interview conducted by John Cumming, Melbourne, 29 November 2000.

Hughes, John, *The Melbourne Filmmakers Co-op*, interview conducted by John Cumming, Melbourne, 20 September 2001.

Hughes, John, *All That is Solid*, interview conducted by John Cumming, Melbourne, 17 January 2002.

Hughes, John, *The early 1970s*, email to John Cumming, Melbourne, 30 May 2002.

Hughes, John, *MFC, Access Video and EMA*, interview conducted by John Cumming, Melbourne, 16 January 2002.

Hughes, John, *Notes on transcript*, email to John Cumming, Melbourne, 24 June 2002.

Hughes, John, *One Way Street*, interview conducted by John Cumming, Melbourne, 15 March 2002.

Hughes, John, *What I Have Written and After Mabo*, interview conducted by John Cumming, Melbourne, 3 July 2002.

Hughes, John, *The Archive Project, synopsis and production proposal*, funding application, Melbourne, 2003.

Hughes, John, *Notes on Treatment*, The Archive Project Proposal, 2003.

Hughes, John, *SBSI and after*, interview conducted by John Cumming, Melbourne, 9 February 2004.

Hughes, John, *The Art of War*, 2005, colour, 4 x 26 minutes, Early Works and SBS Independent, Australia, Producers Betty Churcher, John Hughes, Scriptwriters Betty Churcher, John Hughes.

Hughes, John, *Hidden Treasures*, 2006, 10 x 5 minutes, Film Australia National Interest

Program, Early Works, ABC TV Arts, Producers John Hughes & Philippa Campey, Scriptwriter Betty Churcher, Executive Producer Anna Grieve, Camera Joel Peterson, Sound Mark Tarpey, Steve Best, Music Paul Grabowsky, Editor Uri Mizrahi, featuring Betty Churcher.

Hughes, John, 'Moving History' *A place to think*, online multimedia, Film Australia, ABC, Executive Producers Anna Grieve & Ian Allen, 2007, <http://www.abc.net.au/aplacetothink/?–watch>, accessed 2 February 2013.

Hughes, John, 'Indonesia Calling: Joris Ivens in Australia', *Early Works*, press kit, 9 July 2009, Melbourne, <http://earlyworks.com.au/the–stacks/post/press–kit–indonesia–calling–joris–ivens–in–australia/>, accessed 24 February 2013.

Hughes, John, *Indonesia Calling: Joris Ivens in Australia*, 2009, Digital Betacam, colour and b&w, 90 minutes, Early Works, Australia, Producers John Hughes & Andrea Foxworthy, Scriptwriter John Hughes, Editor Uri Mizrahi. Featuring Graeme Cutts, Andre Stufkens, Susan Geldho, Joesoef Isak, Charlotte Maramis, John Daniell, Maggie Keane, Jan Lingard, Professor Joe Isaac, Arthur Gar Lock Chang & Rabin Hardjadibrata. Produced with assistance from the Australian Broadcasting Corporation, the Melbourne International Film Festival (MIFF) Premiere Fund, Film Victoria & Screen Australia. Distributed by Artfilms, <http://www.artfilms.com.au>.

Hughes, John, 'Indonesia Calling: Joris Ivens in Australia', *Senses of Cinema*, no. 51, 2009.

Hughes, John, *Notes on draft*, email to John Cumming, Melbourne, 23 February 2010.

Hughes, John, *Notes on the Archive project*, email to John Cumming, Melbourne, 30 June 2010.

Hughes, John, *John Hughes*, Melbourne Independent Filmmakers, Bill Mousoulis (ed.) Innersense, Australia, 2010, <http://www.innersense.com.au/mif/hughes.html>, accessed 23 August 2013.

Hughes, John, 'Back Story Update with John Hughes', recording by John Cumming of interview conducted by Kerley, Amanda & William Head, *Generation Next Documentary Conference*, Open Channel & Cinema Nova, Carlton, Australia, 13 October 2011.

Hughes, John, 'After Indonesia Calling', thesis (PhD) exegesis, School of Media and Communication, College of Design and Social Context, RMIT University, Melbourne, November 2012.

Hughes, John, *The Archive Project (book): The Realist Film Unit in Cold War Australia*, Early Works & ATOM, Melbourne, 2013.

Hughes, John, Dion Beebe, Ian Sheath & Dominic Case, 'The Film of the Book', *Cinema Papers*, February 1996, pp. 27–28.

Hughes, John & Open Channel, *Artists' subsidy of the arts*, letter to Cumming, Murray Brown (Cultural Activities Officer AFC) cc'd to John, IFAC, Melbourne, 3 June 1985.

Hughes, John & Martin Friedel, *One Way Street*, music cues, 1992.

Hughes, John & Martyn Goddard, *Nowhere Game*, 1972, 16 mm, b&w, 23 minutes, Magic Dragon Productions, Melbourne, Scriptwriters John Hughes & Martyn Goddard, Camera John Hughes. *Short Films by John Hughes*, distributed by Artfilms, <http://www.artfilms.com.au>.

Hughes, John, Peter Kennedy, Sylvia Lawson, David Malouf & Nancy Underhill, *The Stars Disordered*, Nancy Underhill (ed.), Brisbane, University Art Museum, University of Queensland, 1988.

Hughes, John & Uri Mizrahi, *The Archive Project*, 2006, colour and b&w, 98 minutes, Early Works, Melbourne, Producers Philippa Campey & John Hughes, scriptwriter John Hughes, Editor Uri Mizrahi. Produced with assistance from the NFSA, AFC, Film Victoria, ABC TV Arts and Music and Effects. Distributed by Artfilms, <http://www.artfilms.com.au>.

Hughes, John & Michael Renov, 'Conversation with Michael Renov', Visible Evidence IX Conference, Tivoli Theatre, Fortitude Valley Brisbane, author's notes, 2001.

Hughes, John & Penny Robins, 'More than meets the eye', *Films Used in Changing Schools*, Video Projects, Melbourne, 1985.

Hughes, John & Ben Trudeau, *School: What are the alternatives?*, 25 x 35mm slides and audio cassette, Education Media Australia, Melbourne, 1973.

Hughes, John & Tom Zubryki, *A Filmmakers' Cinema: 20 years of the Filmmakers' cooperatives*, Treatment, Melbourne and Sydney, 2011.

Hughes, John & Tom Zubryki, *A Filmmakers' Cinema: 20 years of the Filmmakers' cooperatives*, Development Proposal, Melbourne and Sydney, 2011.

Hughes, May, Ralton R James & David N Martin, 'Olympic Follies', Tivoli Theatre, Melbourne, 1956. Cinema and Theatre Historical Society, <http://www.caths.org.au/archives/archives.htm>, accessed 11 June 2013.

Hughes, Peter, 'A way of being engaged with the world: the films of John Hughes', *Metro*, no. 93, Autumn 1993, pp. 46–55.

Hughes, Peter, 'The Documentary Project and Postmodernity', thesis (PhD), School of Arts and Media, La Trobe University, Bundoora, 1997.

Hughes, Peter, 'After Mabo', in Keith Beattie and Geoff Mayer (ed.), *The Cinema of Australia and New Zealand*, 24 Frames, Wallflower Press, London, 2007, pp. 177–184.

Hutton, Anne, *Papers of the First Australian Film and History Conference*, Australian Film and Television School, North Ryde, Canberra, 1981.

Ivens, Joris, *The Bridge (De Brug)* 1928, 35 mm, b&w, 14 minutes, Rotterdam, Camera Joris Ivens, Editor Joris Ivens.

Ivens, Joris, *Rain (Regen)*, 1929, 35 mm, b&w, 15 minutes, Netherlands, Producer Joris Ivens, Camera Joris Ivens, Sound version prepared 1932 by Helen van Dongen, Editor Joris Ivens.

Ivens, Joris, *Spanish Earth*, 1937, 35 mm, b&w, 52 minutes, Contemporary Historians, Inc. , New York, Scriptwriters Ivens, Joris & Ernest Hemingway, Camera John Ferno, Sound Irving Reis, Editor Helen Van Dongen.

Ivens, Joris, *The Power and the Land*, 1940, 35 mm, b&w, 33 minutes, US Film Service, commissioned by REA (Rural Electrification Administration), US Ministry of Agriculture, USA, Scriptwriters Edwin Lock, Joris Ivens & Stephen Vincent Benét, Executive Producer William P Adams, Camera Floyd Crosby, Arthur Ornitz, Editor Helen van Dongen.

Ivens, Joris, *Indonesia Calling*, 1946, 35 mm, b&w, 22 minutes, Australasia production, Sydney, Producer The Waterfront Unions of Australia, Scriptwriter Katherine Duncan, Executive Producer Peter Finch, Camera Marion Michelle.

accessed 23 December 2013.

McPhee, Hilary, 'Introduction', in McPhee, Hilary & Ann Standish (eds), *Memoirs of a Young Bastard: The Diaries of Tim Burstall. November 1953 to December 1954*, Melbourne University Press, 2012.

McQueen, Humphrey, 'Walter Benjamin: a life in scraps, quotes & fragments', *ABC Radio 24 Hours*, 1992.

MCTC, *About MCTC, Melbourne Community Television Consortium*, Melbourne, 2010, <http://www.mctcltd.org.au/aboutus.html>, accessed 19 June 2013.

Mekas, Jonas, *Film-maker's Cooperative: a brief history*, The Film-makers' Coop, The New American Cinema Group, 2000, <http://film–makerscoop.com/about/history>, accessed 19 June 2013.

Melbourne Cinematheque, 'Independent Voice: Australian political documentary from the 1940s to the 1980s', Melbourne Cinematheque program notes, 13 July 2005.

Melbourne Cinematheque, *April 20: Australia's John Hughes*, screenings, 2011.

MFC, *Beginnings*, screening flyer, Pinacotheca, Richmond, Melbourne Film-Makers' Co-op, 1970.

MFC, *Formation of a filmmakers co-op*, notice, Melbourne Filmmakers Co-op, Babylon, Melbourne, 3 June 1971.

MFC, *Notice of General Meeting*, Melbourne Film-Makers Co-op, Babylon, Melbourne, 5 July 1971.

MFC, *Alternate Cinema: Australia and USA*, flyer for screening, Melbourne Filmmakers Co-op, circa 1972.

MFC, *Minutes of General Meeting*, Melbourne Filmmakers Co-op, Babylon 161 Spring Street, Melbourne, 1973.

MFC, *Newsletter*, Melbourne Filmmakers Co-op, 1973.

MFC, *Last Ditch Resistance Screening: Menace*, flyer, Hughes, John, Melbourne Filmmakers Co-op, 1977.

MIF, *James Clayden Biography*, Melbourne Independent Filmmakers, Mousoulis, Bill (ed.) Innersense, Melbourne, 2005, <http://www.innersense.com.au/mif/clayden.html>, accessed 9 January 2013.

MIF, *Peter Tammer*, Melbourne Independent Filmmakers, Mousoulis, Bill (ed.) Innersense, Melbourne, May 2008, <http://www.innersense.com.au/mif/tammer.html>, accessed 19 June 2013.

Miller, James, *Koori: A Will to Win*, 1 vol, 2nd edn, Angus & Robertson, North Ryde, 1985. Originally published 1985.

Milner, Lisa, *Fighting films: a history of the Waterside Workers' Federation Film Unit*, Pluto Press, North Melbourne, Vic., 2003.

MIMA, *MIMA Yearbook vol. 1*, 1986, VHS, colour, 56 minutes, Modern Image Makers Association, Melbourne.

Moffatt, Tracey, *beDevil*, 1993, 35 mm, colour, Sydney, Producer Moffatt, Tracey. Produced with assistance from the AFC.

Molony, John N, *The Penguin History of Australia: The story of 200 years*, 2nd edn, Penguin,

Löfvén, Chris, *Filmography*, Melbourne Independent Filmmakers, Mousoulis, Bill (ed.) Innersense, Melbourne, 2012, <http://www.innersense.com.au/mif/lofven.html>, accessed 10 January 2013.

MacCabe, Colin, 'Realism and the Cinema', *Screen*, vol. 15, no. 2, Summer 1974, pp. 7–27.

Maher, Rachel, John Hughes & Megan Spencer, 'Fearless traditions: Australian documentary culture at the crossroads', *Spinach7*, Winter/Spring 2003, pp. 54–55.

Mangiamele, Giorgio, *The Giorgio Mangiamele Collection: Five Provocative Works by an Italian Filmmaker in Post-War Australia*, 2011, DVD, Australia. Distributed by Ronin Films, <http://www.roninfilms.com.au> and NFSA, <http://shop.nfsa.gov.au>.

Mangiamele, Giorgio, *Clay*, 1965, b&w, 85 minutes, Australia, Producer Mangiamele, Giorgio, Camera Giorgio Mangiamele, Sound Bruce McNaughton.

Mangiamele, Giorgio, *Beyond Reason*, 1970, 35 mm, b&w, 78 minutes, Australia, Producer Mangiamele, Giorgio, Camera Giorgio Mangiamele, Sound Chris Tsalikis, Music Enzo Marciano, Editor Russell Hurley, featuring George Dixon, Louise Hall, Maggie Copeland.

Marker, Chris, *La Jetee*, 1962, 35 mm, b&w, 28 minutes, France.

Martin, Adrian, 'All That is Solid', *Filmnews*, August 1988, p. 8.

Martin, Adrian, 'Indefinite Objects: Independent Film and Video', in Moran, Albert (ed.), *The Australian Screen*, Penguin, 1989, pp. 172–190.

Martin, Adrian, 'Collage and Montage in Contemporary Australian Experimental Film and Video, and its Origins', in McIntyre, Arthur (ed.), *Contemporary Australian Collage*, Craftsman House, Roseville, 1990, pp. 49–61.

Martin, Adrian, 'Poetic Politics: A Response to John Hughes' One Way Street', *Photofile*, vol. 43, November 1994, pp. 24–26.

Martin, Adrian, '*The Confessional*, *What I Have Written* and the "Art Film"', *The Week in Film*, ABC Radio National, 13 July 1996.

Marx, Karl & Friedrich Engels, 'The Communist Manifesto', in Tucker, Robert C (ed.), *The Marx-Engels Reader*, Moore, Samuel (trans.), 2nd edn, Norton, London, 1978, pp. 331–362.

Mason, Richard & Jack Lee, *From the Tropics to the Snow*, 1962, colour, 28 minutes, Commonwealth Film Unit, Producer Allan, Jack S, Scriptwriters Morris, John, Cedric Flower & Pat Flower.

Mathews, Bob, *They Chose Peace: Youth Carnival for Peace and Friendship*, 1952, 16 mm, b&w, 28 minutes, Sydney, Realist Films, Camera Bob Mathews, Keith Gow & David Muir, in John Hughes & Uri Mizrahi, The Archive Project, 2006, DVD box set, Distributed by Artfilms, <http://www.artfilms.com.au>.

McKenzie, Brian, *The Last Day's Work*, 1987, 16 mm, colour, Melbourne, Producer Cruthers, John, Scriptwriter McKenzie, Brian.

McLachlan, Donna & David Bates, 'Interview with Arthur and Corinne Cantrill', *Verbatim*, 11 May 5 pm, 2002, ABC Radio National, Australia.

McMurchy, Megan, 'The Documentary', in Murray, Scott (ed.), *Australian Cinema*, Allen & Unwin, Sydney, 1994, pp. 179–198.

McNiven, Liz, 'A Short History of Indigenous Filmmaking', *Australian Screen*, National Film and Sound Archive of Australia, <http://aso.gov.au/titles/collections/indigenous-filmmaking/>,

Kirby, Hon. Michael, AC CMG, 'Whitlam as Internationalist', *Whitlam Lecture*, 2010, University of Western Sydney, 25 February, <http://www.michaelkirby.com.au/images/stories/speeches/2000s/2010_Speeches/2432.Speech–WhitlamLecture–25February2010.pdf>, accessed 19 September 2013.

Kluge, Alexander, *The Patriot/Die Patriotin (The Female Patriot)*, 1979, 35 mm, b&w and colour, 121 minutes, Kairos-Film, Germany, Producers Kluge, Alexander & Willi Segler (ZDF), Scriptwriters Buschmann, Christel, Alexander Kluge & Willi Segler, Editor Beate Mainka-Jellinghaus.

Kracauer, Siegfried, *Theory of film: the redemption of physical reality*, Oxford University Press, 1960.

Kurlantzick, Joshua, *The Ideal Man: The Tragedy of Jim Thompson and the American Way of War*, Wiley, Hoboken, New Jersey, 2011.

Lack, John, 'Seelaf, George (1914–1988)', *Australian Dictionary of Biography*, National Centre of Biography, Australian National University, http://adb.anu.edu.au/biography/seelaf-george-14878/text26068, accessed 28 November 2013.

Lampugnani, Raffaele, *Giorgio Mangiamele: Cinematographer of the Italian Migrant Experience*, Connor Court Publishing, Ballan, Victoria, 2012.

Lander, Ned, *Wrong Side of the Road*, 1981, 79 minutes, Producers Ned Lander & Graeme Isaac, Scriptwriters Ned Lander & Graeme Isaac, Camera Louis Irving, Music No Fixed Address & Us Mob, Editor John Scott. Featuring Ronnie Ansell, Veronica Rankine, Peter Butler, Les Graham, Chris Haywood & Bart Willoughby. Distributed by National Film and Sound Archive.

Laughren, Patrick Gerard, 'Debating Australian Documentary Production Policy: Some Practitioner Perspectives', *Media International Australia*, no. 129, 2008, pp. 116–128.

Laurie, Robin, 'Some Recollections of Life in the APG', *The Pram Factory: Australian Theatre History. The Australian Performing Group at the Pram Factory*, 2005, Suzanne Ingleton, <http://www.pramfactory.com/memoirsfolder/Laurie–Robin.html>, accessed 6 February 2013.

Lawson, Sylvia, 'Such a bloody wonderful place', *Inside Story*, Swinburne Institute for Social Research, Hawthorn, 28 April 2013, http://insidestory.org.au/such-a-bloody-wonderful-place, accessed 16 October 2014.

Leahy, Gillian, 'Collective amnesia: A brief, sporadic history of the first twenty-five years of independent filmmaking in Australia', in Cook, Jefferey (ed.), *Community and Independent Television*, Metro Television Ltd, Sydney, 1993, pp. 52–61.

Lee, Michael, *Critical Overview*, Melbourne Independent Filmmakers, Mousoulis, Bill (ed.) Innersense, Melbourne, 2003, <http://www.innersense.com.au/mif/lee.html>, accessed 9 January 2013.

Léger, Fernand & Dudley Murphy, *Ballet Mécanique*, 1924, b&w, 14 minutes, Paris, Producer Charlot, André, Scriptwriter Léger, Fernand, Camera Dudley Murphy & Man Ray, Music George Antheil, Editor Dudley Murphy, featuring Kiki.

Linnett, Ken, 'Taming of the Left in Australia', film review, *The Melbourne Times*, 5 March 1986, p. 10.

Ivens, Joris, *Joris Ivens and China*, New World Press, Beijing, 1983.

Ivens, Joris, William Klein, Claude Lelouch, Jean Luc Godard, Chris Marker, Alain Resnais & Agnès Varda, *Far from Vietnam (Loin du Vietnam)*, 1967, 35 mm, colour, 115 minutes, Paris, Producers Godard, Jean Luc & Chris Marker, Scriptwriter Marker, Chris, Executive Producers Anne Bellec, Karen Blanguernon, Bernard Fresson, Maurice Garrel, Valerie Mayoux, Marie-France Mignal, Camera Jean Boffety, Denys Clerval, Chislain Cloquet, Willy Kurvant, J Lacouture, Alain Levent, M Loridan, C Marker, F Maspero, R Pic, M Ray, J Sternberg, Kien Tham, Bernard Zitermann, Sound Antoine Bonfanti, Editor Jacques Meppiel. Featuring G Aperghis, M Chapdenat, M Fano. Distributed by Slon.

Jackson, Sue, *When History Meets the New Native Title Era at the Negotiating Table*, A case study in reconciling land use in Broome, Western Australia: A discussion paper, NARU, Australian National University, Darwin, NT, 1996.

Jennings, Sonia, 'Landing a Vote: The past importance of land ownership as an electoral qualification in Victoria', *Provenance: Journal of Public Record Office of Victoria*, no. 6, 11 November 2007, pp. 95–101.

Jones, Dave, *Yackety Yack*, 1974, 16 mm, b&w, 86 minutes, Australia, Producer Jones, Dave, Scriptwriter Jones, Dave, Camera Gordon Glenn, Sound Peter Beilby & Lloyd Carrick. Featuring Dave Jones, John Flaus, Peter Carmody, Peggy Cole, John Cleary, Jerzy Toeplitz, Doug White, Rod Nicholls, Andy Miller. Produced with assistance from the Australia Council, Experimental Film and Television Fund.

Jones, Liz, Betty Burstall & Helen Garner, *History*, La Mama 1988, <http://lamama.com.au/about/history/>, accessed 7 January 2013.

Jones, Stephen, *John Hansen*, D*Hub, Powerhouse Museum, Sydney, 2006, <http://www.dhub.org/articles/150>, accessed 6 February 2013.

Jost, Jon, *Angel City*, 1976, 16 mm, colour, 76 minutes.

Kalina, Paul, 'What I Have Written', *Cinema Papers*, February 1996, pp. 8–10.

Keenan, Haydn, *Persons of Interest: ASIO's dirty war on dissent*, 2013, 4 episodes, Smart Street Films, Sydney, Producer Gai Steele. Featuring Roger Milliss, Michael Hyde, Gary Foley and Frank Hardy. Produced with assistance from SBS-TV. Distributed by Smart Street Films, <http://www.smartstreetfilms.com.au>.

Kennedy, Justice Geoffrey, Sir Ronald Wilson & Mr Peter Brinsden, *WA Inc. Royal Commission*, 1992, Government of Western Australia, Department of the Premier and Cabinet, State Law Publisher, 2000, <http://www.slp.wa.gov.au/publications/publications.nsf/inquiries+and+commissions?openpage>, accessed 22 December 2013.

Kennedy, Peter, *Artist (sculptor), (installation artist), (performance artist) Designer (architect/interior architect/landscape architect)*, Design & Art Australia Online, 2011, <http://www.daao.org.au/bio/peter-kennedy/works/>, accessed 15 September 2013.

Kepley Jr, Vance, 'The Workers International Relief and the Cinema of the Left 1921–1935', *Cinema Journal*, vol. 23, Autumn, 1983, pp. 7–23.

Kesby, Rebecca, 'North Vietnam, 1972: The Christmas bombing of Hanoi', *BBC News Magazine*, 24 December 2012, British Broadcasting Service, <http://www.bbc.co.uk/news/magazine-20719382>, accessed 15 September 2013.

Ringwood, 1988. Originally published 1987 as *The Penguin Bicentennial History of Australia*.

Montsalvat, *Home page*, Eltham, 2010, <http://www.montsalvat.com.au>, accessed 7 January 2013.

Morris, Meaghan, 'Notions of Independence', in Creed, Barbara, John Davies, Freda Freiberg, David Hanan & Kim Montgomery (eds), Papers and Forums on Independent Film and Asian Cinema, La Trobe University, Melbourne, ASSA, AFTRS, 1982.

Morse, Helen and Paul English, The Power of Love, 2013, fortyfivedownstairs poetry readings, <http://www.fortyfivedownstairs.com/events/the-power-of-love>, accessed 16 October 2014.

Mudie, Peter, *Ubu films: Sydney underground movies 1965–1970*, UNSW Press, Sydney, 1997.

Mulvey, Laura & Peter Wollen, *Riddles of the Sphinx*, 1977, 16 mm, colour, London.

Mundell, Ian, 'Joris Ivens', *Senses of Cinema*, no. 37, October–December, 2005, Senses of Cinema, Brussels, <http://sensesofcinema.com/2005/great-directors/ivens/>, accessed 24 February 2013.

Murray, Scott, 'Interview', *Peter Malone's Website*, no. 6, November 1998, 30 May 2012, <http://www.signis.net/malone/tiki-index.php?page=Scott+Murray&bl>, accessed 6 January 2013.

Nash, Margot & Robin Laurie, *We Aim to Please*, 1976, 16 mm, colour, 13 minutes, As If Productions, Melbourne, Producer Anarcho Surrealist Insurrectionary Feminists, Scriptwriters Nash, Margot & Robin Laurie.

Nash, Margot, Judi Stack, Rae Walker, Brian Walsh & Diana Wolthers (eds), *Melbourne Independent Videotape Catalogue* (trans.), Melbourne Access Video and Media Co-operative, Carlton, 1976.

National Archives of Australia, The Wave Hill 'walk-off', Fact sheet 224, 2014, < http://www.naa.gov.au/collection/fact-sheets/fs224.aspx>, accessed 16 October 2014.

National Museum of Australia, 'HC Coombs', Collaborating for Indigenous Rights, < http://indigenousrights.net.au/people/pagination/hc_coombs>, accessed 16 October 2014.

National Portrait Gallery, 'Prime Minister Gough Whitlam pours soil into the hand of traditional land owner Vincent Lingiari (1975) by Mervyn Bishop', *The Portraits*, http://www.portrait.gov.au, accessed 16 October 2014.

NATO, *The Atlantic Charter*, President of the United States, FD Roosevelt, Prime Minister of HM Government in the United Kingdom, W Churchill, North Atlantic Treaty Organisation, 1941, <http://www.nato.int/cps/en/natolive/official_texts_16912.htm>, accessed 12 February 2013.

Nordholt, Henk Schulte, 'A genealogy of violence', in Colombijn, Freek & J Thomas Lindblad (eds), *Roots of violence in Indonesia*, Institute of South East Asian Studies, Singapore, 2002, pp. 33–62.

Noyce, Phil, *Newsfront*, 1978, 35 mm, colour, 110 minutes, Palm Beach Pictures, Producers Noyce, Phil & Bob Ellis, Scriptwriter Elfick, David, Executive Producers Haywood, Chris, Wendy Hughes, Bill Hunter & Gerard Kennedy, Camera Vincent Monton.

Oakeshott, Rob, 'Capitalist punishment', *The Saturday Paper*, 2014, Melbourne, 9 August, p.15.

Open Channel, *Open: Public Television*, program schedule, Melbourne, 1982.

Open Channel, 2013, <http://www.openchannel.org.au>, accessed 14 February 2013.

Owen, Taylor & Ben Kiernan, *Bombs Over Cambodia*, The Walrus, The Walrus Foundation, Canada, 2006, <http://www.walrusmagazine.com/articles/2006.10–history–bombing–cambodia/>, accessed 24 February 2013.

Palmada, 'BLF de-registration is a danger to the union movement', *Tribune*, 12 March 1986, p. 4.

Papastergiadis, Nikos (ed.) *What John Berger Saw* (trans.), ANU Canberra School of Art Gallery, Canberra, 2000, originally published as conference papers in 1999.

Parliament of Australia, *Communist Party Dissolution Act 1950*, Act No. 16, section 25.

Perry, David, *The Refracting Glasses*, 1993, 109 minutes, Sydney, Camera Simon Smith, featuring David Perry, Leon Teague, Tommy Thoms, Taylor Owynns & Alia Karihaloo.

Petit, Christopher, *Radio On*, 1979, Bristol, Producer Griffiths, Keith, Executive Producers Gundelach, Renée & Peter Sainsbury. Featuring David Beames, Lisa Kreuzer, Sandy Ratcliff, Andrew Byatt, Sue Jones-Davies. Produced with assistance from the BFI.

Plater, Diana, 'Documentaries find a new mentor – Aunty', *Sydney Morning Herald*, Monday 21 November 1988, p. 13.

Radnoti, Sandor, 'Benjamin's Politics', *Telos*, vol. 11, no. 3, Fall 1978, pp. 63–81.

Ramsey, Alan, 'A role in the fall of a Labor mate conveniently omitted from the eulogies', *Sydney Morning Herald*, 2005, Fairfax Media, July 20, <http://www.smh.com.au/articles/2005/07/19/1121538972499.html>, accessed 22 December 2013.

Rando, Gaetano & Gino Moliterno, *Celluloid Immigrant: Italian Australian Filmmaker Giorgio Mangiamele*, The Moving Image, ATOM, St Kilda, 2011.

Realist Film Unit, *Prices and the People*, 1948, 16 mm, b&w, 18 minutes, RFU, Melbourne, Scriptwriters Bob Mathews & Jim Crawford, Camera Bob Mathews & Keith Gow, narrator Ken Otway, in John Hughes & Uri Mizrahi, The Archive Project, 2006, DVD box set, Distributed by Artfilms, <http://www.artfilms.com.au>.

Rees, Leslie, *A History of Australian Drama: Australian Drama in the 1970s*, vol. 2, 2 vols, Angus & Robertson, Melbourne, 1978.

Richards, Mike, 'Interview with John Hughes', *ABC Radio*, July 1977.

Rintoul, Stuart, 'Miners and Brian Burke sank land rights hope', *The Australian*, 2013, News Limited, 1 January, <http://www.theaustralian.com.au/in-depth/cabinet-papers/miners-and-brian-burke-sank-land-rights-hope/story-fngr9pxq-1226545827125>, accessed 22 December 2013.

Robertson, Tim, *The Pram Factory*, Melbourne UP, Melbourne, 2001.

Roeg, Nicolas, *Bad Timing*, 1980, 35 mm, colour, UK.

Ross, Caroline, 'It's a video world', *The Sun*, 20 July 1974, p. 24.

Rowley, CD, *The Destruction of Aboriginal Society*, ANUP, Canberra, 1970.

Rowse, Tim, 'Traps: A sympathetic joke on its audience', *Filmnews*, February/March 1986, p. 15.

Rowse, Tim, *Obliged to be Difficult: Nugget Coombs' Legacy in Indigenous Affairs*, Cambridge University Press, Melbourne, 2000.

Rowse, Tim, *Nugget Coombs: A Reforming Life*, Cambridge University Press, Melbourne, 2002.

Rubbo, Michael, *Waiting for Fidel*, 1974, 16 mm, colour, 58 minutes, Producers Daly, Tom,

Colin Low & Michael Rubbo, Editor Michael Rubbo.

Russell, Bertrand, 'Why I Am Not a Christian', in Paul Edwards (ed.), *Why I Am Not a Christian: and other essays on religion and related subjects*, Allen & Unwin, London, 1957.

Santa Barbara Studios & Tig Productions, 1995, Producers Morgan, WT & John Pohl, 8-part television series, *500 Nations*, USA.

SBS Television, 'The Cutting Edge: After Mabo', *Program Publicity*, 6 November 1997.

Scott, John, 'The Celebration (11 September 1973)', *From the Flooded City*, Makar Press, Brisbane, 1981, p. 19.

Scott, John, *The Architect*, Penguin, Ringwood, 2001.

Scott, John, *What I Have Written*, McPhee Gribble, Ringwood, 1993.

Screen Australia, *Development Programs*, Industry Support, Sydney, 2011, <http://www.screenaustralia.gov.au/industry_support/Development.asp>, accessed 21 February 2011.

Screen Australia, *Documentaries Development*, Industry Support, Sydney, 2012, <http://www.screenaustralia.gov.au/funding/documentary/development.aspx>, accessed 23 February 2013.

Screen Australia, Research, *Activity of producers, directors and writers of Australian feature films, 1970–2011*, 2011, <http://www.screenaustralia.gov.au/research/statistics/oefilmmakersffactivity.aspx>, accessed 31 January 2013.

Sculthorp, Peter, 'Earth Cry', conducted by Challender, Stuart, CD, recorded February and July 1989, ABC Classics CD no. 426 4812, Australian Broadcasting Commission, Sydney Symphony Orchestra, 1986.

Shirley, Graham & Brian Adams, *Australian Cinema: The First Eighty Years*, 2nd edn, Angus & Robertson, Sydney, 1989. Originally published 1983.

Sieg, Kent G, 'Marshall Green', in Cathal J Nolan (ed.), *Notable US Ambassadors Since 1775: A Biographical Dictionary*, Greenwood, Westport, 1997, pp. 117–123.

Stilwell, Frank, Obituary: Ted Wheelwright, 1921–2007, The University of Sydney News, 2007, <http://sydney.edu.au/news/84.html?newsstoryid=1868>, accessed 21 December 2013.

Sklan, Carole, 'Interview with John Hughes', *The Stars Disordered*, 1988, pp. 12–13.

Slavin, John, 'The Hole in the Doughnut', *The Age Monthly Review*, May 1989, pp. 12–13.

Smaill, Belinda, 'SBS Documentary and Unfinished Business', *Metro*, no. 126, 2001, pp. 34–40.

Smart, Ralph, *Bitter Springs*, 1951, b&w, 89 minutes, Ealing Studios, UK.

Snider, L Britt, 'Oversight of Covert Action', *The Agency & The Hill: CIA's Relationship with Congress, 1946–2004*, vol. 47, no. 3, ch. 9, 14 April 2007, Center for the Study of Intelligence, The Central Intelligence Agency (CIA), Washington DC, 9 May, p. 281, <https://www.cia.gov/library/center–for–the–study–of–intelligence/csi–publications/books–and–monographs/agency–and–the–hill/The%20Agency%20and%20the%20Hill_Book_1May2008.pdf>, accessed 19 June 2013.

Stein, Eckart, 'Securing working definitions of narrative through discussion of genres of independent filmmaking', AFI Conference: Independent Narrative Filmmaking and Television Marketing, Sydney, author's notes, 1984.

Stern, Lesley, 'Severed Intensities: Conjuring John Hughes' *What I Have Written*', *Cinema Papers*, February 1996, pp. 12–13.

Stevenson, Paul, 'Martin Eslin on Bertolt Brecht', *MSC Newsletter*, vol. 5, no. 8, October 1979, pp. 3–6.

Stewart, Clare, 'SPAA Fringe: independence contested', *Real Time/On Screen*, no. 47, March 2002, p. 17.

Stockwell, Stephen, 'Beyond Conspiracy Theory: US presidential archives on the Australian press, national security and the Whitlam government', Journalism Education Conference, Griffith University, Academia.edu, Brisbane, 2005, <http://www.academia.edu/3518808/Beyond_Conspiracy_Theory_US_presidential_archives_on_the_Australian_press_national_security_and_the_Whitlam_government>, accessed 15 September 2013.

Stokes, Jim, *A brief history of the Royal Commission on Intelligence and Security*, 2013, Website: A brief history of the Royal Commission on Intelligence and Security, National archives of Australia, <http://www.naa.gov.au/collection/publications/papers–and–podcasts/intelligence–and–security/rcis–historyppaper.aspx>, accessed 15 September 2013.

Stratton, David, 'Traps', *Variety*, 26 June 1985, p. 20.

Straub, Jean-Marie & Danièle Huillet, *Introduction to an accompaniment to a cinematographic scene by Arnold Schoenberg*, 1976, 17 minutes.

Sully, François, Marjorie Weiner Normand (ed.), *We the Vietnamese – Voices from Vietnam* (trans.), Praeger, 1971.

Tammer, Peter, *Mallacoota Stampede*, 1981, 16 mm, colour, Melbourne. Distributed by Artfilms, <http://www.artfilms.com.au>.

Tammer, Peter, *Journey to the End of Night*, 1982, 16 mm, colour, Melbourne. Distributed by Artfilms, <http://www.artfilms.com.au>.

Tammer, Peter, *Notes on the Melbourne Filmmakers Co-op*, email to John Cumming, Kyneton, 20 November 2011.

Tange, Sir Arthur, 'Reflections looking back: Whitlam and the Central Intelligence Agency', *Defence Policy-Making: A Close-Up View, 1950–1980*, 2008, Canberra Papers on Strategy and Defence, Demetrius at The Australian National University E Press, Canberra, <http://epress.anu.edu.au/sdsc/dpm/mobile_devices/ch02s25.html>, accessed 22 February 2013.

Thomas, Stephen, 'Hope – Towards an ethical framework of collaborative practice in documentary filmmaking', thesis (MA), School of Film and Television, The University of Melbourne (VCA), Melbourne, December 2010, <https://minerva-access.unimelb.edu.au/handle/11343/36279> accessed 16 October 2014.

Thomas, Steve, *Hope* 2007, colour, 104 minutes, Scriptwriters Brooks, Sue & Steve Thomas. Distributed by Gil Scrine Films, <http://www.antidotefilms.com.au>.

Thompson, Rick, *Conference arrangements*, letter to organisers, ASSA, La Trobe University, Bundoora, 10 March 1982.

Thoms, Albie, 'Ten Years of the Sydney Film-maker's Co-op', in Thoms, Albie (ed.), *Polemics for a New Cinema*, 1978, pp. 346–407.

TOF, *Television Outworkers Forum*, Hughes, John (ed.) Australian Documentary Filmmakers Policy Forum, Melbourne, 2010, <http://lists.culture2.org/cgi–bin/mailman/list info/tof>, accessed 29 June 2010.

Turnour, Quentin 'Giorgio', *Senses of Cinema*, no. 14, June 2001.

Tropfest, *Tropfest Australia. The world's largest short film festival*, Sydney, 2013, <http://tropfest.com>, accessed 13 February 2013.

United Nations, *The Universal Declaration of Human Rights*, Paris, 10 December 1948, <http://www.un.org/en/documents/udhr/index.shtml>, accessed 6 February 2013.

United Nations CERD, *Summary Record of the 1393rd Meeting*, Geneva, 21 March 2000, <http://www.unhchr.ch/tbs/doc.nsf CERD/C/SR.1393>, accessed 24 February 2013.

Verdaasdonk, Dorothee, 'Ivens, Joris', *Film Reference*, <http://www.filmreference.com/Directors–Ha–Ji/Ivens–Joris.html>, accessed 24 February 2013.

Vidal, Gore, 'At Home on the Hudson in the Cold War' in *Palimpsest, a memoir*, Penguin, Melbourne, 1996, pp. 235–238.

Vertov, Dziga, *The man with the movie camera/Chelovek s kinoapparatom*, 1929, 35 mm, b&w, 68 minutes, Kino International Corporation, USSR, Camera Mikhail Kaufman.

Vertov, Dziga, 'Love for the living person', edited and translated by Michelson, Annette, *Kino-Eye: The Writings of Dziga Vertov*, Pluto Press, Sydney, 1984, pp. 147–157. Originally published 1958.

Vincent, Victor, Hartley Cant, Samuel Cohen, Thomas Drake-Brockman, George Hannan, Douglas McClelland & Reginald Wright, *Report from the Select Committee on the Encouragement of Australian Productions for Television*, Canberra, 1963.

Virilio, Paul, *Speed and politics: an essay on dromology*, Mark Polizzotti (trans.), NY, Columbia UP, 1986.

Wahlberg, Malin, 'Wonders of cinematic abstraction: JC Mol and the aesthetic experience of science film', *Screen*, vol. 47, no. 3, 2006, pp. 273–289, <http://screen.oxfordjournals.org/content/47/3/273.full>, accessed 4 September 2013.

Walsh, Martin, *The Brechtian aspect of radical cinema*, BFI Pub., London, 1981.

Walsh, Mike, 'The Motion Picture Distributors Association of Australia and the conversion of Sir Victor Wilson', *Screening the Past*, First Release, Selected papers from the Film and History Conference, Adelaide, November 2002, no. 16, 2004, La Trobe University, 7 May, <http://tlweb.latrobe.edu.au/humanities/screeningthepast/firstrelease/fr_16/mwfr16.html>.

Warner, Chris, Cynthia Connop & Ginny Brook, 'Filmmaking in Australia', *Farrago*, 9 July 1976, pp. 11–14.

Williams, Deane, *Australian Post-War Documentary Film: an Arc of Mirrors*, Intellect, Bristol, 2008.

Williamson, Geordie, 'Love blooms in the afternoon', *The Australian*, April 20 2013, < http://www.theaustralian.com.au/arts/review/love-blooms-in-the-afternoon/story-fn9n8gph-1226623732167>, accessed 16 October 2014.

Wilson, Jake, 'Carlton + Godard = Cinema: An Interview with Nigel Buesst', *Senses of Cinema*, no. 27, 2003, Senses of Cinema Inc., <http://sensesofcinema.com/2003/27/carlton_plus_godard/>, accessed 4 January 2013.

Wollen, Peter, 'The Two Avant-Gardes', *Readings & Writings: Semiotic Counter-Stategies*, Verso, London, 1982. Originally published *Studio International*, December 1975.

Wright, Judith, We call for a treaty, Collins/Fontana, Sydney, 1985.

Wright, Tony, *Fair Go!* 1984, 24 minutes, VTHC Video Unit Melbourne, Producer Robins, Penny,

Scriptwriter Moon, Peter, Sound Tony Wright, featuring Tracey Harvey, Danny Nash, Geoff Kelso, Peter Moon. Produced with assistance from the Legal Aid Commission, Department of Youth, Sport & Recreation and Open Channel.

Youngblood, Gene, 'Jean-Luc Godard: No Difference between Life and Cinema', in Sterritt, David (ed.), *Jean-Luc Godard Interviews*, UP Mississippi, 1998, pp. 9–49. Originally published Los Angeles Free Press, 8 March 1968: 15, 20; 15 March 1968: 5, 25; 22 March 1968: 10–11; 29 March 1968: 24–25, 29.

Zubricki, Tom, 'Documentary: a personal view', in Burton, Geoff & Raffaele Caputo (eds), *Second Take*, Allen & Unwin, St Leonards, 1999, pp. 178–192.

Zuvela, Danni & Albie Thoms, 'The Ubu Moment: An Interview with Albie Thoms', *Senses of Cinema*, no. 27, 2003, Senses of Cinema Inc., Melbourne, <http://www.sensesofcinema.com/2003/27/albie_thoms/>, accessed 24 February 2013.

Appendix V: INDEX:

Entries referring to images or captions are represented in **bold**.

Symbols

16 mm film **4**, 19–24, 31, 33, 44, 69, 80–81, 93, 103, 116, 124, 128, 150, 161, 170, 189, 191, **197**
   newsreel 1, 26–27, **60**, 223
   Super-16 format 161
20th Century Fox 50–51, 90
2000 Weeks 20

A

Aboriginal Advancement League 169
Aboriginal Affairs, Minister for 178
Aboriginal Embassy **170–171**
Aboriginal Reconciliation Convention 1997 174–175
Aboriginal & Torres Strait Islander people 2, 46, 59, 167–186, 222–223
   & non-Indigenous culture 129, 133, 223.
     See also non-Indigenous & European Australians
   land rights campaign 167, 172–175, 178–180, 183, 221–224
   media representation of 167–168, 172, 176, 179
abortion 33, 44, 69
Abortion a Woman's Decision 44
abstract filmmaking 30
Abstract Society, The 43
academic research 220
Acceptable Risk 96
access & equity 43
Access Video and Resource Centre (CAVRC), Carlton 43
access video movement 79–80, 115.
   See community access video
Aceh 228
Action for World Development Exhibition 43
action frames 217
activism & activist filmmaking 3, 44, 101, 201, 205, 215, 229, 231, 233
actuality 9, 85, 105, 117, 130, 135–137, 224–226. *See also* dramatisation, actuality & performance
Adams, Brian 45
Adams, Phillip **6**, 65, 193
Addis, Erika 2, 145
Adelaide Arts Festival 219
Adelaide film festival 92
Adjunct Professor 221
advertising 6, 23, 32–33, 72, 131, 175
advocacy filmmaking 26, 30, 167, 172–175
aesthetic of disruption 194.
   See also Constructivism
After Mabo 2, *13*, 167, 170, 172–179, *181*, 183, 217
   screen designs 177–179, *194*
agitprop 81
agribusiness & meat cartels 93, 172–175, 179–180
Alice Springs 168, 226
allegory 113, 135, 147
Allende, Salvador 59, 73–74, 102
Allies 108, 111
Allison, Edmund 209–210
All That is Solid 121–139, 143, 146, 148–149, 159, 172, 231
All That Is Solid Melts into Air 125
alternative education 95
alternative media 12, 80–82, 84, 113.
   See also access video movement
alternative theatre 13, 45, 105
Alvin Purple 20

amateurs, cine clubs & independent arts practice 14, 79, 152, 189
America. *See* United States of America (USA)
American avant-garde film 21, 34, 44
American guru 31
American War in South East Asia (Laos, Vietnam & Cambodia) 42, 49, 96. *See also* peace movement
  bombing 32, 39
  protest 23
  Whitlam government 41, 59, 61–62
A Moment of Brightness 94
a moment of danger 83
Amsterdam 219
analogue video mixing 68
Anarcho Surrealist Insurrectionary Feminists 84
Anderson, Benedict 228
Angel City 105, 136
angels & bullets 124
Angelus Novus / Angel of History 126, 148
animation 72
Annear, Debra 174
Annotations 21
Anthony, Doug 63
anthropological films 171
anti-semitism 93
Anti-Terrorism Act 2005 198
A Place to Live 189
Aplin, Brett 227
arcades 126
Archival Film Program 93
Archive Project, The (2006) 4, 6, 13, 187–201, 221, 226
Arf-Arf 150
Arriflex **84, 150–151**
Armstrong, Father Jim 24, 26
Arnold Schoenberg 194
art film & art cinema 3, 20
Artfilms 16, 92
art gallery exhibition & installations 22, 33, 124–125, 150, 189–190
  November Eleven 57, 68–70, 72, 75–76
art history programs 191

artists & intellectuals 44, 53, 159–160, 231
Asia Pacific region 59, 63
aspect ratio 195
At Edge 226
Athenaeum Theatre 27
Atlantic Charter 208
ATOM Awards 92, 139 181, 200
audience 8, 15, 21, 105, 108, 135–137, 148, 213
  non-theatrical 81, 103
  positioning 90, 155, 190. *See also* dialectical approach: to audience
  television 92, 123, 131, 221
Audio-Visual Education Centre/Resources Branch (AVEC/AVRB) 140
Australand 184
Australasian Meat Industry Employees' Union 93
Australia at School 94
Australia Council for the Arts (ACA) 27–30, 123, 170, 222
  Aboriginal Arts Board 183
  Film, Radio and Television Board (FRTB) 29, 43, 64, 169
  other boards of 42–43, 68, 93
Australia Day 198
Australian Aboriginal League 192
Australian Bicentennial Authority 124
Australian Broadcasting Commission/Corporation (ABC) 19, 27, 95, 152, 190, 201–202, 224–225. *See also* Documentary Fellowship
  TV Arts 219–220, 224
  TV cine-camera training 1, 19, 42, 72
  TV & creative control 123–124, 140
Australian Centre for the Moving Image (ACMI) 188
Australian cinema 6, 28, 31, 50, 81, 162, 167, 171, 231. *See also* screen culture; *See also* finance & policy
Australian cinema revival/renaissance (1970s) 7, 28–29
Australian Consolidated Press 62

Australian Council for Aboriginal Affairs 222
Australian Council of Trade Unions (ACTU) 70, 83, 92
Australian Defence Department 60
Australian Directors Guild (ADG) 219
Australian Film and Television Development Corporation 29
Australian Film and Television School (AFTS) 29
Australian Film Commission (AFC) 64, 68, 92. *See also* finance & policy: federal; *See also* Documentary Fellowship
   Creative Development Branch/Fund (CDB/CDF) 65, 81, 103, 115–116
   feature films 152, 156, 159–160
   Hughes' films 144–145, 159, 174, 190, 219
   Indigenous Branch 185–186
   negotiations 81–82, 108–109, 145, 185
   No Frills Fund 116
   peer assessment 81–82, 98
   Women's Film Fund 103
Australian Film Institute (AFI)
   Awards 20, 27, 200
   Distribution 92–93
   EFTF 77
   Vincent Library 29
   Visions of Independence 101–102
Australian Law Reform Commission 58
Australian National Film Board (ANFB) 201, 206, 209, 211. *See also* Film Australia
Australian National University (ANU) 93, 223
Australian Screen Production Education and Research Association
Australian Screen Studies Association (ASSA) 92, 99–100, 104
   legacy of 1982 ASSA conference 114–115
Australian Secret Intelligence Service (ASIS) 63
Australian Security Intelligence Organisation (ASIO) 60–63, 93, 198, 202, **216**. *See also* secret security services
   lack of oversight 61
   surveillance by 189–190, 195

Australian Teachers of Media (ATOM) 16. *See also* ATOM Awards
Australian, The 225
authorial voice 110, 113, 231
authoritarianism 15, 32, 45, 73–74, 96, 212
automated new media 44
avant-garde art & theatre 206–207
avant-garde film 15, 19, 28, 65, 75, 115, 148. *See also* experimental film
   American 34, 44, 71–72
   European 30, 85
   terminology 78
awards, honours & dedications 92, 139, 156, 181, 200, 221
A Zed & Two Noughts 166

B

Babylon 23, 32
Bad Timing 160
Ballet Mécanique 72
Balsaitis, Jonas 23
Balwyn Cinema 23
Banff Television Festival 181
Bank of America 72
Banks, Ron 125
Barnett, Chris 124–125, 127
Barta, Tony 150, 195, 196
Bartley, Olivier 227
Batman, John 223
Battle for Bowen Hills, The 98–99
Baudrillard, Jean 126
beDevil 156
Beebe, Dion 160–161
Beginnings 23, 189
Bendinelli, Frank 69–70
Benjamin, Walter 83–85, 137, 149
   Angelus Novus 126, **139**
   collage & quotation 72, 126, 179–180
   One Way Street 143–149, 150, 231
Bennett, Colin 27, 29
Berlin 144
Berlin International Film Festival 161
Berman, Marshall 125, 129

Beyond Conspiracy Theory: US presidential archives on the Australian press, national security and the Whitlam government 59
Beyond Reason 20
big business & government 108, 133, 173–174
Bijedic, Dzemal 60
biopic 144, 146–147, 205, 218
Bishop, Mervyn 223
Bishop, Rod 23, 77
Bitter Springs 171, 178
black-and-white film 161, 195
'black arm band' view of history 176
Blackfire 169
blacklisting 49, 197, 205, 211. *See also* secret security culture
Black Maria 136
Block Arcade 126
Blokker, Jan 218
Blonski, Annette 31, 34, 110, 111, 113, 159, 162
blue-screen 72, 92
Bolex **88–89**, 189, 191
Bradbury, David 123
Brains Trust, the 80
branding 102
Brealey, Gil 20, 35
Breath of Fresh Air, A 21
Breathing Under Water 156
Brecht, Bertolt 30, 44, 69, 85, 105, 135
Brechtian 104, 135–137, 158, 164, 210
Brechtian Aspect of Radical Cinema, The 104–105
Bresson, Robert 135
bricolage 57, 194
Bridge, The (*De Brug*, 1928) 207
Brighton Technical School 15
British & American film corporations 6–7, 90–91. *See also* multinational & transnational corportations; *See also* screen culture: Anglo-American hegemony
British Film Institute (BFI) 30
British Sounds/See You at Mao 30, 44, 85, 166, 170

Bronze Horse Award 161
Brophy, Philip 116
Brotherhood of St Laurence 189
Brubeck, Dave 186
Buck-Morss, Susan 149
budgets 156, 169, 180, 219–220, 224
Buesst, Nigel 9, 21, 34–35, 38–39, 77
Builders Labourers Federation (BLF) 107–108, 113
Bulletins 21
Buoyancy Foundation 24, 26
bureaucracy as coercive force 43
Burke, Brian 173–174, 184
Burstall, Betty 20
Burstall, Tim 20–21
Byrne, David 126
Byrnes, Paul 110

C

cable television 117
Cairns, Jim 62
California 42
Cambodia 39
Camera Natura 150
camera & projection van **86**
cameras
 8mm video 145, 190
 16 mm film 1, 19, 26–27, 128, 150–151
 Arriflex 16mm 84, **150–151**
 Bolex 16 mm **88–89**, 189, 191
 digital 11, 218–219
 J-format video 42–43, 203
 Kinamo 35 mm film 209, 228
 Video-8 & Hi-8 128–129
Cameron, Clyde 63
Cameron, Donna 179
Cameron, Margaret 126, 146–148, 159, 231
Campey, Philippa 191–192, 224
Canadian Film Board 140
Cannes Film Festival 20
Cantrill, Arthur 33–34
Cantrill, Corinne 21, 33, 33–34, 34, 36, 40
Cantrills Filmnotes 33

Cape York Land Council 174
capitalism 46, 73–74, 127, **132**, 221.
 See also neoliberalism
Capitalist Punishment 118
capital punishment 58
Capp, Fiona 221
Caputo, Raffaele 144
career 1, 9, 11, 34
caricature 72, 136
Carlton Access Video and Resource Centre (CAVRC) 43
Carlton filmmakers 19–22, 33, 45
Castle, Jane 129
Cavadini, Alessandro 170
Cavalcanti, Alberto 3
celluloid film **60**, 118, 177, 218.
 See also 16 mm film; *See also* laboratory, film; *See also* Super-8 film
censorship 21, 32, 108, 207
Central Australian Aboriginal Media Association (CAAMA) 129
Central Intelligence Agency (CIA) USA
 CIA & Australia 59–64, 108
 CIA & Chile 59, 76
 CIA cultural policy 21, 71–72
centralised media power 44, 71.
 See also screen culture: Anglo-American hegemony
Centre for Research into Aboriginal Affairs 169
Changing Schools 94–95
Channel 4 102
Chaplin, Charlie 72
characterisation & performance 113–114
Charlot Cubiste 72
Chauvel, Charles 20, 171
Chicago Film Festival 139
Chifley, Ben 45, 210
Chile 59, 76, 102, 106–107, 107, 233
Chinese seamen 208
Chinese students 218
Christmas bombing of Hanoi 61, 76
chroma key 72
Churcher, Betty 181, 186

Churchill, Winston 208
Chytilová, Vera 135
Cinema of Australia & New Zealand, The 177
Cinema Papers 23, 79, 116, 161, 165, 189
cinema thinking 162–163, 231
cinematography 219, 226, 228
cinematographers & camerapeople:
 Erika Addis **2**, **103**, 145
 Dion Beebe 160–161
 Elizabeth Coldicutt **196**
 Graeme Cutts 196–197
 Jane Castle **129**
 Nicolette Freeman **10**, 146, **150–51**
 Jaems Grant **122**, 123, 127
 Keith Gow **88**, 89, **91**, 189
 John Hughes 26–27, 31–33, 169
 John Hughes (newsreel) 1, 19, 22, 24, 41, 71–72
 Joris Ivens 207
 Giorgio Mangiamele 20
 Marion Michelle 209
 Margot Nash **5**, **11**, **82**, 84, **85**, **88**
 Bob Mathews, 189
 Peter Zakharov 174
cinephile 6, 20, 22. *See also* film buff
citizenship 8, 41, 43, 54
clandestine production 209–210
Clarke, Ray 203
class struggle 45
Clay 20
Clayden, James (Jim) 23, 33
Clinton, Bill 39
Coca-Cola 72
Cockcroft, Eva 71
Coldicutt, Elizabeth 196–197
Coldicutt, Ken 188, 190, 196–197
Cold War, The 2, 45–53, 49, 62, 81, 91, 96, 109–110, 187–190, 196–197, 221
 anti-communism 48, 50, 60, 90, 110
 Indonesia 205, 208, 213–215
 US cultural policy 71–72
collaboration. *See also* Kennedy, Peter
 All That is Solid 124–125
 Paul Davies & Carolyn Howard 13, 72,

105–108
WWF Film Unit & *Film-Work* crew 79–80, 84, 87–89, 91
collaborative political process 176
collage. *See* screen design
  of feeling 224
  & quotation 57, 70, 72, 117, 126, 179–180
  within the frame 13–14, 71, 143, **152**, 177, 194–195, 216–217, 231
collective work 34, 91, 96, 105, 189
collectivism 69
colonialism 2, 173, 205, 208–213
colour distortion effects 70
combines. *See* screen culture: Anglo-American hegemony
commercial cinema & TV 161, 168, 179, 207
commercial discourse & subsidy 220. *See also* finance & policy: commercialisation
commercial in-confidence 183
commissioned work 94–96, 202
Committee for International Co-operation and Disarmament (CICD) 15
Commonwealth Employment program (CEP) 93, 96
Commonwealth Film Unit 21, 201–202. *See also* Film Australia
Commonwealth Police 61, 172, 209
communism & anti-communism 62, 73, **101**, 205–209, 211
  Communist Manifesto, The 125
  Communist Party Dissolution Bill 1950 47–50
  Communist Party of Australia (CPA) 45–50, 90, 93, 188–189, 197
  Communist Party of Indonesia (Partai Komunis Indonesia; PKI) 213–215
  Communist Party of the Netherlands, The (Communistische Partij Nederland) 207, 216
  Victorian Royal Commission into Communism (1949) 45–47
community access video 7, 13, 29, 41–44, 54, 71. *See also* community television

community arts & activism 13, 42–43, 80–81, 93–96, 101–103, **109**, 116–117, 183
Community Arts Board 43, 93
community filmmaking 202, 205–215
community schools 95–96
community television 42, 83, 92
computer art 150
concentration camps 49
concentration of wealth & power 102, 233
Conner, Bruce 71
consciousness industry, the 44
conscription, military 32, 41, 58
conservatives & conservatism 32–33, 59, 64, 83, 107, 178–179, 207, 210, 215, 224. *See also* Liberal Party; *See also* neoliberalism
conspiracy theories 59–60, 113
Constituents of a Theory of the Media 44
construction workers 1
Constructivism 12, 69, 73, 85–89, 139–140, 147–148, 198, 226. *See also* dialectical approach
Constructivist theatre 57, 72–73, 135
Contemporary Commonwealth, 2006 188
Coombs, HC 'Nugget' 28, 107, 201, 221–226
Cope, Bill 129, 136–137
Coral Battleground, The 222
Cornell, Joseph 71
corruption 173–174, 213
Costa-Gavras 218
costume designer 125
cottage industry 8–9
Cottle, Drew 209
cotton farming 179–180
Counihan, Mick 53, 109
Counihan, Noel 93
counterculture 7, 15, 21, 31–32, 34, 41, 45, 80, 83. *See also* peace movement; *See also* protests
Country Party 45, 62, 107
coup d'état, constitutional, Australia 1975 57, 59–64, 68, 70–71, 73, 75, 223, 233
  Murdoch prediction of 62

coup d'état, military
   Chile 1973 59, 73–74, 106–107
   Indonesia 1965 62, 213–215
Craven, Marie 116
creative control 3–4, 8–12, 123–125, 140, 182–184, 220. *See also* emerging filmmakers
Creed, Barbara 99–100
crew 125, **146**
crew as cast 32, 87–91
critical collaboration with orthodoxy 96, 144, 176, 232
critically informed practice 16, 21
critics, critique & scholarship 4, 20–23, 27–28, 33–34, 88, 101, 187, 200
   Anglo-American bias 15
   of *After Mabo* 179
   of *All That is Solid* 127, 131–137
   of *Joris Ivens in Australia* 206–207, 210
   of *Love & Fury* 224–226
   of *One Way Street* 146–152
   of *Traps* 106, 110–113, 116
   of *What I Have Written* 161–165
Critique of the Political Economy of the Sign 126
Crowsfoot Films 79, 98
Cruthers, John 156
Cuba 49
Culloden 27
cultural conservatism 224
cultural desert 102
cultural politics & development 7–10, 41–43, 84, 93, 101–102, 115–117. *See also* finance & policy: federal
Cumming, John 9–10, 16, 96
Curran, Wally 93
Cutts, Graeme 10–11, 190, 196–197, 206, 210
Cybernetic Synergy **22**, **28**, 30–31, 41, 159, 231
Czechoslovakia 1968 72

D

Dada 32, 57, 70–73
Daguragu (Wattie Creek) 168, 223–224
Dalmas 19, 31–32, 34, 88, 125, 155
Das, Baba Ram 31
Davies, Brian 21
Davies, John 99–100
Davies, Paul 72, 104–107, 109, 110, 123–124, 127, 135, 145–146, 189
Davis, Eric 50
Dead to the World 156
Deakin University 9
declared persons 49, 211
deconstruction 112, 135–136
defence industry 49
Deleuze, Gilles 162–163
Deling, Bert 77
   MUFS, MFC 21, 23
   Dalmas 31–34
   national access video network 42–43
demilitarisation 58
democracy 28, 46, 50, 54, 59, 73–74, 96, 102, 106–107, 118, 128, 176, 211–215, 232–233
   in education 94–96
   in media production 28, 34, 41–42, 54
   persecution within 197–199, 202, 211, 232
democratic rights 46, 54
Democrats 129
Dendy Cinema 21
Department of Education film unit 140
Department of Employment 171
Department of Foreign Affairs 212
Department of Information (DOI) 90, 201
Department of Interior 50
deregulation 107
Dermody, Susan 114
Der Nederlandsche Filmliga 207
development. *See* project development
Devo 71
dialectical approach 14, 125, 132, 169, 177–178, 183, **187**. *See also* poetics
   to audience 39, 88, 155, 177, 177–178

to education 96
to form 87–90, 106, 110–112, 132
to performance 226
Dialectical Images 148
diary films 32
dictatorship 73
digital activism 201
digital media 33, 44, 205
digital production 177, 216–219
direct address 127
Directors Guild, Australian (ADG) 219
Disher, Norma 81–82, 84, 90–92
distribution 6, 8, 16, 21, 23, 28–29, 67–68, 92, 103–104, 117, 180, 182
  of the films 27, 81, 116
diversity 29, 34, 79, 115
docudrama 105, 110, 112, 125
documentary 160, 220
Documentary Accord scheme 180
Documentary Fellowship 121–124, 131, 139
Documentary Filmmakers Policy Forum, Australian 182–183
documentary theatre 72
documentary traditions 2–3, 70, 78, 79–80, 89
Dodson, Patrick 175–176
Double Take 202
Downtown Community Television (Toronto) 42
dramatisation, actuality & performance 3, 14, 72–73, 104–113.
    See also interviews; *See also* narration
  acting & characterisation 127–130, 143, 159, 180
  in *All that is Solid* 125–127, 130–139
  in ANFB films 202–203
  in *Love & Fury* 224–226
  in *One Way Street* 146–149
  in *What I Have Written* 163–165
  triangulation (performer/audience/text) 136
  Joris Ivens 215–216
Dream Before, The: Homage to Walter Benjamin 148
drug use 1, 24–26, 32
drum roll 53

Dudu, John **177**
Duncan, Catherine 209–211, 216–217
Dutch colonialism in Indonesia 205, 208–213, 228
Dutch Film League.
    See Filmliga, Der Nederlandsche
Dutch tilt 127
DVD 16, 20, 92, 180, 193, 201, 216–217
  menu screens 192, 200–201
Dyson, Cath 93
Dzenis, Anna 149, 162–164
Dziga Vertov 85, 88
Dziga Vertov Group. *See* Godard, Jean-Luc & Gorin, Jean-Pierre

E

Early Leavers scheme 43
Early Works 174, 191
Earth Cry 180
Edgar, Patricia 204
Edison, Thomas 136
editing 24, 74, 89–91, 111, 150, 195, 198–199, 211, 218. *See also* montage
  digital 11, 144, 177, 216
  sound & music 70, 75, 110–111, 111
  video on film 44–45
Edmunds, Lloyd 50
education in politics 84, 94–96
education & racism 170–172
education & training 42, 58, 107, 129.
    See also schools; *See also* Freire, Paulo; *See also* Hughes, John: early life, education & work
education & training media 16, 27–28, 94–96, 103, 140, 170–172, 200
egalitarianism 129
Eight Hour Day 188
Einstein, Albert 207
Eisenhower, Dwight 60
Eisenstein, Sergei 85, **187**, 198
electronic art 29–31
electronic mailing list 182
electronic surveillance 63

elegy & elegiac tone 148, 187, 196, 213, 218
Ellinghaus, Raynor **24**, 26
Elsternwick 19
Eltham filmmakers 20
Emerald Hill 19, 169
emerging filmmakers 2, 8–12, 93, 156, 167–168. *See also* creative control
emotion & feeling 23, 132, 163–165, 221, 224–227, 231–232.
    See also elegy & elegiac tone
Empire Marketing Board 140
engineers 1, 30
English, Paul 14, 225
entrepreneurship 6–8, 21
entrepreneurs in violence 212
environmentalism 59, 83, 167, 221–222, 224–225
environmental reporting award 181
Enzensberger, Hans Magnus 44
essay film 3, 9, 33, 104, 121, 134–136, 148, 150, 163, 221
Esslin, Martin 69
Euripides 126
exhibition 8, 27–30, 67–68, 79–81, 104, 116–117
exhibition - theatrical 219
Exits 72, 104–108, 110–112, 117, 127, 135, 189
Experimenta 150
experimental film 2, 4, 8–9, 15, 21–22, 24, 28–29, 33–34, 71, 148, 207.
    See also avant-garde film
Experimental Film and Television Fund (EFTF) 7, 29–32, 77, 116
experimental narrative & feature films 3, 19, 105, 155–156
experimental video/computer art 150.
    See also video art
experimentation 3, 13–14, 85–86, 121–140, 134, 144, 150, 176, 216, 232

F

Fairfax News 223
Fair Go! 96
fantasy 215
Far From Vietnam 191
Farley, Rick 179
fascism & anti-fascism 46, 48, 50, 73, 81, 83, 96, 144, 149, 206–207
Fearless Vampire Killers, The 27
feature film production 4, 6–8, 19–20, 155–165, 232
  low-budget & experimental 152–153
feminism 83, 99, 110, 232
feminist filmmakers 13–14, 33, 84, 134, 145
Film and History Association of Australia and New Zealand 200
Film and Sound Archive, National.
    See National Film and Sound Archive (NFSA)
Film Australia 50, 201, 206.
    See also Commonwealth Film Unit;
    See also Australian National Film Board
film buff 92, 183. *See also* cinephile
Film Critics Circle of Australia 200
filmed theatre 136
film festivals 16, 92, 103, 201
  as investors 219
Film Finance Corporation
  Documentary Accord 180
  Innovation Fund 219
film form 9, 12–13, 71, 89–93, 104–106, 121–123, 131–140, 143–144, 177–178, 215–216, 221, 232–233.
    See also narrative form;
    See also screen design
  hybrid forms 3, 104, 146–147, 191, 231–232. *See also* dramatisation, actuality & performance
film history 6–8, 81, 83, 206.
    See also Australian cinema;
    See also critics, critique & scholarship
  in Hughes' work 3–4, 16, 79, 92, 171–172, 187–189, 200, 220–221

Film and History Conference 92, 150
Filmliga, Der Nederlandsche 207
Filmmakers' Cinema, A: 20 years of the Filmmakers' cooperatives 220
filmmakers' co-operative movement 4–11, 19, 21, 24, 33, 41–43, 79, 83, 207, 220. *See also* Melbourne Filmmakers Co-operative (MFC); *See also* Sydney Filmmakers Co-operative (SFC)
Filmmakers Handbook, The 77
Filmnews 103, 117, 120, 131
Film, Radio and Television Board (FRTB). *See under* Australia Council
film society movement 6–7, 19–21, 29–30, 45, 79–80, 103, 201
Film Victoria 17, 35, 99, 165, 179, 191, 203, 219–220, 224
Film-Work **4**, 10–11, 79–96, 135, 139, 187
finance & policy: overview 6–8
finance & policy: before federal funding
  grassroots 23–24
  Unifed & SFCV 21, 29
finance & policy: federal. *See also* privatisation; *See also* AFC, ABC, EFTF, SBS
  government policy 27–29, 58, 65, 93
  filmmaker policy input 65, 92, 115, 121–124, 182, 231–232
  subsidy by artists 11, 79, 123, 180, 200
finance & policy: commercialisation 11–12, 20, 28–29, 64–65, 77, 79, 92, 101–102, 115–116, 121, 232–233. *See also* markets & market ideology; *See also* privatisation
  budget inflation 115, 156, 220
  tv presales 124, 145, 152
financing the films
  Nowhere Game 24
  Some Aspects of Australian Racism 169–170
  Cybernetic Synergy 30
  Traps 108
  All That is Solid 124
  One Way Street 144–145
  What I Have Written 156, *159–160*

After Mabo 174–175
River of Dreams 180
The Archive Project 188
Indonesia Calling: Joris Ivens in Australia 219–221, *220–221*
Love & Fury 224
A Filmmakers' Cinema: 20 years of the Filmmakers' cooperatives 220
Finch, Peter 210
Fiske, Pat 102, 145
Fittko, Lisa 147
Fitzgerald, Ann 126
Fitzroy Free Legal Service 42
Fitzroy Residents' Association 43
Fitzsimons, John (Jack) G 189
Five Hundred Nations 181–182
Flaus, John 92, 110–111, 192–193
Flinders Street 190
Flying Wedge 72
Foley, Gary 56, 167–170, 173, 181
Footscray Community Arts Centre 93
Footscray Technical School 96
Footscray Trade Union Clinic and Research Centre 53, 93
Ford Foundation 21, 71
Ford, Gerald 60, 63
Ford, Sue 220
foreign control of national assetts 102, 107–108. *See also* multinational & transnational corportations
foreign policy & foreign interference 58–64, 210
Fortesque Metals Group 184
forty-hour week campaign 48
Foundation, The Walrus 39
found-footage montage 70–72
fragmentation 83, 177
France 156
Frankel, Boris 129
Frankland, Richard 173–176
Fraser, Malcolm 59, 64, 70, 83, 107
freedom of opinion 54
Freeman, Jane 149

Freeman, Nicolette 10, 146, 150
freeze frame 90, 191
Freiberg, Freda 99
Freire, Paulo 42, 73, 82–83, 95–97
French new wave cinema 21, 30, 105
Freney, Denis **101**
Friedel, Martin 190
Friedrich, Zbigniew 111, 240
Fromm, Erich 95–97
From The Tropics to the Snow 202
futurism *See All That is Solid*

G

Gaal, Ivan 140
gallery installations.
    See art gallery exhibition & installations
Gang 364 80
Gaol Does Not Cure 189
Garlick, Bob 21, 35, 38
gender issues 129, 159–160
genre 135, 140, 147–148, 155, 195, 202.
    See also film form
German Expressionism 69
Germany 46, 50, 73, 83, 148, 206
Gibson, Dorothy 50
Gibson, Ralph **44**, 48, **53**
Gibson, Ross 12, 149–152, 156
Gillard, Julia 118
Gill, Michael 106, 108
Glaudini, Bob 136
Glenn, Gordon 23
global entertainment industry 10–11.
    See also screen culture: Anglo-American hegemony
globalisation 74, 102, 127, 133.
    See also multinational & transnational corportations;
    See also neoliberalism
global television event 176
Glynn, Freda 129
Godard, Jean-Luc
    104–106, 135–136, **187**, 191
  dialectical form 89–90, 110–111, 183

  text & sound 88
Godard, Jean-Luc & Gorin, Jean-Pierre 30, 44, 170, 194
  reflexivity, Brecht & Vertov 85, 88
Goddard, Martyn 1, 16, 24, 27, 38
Goldberg, Emanuel 228
Golden Bear Award 161
Golden Holden, The 53
Gorton, John 29, 107, 222
government & big business 108, 173–174
Governor-General of Australia Sir John Kerr 57, 59, 61–62, 64–65, 70, 93
Gow, Keith 4, 80–81, 83–85, 87–90, 191, 198, 201
GPO Film Unit (UK) 140
Grace, Helen 29, 104, 134, 156
Gradman, Eric 124–126
Grant, Jaems 123, 127
graphic history 201
graphics. *See also* text on screen
  as performance 85, 90–91
Gray, Peter 79, 98
Great Barrier Reef 222
Great Depression (1929-32) 15, 48, 50, 85, 133, 206
Greek chorus 31
Greenaway, Peter 166
Green, Marshall 62
grief 213
Grierson, John 140, 206
Grieve, Anna 202
Grosz, George 207
Guattari, Félix 126
Gunana: Homeland of the Mornington Island Woomera Dancers 68–69, 103
Gurindji 169, 223
Guyatt, Kit 21, 22, 32, 34

H

Hall, Barbara 67
Hall, Eva 128
Hanan, David 99–100
hand-held camerawork 226, 228

Hanoi 61
Hansen, John **28–30**, 159
Harden, Fred 23, 33–34
Hardjadibrata, Rabin 210, 212
Hardy, Frank 93
Hawes, Stanley 94, 100, 211
Hawke, Robert 108–109, 114, 117, 173
Haynes, Todd 135–136, 160
health & safety 93, 96
health care *See* universal health care
Heartfield, John 70
Hellman, Lillian 207
Hemingway, Ernest 207
Henson, Bill 160
Herron, John 178
Hewers of Coal 91
Hewson, John 178
Higham, Charles 28
High Court
   Mabo decision 173, 178, 224–225
   Wik decision 175, 178
history award nominations 200
history wars 175
Hoaas, Solrun 220, 226
hobbyist filmmaking 189
Ho Chi Minh 72
Hocking, Jenny 61, 133
Hodsdon, Barrett 21, 135–136, 141
Hodsdon, Bruce 21, 31
Hogg, Geoff 93
Hollywood 28–29
Holmes, Jonathon 73
Holt, Harold 27, 29, **70**, 222
Holt, Jill 240
homophobia 93
Honorary positions 221
Hope (2007) 218
Housing Commission Tenants Union 43
Howard, Carolyn **4**, 72–73, **101**, **104**, 105–107, 109–111, 121–124, 127, 135, 189
Howard, John 173–177, 179, 201, 225
How Does it Strike You? 96
Hoyts Cinemas 50

Hughes, John 1–6, 9, 231–234.
   See also cinematography: John Hughes;
   See also awards, honours & dedications
   as activist & organiser 42–43, 65, 92, 117, 123, 182, 201
   as commissioning editor 181–182
   as historian & academic 144, 165, 211–212, 220–221, 224
   as negotiator 12, 81–82, 145, 220
   as script editor 174
   early life, education & work 14–16, 19, 43, 45
Hughes, John quotes
   on audience & neoliberalism 8
   on community television 92
   on competition 182
   on cultural workers 113
   on *Dalmas* 31
   on directing 165
   on emotion in film 148, 165, 213
   on establishment & avant-garde film 65–66
   on film budgets 219
   on his motivation 143
   on Indonesia coup d'état of 1965-6 213
   on Ivens' *Indonesia Calling* 135, 206
   on memory 160
   on National Indigenous Working Group (NIWG) 174–176
   on *November Eleven* 70
   on propaganda 88
   on schools 47
   on screen design 194–195
   on simultaneity 195
   on The Cold War 47
   on the Documentary Fellowship 123, 131
   on TV news 41–42
Hughes, Kent 48
Hughes, May 15–16
Hughes, Peter 12, 13, 41, 83, 140, 154, 172, 177, 179
Hughes, Stan 14–16, 152
Huillet, Danièle 104, 110, 135, 194
humanism 15, 42
human rights 54, 59, **101**, 107

Humphries, Barry 20
Hungry Miles, The 85
Hyde, Michael 56

I

ideological mask of objectivity 55, 88
ideology 8, 20, 50, 55, 72, 102, 127, 131, 156, 206–207, 216. *See also* capitalism; *See also* communism & anti-communism *See also* mainstream media; *See also* markets & market ideology
IDFA (International Documentary Film Festival Amsterdam) 219
Illich, Ivan 95
immigration 6
impersonal screen 69, 134, 139, 152
improvisation 105
independent film 4–10, 92–93, 101–104, 115–118, 123–124, 152, 231. *See also* filmmakers' co-operative movement; *See also* Carlton filmmakers; *See also* Ivens, Joris; *See also* Waterside Workers' Federation Film Unit (WWFFU); *See also* creative control
   as an industrial sector 114–115, 232
   diversity of 65
   post-war 189–190
   publications 33, 103, 182
   subsidy of, policy impact on 65–68, 156
   the Two Avant-Gardes debate 34
Independent Film Action Committee (IFAC) 10, 105, 114–115, 175, 182
Independent Film Association (IFA) UK 102
Independent Filmmakers Association 77
Independent Voice: Australian political documentary from the 1940s to the 1980s 189–191
indeterminacy 160, 163
indeterminate space. *See* public-private space
Indian seamen 208
Indigenous / non-Indigenous collaboration 167–169, 173–177

Indigenous peoples. *See* Aboriginal & Torres Strait Islander people
individualism 91, 96
Indonesia 62, 205–206, 208–215
   history of violence 212, 228
Indonesia Calling 10, 80, 135, 205–215, 221
Indonesia Calling: Joris Ivens in Australia 2, 4, 205–221, 232–233
Indonesian seamen 208–209, 211–212
industrial disputes
   1945 ban on Dutch ships 208–209
   1948 Pilbara stockmen's strike **192**
   1966 Gurindji Wave Hill station strike 168–169
   1977 Victorian power workers' strike 79
   education about 96
industry 117
In My Beginning: A story of New Education 94
installations. *See* art gallery exhibition & installations
institutional racism 169
intellectuals. *See* artists & intellectuals
interactivity 44, 205
intergenerational equity 222–223
Interim Council for a Film and Television School (ICFTS) 29, 42
international affairs 58
International Documentary Film Festival Amsterdam (IDFA) 219
International Inquiry into US War Crimes in Indo-China 42
international intelligence community 61, 64
internationalism 15
international markets 11
internet, the 16, 44, 182, 201–202. *See also* streaming
intertextuality 105, 111. *See Exits*
interviews 149, 200
   as portaiture 128–133, 196
   off-camera voice 91
interwar years 206
In the Future 126
In This Life's Body 33

Introduction to an accompaniment to a cinematographic scene by Arnold Schoenberg (1976) 194
Isaac, Prof. Joe 212
Isak, Joesoef 212–213
Is It Working? George Seelaf for the record 54, 94–95, 158
Italian neo-realism 20
Italy 73, 161
Ivens, Joris 2, 4, 10, 12, 70, 79, 135, 205–219

J

Jacka, Liz 114
James, Ralton R 18
Japanese imperialism 78, 207, 208, 212
Jason 126
Jedda 20, 171
Jennings, Michael 148
Jesuit quality 82
Jewish 83, 143, 146
J-format video 69, 203
Joint Defence Space Research Facilities 63
Jones, Dave 31, 155
Jones, Ian 20
Joris Ivens in Australia. *See Indonesia Calling: Joris Ivens in Australia*
Jost, Jon 40, 105
journalism 101–113, 159, 192, 212, 225
 & political interference 78, 108
Journey to the End of Night 104
Julian, Isaac 135
Jump Cut 30, 69

K

Kalina, Paul 157, 165–166
Karavan, Dani 144, 159
Karen Carpenter Story, The 135
Kate, Hetty 227
Kaufman, Tina 117, 120
Keating, Paul 107, 172–173, 179
Kennedy, John F 49

Kennedy, Peter 77, 117
 MFC banner 67–68
 November 11 banners 70, 73
 November Eleven: On Sacred Land 74–75
 The Stars Disordered 124, 130
Kennett, Jeff 179
Kerr, Sir John 57, 59
Kesselschmidt, John 96
Keuken, Johan van der 218
Keys, Angela 209
Kiernan, Ben 39
Kimberley Diamond Company 184
Kinamo camera 209, 228
kinetic video 30–31
Kisch, Egon Erwin 69
Kissinger, Henry 61–62
Klee, Paul 126
Klimionok, Reverend Reginald 128–130
Kluge, Alexander 104, 109–110, 132, 135, 192–193
Kluge, Alexandra 110
Know Your Friends, Know Your Enemies 79
Kodak 209
Koman, Jacek **158**, 164
Koornong school 94
Korean War 48
Koval, Ramona 225–226
Kracauer, Siegfried 135, 224
Kulinma: listening to Aboriginal Australians 223

L

laboratory, film 21, 24, 104, 161, 177
Labor Party & Labor Governments 28, 41, 43, 45, 55, 58–63, 105–109, 114, 117–118, 133, 172–177, 179, 210, 222, 225
labour movement. *See* trade union movement
Lacey, Betty 188
Lacis, Asja 153
Lack, John 93
La Jetee 160
Lake Tyers 32
La Mama theatre 20–21, 39, 56

Lander, Ned 171
Lane, Garry 79, 98
Langer, Albert 56
Langton, Marcia 175, 179
Last Year at Marienbad 166
Lathouris, Nico (Nick) **10**, 124–125, 130–131, **134**, 140, 146–148
La Trobe University 23, 43, 92, 144
Laughren, Pat 72, 105, 109, 135, 189
Laurie, Robin 231
   Dalmas 32
   Flying Wedge 72
   Menace 47, 53
   national video network 42
   Nowhere Game 24
   We Aim to Please 84
Laurie, Ted 42, 45, 231
Lawford, Ningali 180–181
Law Reform Commission, Australian 58
Lawson, Sylvia 124, 224
Laycock, Don 23
Learning Exchange 42.
   See also Video Exchange
Leary, Timothy 31
Lee, Michael 23
left-wing 15, 45, 60, 62, 206
  orthodoxy 109–110, 115, 196
legal aid 58
Léger, Fernand 72
Leipzig Film Festival 92
Lenin, Vladimir Ilyich (Ulyanov) 73, 207
letters 216, 222, 224–226
Levy, Jerome (Jock) 81–82, 84–85, 90–91
Levy, Sandra 21
libel laws 108
liberal 107
 -capitalist 73
 conditions of production 29, 123, 140
 -humanist 15
 -left 206
liberal democracy 233
Liberal Party & Liberal Governments 27, 29, 45, 48, 50, 59, 62, 64, 70, 83, 107, 173–177, 201, 225.

   attitudes to native title 178–179, 222–223
liberation movements 208, 212
libertarianism 71–72
Life as a Project of Montage 150
lightshows 21, 29–30, 30
lines of flight 134
Lingiari, Vincent 223–224
Lippmann, Lorna 169
Lipsett, Arthur 71
Lissitzky, El 44, 69, 87
listener-viewer 88, 90, 225–227, 227.
   See also audience
live global television event 144
lobbyists 184. *See also* IFA & IFAC
Löfvén, Chris 37
London Filmmaker's Co-operative 21
Longford Cinema 117
Longmore, Pat 33
long-take shots 26, 31
Love & Fury: Judith Wright & 'Nugget' Coombs 13–14, 221–227
low-budget & experimental feature films 105
LSD 32
Lye, Len 71
Lygon Street cinema 67

M

Mabo, Eddie 173, 223
Mack, Andrew 129
magical thinking 125
magic lanterns 170
Maher, Rachel 182
Maidens 83
mainstream media 1, 21, 41–42, 46, 107, 201. *See also* mass media
 power & ideology 50, 55, 71, 215
Makavejev, Dušan 135
make-up artist 125
Malaka, Jan 213
Mallacoota Stampede 105
Malouf, David 124
Mangiamele, Giorgio 19–21, 155
Maoism 45, 56, 72

Mao Tse-tung 208
Maramis, Charlotte 211
maritime workers 79, 208–209, 211–212
Marker, Chris 160
marketing 27
markets & market ideology 7–10, 156,
　　202. *See also* finance & policy:
　　commercialisation
　ascendence & globalisation
　　of 101–103, 106, 117, 133,
　　202. *See also* globalisation;
　　See also neoliberalism;
　　See also privatisation
　digital 16, 117
　television 150–152, 233–234
Martin, Adrian 131–137, 148–149, 165
Martin, David N 18
Marxism 133, 196
Marxist cultural avant-garde 30, 69, 73, 85
Marx, Karl 73, 125–126
Masculin féminin 105
masculinism & male-domination 11, 24,
　　32–33, 84, 110, 231
mass executions 205
mass media 44, 69.
　　See also mainstream media
materialist cinema 30
Mathews, Bob 81, 89, 188–191, 196
Mathews, John 32
May 1968 44
May Day march **54**
Maza, Bob 170–171, 225
McCarthyism in Australia 41, 47–50.
　　See also declared persons
McGauchie, Donald 178–179
McGregor, Craig 129
McGuinness, Bruce 169–170
McKenzie, Brian 9, 142
McLuhan, Marshall 44
McMahon, Sonia **62**
McMahon, William **62**, 222
McMurchy, Megan 81, 115–116, 124
McQueen, Humphrey 108, 146, 149
McRae, Ian 23

Meat Industry Employees' Union 93
mechanisation 83
Medea 126–127
media 41–44, 101, 210, 215.
　　See also television; *See also* alternative
　　media
Media Access Centre (California) 42.
　　See also community access video
media art 77, 114–115, 150
Medibank & Medicare 58, 107
Medium Cool 105
medium is the message, the 44
Melbourne Cinémathèque 19, 189
Melbourne Conservatorium of Music 221
Melbourne Filmmakers Co-operative (MFC) 9,
　　22–24, 27–33, 41–45, 98–100, 125, 182,
　　232. *See also* filmmakers' co-operative
　　movement
　women in 24, 32
　demise of 67–70, 92
Melbourne Fringe Festival 116
Melbourne (International) Film Festival (MFF/
　　MIFF) 21, 29, 38, 92
　MIFF Premier fund 219
Melbourne Olympic Games of 1956 14–15
Melbourne Peace Congress (1950) 191
Melbourne State College/College of Education
　　(MCE/MSC) 43–44, 68–69, 79, 103, 170
Melbourne Times 149
Melbourne University Film Society (MUFS)
　　19–22, 21, 24, 29–30. *See also* University
　　of Melbourne, The
Melbourne Women's Film Group 33
memory 16, 83, 87, 160
Menace 41–56, 67, 79–80, 82, 93, 104, 231
　Nash & Laurie 11, 84
　origin & themes 2, 57, 187, 206–207, 211,
　　232
Menzies, Robert 48–50, 83, 211
Meriam people 173
Merri Creek 223
Metro magazine 149, 162
Michelle, Marion 209–210
Mickey Mouse 128

middle class 45
MIFF 187
Miliken, Angie 163–164
military & militia 19, 58, 129, 206, 208, 213–215, 228, 233–234. *See also* United States of America (USA): US military bases in Australia; *See also* coup d'état, military
Milner, Lisa 80–81, 83
Mind's Eye Cinema 23
mining industry 107, 172–173, 184
Mirimbiak Nations Aboriginal Corporation 174–175
mise-en-scène 87, 90, 130, 136, 143
Mizrahi, Uri 146, 171, 177–179, 191–192, 194–196, 216–217, 224
mode of address 172
mode of representation. *See* film form
modernism 72, 125, 139, 207
Moffatt, Tracey 156
Molecular Revolutions 126
moment of danger 83–84
Moments Like These 167, 170–172, 225
Monash University 45, 72, 144, 156, 165, 169, 187
montage 68, 111, 132, 194, 198, 216. *See also* musique concrète; *See also* screen design; *See also* editing
Montgomery, Kim 99–100
Monthly, The 221
Montparnasse 218
Montsalvat artists' colony 20
Moore, Robert 70
Mornington Island 68
Morris dancers 130
Morris, Meaghan 99–100
Morse, Helen 14, 225–226
mosaic structure 132, 148. *See* montage
Moscow 48
Motion Picture Directory, The 81
Mousoulis, Bill 116
movie theatre 172
Movietone News 90
Moving History website 188, 201–202, 221

multiculturalism 205, 215
multimedia 72. *See also* performance art
multinational & transnational corportations 6–7, 10–11, 16, 107, 133, 172–173, 184. *See also* markets & market ideology: ascendence & globalisation of
in media & entertainment 7–10, 92, 102
multiplatform projects 75, 188
multi-screen projection 23, 33
Mulvey, Laura 104, 135
Mundell, Ian 210
Murdoch, Rupert 62
Murphy, Lionel 60, 133
Murray Islands 173
Murray, Scott 23
musical theatre 15
Music and Effects 191
music & composers 15, 139, 148, 180, 227–228. *See also* sound; *See also* songs
Brett Aplin, Hetty Kate & 'Olympia' (Olivier Bartley) 227
editing of 111
electronic 29
Eric Gradman 124
Laurie Anderson 148
Martin Friedel 190, 193
Paul Grabowsky 203
Steve Reich 148
Take Five 186
music videos 71, 115
musique concrète 70
Mystfest 161

N

narration 195, 206, 209–210, 216, 224–226
conventioanl use of 47–48, 162, 169, 200
first-person 107, 110, 193–194
narrative 105–107, 116–117, 195, 213, 218
in MFC films 22–23, 33, 34
narrative form 94, 101, 113, 126–127, 131–132, 136, 155–157, 192
Nash, Margot 4, 11, 84–91, 189
National Archives of Australia 201

National Farmers Federation (NFF) 175, 178–179
National Film and Sound Archive (NFSA) 188–191, 201
National Gallery of Australia (NGA) 181
National Gallery of Victoria (NGV) 188
National Gallery School 23
National Indigenous Working Group (NIWG) 174–176
National Liberation Front of South Vietnam (NLF) 56
National Library of Australia 224
national park 179
National Party 63, 64, 118, 173, 223
national security agencies & the Whitlam government 60
national video network 43.
   See also community access video
Native Title Act 173, 175, 179.
   See also Aboriginal & Torres Strait Islander people: land rights
naturalism 106, 112, 136, 147, 164
Nazism. *See* fascism & anti-fascism
Neave, Bill 104
neocolonialism. *See* United States of America (USA): US neocolonialism
neoliberalism 98, 101, 107–108, 114, 129, 233. *See also* finance & policy: commercialisation; *See also* markets & market ideology: ascendence & globalisation of
neorealism 20–21, 85. *See also* realism & realist filmmakers
Netherlands East Indies. *See* Indonesia
Netherlands Parliament 217
New American Cinema 21, 71
New Deal 208
new digital freedom 11
New Education movement 94–96
New German Critique editor Anson Rabinbach 147
New Left 44–45
New Left Review 69
new media 41, 44, 54

Newsfront 110, 117
New Sobriety 1914-33, The: Art and Politics in the Weimar Period 69, 72
Newsreel collective 40
newsreels 42, 47, 56, 72–73, 110, 135, 218
   anti-union 83
   racist 171
New Theatre 80–82, 90, 188–189, 193
New Theatre League 209
new wave. *See* French new wave
New York 34, 207
New York Film-maker's Coop 21
Nield, Clive 94
Ningla A-Na 170–171
Nixon, Richard 61–62, 64
no-budget production. *See* finance & policy: federal: subsidy by artists
non-commercial film 65
non-feature filmmaking 4, 64, 155
non-Indigenous & European Australians.
   See also racism; *See also* treaty campaign
   culture of cheating 129, 133
   filmmakers & protocols 167–169, 172, 174–175
   perceptions 167, 172, 178, 180.
      See Aboriginal & Torres Strait Islander people: media representation of
non-linear use of film 216–217
non-narrative 21, 23
non-profit organisations 23, 67, 104
non-proliferation of nuclear weapons 59
non-theatrical exhibition 104
Nordholt, Henk 213
Northern Territory 173
November Eleven 6, 7, 57, 68–72, 105, 129, 156, 189
November Eleven: On Sacred Land 74–75, 111
November Eleven: Work in Progress 72–74, 105, 107–108, 111–112
November Victory 91
No Way to Forget 174–175

Nowhere Game 19, 24–27, 34, 36, 38, 55, 135
Noyce, Phillip 39, 110
NSW Trades and Labour Council 83
nuclear weapons or war 59, 129, 208
Nurrungar 63

O

Oakeshott, Rob 118
objectivity 41, 69, 88, 105
observational technique 26, 106, 216
oil crisis of 1973 59
'Olympia' (Olivier Bartley) 227
Olympic Follies 15
One Way Street: Fragments for Walter Benjamin 2–3, **10**, 13, 143–153, 193. *See also* dramatisation, actuality & performance
  references to 134, 136, 158, 159, 175–177
online 220
online distribution 8–9
online filmmaking 201–202
online television 202
Oorthuys, Cas 212
Open Channel 171
Operation Linebacker II 76. *See also* Christmas bombing of Hanoi
oppositional practices 9–11, 37, 80, 89–92, 99, 201, 207, 209. *See also* community access video; *See also* activism & activist filmmaking
optical effects. *See* laboratories
oral history 93, 193, 202
Order of Australia 93
Ord River 180
Oshima, Nagisa 135, 218
The Other Cinema 166
outsourcing 101, 117. *See also* Television Outworkers Forum (TOF)
outtakes 94, 111, 218
Ownership & control of Australian companies 133. *See also* screen culture: Anglo-American hegemony

Oxfam 102

P

Packer, Sir Frank 62
painting 68, 70, 74, 124, 223
pamphleteering 82
Paris 44, 144–145, 156
parochialism 215
parody 131, 134
Parr, Mike 68, 75
participatory democracy 54. *See also* democracy
pastiche 202
pastoral leaseholds 174–175
Pate, Michael 178
Patriot, The 110
Patterson, Rod 24, 26, 44, 54
Peace Congress, Melbourne 1950 191
peace movement
  American War in South East Asia 15, 23, 32, 45, 56, 61, 72–73, 133
  Cold War 48–49, 189–191
Pearson, Noel **174**, **176**, **180**
Pecze, Andrew 23
Pedagogy of Hope 73, 96
Pedagogy of the Oppressed 42
pensions 48
Pentecostal 130
Penthesilea, Queen of the Amazons 135
performance art 23, 33
performance ensembles 121–124, 135–136, 146–147
  Paul Davies & Carolyn Howard 72, 104–107, 127–128
Perkins, Roberta 129–130
Perry, David 34, 150, 195–196
persona 106, 136
personal approach 10, 14–15, 19–22, 32–33, 91, 137, 139, 152, 192
  to film criticism 162
  to performance 105, 169, 172, 212, 224–226

personal politics 48, 101, 113–114, 126–127, 134
Petit, Christopher 160
Phallic Forest 32
Philosophy of History, Theses on 126, 148
Photofile 148
'photographed reality' 135
photography 87–89, 183, 223.
   See also cinematography
photojournalism 212
photomontage 68
picure in picture 130, **177**, 180.
   See also screen design
Pinacotheca art gallery 22–23
Pine Gap 63–64, 129
Pinochet, Augusto 59, 107
Piscator, Erwin 72, 105
pluralistic society 43
Podorogawho, Valery 153
poetics 13, 20–21, 150, 207, 221, 231.
   See also cinema thinking
   in *All That is Solid* 132–137
   in *Indonesia Calling* 210, 212, 215, 231
   in Marx 125
   in *One Way Street* 143, 147, 150
   in *What I Have Written* 163
Poignant, Axel 211
Poison 135–136, 160
Polanski, Roman 27
Polaroid photography 87–89
police 61, 172, 198
political art 233–234
Political Essays 127
political policing 106, 108, 232.
   See also blacklisting
Politics and the Image Industry 23
politics as entertainment 108
Pollard, Bruce 23
Portapak 43
Portapak video 43
Portbou, Spain 144
Portola Institute (California) 42.
   See also community access video
postcards 68
post-colonial Australia 167
Post Industrial Utopians 129
postmodernism 133
post-punk 115
post-war period 19–22, 29–30, 41, 49, 80, 187, 202, 205, 215.
   See also Cold War, The
poverty 189
Power and the Land 208
Prahran College of Technology 23
Pram Factory, The 49–50, 105, 125
Precious Metals Australia 184
Premier's Plan, the 48
press & media 60, 161
Preston Institute of Technology (PIT) 23, 77
Prices and the People 188, 193
private life on screen 137, 148–149, 226
privatisation 101–102, 107, 114, 117–118, 211. *See also* neoliberalism
Prize, The 20
product endorsement scene 218
production design 125, 160
production & producing 3–15, 19–21, 32, 41, 68, 79, 80–82, 92–93, 121–125, 144–146, 152–153, 156, 159–160, 165, 174–176, 179–182, 191–192, 201–202, 209–210, 218–223, 233.
   See also finance & policy
production value 224
production workshops model (UK) 92
progressive
   artists & thinkers 83–85, 207, 231
   education 94–95
   images 215
   politics & art 41–42, 57, 91–92, 96, 107, 206–207, 217
project development 108–109.
   See also research
   All That is Solid 124–126
   One Way Street 145–146
   What I Have Written 156–161
   After Mabo 174–177

River of Dreams 179
The Archive Project 188, 190–191
Joris Ivens in Australia 219
project of montage 152
projectors & projection 23, 68, 86
propaganda 158
propaganda & manipulation 55, 87–88, 207, 215, 221, 223
  anti-communist 50–51, 90
  anti-union 81, 83
Propaganda Then and Now 88
protests 23, 44–45, **54**, 70–72.
  See also peace movement
  2005 legislation to curb 198
psychological realism 106, 113
psychologism 69, 165–166
Public Access and Community Television broadcast (1982) 92
public broadcasting 8, 12, 92.
  See also community television
public-private space 14–15, 90
public service 43, 98, 102, 107, 183, 211, 222
public speaking
  attempt to ban 49
Pudovkin, Vsevolod 85, 207

Q

Queen's Counsel 45
quotation 147–148. *See* collage & quotation

R

Rabinbach, Anson 3, 147
racial segregation 168
racism 2, 20, 58, 167–179
  Australia's reputation for 210, 215
  Dutch 212
  institutional 169, 183
radio 41, 63, 70, 76–77, 107, 202–203, 209, 226
Radio 3RRR 109
Radio and Television Board (FRTB) 169
Radio On 160

Rafferty, Chipps 178
Rain (*Regen*, 1929) 207
Randall, Robert 69–70
Rayson, Hannie 105
realism & realist filmmakers 30, 34, 84, 85, 89, 105–107, 112–114, 136–137, 216
  in What I Have Written 155, 161, 165
Realist Film Association, The (RFA) 79, 187–188, 193, 195, 197, 203, 207
Realist Film Unit, The (RFU) 13, 80–81, 94, 188–192, 197–199, 202
RealTime 120
reconciliation 174–175, 223
rectitude of sentiment 165, 221
Red Army 208
redemption of physical reality 135–136, 224. *See also* actuality
Red Ted. *See* Laurie, Ted
red wedge 87
re-enactment & reconstruction 9, 135, 210, 216. *See also* dramatisation, actuality & performance
Reeves, Andrew 94
referendum to control prices & wages (1974) 59
reflexive & self-reflexive practice 31–32, 85–91, 94, 98, 104–105, 110, 130, 135–138, 191–193, 202, 210
  in education 94–96
Refracting Glasses, The 150
refugees 50
Regan, Ronald 114
rehearsal process 160
Reich, Steve 148
relationships in Hughes' films 53, 114, 131, 156–159, 162–165
religion 46, 93
reportage 69, 216
research 101, 125, 144, 158, 171, 203, 220
Reserve Bank 107, 222–223
Residents' Association, Fitzroy 43
Resnais, Alain 166
reviews. *See* critics, critique & scholarship
Riddles of the Sphinx 104

right-wing 106, 206
risk-management 115
River of Dreams 167, 179–183, 194
RMIT University 23, 77, 221
Robins, Penny 93, 96
Roeg, Nicolas 160
Rogers, Mark 124, 126–127, 130, 146–147
role-play 96
romanticism 146
Ronin Films 92, 180
Roosevelt, Franklin D 208
Ross, Caroline 44
Rowley, CD 169
Rowse, Tim 110, 113, 221, 223
Royal Commission into Communism, Victorian Government 45–46
Royal Commission into Exploratory & Production Drilling for Petroleum in the Great Barrier Reef 222–223
Royal Melbourne Institute of Technology (RMIT) 23. *See also* RMIT University
Rusden State College 9–10, 96
Russell, Bertrand 15
Russia 1, 46, 85, 207. *See also* Soviet Union
Russian constructivism 69

S

sacred sites 173
Sainsbury, Peter 144–145, 156, 159, 166
Sardjono 216–217
satellite links 144
Saunders, Wal 185
Save a Starving Film 98
Save the Film Co-op banner 68–69
schools 15, 47, 94–96, 170
scientists 221
Scollo, Andrew 69–70
Scott, John 70, 156–159, 162, 164–166
scratch video 70–72
Screen 69
Screen Australia 219, 224. *See* Australian Film Commission (AFC)
screen culture 2, 4–8, 13–14, 16, 19, 156. *See also* critics, critique & scholarship; *See also* film history; *See also* finance & policy
 Anglo-American hegemony 6–7, 21, 50–51, 79, 90–91
 1920s 207
 1940s 20–21, 79, 187–188, 201
 1950s 19–20, 79–85
 1960s 19–23, 28–29, 34, 80, 105, 202
 1970s 29–33, 41–54, 64–65
 1980s 68, 71, 101, 117, 155–156, 231
 1990s 152, 156, 165
 2000s 182–183, 219–220, 233–234
screen design 13–14, **31**, **65**, 72, 87, 136, **169**, 177–183, **187**, 231. *See also* collage & quotation; *See also* collage-within-the-frame & cinema thinking 3, 231
 film in film 90, 194–197
 graphics in 90–91, **144**, **169**, 216–217
 web page 201–202
Screen NSW 220
Screen Sound. *See* National Film and Sound Archive (NFSA)
Screen West 179
Scripsi 156
scripts **3**, 124, 146, **160**, 164–165, 172, 186, 209, 216, 225–226
script writing & editing 31–32, 110, 146, 149, 158–160, 174
Sculthorpe, Peter 180
Seamen's Union of Australia 208
Sebastian the Fox 20
Second World War 104
secret security culture 61–64, 202–203, 232. *See also* blacklisting; *See also* political policing
secret security services 2, 201–202, 209–210, 211, 216, 221. *See also* Central Intelligence Agency (CIA) USA; *See* Australian Security Intelligence Organisation (ASIO)
Seelaf, George 53–54, 54, 93–94
See You at Mao.

See *British Sounds/See You at Mao*
self-funded production. *See* finance & policy: federal: subsidy by artists
September 11, 1973 59
Serious Undertakings 16, 104, 134, 156
Sharp, Nonie 223
Shaw, George Bernard 207
Sheath, Ian 161
Shirley, Graham 45
shooting ratio 205
shop window displays 14, 152
short film 8, 10, 15, 19–20, 156
simultaneous visual & aural text 169
site-specific theatre 105
skepticism 14–15
Sklan, Carole 125
Slavin, John 128, 131–133
slide projector 129
sloganeering 70
Slums Are Still With Us, The 192
Smith, Louise 124, 126–127, 146–147
social
  advocacy 26, 49
  change 34, 41–43, 83, 232
  justice 8, 42
social-documentary & social conscience film 22, 84, 96, 167–168
socialism 44, 73, 90
social issues 167–168, 189
socialist newspapers 130
social media 183
social mode of production 176
social realism 84, 87, 89, 194
social welfare 107
solidarity 205, 212
Some Aspects of Australian Racism 167–170, 174, 183, 216
  screen design 13, 177, 231
songs
  I believe in miracles 130
  In the Future 126, 139
  The Dream Before: Homage to Walter Benjamin 148
  Visions of Johanna 37

sound 50, 87, 110–111, 130, 190, 211. *See also* editing
  recording 84, **88**, 145, 174, 226
  re-creation of sound tracks 193–194, 200
sound, image & text 88, 177, 196
sound poetry 150
South East Asia. *See* American War in South East Asia (Laos, Vietnam & Cambodia)
sovereignty of nations 232
Soviet cultural avant-garde 30, 69, 73
Soviet imperialism 72
Soviet Union 46–48, 49, 72–73, 109, 207, 209
spacecraft 63
Spain 73, 144
Spanish Civil War 50, 81, 188, 207
Spanish Earth 207, 215
Speaking Directly 191
Special Broadcasting Service Independent (SBSI) 180–181
Special Broadcasting Service (SBS) Television 12, 152, 174–175, 179–180
Speed and Politics 126
Spencer, Baldwin 171–172
Spencer, Megan 182–183
sponsored documentary 81, 93–94, 96
Spring Street 23, 32
Stalin, Joseph 46, 48, 53, 73
  Stalinism 109–110
Stallings, Richard 63
Stanford University 69
Stanislavski 224
Stanner, Bill 223
stars & hearts 124
State Film Centre of Victoria 21
Steenbeck 16 mm film editing machine 4
Stein, Ekhart 101–102
Stern, Lesley 99, 161–163, 166
Stewart, Clare 11
Stockholm International Film Festival 161
stock shots 224
Stockwell, Professor Stephen 60, 63
stolen generation 181
Stollman, Sarah 160

Storm, Esben 220
Storming Mont Albert By Tram 105
Stratton, David 92, 112
Straub, Jean-Marie 104, 110, 135, 194
streaming video 16, 201
street theatre 72, 130
Stretton, Hugh 127
strikes. *See* industrial disputes
structural aspects/approach. *See* film form
student organisations 21, 198.
    See also Melbourne University Film Society (MUFS)
student protest 23
students 9, 44–45, 77, 94–96, 105, 183, 218
studio scenes 72, 92
stylisation 13, 87, 106, 135, 146–147, 155
suburbs 45, 54
Suharto 212–213, 215
Sukarno 208, 213
Sun, The 44
Super-8 film 23–24, 33, 68, 69, 116, 118, 128, 153, **160**
Supreme Sound 209
surrealism 30, 84, 161
surveillance 187, 190–191, 195, 198, 211, 232
Swinburne Community School (SCS) 95
Swinburne Technical College 23
Sydney 188–189, 203, 209
Sydney Film Festival 92
Sydney filmmakers 28–29, 32–34, 42, 65, 79, 81, 134, 209–212
Sydney Filmmakers Co-operative (SFC) 21–23, 28–29, 33, 92, 99, 103, 220.
    See also filmmakers' co-operative movement; *See also* Filmnews
  demise of 67, 117–118
Sydney Symphony Orchestra 180
Sydney Underground Movies 21–22
Sydney University Film Group 21
synthesised video imagery 30–31

T

Take Five 181
Tammer, Peter 9, 16, 21–23, 33–34, 104–105
Tange, Arthur 60
tape recorder 82
tax avoidance 106
Taylor, Andrew 93
teachers 15, 94
technology 19, 44, 69, 128, 170, 177, 216–219. *See also* video; *See also* celluloid film; *See also* cameras
  film/video hybrid 44, 68
  instantaneous analogue 72, 87
  online 182, 202, 220
Ted Laurie on American War Crimes in Vietnam 41. *See also* American War in South East Asia (Laos, Vietnam & Cambodia)
Ted Wheelwright 130, 133
telecine 170
telegraph cable 217
television 15, 28–29, 72, 83, 92, 102, 117, 149. *See also* Australian Broadcasting Commission / Corporation; *See also* Special Broadcasting Service (SBS) Television; *See also* community television
  innovative concepts 144, 176–177
  tv arts programs.
    See Archive Project, The; *See* Churcher, Betty; *See Love & Fury*
  tv news 1, 3, 41–42, 54, 178
  tv training 19, 42
television & independent production 16, 20, 101–102, 117, 123, 131, 140, 145, 152, 221
Television Outworkers Forum (TOF) 182–183. *See also* privatisation; *See also* finance & policy: commercialisation
televisual convention 33, 144, 176–177, 187–188, 200–201, 218
  parody of 131, 134

Telos 69
tenants union 43
Ten-Point Plan 175
terra nullius 173
terror tactics 50–51, 108
text on screen 72, **144**, **169**, 177–179, 195, 216–217
texture 128, 194, 231
Thatcher, Margaret 102, 107
theatre 13–16, 20–21, 23, 32–33, 39, 45, 53, 57, 72, 90, 106–107, 117–118, 124, 135–136, 172
 & protest 45, 72, 130
Theatre Works 105, 119
theory, film 20, 188
These Are Our Children 189, 192
Theses on the Philosophy of History 126, 148
They Chose Peace 189
Third World 96, 167
Thomas, Steve 218
Thoms, Albie 22, 29, 220
Thornburn, Gretchen 145
Thornley, Jeni 83
Thread of Voice 150
Tickell, Gerry 95
time-based art 200
Time To Go John 201
Tivoli Theatre 15
Toffler, Alvin 95
topical international event 15
Toronto, Downtown Community Television 42
totalisation 73, 109, 180
Tout va bien 194
Townsville Aboriginal and Islander Media Association (TAIMA) 171
Trades and Labour Council (NSW) 83
Trades Hall Council, Victorian (VTHC) 78, 123, 188
 Film and Video Unit (VTHCVU) 93–94, 98
trade union arts & media 4, 21, 79–83, 91–94, 102, 188, 233
Trade Union Clinic and Research Centre 53, 93
Trade Union Film Festival & Film Society 92

trade union movement 47–50, 53–56, 188, 205, 207–208, 211, 213
 mythologies 57, 73, 113
 security agency interventions 64, 78, 198
traditions of filmmaking 135–136, 232.
 See also documentary traditions
transformational images 215, 221
Traps **2**, **4**, 101–117, 153
 dramatisation in 13, 125, 134
 other references to 123, 127, 132, 141, 158–159, 170, 231
trauma & testimony 150, 169, 212–213, 213
travelogue films 202
treadmill stage 72
treatment 158, 159, 174, 191.
 See also scripts
treaty campaign 223
Tribe 31–32
Tribune 101
Trikojus, Sasha 21, 23, 31, 42–43
triptych of Hughes' films 2, 4, 80, 187, 205
Tropfest film festival 11
Trudeau, Ben 95
TS Eliot 94
Two Avant-Gardes, The 34

U

Ubu group 21–22, 34
U-matic video 68
Uncivilised 171
underground film & video 21, 34
Underhill, Nancy 124
unemployment 59
Unfinished Business 181
Unidad Popular 59
Unifed 21, 29, 33, 38, 219
Union of Soviet Socialist Republics (USSR) 48. *See also* Soviet Union
unions. *See* trade union movement
union theatres 21, 32, 80.
 See also New Theatre
United Nations 59, 181, 210
United States of America (USA) 39, 49,

60–64, 114, 207-208.
US Ambassador to Australia & Indonesia 62
US bombing of Hanoi & Haiphong 61–62
   See also American War in South East Asia (Laos, Vietnam & Cambodia)
US film corporations.
   See British & American film corporations
US flag 90
US-led 2003 invasion of Iraq 221
US military bases in Australia 61–63, 129
US National Security Council 60
US neocolonialism 48, 90, 107–108.
   See also screen culture: Anglo-American hegemony
US presidential archives 59–60
US Secretary of State, Henry Kissinger 61
US Senate Committees on Intelligence 64
universal health care 58, 107
University of Melbourne, The 20, 32, 45, 94, 221. *See also* Melbourne University Film Society (MUFS)
US national security state 49
   See also Central Intelligence Agency (CIA)
utopianism & hope 130, 134, 179, 196, 212, 215, 221

V

Valentine, Senator Jo 129
Variety 112
vertical integration 6. *See also* screen culture: Anglo-American hegemony
Vertov, Dziga 85, 88, 135–136
Veterans Against the War 133
vice squad 32
Victorian
   filmmakers 21–22
   government & big business 108
   political policing 108
   power workers' strike 79
Victorian Amateur Cine Society 189
Victorian College of the Arts 221
Victorian Department of Education 94–95
Victorian Department of Health 27, 32

Victorian Royal Commission into Communism (1949) 45–47
Vidal, Gore 49
video
   See also cameras;
   See also independent film
   chroma key 72
   digital 8–10, 16, 177, 219
   distribution & streaming 16, 104, 201
   early technology & recordings 22–23, 30–31, 41–44
   & social change 42, 54
video access & media centres 42–43, 102–103, 103, 115.
   See also access video movement
video art 30, 33, 41, 54, 57, 68–72, 72, 75, 116, 150. *See also* art gallery exhibition & installations
Video Exchange 42–43. *See also* community access video; *See also* Learning Exchange
video monitors & projection **57**, **93**, 130, 189
Video Projects 96, 188
videotapes 57, 70, 73–74, 171, 175, 177
videotape technology 42, 44, 116, 161
   reel-to-reel J-format 69, 195, 203
   U-matic 68–69
   VHS & Beta cassettes 104
   Video-8 & Hi-8
      128–129, 144–145, 153, 190
Vietnam War
   See American War in South East Asia
Vincent Library 29
Vincent Report 28
Virilio, Paul 126
Visions of Independence 101–102
visual art & visual artists 19, 22–24, 34, 57, 67, 75–76, 115, 152, 179
visual synthesiser 30
vital industries 49
vocation 9
voice-over 225–226
volunteerism 8, 10, 23, 41, 43, 67, 152, 188, 205, 210, 225

W

wages & conditions 32, 48, 59, 93, 115–116, 123, 131, 188
Wahlberg, Malin 207
WA Inc. 173–174, 184
Wainer, Dr Bertram 44–45
Walkley Awards 225
Walsh, Martin 104
war. *See* American, Cold, Dutch, Korean, Spanish & World wars; *See also* protests; *See also* peace movement
War Game, The 27
War on Terror 187, 221, 232
Warrandyte 94
Watergate scandal 62
Waterside Workers' Federation (WWF) 208
  Film Unit (WWFFU) 80–93, 135, 140, 207–208
Watkins, Peter 27
Watt, Harry 210
Wave Hill walk-off & Wattie Creek (Daguragu) 168–169, 223–224
way of being engaged with the world, a 150
We Aim to Please 84, 189
weapons 49, 59, 62–63, 208
web page design 177, 187–188, 202–203
We call for a treaty 223
Weimar Republic 72, 206
Weir, Peter 202
Welshman, John 153
West Australian Workers Star 211
Western Australian government & big business 173–174, 184
Western Suburbs Community Health Centre. *See* Footscray Trade Union Clinic and Research Centre
Westgate Bridge Disaster 1, 23, 32
West, Katharine 129–130
Wexler, Haskell 105
wharfies 82
Whatever Happened to Green Valley 202
What I Have Written V, 14, *155–165*, 231–232, *232*
  narrative *156–157*
  characters & themes *159–160*, 164–165
  financing *159–160*
  design & cinematography *160–161*
  release & reception **161–163**
  other references to 1–2, *13*, *143*, *152*
What John Berger Saw 150
Wheelwright, Ted 130–133
White Australia 215. *See also* racism
Whitlam, Gough 28, 41, 43, 45, 55, 58–63, **68**, 70, 105–107, 133, 222, 225. *See also* coup d'état, constitutional , Australia 1975
  on US bombing of Vietnam 61
Whitlam, Margaret **70**
Whitteron, John 84, 92
Why I Am Not a Christian 15
widescreen 194–195
Wik decision. *See* High Court
WikiLeaks 62
Wilkinson, Marion 108–109
Willett, John 69, 72, 105
Williams, Deane 187–188, 190, 196, 206
Williamson, Geordie 225–226
Wilson, Jim 23
Windmill, Chris 116
Wiseman, Gwenda 107, 111–114, 231
witch-hunts 205
Wolf, Virginia 192
Wollen, Peter 34, 104, 135
women filmmakers 33, 205
women's cinema groups 84. *See also* Australian Film Commission (AFC): Women's Film Fund
women's liberation 33. *See also* feminism
Wookey, Ann 32
words used to create images 195–196
workers' cultural groups 80–81, 96
Workers International Relief (WIR) 81, 207
working-class life, people & culture 44, 46, 80, 207–208. *See also* trade union movement
World Heritage 222
World War I 15, 32, 46

World War II 15, 19, 39, 96
World War II veterans 61, 80, 104, 133
world war III 48–49
Wright, Judith 221–226
Wright, Tony 93, 96
writer-directors 8
Wrong Side of the Road 171
Wurundjeri elders 223

X

xenophobia 215

Y

Yackety Yack 31, 155
Yarra River 1
Yellow House 21
You go to my head 227
Young-Bruehl, Elizabeth 149
Youth Carnival for Peace and Friendship 189
YouTube 1
Yugoslavia 60
Yunupingu, Galarrwuy **176**

Z

Zakharov, Peter 174
ZDF television 101
zeitgeist 15, 44, 231
Zijderveld, Anton C. 43
Zubrycki, Tom 42, 220